Teaching Science in the Elementary School

Donna M. Wolfinger
Auburn University at Montgomery

Teaching Science in the Elementary School

Content, Process, and Attitude

Little, Brown and Company
Boston Toronto

Library of Congress Cataloging in Publication Data

Wolfinger, Donna M.

Teaching science in the elementary school.

1. Science—Study and teaching (Elementary)

I. Title.

LB1585.W63 1984 372.3'5044 83-16203

ISBN 0-316-95101-3

Library of Congress Catalog Card No. 83-16203

ISBN 0-316-95101-3

9 8 7 6 5 4 3 2 1

HAL

Published simultaneously in Canada by Little, Brown & Company (Canada) Limited

Printed in the United States of America

Photo Credits

Page xx: Copyright The Exploratorium/Photo by Nancy Rodger. *Page 84:* Barbara Alper/Stock Boston. *Page 160:* Elizabeth Hamlin/Stock Boston. *Page 336:* Copyright The Exploratorium/Photo by Nancy Rodger.

To H. Seymour Fowler

Preface

In the 1950s we read about science. In the 60s we discovered Piaget and learned to do science. In the 70s we went back to basics and found that science was not a basic. Now, in the 80s, we see attention being focused on the quality of science education in our schools. Our past experience with science instruction will have an impact on how we face the challenges of teaching science in the remainder of this decade and into the next. As prospective teachers or practicing teachers, we must consider how best to facilitate children's learning of science — its concepts and attitudes — and how to guide children in coming to realize the excitement of science.

The research scientists who enter the laboratory do so with a thorough foundation of understanding gained not only through the use of a microscope, balance, or test tube but also through reading, listening, and discussing. To portray science in the 80s as merely one manipulation of materials after another or as one act of discovery after another is to show modern science in a false light. Also, it is not accurate to conceptualize elementary school science as being only discovery or simply a reading exercise. It is the aim of this textbook to provide preservice and inservice teachers with information about children, the nature of science, and the methods of science teaching that will enable them to make informed decisions about which teaching methods and strategies would be most appropriate in a particular situation.

In order to help teachers make logical decisions about teaching strategies, the material in *Teaching Science in the Elementary School* has been divided into four parts. Each part investigates a particular aspect of science teaching and provides ample opportunity for the reader to put into practice the content of the section. The Learning Activities in each chapter involve working with children, with science, with materials, and with elementary science textbooks.

Part One, "Helping Children Learn Science" (Chapters One and Two), deals with two basic elements: the nature of science and the characteristics of children from preschool through sixth grade. The first discussion of how children can be helped to learn science is based on these characteristics of children. Although a Piagetian perspective on how children learn the processes of science is evident, extensive material on Information Processing Theory is also utilized in order to develop a broader understanding of how the content of science is learned. Memory, concept development, hemispheric processing, and problem solving skills are important.

Part Two, "The Processes of Science" (Chapters Three through Five), discusses the investigative processes used in science and, in turn, which should be used by children. Each process is considered not only as a means of gaining experience in investigating natural phenomena but also as a means of developing the content of science. Learning Activities here allow the preservice or inservice teacher to develop expertise in the use of the processes of science from observation through true experiment.

Part Three, "Methods of Teaching Science" (Chapters Six through Ten), covers the multiplicity of methods that can be used effectively in helping children learn all three aspects of science. Special attention is given to ways of working with mainstreamed handicapped children and with the gifted as well as to the changing roles of girls in science. The scientific attitudes and the methods for developing these attitudes receive extensive treatment. *Part Three* concludes with a discussion of the use of textbooks in the classroom and with the growing role of microcomputers in science teaching. Included are examples of long-range planning for both content and process teaching sample lesson plans that illustrate each of the teaching methods.

Part Four, "Activities for Teaching Science" (Chapters Eleven through Thirteen), provides activities that can be used to enhance any science program. Although the activities are process oriented, the related science content is indicated so that the teacher can choose activities related to the content being studied by the class.

A great many individuals were particularly helpful in the writing of this textbook. In particular, I would like to mention Ronnie Carr for her aid in locating and understanding the material on mainstreaming and special education in general; Ann Mobbs and Pam Tucker for their help in obtaining information on the use of the microcomputer in schools; and Barbara Rouse for making sense out of the pieces of paper, arrows, and penciled-in sentences that were the original manuscript. Also, many thanks go to the students in classes on methods of teaching science who tried out the learning activities and who listened to the lectures on which this textbook is based. Finally, I wish to express my sincere appreciation to the following colleagues for reading the manuscript and offering their criticisms and suggestions: Shirley A. Brehm, Michigan State University; Willis Horak, The University of Arizona; Richard D. Konicek, University of Massachusetts, Amherst; Robert L. Steiner, University of Puget Sound; and Alan M. Voelker, Northern Illinois University.

Brief Contents

Contents

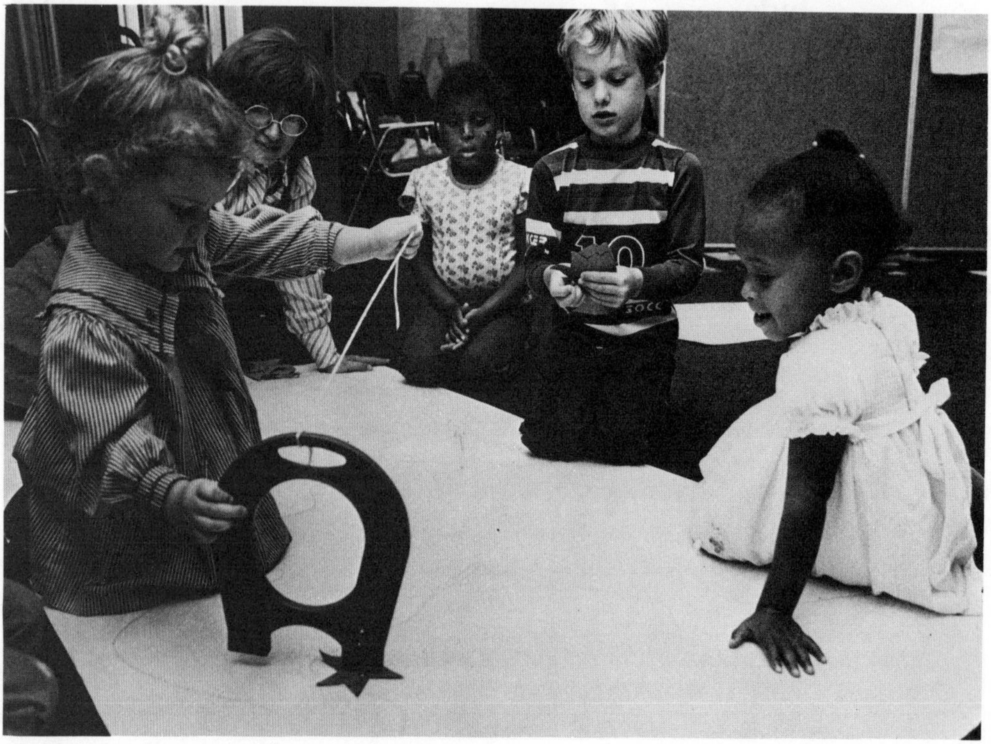

Part I

Helping Children Learn Science

Human beings are, understandably, highly motivated to find regularities, natural laws. The search for rules, the only possible way to understand such a vast and complex universe, is called science.

— Sagan, 1974

1 The Child and Science

Chapter Objectives

Upon completion of this chapter you should be able to

1. define science and identify each of the three major components of science;
2. list the similarities and differences between the scientific approach of the research scientist and the investigative approach of the child;
3. compare the characteristics of the preschool child to those of the primary grade child and to those of the intermediate grade child;
4. demonstrate how the characteristics of children at various ages affect the approach taken to science teaching;
5. identify the three major influences on the modern elementary school science curriculum.

"Teaching science is easy," a fifth-grade teacher once told me. "All you do is treat it like a reading lesson and the kids don't have any trouble . . . and neither do I."

This teacher had made a decision about science teaching that suited *her* needs and which made *her* feel very comfortable with the science textbook. Her reasoning might have followed the pattern: I don't know much about science teaching. But, I do know how to teach reading. I'm a good reading teacher. My science textbook is very similar to my reading textbook. So, I'll just pretend that science and reading are the same thing and teach two reading lessons each day.

This teacher felt good about her decision, and she felt good about her method of teaching science. But had she known more about science and the methods of teaching science she might not have been so willing to talk about her way of solving the problem of science teaching. By basing her decision on how well she taught reading rather than on the nature of science this teacher not only was showing her students only a small part of science but also was depriving them of the chance to experience the excitement of science.

Decisions on how to teach science, or any other subject, should be based on solid information. This chapter is designed to develop that kind of information, which is the foundation for any informed decision about teaching science in the elementary school.

This foundation for decision making is based on the nature of science, the characteristics of children, and the development of the science curriculum into its present form. This chapter considers each of these topics, so that you will have the background to realize that reading in the science textbook is satisfactory as far as it goes, but it should not be considered the entire program.

The Nature of Science

When I was a teacher of science to children in the first seven grades, I asked those children to define the word *science*. The first grade was almost unanimous in its definition. Through shrugs, shakes of heads, and comments, they conveyed one definition: "We don't know." For many of these children, even the word *science* was totally new. Although the kindergarten teacher had had the children grow plants, look at rocks, and take care of a classroom aquarium, these experiences had come as a part of their daily routine rather than being grouped under a particular area of the curriculum.

In the higher grades, however, the children did have a number of definitions to offer:

1. It's studying about animals.
2. It's what *you* teach.
3. It's what my dad does. He's a scientist. He looks for fossils.
4. It's looking through a microscope.

5. Science is when you do an experiment and you find out about something.
6. It's learning about rocks and chemicals and plants and stuff.
7. Science is what you do in science.

These children attempted to put into their own words the experiences they had had in that segment of the curriculum presented to them as science. Their definitions were not as sophisticated as the definition many students were forced to memorize in junior or senior high school: "Science is an organized body of knowledge." But the definitions offered by the children were, perhaps, closer to the actuality that is science.

The limited scope of the definition of science as an organized body of knowledge led many teachers to treat science as yet another time for reading. One began on the first page of the text and read through to the last page of the text, hoping that the end of the book and the end of the school year arrived at about the same time. Periodic tests assured that the children actually read and memorized the printed material.

Such a presentation of science as reading actually showed less of an understanding of science than the children showed in their definitions. Science is as much studying about animals and plants as it is studying about rocks and chemicals. And, science includes the human activities of looking through a microscope, searching for fossils, and trying to find out about something. Thus science is also doing: experimenting, observing, trying things to see what will happen. In essence, science is a search for understanding.

The Three Aspects of Science

In its search for understanding, science does develop a body of knowledge. But that body of knowledge is the result of certain attitudes and the product of human activity. Science, then, consists of three aspects: content, process, and attitude.

Content. Content is defined as all of the factual information and theoretical information gained by human beings as they attempt to understand the universe. The content of science changes continuously as new experiments lead to new understandings and new questions.

For example, in the writings of many ancient peoples are wondrous tales of the origins of simple animals. Flies were supposed to be the product of rotting meat or excrement. Snakes came from river reeds, and certain trees had fabulous blossoms: they dropped living lambs from beneath their petals. Later when such tales were found to be the product of active imaginations or erroneous observations, the theories were changed. At first, such theoretical changes held that lower forms of life only, like flies, could be generated spontaneously from inanimate matter or from unrelated animate matter.

Not until Francesco Redi turned his attention to the problem in 1668 was the theory of spontaneous generation systematically attacked. Redi carefully controlled his experiments and was able to show that maggots would not appear unless adult flies had access to meat. Using three containers, Redi covered one with parchment and one with gauze, leaving the third open. Only in the open container, in meat where flies had laid eggs, did maggots develop.

Scientific theories constantly change to accommodate new, more accurate information, but the process of change requires many years, even when the experimental evidence is overwhelming. But, once the evidence accumulates, and change does occur, the once strongly held theory of yesterday may become the myth of today. Content in science is changing and accumulating today more rapidly than ever before.

But whatever content is taught, it should permit the final development of children in three important areas:

> First, children should be helped to understand the nature of physical laws: what they are and what they are not, what they can tell us about the physical world and what they cannot, how they are arrived at, and in what sense they are true. Second, students should have some grounding in the laws of probability and chance, and thus some understanding that in a world as complex as ours both statistical fluctuations and the accidental coincidence of unrelated events happen all the time. Third, the idea should be conveyed that science is not a collection of isolated facts but a highly unified and consistent view of the world. (Saxon, 1982, p. 846A)

A part of this suggested content, the ability to determine probability and chance as well as to determine what is due to coincidence and what due to cause and effect, can be developed through the second aspect of science — process.

Process. Process involves the use of the methods of science to gain an understanding of the physical world. Through observation, inference, conclusion, classification, and experimentation both the scientist and the child can gain first-hand understanding of the operation of the physical world. The most powerful form of the method of science is the controlled experiment, in which a single factor, perhaps out of hundreds, is manipulated so that its effect may be determined. The isolation of a single food as the cause of an allergy, the testing of water to determine why fish are dying and the concomitant isolation of a single pollutant, the identification of a type of virus as the cause of a disease, all are examples of the method of science as it is used in the daily solution of problems. Through the experimental method and the use of the processes of science the content of science is learned, changed, and supplemented.

In the laboratory or in the field the scientist is concerned with the method used to attack and solve a problem. He is as concerned with this method as he is with the final outcome: the bit of knowledge that he will gain. For children, it is possible that the process used for learning is more important than the final result of the activity. There is a growing body of evidence that children are better able to learn to investigate the common phenomena of their world than they are to learn the cause of a particular phenomenon.

This may be particularly true in the case of young children, who cannot easily determine appropriate cause-and-effect relationships. A young child can observe that a white pebble, a white marble, and a white toy all sink in water. The conclusion drawn by the child may be that the color of the object is the major factor: white things sink. The idea that there is more to floating than the color of the object is not considered by the child. Requiring that the child know the correct cause of floating can only result in rote memorization of an essentially meaningless fact. Allowing the child to work with many objects, to observe their characteristics, and to determine whether or not they sink or float will result in the child eliminating color as the cause of sinking and, after much activity, in gaining an understanding of the cause of floating. In this case, the child will have learned, not memorized.

Science, then, may be considered as a means of learning through active involvement in the solution of a problem. Science may also be considered as facts, laws, theories, and principles. These two aspects of science, content and process, complete two-thirds of the total picture. But science has a crucial third component; it is also a set of attitudes.

Attitude. The scientist is willing to suspend judgment until all of the facts are known. The scientist is noted for a lack of superstition, for a high degree of curiosity, and for the ability to look at the world with an open mind. These attitudes are not, however, a part of the typical child's repertoire. But through an elementary science program such attitudes can become a part of the child's approach to the world.

Scientific attitudes can develop in children only if the teacher permits them to develop. Curiosity fades if the teacher provides every answer to every question or refuses to allow the investigations implied by the frequently voiced: "What would happen if . . . ?"

The attitude of open-mindedness is lost in a classroom where only the right answer is permitted and where creative deviations from the norm are punished by being rejected or ignored by the teacher.

A willingness to suspend judgment cannot grow if only a single authority exists, whether text or teacher, that gives an answer fitted into the allotted time for science in the daily schedule.

The nature of science as a fusion of content, process, and attitude should govern how science is approached in the elementary school. Without knowing content, the child cannot understand the grandeur of the universe; without learning process, the child cannot experience the excitement of the search. Without the attitude of a scientist, the child cannot value content and cannot appreciate the search.

An elementary science program should permit the child to encounter the world on a level where understanding can develop. If children are to learn science, they must experience it in all of its facets.

The Scientist and the Child: A Comparison

Children are curious. This curiosity, this desire to learn about the world, has led to the assumption that children are scientists by nature. But is such a statement a valid premise? Can the teacher expect children to understand intuitively how to investigate the common phenomena presented in a textbook or other content-oriented approach to science teaching? To answer these questions, we will consider a recently published piece of scientific research and a description of a typical child attempting to solve a science problem.

The Work of the Scientist

In this particular piece of research, the investigator was attempting to determine the way in which children interact with science materials when those materials are presented in nonstructured learning situations. The children involved in the research were enrolled in a preschool program and ranged from three to six years in age.

The subjects included twenty-one boys and eighteen girls, with twenty-four of the children white, eight of the children black, and seven of them Spanish-speaking. Although the children came from two classrooms, they were taught by the researcher and an assistant in groups of six for one thirty-minute period each week for thirteen weeks. The children did not work with the same group each week but were assigned to different groups for each of the teaching sessions.

The science activities that these children worked with were included in the regular program for the preschool. Each of the six children in the group had a full set of materials with which to work, but the children were encouraged to interact with one another.

The activities presented to the children included:

1. *Marbles:* Children used these to investigate the interactions of one object with another, beginning with the question, "How can you make a big splash using the marble and water?"
2. *Balances:* Children used balances and objects to investigate the concepts of more, less, and equal, beginning with the question, "How can you make one side of the balance heavier than the other?"
3. *Water:* Children used water and objects to investigate the concepts of sinking and floating, beginning with the question, "Which of these things will float?"
4. *Pulley Systems:* Children used pulleys to investigate concepts of motion, beginning with the question, "How can you get two wheels to move at the same time?"

The materials were made ready for the subjects before the teacher gave a brief verbal introduction. During the three to four minute introduction, unfamiliar objects were named and unfamiliar words were defined with reference to materials. At the end of the introduction, the beginning question for the materials at hand was posed to the children. In order to allow as much freedom to investigate as possible, the subjects were given no hint as to how to answer the questions.

While the children worked, the researcher and the assistant observed the children, watching how they interacted with the materials and making notes of the children's comments. After the thirteen weeks of instruction were completed, the researcher reviewed and analyzed the written records to determine the kinds of interactions which took place between the children and the objects.

From this analysis of the data, the researcher proposed four stages in the development of the use of materials:

1. *Exploration:* At the beginning of each of the sessions with materials, the subjects interacted with all of the materials by rolling, dropping, bouncing, smelling, tasting, feeling, piling, knocking down, squeezing, and banging. The degree of familiarity with the materials made no difference since objects like rubber bands received as much attention as did pulley wheels. Four of the children continued this kind of exploratory behavior throughout the entire thirteen weeks.

2. *Representation:* At the representation level subjects used the materials in fantasy play rather than to investigate the question which was given. Popsicle sticks became sharks and floating objects people. Pulley systems were helicopters, police cars, or record players. Spontaneous bursts of singing "Row, Row, Row Your Boat" occurred whenever water was used. Fantasy play involved more than one child. Four children remained at this level throughout the thirteen weeks.

3. *Investigation:* At this level the subjects would notice some unexpected occurrence: an object that floated when placed gently on the water but sank if dropped; two objects that appeared different but balanced. When this occurred, the subject would repeatedly test all of the objects to determine whether the same thing would happen with every object. After the certainty of the unusual happening was established and other objects tested, the child would then demonstrate it for others. Only six children progressed beyond this stage to the last stage of object use.

4. *Generalization:* At this stage the subject began to develop a verbal generalization consistent with the result of the investigation of the unexpected event. These generalizations were consistent with the observations made by the subject but were not necessarily scientifically correct.

In general, this piece of research indicated the necessity for children to interact with materials if they were to be able to use these materials in a meaningful way to investigate common scientific phenomena. With this description of a piece of research as a basis, we can consider the actual steps investigators use in conducting research.

Research Procedures. The following indicates a highly generalized and idealized step-by-step sequence of events used in the development of an experiment. This sequence is changed by the individual scientist to fit a particular project or to reflect individual idiosyncrasies, but it does give a good indication of what is done during research and does provide a basis from which to begin an analysis of the research described.

Step One. The first step in any research is to develop a question which can be solved through the use of the experimental method. In the research presented, the scientist asked the question, "How do preschool children interact with science materials in an unstructured setting?" Once this question was established, the researcher moved on to step two.

Step Two. The researcher read all available, pertinent information relevant to the research question. The purpose of this step is to determine whether the question has already been fully answered and also to determine whether there are any established procedures for the solution to such a question. In addition, reading the material helps one to develop background information that may be useful in establishing a procedure or in interpreting the data which are collected.

Step Three. In step three, the researcher plans the procedure that will be used to determine the answer to the research question. The procedures are established so that the researcher knows precisely what steps are to be followed, how the material is to be presented to the subjects, and what data are to be collected. In addition, the procedure allows the researcher to keep all factors the same for each of the repetitions of the experimental procedures. The procedure also permits duplication of the experiment under other conditions and by other scientists.

Step Four. In step four, the procedure is used and the desired data are collected. In this case the data were collected in the form of observations of the children while they worked. In other cases, the data may be in numerical form.

Step Five. In step five, the data collected during the experiment are analyzed to determine what has actually occurred. In the case of the experiment described, the data indicated stages through which children passed as they worked with science materials. In other cases, the data may indicate that the scientists' ideas were valid or invalid.

Step Six. In the final step, the researcher draws a conclusion. In this case the conclusion was in the form of the four stages that the children evidenced as they worked.

In this particular piece of research, there was no need for two common experimental factors: a control group and the development of an hypothesis. A control group is used for comparison purposes, to determine whether a change in procedure causes a change in the subjects of the experiment. In this case, the researcher was trying to describe what children did naturally and not attempting to introduce a change. Consequently, no comparison group was needed. The researcher could have indicated an hypothesis for this experiment, perhaps stating: "Children given science materials in an open environment will use those materials in an organized fashion to directly research the question given." In this case, the hypothesis would have been shown to be incorrect.

Keep in mind this research as we consider a typical child researching a problem that many children identify: insects collected and placed in jars with tight lids quickly die.

The Work of the Child

No matter what this particular child does, no matter how carefully she places the "bugs" in jars, they die by morning. This child, a six-year-old named Lucy, quickly notices what happens and brings the jar with a dead butterfly to her father and asks: "What made it die?" Father, unable to answer the question, sends Lucy to her teacher. The teacher suggests that she try to find out for herself. Unable to read well enough to find an answer, Lucy decides to turn to the jars, the insects, and her own judgment of what to do to learn why the insects always die. Five jars, all that she could find in the house, are soon lined up on the window sill of her bedroom. In the large mayonnaise jar is a monarch butterfly. The eight-ounce mushroom jar holds a Japanese beetle, and the liter sized soda bottle holds a praying mantis. The peanut butter jar has a moth; the vitamin bottle a ladybug.

Deciding to see if the bugs die because they need food, Lucy stuffs four sycamore leaves into the first two jars. But, she thinks, maybe they are not hungry; maybe the bugs cannot breathe. Leaving the jars with the leaves as they are, Lucy goes to find a hammer and nail to punch holes in the jar lids.

One television program and a game of checkers later, she returns to the jars and punches three holes in one jar lid and eleven in the next. The ladybug escapes. The praying mantis looks thirsty. Lucy splashes a little water into the jar along with the leaves. With all of the jars ready, Lucy goes off to play. Three days later, she remembers to check the jars. By then all the bugs are dead, so the jars are emptied and rocks replace the insect collection.

Similarities and Differences Between the Child and the Scientist

How similar is this child's investigation to that of a research scientist? The first step of the scientist is to determine a research question. With this defined question, the scientist reads pertinent information. On the first count, the child and the scientist are equal: both have a question for which they want an answer. After this initial similarity, however, differences emerge.

Background. Unable to read well, the child must seek information orally. She does this not as the scientist does it — to seek background information — but to obtain a final answer to the question. Only when no specific solution can be obtained does the child turn to a different means for determining the answer.

Materials. To find the answer to her question, the child turns to materials and to an activity that will give her an answer. She plunges into an experiment without hesitation. She does not refine her general question into a more specific question or into an hypothesis. This plunging, do-it-now approach leads to less than methodical work.

Control. Without a plan, there is no control. Five differently sized jars with five different species of insects seem appropriate to this child. The testing of food in two cases, air in two cases, and both air and water in another case is no problem. The escape of one of her experimental insects causes her no concern whatsoever. Having another insect for comparative purposes never even occurs to Lucy.

Results. The scientist's systematic, methodical work in observing the results of an experiment is neglected by this child in favor of television programs and games. Records of results are not kept, even though pictures could be used by the child who does not write well enough to keep a written record. In fact, since the project was forgotten for three days, no data could be collected. It is not unusual for a six-year-old child to start a project with great enthusiasm and leave it uncompleted in favor of some new activity.

Naturally, there are children who are more methodical than the fictitious Lucy. There are children who not only collect rocks but also classify them according to some system. Most children, however, are akin to Lucy rather than to the mature scientist.

Learning Activity 1–1

Investigating How Children Solve Problems

Using one of the simple questions listed below design an experiment that you could use to determine the answer. Remember to control all possible factors other than the one which you are researching and to have a control with which to compare your experimental results. After you have designed and carried out your experiment, ask a child of four, a child of eight, and a child of eleven how he or she would solve the same problem. Record the child's responses in each case. Compare the responses of the children to each other and to your own method. What similarities and differences emerge?

1. What caused the "bugs" in the jar to die?
2. What caused the water in the aquarium to turn green?
3. What causes bread to get moldy?
4. What causes an ice cube to melt?
5. What causes a plant on the window sill to grow better than a plant in a closet?
6. What causes one paper airplane to fly farther than another?
7. What causes one soap bubble to be larger than another?

Note: It will be particularly helpful, if, when you interview the children, you have moldy bread, an ice cube, plants, or other materials so that they can see and handle them while talking.

Is the child, then, a scientist by nature? These scenarios of the child and the scientist seem to indicate that there is little in common except the desire to find an answer through the use of materials. Yet, the characteristics of child research are similar to the characteristics of adult research in more ways than simply the isolation of a question. It is the quality of the research more than the content that causes the greatest differences between the child and the adult. The desire to know, the willingness to set up some activity to answer a question, and the curiosity of the child all are akin to the scientist.

The kinship which does exist is one of attitude rather than one of method. The ability to work as the adult scientist works, to use the scientific method, does not develop naturally. It is not a simple product of either age or exposure to the content of science. Rather the ability to work in a mature and methodical manner must be developed gradually through a school science program suited to the needs, abilities, and characteristics of children. It is a method that needs to be gradually presented and refined as the child matures and learns. It is also a method that needs to be used with great frequency.

The traits of the children in a classroom at each level from preschool through sixth grade provide the first clue to the sequence in learning the scientific method that may be most effective with children.

Between Three and Five: The Preschool Child

The preschool-kindergarten classroom is an excitingly dynamic place where young children are able to interact with a wide variety of materials as well as with each other and with adults. The learning that occurs is difficult to categorize into tidy subject matter areas. Three-, four-, and five-year-olds move rapidly from one activity to another utilizing skills gained in one area to work in a second. Therefore, science may emerge as children fashion clay animals, listen at story time, or socialize in the playground sandbox.

An observer quickly notices differences between those who are in the three- and four-year age group and those who have reached five years of age.

Threes and Fours

Language. Threes and fours generally have a limited, though functional, vocabulary of about 2,000 words. This vocabulary tends to be extensive enough by four so that preschoolers are able to understand simple explanations and reasons. Since questions and answers seem to make up the bulk of child to adult conversation, the ability to understand explanations is a strong point. It is far too easy, however, for teachers of threes and fours to provide all of the answers or to provide more of an answer than is really needed.

Investigative Behavior. The alternative to providing verbal answers is fairly easy, because threes and fours are curious. They are also beginning to show the initiative that will allow them to investigate their own questions and to supply their own answers. Planning and beginning an investigation tends to be as interesting for the preschooler as actually investigating. For teachers, however, the problem with preschoolers is that they plan and start but frequently do not finish.

Investigations for threes and fours should be play oriented rather than work oriented, because it is through play that young children learn. Using small muscles like those of the hands is difficult for young children, because these muscles are not yet mature. By four, however, children can be expected to use scissors to cut on a straight line or to use a pencil to draw crude letters. But consistency in such skills cannot be expected at this age level.

More appropriate for young children, both because of their stage in muscle development and because play is a primary means of learning, are large muscle activities: running, jumping, hopping, throwing, catching, and skipping. Even when small muscle use may be appropriate, these children tend to use large muscles.

Cooperation and Sharing. Threes and fours tend to enjoy being with other children. Threes often play together without actually interacting in a relationship known as parallel play. Fours also play together in this way, but they are also beginning to cooperate and share. But, whether playing or working, threes and fours tend to do best in an atmosphere that provides security, guidance, clear routines, and the opportunity to make decisions within a limited framework.

Fives

Cooperation. The five-year-old moving into the kindergarten has progressed to the point where language can be used for true interaction and discussion. Show-and-tell becomes a popular part of the school day. Perhaps because of the increased ability to use language, the five-year-old is able to play and to work cooperatively with others. Most frequently, fives will choose one other child or a small group of five or six for cooperative ventures.

Independence. Along with the increased ability to cooperate, five-year-olds show increasing independence. They are able, with teacher help, to plan a total group activity. They can follow directions. They can concentrate on a single activity for twenty minutes or more and even carry a project over to the next day.

Large muscle coordination is so improved over threes and fours that even walking a balance beam is possible. Small muscle coordination is also improving. By five children can be expected to fold a paper on a corner-to-corner diagonal; copy a square, triangle, or design; and draw easily recognized letters or numbers. Children of five also enjoy rhythms, songs, dramatic play, and stories that feature real children or animals that behave like children.

Atmosphere. Fives seem to thrive on an atmosphere of activity and freedom to use and develop personal abilities. Guidance is necessary so that the five-year-old begins to develop the skills that will be needed in the first grade.

Science in the Preschool and Kindergarten

The natural curiosity of children in the preschool and kindergarten lends itself to an interest in the study of science at these age levels. The characteristics of the preschool-kindergarten age child give some indication as to how activities can be presented so that the experiences of science can be most beneficial to three-, four-, and five-year-olds.

Open-ended Activities. Since the preschooler is generally not concerned with reaching a specified end-point, activities for science should be open ended. The child engaged in open-ended activities can choose to continue with the activity or to end, depending on interest and preference. Because the activity is open ended, the child cannot be considered to have failed in any way by not bringing the activity to closure.

Autonomy. Providing a variety of science activities, limited to two or three choices for three-year-olds and moving to a wider variety for five-year-olds, will help in developing the child's ability to make choices and will also complement the child's growing sense of autonomy. The child's growing sense of autonomy can also be encouraged if children obtain their own materials from a central location and return those materials to that location when they are finished. Even the youngest child is capable of obtaining and returning materials, thus saving the teacher's energy for more important tasks.

Method. Although the preschooler's verbal ability is increasing and can be effectively used in interpersonal communication, verbal methods of science teaching are inappropriate for preschoolers. Manipulative materials that involve many senses, involve large muscles, and encourage small muscle development should be provided. Threes and fours should have individual sets of materials with which to work, even though they will enjoy sitting with friends while working. Fives should also have their own materials, but on occasion they should be encouraged to cooperate with others and share materials. As children work with materials, they should also be encouraged to talk with one another, to demonstrate for each other, and to communicate with one another their discoveries. In this way children can uncover discrepancies that need further investigation and affirm rules that they discover through manipulation.

Questions. Children frequently ask questions that lend themselves to investigation with concrete materials. The teacher should encourage such scientific investigations rather than providing an explanation. The teacher's role, then, is to act as a guide, to help the child plan, to be available when needed in order to help, and to listen to the exciting results if the activity comes to closure. Some questions will also lend themselves to resolution with written information as well as with investigation. At such times, the teacher is encouraged to locate and read to the class or to small groups of interested children information written on an appropriate level. Many picture books deal with science-oriented topics which children investigate.

Atmosphere. The teacher needs to develop an atmosphere in which the preschool or kindergarten age child is able to experience success in science-related activities. An understanding that for the younger child finishing is not as important as starting should help the teacher avoid criticizing when a child fails to complete a task. An understanding that small muscles are not well developed can prevent the teacher from supplying materials that require too many small manipulations or from expecting adultlike perfection in the finished product.

Correlation. In the preschool and kindergarten, the science aspect of the school curriculum should be integrated as much as possible into the total activity of the day. Playground activities can lend themselves to the study of the human body, energy, and simple machines. Sand and water play can be used to develop understandings of matter, and music can help to develop an understanding of sound. Rather than attempting to compartmentalize science into a distinct aspect of the day for young children, the teacher should use ordinary activities as a means for developing science-related topics.

A Preschool Science Lesson

Ten Headstart children sat in a circle on the tile floor of their classroom curiously turning to look at the newspaper-covered tables behind them where basins of water and flour waited. Almost equally interesting, however, were the basin of water and the closed box on the floor in front of the teacher.

The teacher shook the closed box and quickly gained the attention of the four- and five-year-olds.

"Listen again. What could I have in my box?" she asked as she shook the box several more times.

The children responded eagerly.

"Stones."

"Balls."

"Marbles."

"Pennies."

"Little sticks."

After all of the ideas were given, the teacher dumped the contents of the box on the floor: a stone, a large ball bearing, a marble, a solid rubber ball.

"What would happen if I held the marble here and let it fall into the basin of water?" the teacher asked.

"It will splash!" the children replied, giggling.

"Let's see," the teacher said and dropped the marble into the water. "How far did the water splash?"

Five of the children pointed to water spots on the table top.

"Which one of the splashes is the farthest from the basin?"

"This one," Jamie said. He marked his splash mark with a small block that the teacher handed him.

"Now, let's look at these other objects," the teacher said and held up each object. "Which of these do you think will splash the farthest?"

The objects were ordered and left where they were placed. "At the tables are some basins of water and flour. Let's try out each of the objects and see which splashes the farthest. Please try not to mix the water and the flour together."

While eight of the children dropped objects into the water, and also learned that flour could splash as well, one child immediately dumped the water into the flour and began to mix them together.

"What are you finding out, D.J.?" the teacher asked.

"When you mix them together, they get squishy, and gooey, and like stretchy and the stuff makes things stick all together."

While D.J. investigated the water and flour mixture, Inez first tried splashing, tried wetting each object, rolling it in the flour, and then tried to see if the object would bounce. She continued caking the objects with flour, each time a little thicker, trying them over and over. "When you bounce them the stuff falls off and gets all over the floor," she announced.

"Teacher, it itches and gets real skinny and falls off when it dries up," D.J. reported holding out water and flour-caked arms.

"How is the dry flour and water different from the wet kind?" he was asked.

"I'll go look."

"Teacher, look how far mine splashed."

"Mine went even farther."

"Flour doesn't splash much," Janey, nearly covered with flour, reported.

"If you throw the marble it splashes more than the ball, but if you just drop them, the ball is splashier."

The group was called back to the circle. D.J. and Inez reported on their unique investigations. Then the group tested the order of the objects marking the longest splash for each object; the original ranking was changed to suit the new evidence. A few children reported differing results from their own investigations and were asked to demonstrate how they had dropped the objects.

The class decided to keep the order they had found together and to try different ways of dropping the objects the next day.

"What do we do now?" the teacher asked.

"Clean up all the mess," the children chorused. They did.

Between Six and Eight: The Primary Grade Child

The primary grade classroom may be similar to the preschool-kindergarten or may have a totally different atmosphere. In some cases, primary grade children are in classrooms where a great deal of free movement is permitted, where games and materials are abundant, and where children choose which activity to do at a particular time. In other cases, primary grade children are in classrooms where each child is provided with a desk, where learning is word oriented, and where a uniform daily schedule is followed by everyone. Whether the child learns in a structured classroom or in an open environment, the characteristics of the child remain the same.

Sixes

Physical Activity. The six-year-old entering the first grade is very similar in a number of ways to the previous year's five-year-old. Physical activity is still highly important so that these children tend to be exuberant, active, and aggressive. They tend to throw their entire bodies into any activity. Though there is steady improvement, sixes are still inept at the use of small muscles. And, since these small muscles are not well developed and the eyes are not yet mature, fatigue follows prolonged attempts at hand-eye coordination.

Cooperation. Also like fives, sixes enjoy working with other children. It is difficult, however, for sixes to take turns. It is also difficult for them to follow group rules: sixes will often withdraw from an activity if they do not get their own way. But, even when the child does not withdraw, it is not unusual for a six-year-old to leave an activity unfinished.

Behavior. By six, the child is trying to identify with older children and to leave behind the "babies" found in the kindergarten. This change in outlook causes six-year-olds to want both the responsibility of increased maturity and the security of an established routine. They are eager to learn new things, especially about the immediate environment, but they are also contented with whatever is occurring at a particular time. They are keenly competitive, yet criticism causes them to wilt. Sixes can best be described as a bundle of contradictory behaviors.

Sevens

Behavior. By age seven, many of the contradictions found in the six-year-old have been eliminated. Sevens are still active and in need of large muscle activity, but they are also better able to use small muscles for tasks like writing than are sixes. Eyes are more mature so that reading is not quite so tiring, but fatigue still follows prolonged use of the eyes. As reading and writing skills develop, so do oral language skills. Sevens are talkative and frequently exaggerate as they tell stories. They enjoy many verbal activities: songs, fairy tales, myths, nature stories, comic books, television, and motion pictures. Factual stories about machines, electricity, rockets, space, and animals are also enjoyed.

Maturity. Sevens, like sixes, are making the break from the world of little children to the world of adults. Striving for greater maturity, the seven-year-old will both stand up for his rights and reach out for the assurance of adults. Because of these traits, guidance is needed, so that the seven can gain in independence but within a secure environment. In their desire to please adults, however, seven-year-olds can easily become overly dependent upon those adults. Guidance should, therefore, be limited.

Abilities. Although the preschool and kindergarten age child may evidence some differences in ability from other children, these differences do not become great enough for the teacher or the other children to notice them until the age of seven. These differences will not be too great at this time, but the teacher does need to treat each student as an individual.

Eights

Behavior. Compared to the younger primary grade children, the eight-year-old seems very mature. Their small muscles are better developed and their eyes are mature. Reading now is an important way to get information. Writing is becoming more usable for conveying information. Because reading is becoming an important means of learning, any reading difficulties that arise begin to pose a real problem.

Peer Influence. At about eight years of age, the peer group begins to gain in importance. Gangs are starting to develop, particularly same-gender gangs; boys and girls are starting to pull apart from one another. Group activities, spontaneous and organized games, and group dramatics are popular. Planning for the entire group can be done with a minimum of difficulty and implemented with a minimum of teacher assistance.

Increasing identification with the peer group has a number of ramifications. First, in cases of conflict, allegiance with other children rather than with adults occurs. Second, awareness of individual differences becomes more developed. At this point, guidance is needed constructively to channel this awareness of differences. And, third, there is a great desire to belong to the group. Outcasts first begin to develop among eight-year-olds. But, even though peers are highly important, children still look to adults for praise and for encouragement.

Work Habits. For the first time, the child derives as much enjoyment out of completing a task as out of beginning one. The eight-year-old seems to enjoy bringing an activity to closure and is willing to tackle almost anything. At this age level, collections begin to become interesting and seem to serve as a symbol of the eight-year-old's ability to categorize, organize, and complete an activity.

Science in the Primary Grades

The reading interests of children in the primary grades give an indication of the interest in science-related topics that exists at this age level. Nature stories, stories about space and rockets, as well as stories about machines are all enjoyed. Although such stories are read and enjoyed, there is still a need for activities and for presentation of science in a manner consistent with their basic characteristics.

Multisensory Activities. Science activities should be multisensory in nature. That is, the activities should involve the child through as many senses as possible and should include large muscle activity. As the child progresses from first through third grade, more small muscle manipulations can be called for.

Open-ended Activities. Activities will still need to be open ended, although some activities that reach closure should be included for eight-year-olds. There are a number of reasons for retaining open-ended activities in the primary grades. First, children at ages six and seven are not yet ready for activities that require closure. Second, as differing ability levels emerge, children should be able to work at a level that is individually appropriate. Open-ended activities allow for varying ability levels by also allowing the child to stop at a point before the child reaches frustration. And, third, open-ended activities play upon children's initiative by allowing them to plan their own courses of action.

Grouping. A variety of grouping arrangements and materials arrangements should be used in the primary grades. Younger primary grade children should each have his or her own set of materials for science activities. Such arrangements can allow a child to withdraw from an activity planned as a group endeavor and still continue with the activity. Later, as eights show the ability to plan for a large-group experience, a single set of materials can be provided and divided for group use so that each member of the group investigates a part of the problem. However, large groups with a single set of materials should not become the only pattern for teaching science to eight-year-olds. Eights should also have access as frequently as possible to individual sets of materials.

Reading. Most children now have enough reading skill so that written directions for science activities can be used. However, alternatives must be provided for those children who are not able to read well enough to comprehend what is to be done: tapes, drawings, teacher or other student demonstrations of the procedures are all appropriate. No child should be forced to fail in science because of weak reading skills.

The reading skills of the eight-year-old, as well as those of other primary grade children, can also be used to develop background information prior to science activities as well as to provide additional information not available through simple science activities. A wide variety of selected textbooks and tradebooks should be made available to primary grade children so that their reading can be directed to some purpose.

Written and Oral Communication. As skill in writing is developed in the primary grades, children should use that skill in the science program. Written and oral communication skills can be used by primary grade children as they collect and organize data during activities. Oral skills can be developed by giving reports of results to others in the class. Simple charts can be filled in by students, but, once again, alternatives need to be provided when a child does not have a given language skill.

Collections. Developing collections is an interest of the eight-year-old; hence, class and individual collections should be encouraged. Such collections provide a natural starting point for the development of classification skills and frequently lead to questions that can be answered through the use of concrete materials or by exercising reading skills.

Atmosphere. As with preschoolers and kindergarteners, the teacher needs to provide an atmosphere conducive to success by tailoring expectations to children rather than molding children to expectations. The teacher should delegate an increasing amount of responsibility, beginning with limited choices and extending to students' planning their own science activities around subject-matter limitations. In essence, the atmosphere of the primary grade science class should be one of "let's find out."

A Primary Grade Science Lesson

The second graders were studying a unit on matter and energy. From their observations of rocks, each other, toys, desks, and plants, the children had decided that matter was something that they could hold in their hands and that felt heavy. After reading their textbooks, they redefined matter as something that took up space and was heavy. The textbook phrase "has mass" was rejected because the children were not quite certain what that meant.

Their next task was to begin to define energy. The children came to school and found a large box, taped securely closed, at the back of the classroom.

"What's in the box?" Tommy asked.

"Wow! It's heavy," Jim said pushing on the side.

"It's taped closed. Before I can open it, I need to get the box from the back of the room to the front of the room. How could I do that?" the teacher asked.

The children began to give their ideas. Each idea was listed on the board as it was given: roll it, push it, get a rope and drag it, slide it, get a big bunch of people and carry it, get a real strong guy to carry it, get a strong chain and a horse, hook the chain to the horse and around the box, and have the horse drag it.

After all the ideas were given the children tried the feasible ideas and finally managed to get the box to the front of the room.

"Good job! Is that box matter?"

"Yes."

"Now, what about the *ways* we used to move the box? Are *they* matter?"

"Yes."

"Let's look at that. What did we do to move the box?"

"Pushed, pulled, dragged, and rolled," the children answered.

Eric came up to push the box. While he pushed, the teacher tried to grab hold of his push. The children agreed that she could not catch and hold it. The same thing was done while other children tried to pull, drag, or roll the box. Not once could the teacher or any of the children catch a push, drag, pull, or roll.

From this information, the children inferred that they could not catch hold of these things. They did not take up any space and certainly were not heavy. They were all something, but they were not matter.

"What could all of these things be?" the teacher asked.

"Well, you can push or you can pull," Betsy said.

"Or drag," Lisa added.

"Drags are just like pulls," Jim decided.

"All right, all these are pushes or pulls. There's a special word for these things. We call all of them energy. Let's think for a minute. What other things do we know about that are energy?"

Between Nine and Twelve: The Intermediate Grade Child

Like the primary grade classrooms, those of the intermediate grades may have a number of different appearances. The classrooms can be open or structured like those of the primary grades, and a third variety is sometimes seen. Many intermediate grade children are in departmentalized or partially departmentalized programs in which they move from classroom to classroom and teacher to teacher as the various subject areas are encountered. Recall again that it is the classroom structure that changes and not the characteristics of the children in those classrooms.

Nines and Tens

Behavior. Nines and tens are better able to handle a variety of teachers and techniques than are younger children. They tend to be decisive and responsible, dependable and reasonable. By this age children are able not only to plan and complete an activity but also to do both without a great deal of adult supervision.

Perfectionism. The careless eight-year-old vanishes by nine or ten to be replaced by the perfectionist. Papers are done and redone until they are beautiful in appearance and as accurate as the child can manage. The child of nine or ten wants to do well and frequently becomes demoralized if there is too much pressure or discouragement. But this perfectionism can also lead to conformity. The child wants to fit into a peer group even though the group to which the child belongs may change frequently. Nines and tens find it hard to accept those who are different, yet they are beginning to realize that a number of differing opinions can exist and that all may be equally valid.

Individual Differences. Individual differences are quite apparent among nines and tens. Physically, girls are more mature than boys. But, perhaps more important, their physical maturity is accompanied by differences in interests and abilities. It becomes possible for teachers, parents, and other children to point out the interests of individual children as well as to play upon these interests in both constructive and destructive ways.

Reading. Reading now becomes a source of discouragement for many children. The emphasis of the intermediate grades is too frequently on gathering information through reading. Children with reading problems, more frequently boys than girls, are under great pressure to succeed in reading so they can succeed in other areas.

Responsibility. At nine and ten children are beginning to show the half-adult, half-child behaviors that teachers find so frustrating. They want responsibility, but also need to be able to fail in their responsibilities without too much reminder that they did fail. These children are able to learn from their mistakes; are able to handle deserved punishment. At this age, too, children strongly resent adults who talk down to them.

Elevens and Twelves

The perfectionism of nines and tens seems a prelude to the awkwardness of the preadolescent elevens and twelves. This change from child to adolescent can be characterized by such adjectives as awkward, restless, lazy, changeable, overly critical, rebellious, uncooperative, self-conscious, independent, and curious. Elevens and twelves are all of these things, sometimes within the same hour. Their very changeableness makes them one of the most challenging and most interesting of age groups to teach.

Peer Pressure. The peer influence of the eight-year-old becomes the peer pressure of the eleven- and twelve-year-old. For the first time, the opinion of the peer group is beginning to be more highly valued than that of adults. The peer group becomes the socializing agent providing a better gauge of behavior than parental norms can provide for the child. Peer pressures can also have a negative effect on the preadolescent causing the individual to doubt his or her own judgment and to change from a correct to an incorrect idea in order to conform. The preadolescent will frequently go along with the group rather than stand on his or her own convictions.

Curiosity. The preadolescent period is also the time when curiosity is high. Curiosity, at this level, is highly correlated with self-esteem. Very curious children tend to be more self-reliant, less prejudiced, more socially responsible, and to have a greater sense of belonging. It is possible that children with poor self-esteem do not appear to be curious because they expect to fail. From the opposite side, it is also possible that children who are not curious may not explore their surroundings as much as curious children and so may fail to learn those things necessary to help them gain in self-esteem.

Language. At this stage, language is beginning to take on a function that extends beyond simple communication. The preadolescent is making a transition from thought stimulated by concrete objects to thought using abstractions as a basis. This transition is beginning to permit the child to think and to learn in an adult manner. The child thus has a strong need for independence and increased responsibility, for treatment as an adult, and for freedom from condemnation for acting like a child. Both independence and responsibility need to develop in an atmosphere without nagging and among adults who are able to demonstrate affection and a sense of humor.

Science in the Intermediate Grades

It is the nature of the preadolescent to be both responsible and irresponsible, mature and immature, independent and dependent, cooperative and uncooperative. In order to allow for the changeable nature of the preadolescent, the science program needs to be an open and accepting one, where discussions can be held that demonstrate a wide variety of opinions and where activities can be conducted that lead the child toward more adult modes of thought.

Individualization. The preadolescent level is characterized by a wide range of maturity levels as well as a wide range of interests. In order better to assure suitability of the program, greater individualization of content and activity is needed than ever before. Students at the preadolescent level should have the opportunity to select areas of science study from a variety of equally valid experiences or at least to choose the order of specified areas to suit personal needs and preferences.

The need for individualization is also reflected in the requirement that children of eleven and twelve be able to plan and carry out activities in science without adult interference. Preadolescents need to be given the latitude to develop as individuals as well as the freedom to pursue topics of interest. This requires that the teacher be present to provide advice and assistance but not consistently to take over the activity.

Discussions. Among preadolescents, peer pressure to conform is so strong that opinions can be changed solely by pressure from other children. Consequently, attention during science should be given to collecting factual data, to drawing conclusions from that data, and to supporting one's conclusions with data. All three of these activities can occur during discussions of experiments, activities, and reading assignments.

Other discussions, not concerned with hard data from experiments or reading matter, should also take place with preadolescents. The topics and the structure of these discussions should be such that a variety of opinions can be elicited without any final, absolute decision possible. The preadolescent needs to become aware of the variety of possible opinions on science-related topics so that the idea grows that it is normal and natural to have a variety of opinions, that everyone need not think alike. The atmosphere during such discussions must be such that students listen to one another with respect and wait to present opposing data and opinions. Openness and acceptance must be the key words.

Abstract Thought Processes. The movement toward abstract thought that begins to develop among elevens and twelves needs careful nurturing if it is to develop fully. Although some students will continue to need concrete materials as an aid to conceptual development, others will be reaching toward abstraction. Those abstract thinkers, as well as those who are mature enough to make the transition to abstractness, should conduct true experiments in the science class with control of variables and the use of a control group. The preadolescent is also becoming more able to use mathematics as a meaningful part of a science experience. Consequently, mathematics should be integrated into science experiences whenever they are appropriate.

Abstract thinking abilities are not, however, fully developed in any single child or even evident in all children. Consequently, although the use of experimentation in science should be included, students should also have the option of returning to activities which do not require control of variables whenever they need to do so.

Verbal Learning. The development of abstract thought processes means not only an ability to learn from the true experiment but also an ability to learn more from written materials than ever before. Although a steady diet of reading is not appropriate to the spirit of science, reading can help preadolescents determine how to plan for an experiment by providing background information and supplying missing theoretical information that will allow for a fuller understanding of experimental results. A wide variety of textbooks, tradebooks, magazines, and films or film strips should always be available to the eleven- or twelve-year-old so that the research scientist's need to keep up on current information may be developed in the child.

Although children have reached the mental stage where reading is a common source of information, reading problems frequently make reading a difficult means for learning for many children. Alternatives to reading should be provided, both for the child to understand activity or experiment directions and for information. But even those children who read well may need some assistance as the fifth and sixth grades are reached. Even in the best science textbook for teaching, content becomes more technical and more filled with unfamiliar vocabulary.

Terms that are new to children must be defined if written material is to be understood. An effective sequence for the development of meaning provides concrete experiences that will develop the underlying concept and then moves to the verbal definition of the term. In any case, terms themselves should probably receive less emphasis than the concept named by the term.

Curiosity. Curiosity needs to be cultivated during the preadolescent period since it is so closely tied to self-esteem. The child will need to have the satisfaction of following up on an item of individual interest rather than always following what everyone else is doing. The child will need to have the satisfaction of coming to a conclusion that may be verified by others through further experimentation or through reading of sources. In addition, the teacher will need to be willing to make adjustments in schedules in order to accommodate sudden, intense interests. At this period, it is important to pick up on ideas rather than defer them to a later, more convenient time. Preadolescent changeability may make something highly interesting at one point in time though not at another. As we teach children to develop experimental skills in science, content means a great deal less than the actual process of experimentation. In many cases a real problem that evolves from student interests is more valid for teaching science than is an artificial problem situation found in a textbook.

An Intermediate Grade Science Lesson

The sixth grade had been studying simple chemistry, learning about physical and chemical changes, compounds and elements, mixtures and solutions. As they dissolved various materials in water to find out how much sugar, salt, alum, or Epsom salts would dissolve in 100 milliliters, some of the children began to wonder whether the temperature of the water made any difference in how much of the solid would dissolve.

Under the direction of the teacher they wrote a hypothesis: "If the temperature of the water changes, then the amount of sugar, salt, alum, or Epsom salts that dissolves in the water will change."

The students divided themselves into groups of three or four to try and decide what they would do to test the hypothesis. One group decided to raise the temperature of the water ten degrees at a time using an alcohol lamp to see how much salt would dissolve. A second group decided to use a similar idea for raising the temperature but to use sugar instead. Groups three and four were more interested in what would happen if the water were colder and so decided to add ice to the water. Group three would test alum and group four would test Epsom salts. At that point the members of group five raised the question of how they could compare the results if everyone was trying different materials and different temperatures. As a group the class decided that each of the materials should be tested once in water where the temperature was increasing, and once in water where it was decreasing. Since there were nine groups, one group decided that it would be the control group and try once again to see how much of each solid would dissolve in water at room temperature.

Once the results were determined, the problem of how to compare all of the data arose. Some of the children wanted to collect all of the weights and the temperatures into a single giant chart and then look at all of the data. Others thought it would be better for each group to graph its data and then compare the various graphs. A minority wanted to graph all of the information on a single graph using differing colors for each of the experiments.

Because no consensus could be gained, the three factions each presented their data in their own way. When everything was finished, the groups each presented their conclusions. The groups all agreed that the hotter the water the more of the solid would dissolve. But, the problem remained as to which method of presenting the data was easiest to use. After a discussion in which each of the groups was asked to present the strengths of its particular method, the class evaluated the methods. They concluded that the graph of all of the data using different colors allowed them to draw a conclusion the most easily, but that the giant chart had the advantage of showing exactly what changes occurred and how they occurred.

Learning Activity 1–2

Investigating Learning Characteristics of Children

The preschool child, the primary grade child, and the intermediate grade child differ in their physical characteristics, their relationships to other children, and their approaches to learning tasks.

Observe three children in a school setting: one between three and five, one between six and nine, and one between ten and twelve. Compare the three children in terms of

1. physical characteristics,
2. movement,
3. length of time on task,
4. interests displayed,
5. dislikes,
6. use of materials,
7. dependency on teacher or caregiver,
8. interactions with other children,
9. use of words to communicate,
10. completion of tasks.

Science in the Elementary School

Just as the methods of science must be appropriate to the children being taught so must the content conveyed by those methods be appropriate. Thought on what is appropriate to the child has changed many times during the twentieth century. Nature study with its emphasis on biological science gave way to a program of topics in all areas of science. The topics approach was then supplanted by attention to conceptual schemes, which in turn gave way to process as the sole content of the elementary science program.

Nature Study

The Characteristics of Nature Study. Nature study, the first of the trends, began in the late nineteenth century and extended into the first three decades of the twentieth century. At the height of this movement, Anna Bosford Comstock in the *Handbook of Nature Study* defined nature study in the following way:

> Nature study is, despite all discussion and perversions, a study of nature; it consists of simple, truthful observation that may, like beads on a string, finally be threaded upon understanding and thus be held together as a logical and harmonious whole. Therefore, the object of the nature study teacher should be to cultivate in the children powers of accurate observation and to build up, within them, understanding. (Comstock, 1911, p. 1)

Nature study took children out of their classrooms and into the natural world to observe, make inferences, and draw conclusions about fish, birds, reptiles, mammals, insects, plants of all varieties, the Earth, and weather.

Children were to develop knowledge, to grow in both imagination and in perception of what is true, to mature in a love of beauty, and to develop a sense of companionship with nature. Nature study, then, attempted to accomplish goals within the cognitive and affective domains of learning through attention to the biological world.

The Legacy of Nature Study. Although nature study as a movement began to wane in the 1930's, its legacy has remained. Elementary science, particularly in the primary grades, remains top-heavy with biological science. Topics such as the four seasons, plants, animals, growing things, and the various subdivisions of the plant and animal kingdoms tend to make up the bulk of the content-oriented textbook's material. The legacy of nature study remains, though the movement gave way to a topical, more balanced form of content.

Gerald S. Craig and the Content of Science

Gerald S. Craig's 1927 doctoral thesis, "Certain Techniques Used in Developing a Course of Study in Science for the Horace Mann Elementary School," listed topics that Craig determined would satisfy the major functions of the elementary science program. The first of these functions was to allow children to answer questions dealing with the world around them, the second was to contribute to life through health, safety, and technology. These two functions, according to Craig's study, could best be fulfilled if children received information from ten content areas:

1. health and nutrition,
2. living things,
3. conservation and the balance of nature,
4. rocks and soil,
5. atmosphere and weather,
6. chemical and physical changes,
7. motions, mechanics, and technology,

8. electricity, magnetism, and technology,
9. energy from the sun,
10. earth and sky.

The Legacy of Craig's Topical Approach. Craig's list of topics is still very much in evidence in current content-oriented textbooks. Teachers, who were taught themselves in a units or topics approach, frequently plan their content around this listing of topics. The listing cannot become out of date because of its very comprehensiveness. Only the actual information within the topic area would require updating to permit it to be used today.

Learning Activity 1–3

Investigating the Content of Science Textbooks

Review the kindergarten or first-grade through sixth-grade textbooks of a science series. Note the topics that are included in each of the textbooks. Compare the list of topics that you find with the list developed by Gerald S. Craig.

1. What similarities in topics do you find?
2. What topics are included in your list that are not a part of Craig's list?
3. What proportion of the topics is biological in nature?
4. Do you consider the topics which are included in Craig's list appropriate for today's children? Why? Why not?
5. What topics might you include which are not a part of either your list or the list developed by Craig?
6. What topics might you decide to delete from the textbooks which you reviewed? What are your reasons for these deletions?

Now, find three or four others who reviewed different series of textbooks. As a group compare the topics considered at each level and compile a listing of those topics that are most frequently found at each of the grade levels of a modern science program.

Craig's listing does, however, suffer from one particular flaw: it tends to fragment the content information rather than to develop interrelationships among the topics. At the end of the 1950's, such fragmentation began to be challenged. It appeared that students were unable to relate information from the various topic areas so that it could be used in problem solving. Those who began this challenge suggested that the topics approach to content selection be replaced by one which emphasized the nature of science.

Jerome Bruner, one of the outstanding spokesmen for the approach to curriculum development that emphasizes the nature of the discipline, wrote in 1963:

> The curriculum of the subject should be determined by the most fundamental understanding that can be achieved of the underlying principles that give structure to the subject. Teaching specific topics or skills without making clear their context in the broader fundamental structure of a field of knowledge is uneconomical in several deep senses. In the first place, such teaching makes it exceedingly difficult for the student to generalize from what he has learned to what he will encounter. In the second place, learning that has fallen short of a grasp of general principles has little regard in terms of intellectual excitement. (Bruner, 1963, p. 31)

Theory into Action: The Underlying Structure of Science

In 1964, the National Science Teachers Association (NSTA) issued a position paper, *Theory into Action in Science Curriculum Development.* In this paper the underlying principles that constitute the fundamental structure of science were discussed in the form of twelve themes. Seven of these themes, which were to be used for curriculum development, were concerned with the conceptual basis of science.

Children were to learn basic concepts of matter and energy that could be applied to all branches of science. Concepts of interaction among units of matter as well as concepts of hierarchical classification as an organizational tool were also considered. The idea of change as the result of interactions over a period of time was discussed. These conceptual schemes were to serve as a framework for content selection. All branches of science were to contribute to a total understanding of the overarching conceptual patterns.

This NSTA position paper also covered a second aspect of science. The nature of the scientific enterprise was to be demonstrated through attention to the five processes of science. Children were to learn that science was not a finished product, that there was still much left to be learned. Children were also to learn that what we know now was discovered piecemeal by scientists working in many different places and, often, in many different times. The children were also to learn that measurement formed an integral part of science and that precise measurement frequently leads to an understanding of the laws which govern the universe.

The NSTA themes caused a great deal of rethinking about the science program for the elementary school. But the changes were not to stop at this point.

Process as the Content of Science

Until the early 1960's, the thrust of the science curriculum was toward the content of science: its facts, laws, principles, and theories. The nature of science approach to curriculum development provided another, valid possibility. Rather than a content focus, advocates proposed a process focus. The content of the science curriculum was to be the methods used by the research scientist in the pursuit of knowledge.

The American Association for the Advancement of Science in its elementary science program, *Science — A Process Approach* (SAPA), defined thirteen processes that could be used as the basis of a science program. In the kindergarten through third grade, SAPA developed the child's skill in the processes of observing, using numbers, predicting, inferring, classifying, communicating, using space/time relations, and measuring. These eight processes were viewed as the basis upon which more complex processes could be built.

The intermediate grade child, after establishing a basis in primary processes, could then begin to work with five advanced processes: formulating hypotheses, interpreting data, controlling variables, experimenting, and defining operationally.

In this text some of the SAPA processes as well as processes identified in other sources will be used. The total list of processes consists of

communicating
observing
using numbers
predicting
inferring
concluding
classifying
using space relations
interpreting data
formulating hypotheses
controlling variables
experimenting
defining operationally
asking operational questions
seeking cause and effect
using interaction and systems.

Appropriateness of the Processes. All of the processes of science are not equally appropriate for all ages or grade levels within the elementary school. Although very young children can make observations and investigate operational questions, it is not until the fifth or sixth grade that children can be expected to conduct true experiments and control variables. Also, within most of the processes are a number of levels of difficulty. Thus, in the process of prediction, children at an early level can make predictions from concrete objects but not from theoretical material. Table 1–1 indicates the definition of each of the processes and the practical levels within each of the processes.

Table 1–1 The processes of science

PROCESS	DEFINITION	LEVELS
Communicating	Interpreting and conveying information in oral, written, pictorial, or numerical form	1. Oral and pictorial communication are level one. 2. Written forms of communication are level two. 3. Numerical computations are level three.

Table 1–1 Continued

PROCESS	DEFINITION	LEVELS
Observing	Obtaining information through all of the appropriate senses	1. Only one level will be considered for practical classroom use.
Using numbers	Using numbers other than length, area, weight, and volume to describe the outcome of an activity or an experiment; includes graphs	1. Level one consists of counting. 2. Level two uses numerical computations. 3. Graphing may consist of object graphs, string or paper graphs, bar graphs, or point graphs.
Predicting	The process of anticipating future events based upon past observations and experiences	1. Level one uses concrete objects as the basis. 2. Level two uses theories and abstractions as the basis.
Inferring	The process of interpreting direct observations; past experiences are frequently used as a basis	1. Level one uses nonnumerical data. 2. Level two uses numerical data.
Concluding	A special type of inference generally based on a large amount of data and describing a pattern that exists within the data; less likely to change than are inferences	1. Level one uses nonnumerical data. 2. Level two uses numerical data.
Classifying	Grouping of objects and phenomena on the basis of likenesses and differences	1. Level one uses concrete objects grouped through the use of a single property. 2. Level two uses concrete objects grouped through the use of more than one property. 3. Level three uses concrete objects in a hierarchical form of classification. 4. Level four uses nonconcrete phenomena as the material for classification.
Using space relations	The process of using basic plane and solid geometric shapes as well as length, area, weight, and volume as a part of observation	1. Shapes: a. Level one uses the solid geometric shapes. b. Level two uses the plane geometric shapes 2. Geometric factors: a. Level one uses direct measurement of length. b. Level two uses direct measurement of area. c. Level three uses direct measurement of weight.

Table continues on following page.

Table 1–1 Continued

PROCESS	DEFINITION	LEVELS
		d. Level four uses direct measurement of volume. e. Level five uses indirect measurements. f. Level six uses computations.
Interpreting data	The process of using numerical or other forms of data to determine the validity of an hypothesis or to answer a question	1. Level one uses nonnumerical, descriptive data. 2. Level two uses numerical data.
Formulating hypotheses	The process of developing an if . . . then statement, which will then be tested by conducting an experiment	1. Only one level will be considered here for practical classroom use.
Controlling variables	The process of holding all factors constant except the single factor being tested through an experiment	1. Level one consists of identification of variables already controlled in a previously planned experiment. 2. Level two consists of identification of all variables in a research situation. 3. Level three consists of identification of the variables in a situation and the planning of a controlled experiment around those variables.
Experimenting	The process of verifying an hypothesis through the use of materials and the control of variables	1. Only one level will be considered here for practical classroom use.
Seeking cause and effect	The process of correctly attributing Factor *A* to Factor *B*	1. Only one level of true causality is found.
Asking operational questions	The process of asking questions which contain within them the means for using concrete materials to find the answer to the question	1. Only one level will be considered here for practical classroom use.
Using interaction and systems	The process by which all parts, objects, or phenomena involved in a particular occurrence are identified and their relationships determined	1. Level one uses concrete objects and emphasizes the parts of the system. 2. Level two uses concrete objects and emphasizes both identification and interaction. 3. Level three uses both concrete objects and nonconcrete phenomena.

Advantages of Process Teaching in Science. The process approach has a number of advantages over a pure content approach to science in the elementary school. First, the process approach requires that children be involved with concrete materials and so is more closely attuned to the learning style of children than is a completely verbal approach. Second, the process orientation to science requires that each child participate cognitively in the learning process. The child is able to structure information according to individual understanding. The child actively manipulates materials and actively pursues the ideas that are generated by those materials; ideas are generated and investigated rather than memorized. Third, children are less likely to experience failure in a process-oriented program. Activities may be more open ended to allow a more able student to pursue a topic further than a less able student. The less able student is more likely to be working at his or her appropriate level. Fourth, activities tend to be such that a conclusion, for example, that follows directly from data although incorrect scientifically may be correct in practice, because it is a logical conclusion for that set of data. It is the latter aspect that is important. Students cannot fail in a process-only program. Fifth, recent research has shown that a process approach in which students use materials develops skills that are applicable to all branches of science, not only the one area being studied, and can be applied to other branches of knowledge. Being able to make inferences or draw conclusions in science may help the child in reading to understand the cause and effect of a story. Being able to point out the variables in an experimental situation may help the child to identify, for instance, the variables that contributed to the development of a democracy in one nation and a dictatorship in another.

Science in the Elementary Curriculum

Science is one among many subjects that the child confronts each day. Those few minutes that are set aside for science study in the daily schedule need to be used as productively as possible. Trying to teach a little biology, a little chemistry, a little geology results in fragmentation and, all too often, leads to dependence on memorization and reading as teaching methods. Trying to use the items of interest that the children bring to class can result in a program that is not only fragmented but also a hodge-podge.

The Integration of Process and Content in Elementary Science

Science is a search for understanding. If the science program of the elementary school, on the one hand, addresses only the processes of science, teaching children only to emulate the actions of the scientist, then the child cannot develop the understanding of the universe that science tries to achieve. On the other hand, if only content is taught, children cannot develop the ability to investigate the unknown and to seek out answers to their questions. Balance must be the watchword of the elementary science program.

Yet children in the preschool and early primary grades find it difficult to understand causal relationships and may be unable to comprehend the content of science. Rather than attempting to thrust the child into a science curriculum beyond his or her cognitive abilities, the teacher should present a science curriculum that develops in a stage-by-stage pattern permitting the child appropriately to develop understandings.

Preschool and Kindergarten Science. The preschool-kindergarten child is generally not ready for the content of science. Such content tends to consist of abstractions developed from observations, which at this age can only be memorized by the child and parroted back in a rote manner. Children at the preschool-kindergarten age level would be better occupied in making their own observations, inferences, and predictions; in learning to classify; and in learning to communicate what they have seen, felt, and heard. By manipulating a variety of objects, young children can begin to develop the experiential background they will need for later understanding of content.

This is not to say that there should be no content in the preschool-kindergarten program but rather that such content should be directly derived from observations made by the children. Thus, rather than being asked to show why there are four seasons, children should be determining the characteristics, by observation, of the four seasons. Rather than trying to show that dinosaurs lived millions of years ago and became extinct, children could be observing pictures and models and finding similarities and differences between dinosaurs and modern animals.

At the preschool-kindergarten level, process should be more important than the factual knowledge of science.

Primary Grade Science. As the child moves into the primary grades, process and content should be more systematically attacked in the science program. With the processes serving as a unifying theme, the primary grade child should be introduced to the use of these processes in a variety of content situations. A unit for the primary grades on classifying could include various materials which illustrate how classification is used to arrange the content of science: animals, plants, stones, cloud types, even the children themselves could all be used.

At the primary grade level, both process and content could be emphasized. But the unifying theme would still be the various processes that would be used to gain content information.

Intermediate Grade Science. At the intermediate grade level, both more complex processes and more complex content can be considered. Now, however, the content of science should become the unifying theme for the program. Rather than offering a unit on experimenting, the teacher could present a unit dealing with simple machines, weather, rocks and minerals, or other topics, along with the process of experimentation used to generate information dealing with the content topic of the unit.

On the intermediate grade level, when children have developed the ability to understand cause-and-effect relationships, to use concrete as well as abstract knowledge, and to use the experiment as a means for solving content-oriented problems, their science program should reflect this maturity. At the intermediate level, the child is indeed ready to work as the research scientist works: developing information by experimentation and reading for background knowledge.

The flow of learning in the elementary school should, then, move from simple processes with little attention to content to more complex processes developed within the framework of content. Such a flow more closely parallels the characteristics of developing children than does either a purely content approach or a purely process approach. The combination of process and content in teaching also more closely reflects the nature of science as a search for understanding.

Summary

The basic behavioral characteristics of preschool through elementary grade children provide some guidelines as to the kinds of science activities which will be most appropriate. For all age levels four factors remain constant:

1. Process as well as content should be emphasized.
2. Activities should be open ended so that individual students have the opportunity to stop at a point most appropriate to them.
3. Concrete materials should be used on all levels to encourage activity and experimentation as well as to allow students who do not function verbally to succeed in the science program.
4. The focus of the science program should be on students structuring their own knowledge rather than on reading and listening to answers.

Certain other factors change as children mature:

1. Young children should engage in process-oriented activities that will lead to easily observable content, whereas older children should be using the processes of science to develop more detailed and abstract content-oriented information.
2. For younger children, small muscle activities should be limited and large muscle activities emphasized. Older children will be able to manipulate small objects and to keep written records.
3. The higher the grade level the greater the individual differences that will manifest themselves. Upper grade students should have alternative ways of getting instructions and of gathering information so that their inability to read or to conduct experiments does not hamper success.

Selected References

American Association for the Advancement of Science. *Science — A Process Approach.* Lexington, Mass.: Ginn, 1975.

Bruner, J. *The Process of Education.* New York: Vintage Books, 1963.

Comstock, A. B. *Handbook of Nature Study.* Ithaca, New York: Comstock Publishing, 1911.

Craig, G. S. *Certain Techniques Used in Developing a Course of Study in Science for the Horace Mann Elementary School.* Bureau of Publication, Teachers College, Columbia University, Contributions to Education, No. 276. New York, 1927.

Gerlich, J. A., G. Downs, and G. Mangrane. How essential is science at the elementary level. *Science and Children, 19,* 3, 1981.

Goldberg, L. Elementary school science: Learning how to learn. *Science and Children, 19,* 7, 1982.

Hymes, J. L. *Teaching the Child Under Six.* Columbus, Ohio: Merrill, 1981.

National Science Teachers Association, Curriculum Committee. *Theory into Action in Science Curriculum Development.* Washington, D.C.: National Science Teachers Association, 1964.

Sagan, C. *Broca's Brain.* New York: Random House, 1974.

Saxon, D. S. Liberal education in a technological age. *Science, 218,* 4574, 1982.

Smart, M., and R. C. Smart. *Preschool Children: Development and Relationships.* New York: Macmillan, 1982.

Wolfinger, D. M. Interaction of young children with science materials in a free setting. Unpublished manuscript, 1982.

You take the most primitive man you ever met in the most backward society you can find, and there is such elegance and depth to this being's mind that his life is precious.

— Hunt, 1982

2 Psychology and Science Teaching

Chapter Objectives

Upon completion of this chapter you should be able to

1. relate the cognitive psychology of Jean Piaget to the teaching of the processes of science: classification, cause and effect, observation, inference, data interpretation, modeling, and experimenting;
2. discuss the levels within the processes of science as they apply to the classroom;
3. relate the information processing theory of psychology to science teaching particularly as it relates to memory, concept development, and problem solving.

In recent years, the predominant psychological theory considered by educators has been that of genetic epistemologist Jean Piaget. So pervasive has Piaget's theory become that it is the basis of many textbooks and programs in elementary science. The inclusion of a larger number of concrete experiences in the elementary school science curriculum is, in part, an outgrowth of Piaget's work.

In particular, the science teacher can use this work to help determine when mastery of certain science-process skills can be expected of children. Although Piaget has not considered all of the scientific processes, he has studied classification, cause and effect, observation and inference with data interpretation, mental modeling, and experimentation.

The processes of science do not, however, make up the entire science program. Content must be taught if the program is to be balanced. Although some of Piaget's work can be applied to the teaching of science content, a second psychological perspective can be of more aid to the teacher. The relatively new psychology of information processing deals with content-related aspects of science teaching: memory, concept development, and problem solving.

This chapter will consider both the process-related theory of Piaget and the content-related theory of information processing.

Piaget and the Processes of Science

The work of Jean Piaget, begun in the 1920's, is based upon three assumptions. First, it is assumed that the activity of a child is the primary source of new knowledge. Second, knowledge is assumed to have as its major function adaptation. And, third, the structures that are created through the action of a child are considered to form a continuous and invariant sequence (Kagan, 1980). The four developmental stages for which Piaget is most widely known are based on this latter assumption.

The Four Developmental Stages

The four developmental stages encompass the ages from birth through adulthood showing a gradual development of mental processes in children. The following age approximations are widely used:

1. sensorimotor stage: birth through eighteen months,
2. preoperational stage: eighteen months through six and one-half years,
3. concrete operational stage: six and one-half years through eleven or twelve years,
4. formal operational stage: eleven or twelve years throughout adulthood.

Each of these stages will be briefly discussed here and will also be found summarized in Table 2–1.

The Sensorimotor Stage. Comic strip children still in the diaper stage seem to have a wonderful means of communication with the readers of those comic strips. They sit in their playpens unable to talk, yet they seem to think in words and phrases that would put many adults to shame. Mothers attempt to make crying infants of five or six months of age stop by shouting, "stop that," and then grow angry because the child continues to cry. Children without a spoken language cannot be made to govern their behaviors by listening to words. How, then, do these preverbal children think?

Adults who possess a language think through the use of words — symbols for the actions and objects which are a part of thought. Children without words think by means of actions.

At the age of seventeen or eighteen months, many children become interested in building with blocks. They construct towers by placing one block atop another until the entire construction topples over. The following is an example of sensorimotor thinking on the part of a child of about seventeen months:

> E. brought one block at a time from his bedroom and placed them on the dining room table. After he had four blocks on the table, he began to pile them one on top of another until he had a tower about seven inches high. E. went back to his room for another block, piled it on the tower, then went for one more block. This time the tower was too tall for him to reach the top. He looked at the block in his hand, at the tower, then back at the block once again. He tried to reach the top once more. Then, he jumped up and down a few times as well as he was able. Placing the block on the table, he ran to his bedroom and returned with a pounding bench. He placed it on the floor and climbed onto it. He was then able to reach the top of the tower and add the block.

The child in this example did not have the words with which to think through the problem. Instead, he thought through the problem in actions using a physical movement, jumping, as the link between the needed height and the bench that was among his toys.

The development of this ability to think through a problem with actions rather than with words is the culmination of a process which begins at birth when only the reflexes are present. The end of the process of thought without words is the beginning of language in the child. At about two years of age, or at the point where language begins, the child enters the preoperational stage.

The Preoperational Stage. The preoperational stage is divided into two substages: the first is called the preconceptual and lasts from the onset of verbal ability until about four and one-half years of age; the second is termed the intuitive and lasts from about four and one-half years to about six or seven years. Although the thinking processes of the preoperational child do depend on the use of words, these processes differ from those of the adult in six important ways: egocentrism, conservation, reversibility, centering, transduction, and concreteness.

Egocentrism. This term refers to the fact that the child sees the world as revolving around himself. It is nearly impossible for the child to take the point of view of another individual, to accept as equally valuable or valid the ideas of another if those ideas do not agree with his own. Young egocentric children use words whose referents may be clear only to themselves. Thus, the preoperational child tells about his play time by saying, "he did it with me." The child cannot, then, comprehend why his listener does not automatically know who "he" is or what "it" was.

Gradually, the child begins to realize that others do not necessarily have the same knowledge or the same ideas that he or she has. And, as interaction with others who have differing views occurs, the child begins to take other views into account. Egocentrism decreases with repeated social interaction.

Conservation. Conservation is the ability to realize that a change in the appearance of an object does not change the quantity of that object. For example, a child is given two balls of clay, *A* and *B*, that are exactly the same size. She is permitted to touch the clay, to pick up the two balls, and generally to satisfy herself that they are equal. Then, as she watches, clay ball *B* is flattened into a "cookie."

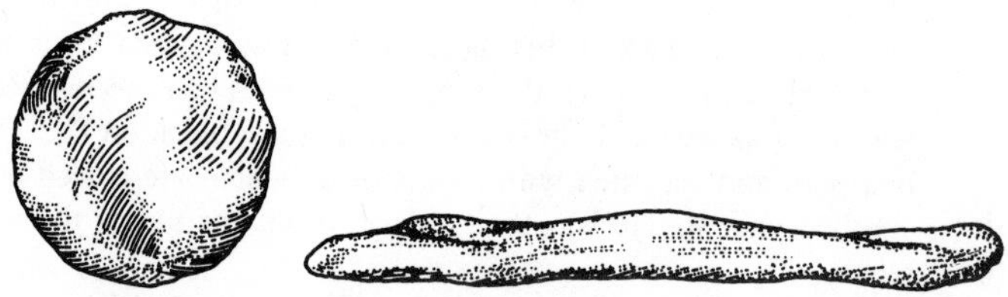

Although nothing has been added or taken away, the child will claim either (1) that *A* is bigger or has more clay than *B* because *A* is taller or (2) that *B* is bigger than *A* or has more clay than *A* because it is wider. If *B* is rolled back into a ball, it becomes the same size for the child as *A* once again.

This procedure tests the young child for conservation of substance. The six commonly considered types of conservation and the average ages of attainment are listed below (note that conservation of number is attained at the end of the preoperational stage as a herald of the end of that mode of thinking):

1. conservation of number: about six years of age,
2. conservation of substance: about seven years of age,
3. conservation of length: about eight years of age,
4. conservation of area: between eight and eleven years of age,
5. conservation of weight: about ten years of age,
6. conservation of volume: between eleven and fifteen years of age.

Because the preoperational child cannot answer the majority of the conservation tasks correctly, the child is described as a nonconserver. One of the major reasons for the inability of the child to conserve is the child's inability to coordinate variables. The child cannot see that a change in the thickness of clay is compensated for by a change in the length.

Centering. The focusing of the preoperational child on one property to the exclusion of others is known as centering. Because of this tendency to center, the child is unable to shift attention from one characteristic to another while retaining the memory and use of the first characteristic. Centering is also a major reason why the preoperational child cannot correctly answer the conservation tasks.

Reversibility. Reversibility of thought allows an individual to begin at point *A*, travel through the thought processes to point *B*, and then return to point *A* once again. This is the defining characteristic of reversible thought. It is not a characteristic of the thought processes of the preoperational child.

The preoperational child, without reversible thought, thinks in the following manner. A four-year-old girl is asked:

"Do you have a sister?"
"Yes."
"What's her name?"
"Jeannie."
"Does Jeannie have a sister?"
"No."

This four-year-old can manage the forward relationship of herself as having a sister named Jeannie. She has traveled from point *A* to point *B*. But the same child cannot reverse her thought patterns to travel backward from point *B* to point *A* and so can only conclude that her sister Jeannie does not have a sister.

Transductive Reasoning. Adults tend to reason from particular facts to general conclusions as in induction or from a general statement to particulars as in deduction. The preoperational child, on the other hand, reasons in neither of these ways, but from specific to specific. Two special cases of transduction — reasoning from specific to specific — are (1) syncretism, or the linking together of two things which are unrelated (usually because those things are close together perceptually) and (2) juxtaposition, or the giving of successive unrelated judgments.

Concreteness. The final difference between preoperational thought and adult thought is the child's necessity for concreteness. Adults tend to think in terms of words and symbols; the concepts that they learn tend to be learned through the use of words rather than through the use of objects. Preoperational children, on the other hand, develop new concepts through the use of real objects rather than through the use of words. The adult can read about series and parallel circuits and gain a concept of those types of circuits; the child must connect bulbs, wires, and batteries to gain the same concept.

The Concrete Operational Stage. The concrete operational stage begins at about seven years of age and, according to Piaget, lasts until approximately eleven to fifteen years of age. During the concrete operational stage of intellectual development, children develop the thought patterns which permit them to answer all of the conservation tasks correctly. Other characteristics of this period are

1. the appearance of operations,
2. an inability to use verbal reasoning,
3. a decrease in egocentricity,
4. the appearance of reversibility.

Operations. An operation is "an action that can return to its starting point and that can be integrated with other actions also possessing this feature of reversibility" (Piaget and Inhelder, 1956, p. 36). This action takes place internally rather than externally with objects. Having the ability to use operations, the concrete operational child is able to master some very complex relationships which obey certain laws. These laws are:

1. When elements of a grouping are combined, they produce a new element of some kind.
2. Every change is reversible.
3. An operation combined with its opposite is annulled.
4. Combinations of operations obey the associative property.
5. A class added to itself results in the same class.

Verbal Reasoning. Although the concrete operational child is better able to use language than the preoperational child, verbal reasoning is still limited. Reasoning from a premise is still not possible for the concrete operational child. Consequently, when presented with a question like, "What would happen if the sun did not come up tomorrow?" the concrete operational child is likely to answer that the sun always comes up.

Part of the difficulty that concrete operational children have with this type of question is due to their inability to use language effectively in thinking. This is also evidenced in the difficulty children have in explaining proverbs like, "Still waters run deep." Children at this stage also have problems in defining words.

Reversibility of Thought. A third change in the concrete operational child's thinking processes also demonstrates a distinct difference from the preoperational child. During the seven- to eleven-year age period, reversibility of thought develops. The concrete operational child now knows that she is Jeannie's sister and that Jeannie is her sister. This ability to use reversible thought allows the child to coordinate variables in the various conservation tasks and so to answer those tasks correctly.

Egocentricity. The final major development of the concrete operational period is a decrease in egocentricity. The development of concrete operations, with an increasing mobility of thought, permits the child to shift rapidly back and forth between his or her own viewpoint and that of another person. Decreased egocentricity also makes possible sharing of goals and group cooperation on projects.

The Formal Operational Stage. During the formal operations stage, beginning at about eleven years of age and extending throughout adult life, truly logical thinking processes are perfected. These logical thought processes characterize the reflective intelligence of the adult.

The formal thinker can envisage all the possible relations which could hold true for a set of data and then can, through a combination of experiments and logical analysis, find which of the relations do, in fact, hold true. The formal operational thinker can develop an hypothesis and then through the control of all variables, except that one which must be changed to determine its effect, test that hypothesis in an experimental situation.

Formal thinking is propositional thinking. The formal thinker in the process of reasoning manipulates either assertions or statements which contain the new data from which the assertions were developed.

Factors Influencing Passage Through the Stages

What is it that enables the individual maturing from infant to adult to pass through these four, seemingly invariant, stages? Piaget hypothesized four factors of utmost importance. Three are common to most developmental theories, whereas the fourth is uniquely Piagetian.

Biological Maturation. Biological maturation, the physical maturity of the individual, determines, in part, when a particular pattern of behavior will occur. For example, muscular and neurological development must reach a certain level before a child walks. A three-month-old is not physically mature enough to walk, whereas a thirteen-month-old is.

Experience with the Physical Environment. Experience with the physical environment is the second factor influencing passage through the stages. The child must explore and interact with the environment. Piaget considers exercise, physical experiences, and logical-mathematical experience to be the major types of exploration in which the child can engage. The latter, logical achievements, are of particular importance as the child moves from one period of development to another.

Experience with the Social Environment. The third factor is experience with the social environment. The social environment provides an opportunity for the child to learn many kinds of activities, concepts, and relationships such as cooperation, competition, mutual respect, folkways, and cultural mores.

Equilibration. Equilibration, the uniquely Piagetian fourth factor, is considered the fundamental developmental factor. Development of an equilibration involves four steps. In step one, the individual, when confronted with two opposite properties, *A* and *B*, tends to center only on property *A*. In step two, the individual centers only on property *B* to the exclusion of property *A*. Step three involves a consolidation process. During this step, the alternation of centering found in steps one and two results in the conjunction of these properties. The individual becomes able to differentiate between *A* and *B* and seems to consider the two properties simultaneously. Finally, in step four, the individual attains the ability to attend to the transformation of properties *A* and *B* and to associate these transformed properties in various ways while continuing to maintain the original properties, *A* and *B*, as a part of a cognitive structure.

Finally, in step four, the individual is able to attend to the transformation of properties *A* and *B* and to associate these transformed properties in varying ways. At the same time, however, the individual is able to maintain the original properties, *A* and *B*, as a part of the cognitive structure. In this step the child can see the thick sphere of clay flattened into a thin, flat pancake. Property *A*, thickness, has been transformed to thinness. Property *B*, sphericity, has been transformed to flatness. But, in the child's cognitive structure, the memory of the round, thick ball of clay is retained.

Assimilation and Accommodation. The mechanisms through which these four steps and equilibrium itself are attained are the processes of assimilation and accommodation. Assimilation requires that incoming information be changed by the individual so that it can easily be incorporated with the information already possessed by the individual. Such modifications of input allow new information to fit smoothly into what is already known and understood by the individual. In accommodation, the existing information is modified to suit the new information. In this way the individual changes his beliefs, attitudes, or factual knowledge to reflect newly acquired information.

The preoperational child is unable to accommodate new information by coherently assimilating it to the old. Each successive input of new information results in the destruction of any previously existing equilibrium.

The maturation of the preoperational child into the concrete operational child results in increasing stability in the equilibria that are formed by the child. The attainment of reversibility during the concrete operations stage is a major advance over the preoperational stage and is a by-product of the equilibration process, since reversibility provides the balancing and compensating functions that are necessary to achieve equilibrium.

Although these stages do provide teachers with a great deal of information about the cognitive capabilities of children at various ages, the most direct

Table 2–1 Major characteristics of Piaget's four developmental stages

SENSORIMOTOR	PREOPERATIONAL
1. Age birth through eighteen months.	1. Age eighteen months to four and one-half years.
2. Preverbal stage.	2. Egocentric viewpoint.
3. Thought is through action.	3. Lacks ability to conserve all but number.
4. Development of object permanence.	4. Lacks reversible thought.
5. Development of primary, secondary, and tertiary circular reactions.	5. Centers on one trait at a time.
	6. Transductive reasoning is used.
	7. Concrete objects are needed for thought.

CONCRETE OPERATIONAL	FORMAL OPERATIONAL
1. Age six and one-half through eleven or twelve.	1. Age eleven or twelve through adult.
2. Egocentricity decreases.	2. Logical, deductive thought processes available.
3. Can use more than one trait at a time.	3. Logical causality used.
4. Begins to develop logical causality.	4. Can control variables.
5. Conserves in all areas except volume.	5. Can use abstract, propositional thought.
6. Needs concrete objects for thought.	6. Able to comprehend that many sides of the same problem can exist and that there can be many valid solutions to the same problem.

application of Piagetian theory to science teaching comes through the skills associated with each process rather than through the development of content. Each of those process skills will be discussed in the following pages.

The Process of Classification

Through his investigations into the abilities of children to classify objects, Piaget showed that the ability to classify develops through various stages until the child is able to classify in the form of a true hierarchy. Even two- or three-year-olds will order their toys in a simple system from smallest to largest, showing the start of a classification scheme. It is not, however, until the fifth or sixth grade that children reach the point where they are able to use the more complex forms of classification.

Simple Forms of Classification. Very young children presented with a collection of squares, rectangles, circles, and triangles and asked to put these shapes into groups, do not actually form classificatory groups with the objects. Instead, many young children form patterns or pictures from the shapes and consider those patterns to be groups. These patterns or pictures may take the form of:

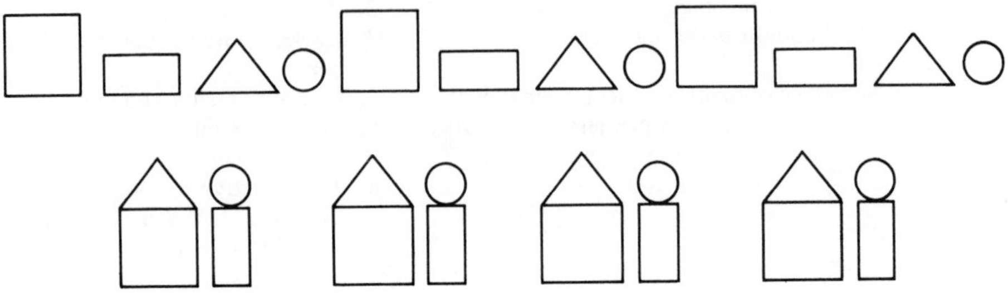

At about five years of age, however, children do begin to actually classify shapes or other objects into groups. These groups do not have a great deal of stability, and the child frequently changes the characteristics on which the grouping is based. The child may start gathering triangles but notice that the second triangle is blue; then the child may select the next object after the triangle because it is also blue, but a blue circle. The child may change the trait with each of the objects or keep the same one for a few of the objects before changing to something else. Consequently, all of the original pile of objects may end up in a single pile again. A second feature of this stage is that the child may not classify all of the objects that he or she is given. This occurs either because the remaining objects do not readily fit into the current grouping property used by the child or because the child has grown tired of the task.

By the time a child has reached the age of eight, the groupings he or she chooses have become stable provided that the child is attempting to classify by a single trait. Between five and eight years of age, the child is able to choose a single characteristic and to classify on the basis of that characteristic but finds it difficult to use more than one characteristic at a time. The child will be able to classify on the basis of either color or shape but not on the basis of both color and shape. During this period, the child does become able to classify all objects and is said to be able to use exhaustive sorting.

At about eight years of age, the child becomes able to classify using two or more characteristics at a time and continues to use exhaustive sorting. At the end of this stage, the child is able to classify using more than two traits and to coordinate the characteristics being used so that errors in classification are rare. When the child is able to use multiple traits in classification, the transition to hierarchical classification is possible.

Hierarchical Classification. Only after the child uses multiple trait classification can the child be expected to use a hierarchical form of classification. The system in Figure 2–1 could be used to classify the children in a fifth or sixth grade classroom. Trying to teach the use of hierarchical classification before about the fifth grade is very difficult. While trying to classify hierarchically with third graders, I quickly learned that it was my own guidance rather than the understanding of the children that allowed the system to be used. The class could not answer a simple question, "Are all of the red-haired children boys?" simply by looking at the chart developed. Instead the children looked around the room, then answered the question on the basis of their observations of the children. Trying to classify a group of objects on a table, this same group was able to name one major category and some very obvious secondary characteristics of a second category. They were not, however, able to go any further than that second level in their classification system.

Criteria for a True Hierarchical Classification System. A true hierarchical classification system has ten criteria which must be met if the system is to be correct in all ways:

1. All objects must be classified even if a unique object must be placed in a class by itself.
2. No class can be isolated from the rest of the system.
3. A class includes all objects having a certain, specified characteristic.
4. A class can include only those objects that have a certain, specified property.
5. All classes of the same rank in the system must be disjoint (detached and distinct).
6. A complementary class has its own characteristics, which are not possessed by its complement.
7. A class is included in each higher ranking class that contains all of its objects.
8. The objects included in a class are the minimum compatible with the defining properties of the class.
9. Similar characteristics are used to distinguish classes of the same rank.
10. Classes must be divided symmetrically so that if class B_1 is subdivided into classes C_1 and C_2 then class B_2 must be subdivided into classes $C_{1'}$ and $C_{2'}$.

Figure 2–2 illustrates a classification system which is consistent with these ten rules. The objects used for this classification are tennis ball, golf ball, soccer ball, football, basketball, globe, glass marble, steel ball bearing, spherical sponge, b-b shot, wooden sphere, styrofoam ball, foam rubber ball, plastic bead, and wooden bead. Before looking at Figure 2–2, develop your own classification system for these objects. Using the ten classification rules as well as the figure as a model, critique your system.

Figure 2–3 illustrates a classification system which violates a number of the classification rules. As you look at the system, see if you can determine which of the rules have been violated. The objects used for the classification are tennis

Figure 2–1 Hierarchical classification

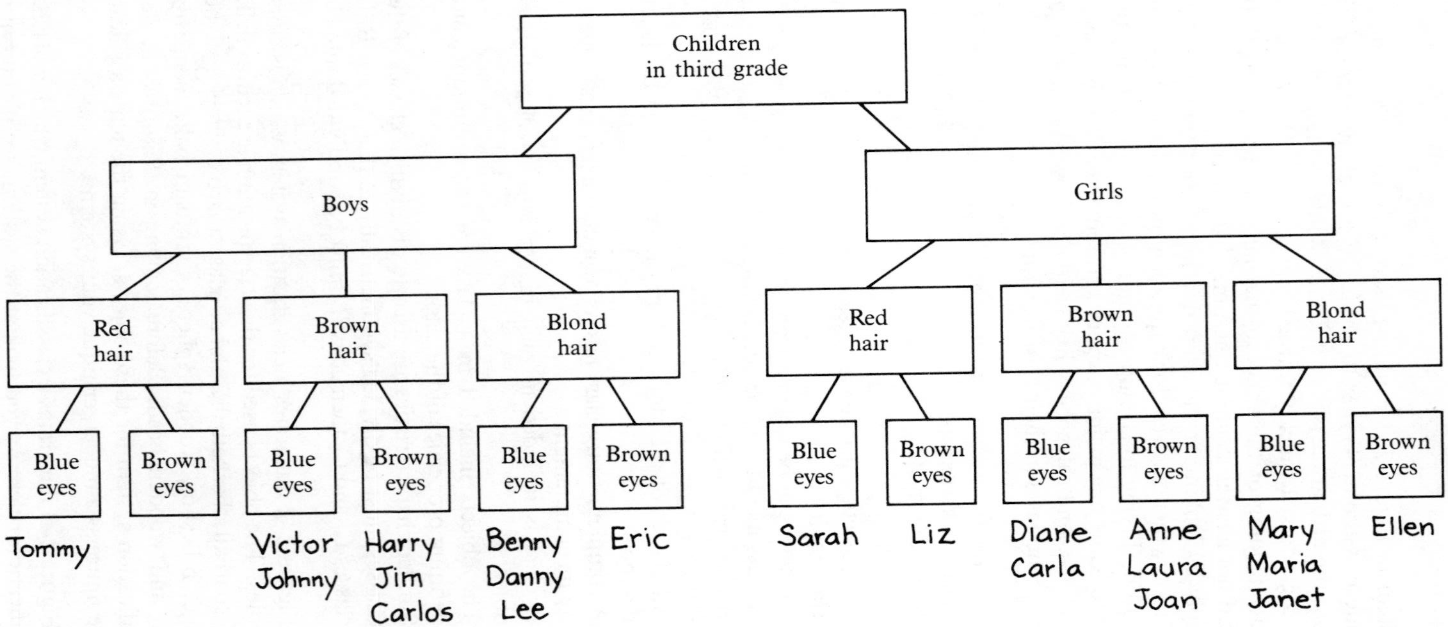

Figure 2–2 Hierarchical classification

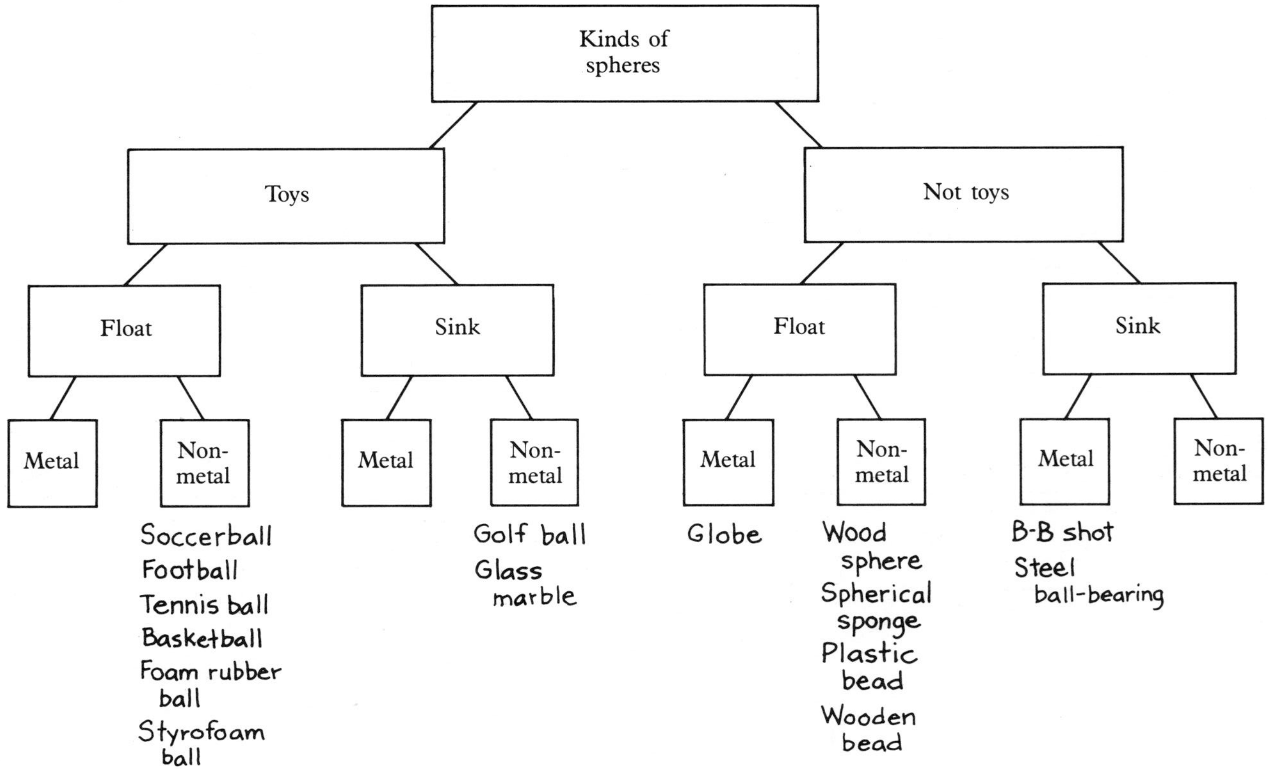

Note: In both cases, float and sink, there are no metal toys. There is nothing wrong with having an empty group within the system. An empty group in a classification system corresponds to an empty set in mathematics.

Figure 2–3 Violation of the classification rules

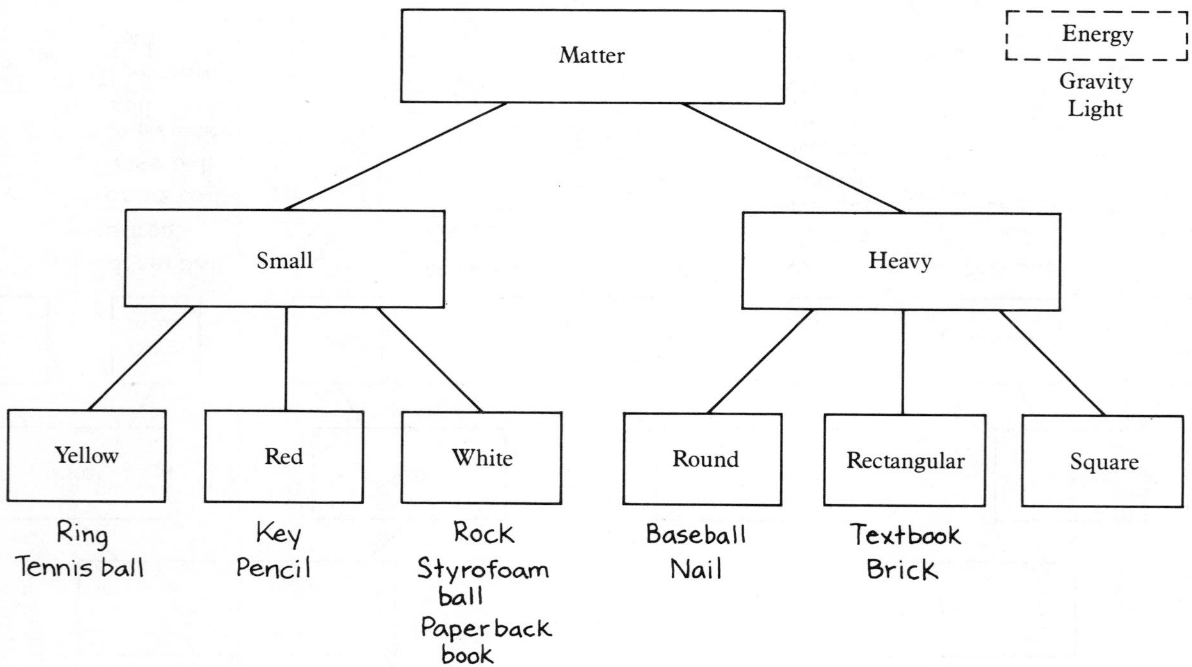

Note: Small and heavy are not disjoint classes. The nail and the key are both small as well as heavy. The ring is classified as small, but is heavier than the nail. Both the small/heavy level and the next lower level do not use similar characteristics. The small/heavy level uses linear dimension in one case and weight in the other. Shape and color are used on the next level. The paperclip is omitted on this shape/color level since it does not fit into any category. Energy is an isolated class. Since energy is not an object it can only be put aside on its own apart from the rest of the system.

ball, baseball, brick, rock, pencil, textbook, paperback book, paper clip, nail, ring, key, styrofoam ball, gravity, light.

The process of classification develops from a very simple form to a highly complex form. Piaget's work on classification indicates the kinds of classification experiences which children can be given as a part of the elementary science program and the kinds of experiences which will allow children to succeed. Likewise, the Piagetian view of causality gives an indication of what can be expected of children as they try to understand and apply the cause-and-effect processes of science.

Cause-and-Effect Processes

Through his research into how children explain common occurrences Piaget discovered that children do not see cause-and-effect relationships in the same way as adults see them. In fact, young children find it difficult, if not impossible, to separate from true origins and causes such ideas as that all things are living or that people made all objects. Until the child reaches about ten years of age, his or her explanations of the "whys" of the world may not be logical.

Very young children, up to about four years of age, often use magical kinds of explanations. These children are certain that their words and gestures influence events occurring around them; wishing, they think, can make something happen. Piaget refers to this type of explanation of causality as psychological.

The child interpreting the world in terms of psychological causality may, if faced with the prospect of broccoli for dinner, try wishing very hard for it to turn to ice cream. Although this may sound to us like a child's typical fantasy approach to life, the child who uses psychological causality really believes that wishing will cause a change. The world of the preschool child is truly magical. But gradually the magical approach to reality disappears, and the primary grade child emerges with different forms of causal explanations.

Causal Explanations by Primary Grade Children. The primary grade child, up to about seven years of age, relies upon a variety of different kinds of causal explanations. Table 2–2 outlines the seven types of precausal explanations used by primary grade children. Three of these will be discussed here, because they tend to be more frequently used than the others: phenomenism, artificialism, and animism. All of these explanations are called precausal by Piaget, that is, they do not show a logical approach to cause-and-effect relationships.

Phenomenism. A causal explanation that relies on phenomenism makes it very difficult for the early primary grade child to draw conclusions from the data he or she collects during an activity. Water boils because it is in a pot. A boat floats because it is white. A seed grows because it has wrinkles.

The kind of explanations given by the child using phenomenism indicate that the child is apt to attribute causation to anything that the child perceives

Table 2–2 Types of precausal explanations

TYPE	DEFINITION	EXAMPLE
Motivation	Causality is the result of a divine plan.	God causes clouds to move; boats to float, etc.
Finalism	Causality is a simple fact without origin or consequence.	A magnet picks up tacks because it just does.
Phenomenism	Anything may cause anything.	Water runs downhill because there are fish in the stream.
Participation	Two things can act on one another over a distance because of some invisible emanation.	The sun moves because the child walks down the street.
Moral	Phenomena are a result of moral necessity.	Boats must float because people would drown if they did not.
Artificialism	Events and objects are the result of human activity.	How was the Earth formed? People made it.
Animism	All events and phenomena are seen as alive and conscious.	A car moves because it is alive.
Dynamism	Forces are confused with life.	Water runs downhill because the mountain pushes it.

as important. Such explanations make it difficult for the child to consider the information collected during an activity with any sort of logic.

Artificialism. A second possible precausal explanation used by primary grade children is artificialism. For the child who relies on artificialism, people are seen as the cause of all things. How did the Earth originate? People made it. How did a mountain form? People built it. What causes waves in the ocean? People swimming. Such explanations can be frustrating to the teacher particularly during units of study dealing with the planets, stars, or the Earth.

Animism. The final type of precausal explanation to be considered here is animism — the most pervasive of the three types. Under the influence of animism the child conceives of all things as alive and conscious. Children at this level of causal development tend to see the characteristic of movement as the major criterion for determining whether or not an object or phenomenon is alive. A second criterion is the usefulness of the object or phenomenon to human beings.

A car is alive because its wheels move. A cloud is alive because it moves across the sky. A desk is alive because a man can write on it. These types of explanations may last until the child reaches eight years of age. A full understanding, that only plants and animals are alive, may not be reached until the child is eleven years of age.

Learning Activity 2–1

Investigating Animism in Children

Using the following questions taken from a Piagetian interview, interview three children, one of preschool or kindergarten age, one of second or third grade age, and one of fifth or sixth grade age. Questions can be changed if children do not seem to understand. However, be careful not to lead the child to answers that you want to hear. Also, be certain to show no negative reactions to responses given by the children. Record all answers verbatim.

Following your interviews, compare the responses given by the children. At what level do you see the strongest indication of animistic reasoning?

1. What does it mean when you say something is alive?
2. Tell me the names of some things that are alive? (Three is sufficient.)
3. Is this table alive?
   What makes you say this table is/is not alive?
4. Is the sun alive?
   What makes you say the sun is/is not alive?
5. Is a mountain alive?
   What makes you say the mountain is/is not alive?
6. Is a car alive?
   What makes you say a car is/is not alive?
7. Is a cat alive?
   What makes you say a cat is/is not alive?
8. Is a cloud alive?
   What makes you say a cloud is/is not alive?
9. Is a lamp alive?
   What makes you say a lamp is/is not alive?
10. Is my watch alive?
    What makes you say my watch is/is not alive?
11. Is a bird alive?
    What makes you say a bird is/is not alive?
12. Is the wind alive?
    What makes you say the wind is/is not alive?
13. Is a flower alive?
    What makes you say a flower is/is not alive?
14. Is a tree alive?
    What makes you say a tree is/is not alive?

Causal Explanations by Intermediate Grade Children. As the child moves into the intermediate grades, he or she begins to recognize natural relationships and attempts to make logical explanations. The six types of causal thinking used by children between seven and ten years of age are found in Table 2–3. Both maturity and experience are necessary if children are to develop the ability to use logical forms of causality. Finally, sometime after ten years of age, children develop the ability to make logical explanations about cause and effect. They can finally make logical deductions from the observations made during an activity or experiment.

The ability to draw logical cause-and-effect relationships develops over the years of elementary school until the child is finally able to determine the actual cause-and-effect relationships in an activity or an experiment. The child's ability to determine causality helps him or her understand the processes of interaction and systems, cause and effect, inference, prediction, and conclusion. The work of Piaget again gives insight into what the teacher may expect from children at the various grade levels.

Table 2–3 Transitional forms of causality

TYPE	DEFINITION	EXAMPLE
Reaction of surrounding medium	The first genuinely physical explanation. The need for contact as a cause is seen so the surrounding medium is used.	Clouds move because, after some mysterious start, the air behind the cloud continues the motion.
Mechanical	Contact and transference of movement are used as explanations	The motion of a bicycle is caused by the pedals. No chain is needed.
Generation	An extension of animism with the added idea that matter can be changed from one form to another.	Clouds form from smoke which grows, like a living thing, into a cloud.
Substantial	Like causality by generation but without the ability to grow.	The sun is a ball of clouds rolled together, but there had to be enough clouds at the start since clouds cannot grow.
Condensation and rarefaction	Matter which makes up objects is more or less condensed depending on its type.	A stone is condensed and wood is rarefied so stones sink and wood floats.
Atomistic	Objects are made of tiny particles tightly or loosely packed together.	Water can be poured because it is made of tiny pieces.

Learning Activity 2–2

Piaget and Causality

Piaget's work into the development of causal thinking in children gives a great deal of insight into how children develop the ability to identify logical cause-and-effect relationships. Choose one of the following books and read one or more chapters dealing with the original work of Piaget into causality.

1. *The Child's Conception of Physical Causality,* Jean Piaget (translated by Marjorie Habain), Littlefield, Adams, and Company, 1972. This volume details experiments into the nature of air, the origins of wind, the movement of clouds, the cause of floating, the cause of shadows, the mechanisms of bicycles, steam engines, trains, cars, and airplanes. The reported interviews give a good view of how children think at various ages.
2. *The Child's Conception of the World,* Jean Piaget (translated by Jean and Andrew Tomlinson), Littlefield, Adams, and Company, 1975. This volume details interviews dealing with the nature of thought and dreams, the concept of animism, the origin of the sun, moon, water, trees, mountains, and the Earth. The interviews are particularly good in illustrating the causal relations of animism, artificialism, and moral necessity.
3. *Causal Thinking in the Child,* Monique Laurendeau and Adrien Pinard, International Universities Press, 1962. This report of an experimental study reviews Piaget's original work and adds to the material dealing with dreams, life, origin of night, movement of clouds, and floating and sinking. Interviews are included as well as interpretations of those interviews.

Learning Activity 2–3

Investigating Causality in Children

The following are starting questions for interviews with children dealing with the transitional forms of causality. These are only starting questions since the answers given by children will vary greatly. As you talk with children, your follow-up questions should grow directly out of the answers given by the child and should probe more deeply into what the child is telling you. For example, if you ask, How did the sun start? and the child answers that it came from fire a follow-up question could be, Where did the fire come from? or, How did the fire start?

Interview three children of various ages from preschool through sixth grade trying for at least two years' difference in their ages. Record the answers given by the children verbatim. Once you have finished with the interviews, try to determine the kind of causal relations being used by each of the children. Try two or more of the interviews below.

1. How did the sun begin? Has there always been a sun? What is the sun made from?
2. Have you ever looked at the moon? What does the moon look like? Does the moon always look the same? What causes the moon to look different at different times?
3. What causes a boat to float?
4. How does a bicycle work? What causes it to move?
5. Where do clouds come from? What are clouds made from? How do clouds move?
6. How did mountains form? Were mountains always there?
7. How does a car work? What causes a car to move?

Note: Prior to conducting these interviews, review the interviews detailed in the suggested readings of Learning Activity 2–2. These will give you a good idea of the kinds of questions to ask as well as how to respond to the answers which the children give.

The ability to determine causal relations is directly related to cause-and-effect processes, but Piaget has also spoken directly to the processes of inferring as he considered observation, inference, and data.

The Process of Inferring

Observation, Inference, and Data Interpretation as Processes. Observation and inference are the basic scientific processes, because they form the basis for the gathering and interpretation of data. The skills appear to develop for these processes with the four developmental stages. The sensorimotor stage will not be discussed here.

The Preoperational Child. Children in the preoperational stage find the use and collection of data difficult. These children are likely to have their observations colored by immediate perceptions rather than by actual occurrences of the activity. As these children interpret the data from an activity, their interpretations are likely to be egocentric and anthropomorphic in nature. In addition, the preoperational child is unlikely to see possible contradictions between perceptions and the actual data. The information that is collected by the preoperational child will be hard for that child to order. What occurs first, second, third, etc., will be hard for the child to determine after the activity has ended.

The Concrete Operational Child. The concrete operational child will have advanced over the preoperational child in his or her ability to determine the sequence of data and observations. Now the child will be able to determine what occurred first, second, etc. In interpreting the data from an activity, the concrete operational child will tend to look at a single characteristic during the early part of the developmental stage but, by the end of the stage, will be able to take several aspects of a system into account, although looking at each aspect separately, and interpret the effect of each of those aspects. In a situation that is written rather than concrete, the concrete operational child will stay within the confines of the description and merely redescribe the situation when asked to make inferences from the description.

The Formal Operational Child. The formal operational individual is fully capable of making objective observations and of considering a variety of factors during those observations. In addition, the formal operational individual will be able to take a written description of an activity and account for all of the relevant features of the account. The formal operational individual will also be able to go beyond that description to make inferences using not only the data given in the description but also relevant past experiences.

Modeling as a Process

The ability to form and to use both mental and physical models is not truly a process of science, yet the ability to form and use models allows the individual to hypothesize, infer, and experiment. As with observation, inference, and data interpretation, the ability to use models develops along with the developmental stages.

The Preoperational Child. The preoperational child tends to be unable to build a mental model through the consideration of specific facts. The preoperational child tends to be tied by transductive reasoning to a consideration of specifics rather than generalizations.

The Concrete Operational Child. The concrete operational child in the early phases of this developmental stage will be able to develop mental models of scientific content, but only when those models are developed around the processes of seriation, classification, and simple one-to-one correspondence. During this early stage, children also find it difficult to use models of objects because they tend to equate the model with reality. Consequently, use of a balloon to represent a human lung may be interpreted by the child to mean that the lung is a balloon.

In the late concrete operational stage, the child will be able to use mental models as well as physical models provided that the mental models are founded in concrete experiences and the physical models correspond exactly to reality. The late concrete operational child will no longer consider the model the real thing, but the child will not be able to make a correspondence between reality and something which does not look like the real object.

The Formal Operational Child. By the formal operational stage, the child is able to use all mental models of reality. In the early phase of formal operations, the child will have difficulty comparing two models, such as the wave theory and the particle theory of light, which account for the same phenomena. Each of the models will be considered as representative of reality, and confusion may result from the consideration of both models. By the late formal stage, the child is able to go beyond known explanations to search for explanatory models, to extend models, and to compare alternative models of reality in order to account for the data obtained during an experiment or an activity. When using physical models, the formal operational child will be able to consider and use models in which the parts bear little or no resemblance to actuality.

The Process of Experimenting

The process of experimenting is the last of the scientific processes considered in detail by Piaget. This is a skill which develops during the formal operational stage of development, but its development is preceded by acquisition of certain skills on the part of the preoperational and concrete operational child. The process of experimenting, with particular attention to control of variables, will be discussed below in Chapter 5. A general developmental sequence is considered here.

The Preoperational Child. Although the preoperational child is unable to carry out or to understand a true experiment, the child at this level is able to concentrate one at a time on particular factors or features of an activity. This ability is a prerequisite to the development of an ability to isolate and control variables.

The Concrete Operational Child. Although the child in the early concrete operational stage does not have a particular strategy for controlling variables during an activity, the child at this stage of development will be able to reject activities where a factor is uncontrolled when that factor is actually or intuitively obvious. In other words, the child at this level will realize that the effect of the surface on the height to which a ball will bounce cannot be tested if a ping-pong ball is used in one trial and a basketball is used in another.

By the late concrete operational stage, the child will attempt to carry out an experiment but will vary more than one factor at a time or may vary one factor while saying he is varying a different factor. Although the late concrete operational child will be able to order the data gained through an experiment, he or she will find it impossible to exclude the effect of interfering variables in interpreting that data.

Although the late concrete operational child frequently arrives at the correct effect of a particular variable, this conclusion is often based on intuition and on faulty reasoning rather than on interpretation of the data actually collected during the experiment.

The Formal Operational Child. The child in the early formal operations stage will be able to control the variables in an experiment but may have difficulty in isolating those variables which are not obvious perceptually. At this point the child sees the necessity for making an hypothesis, planning controlled experiments, and collecting data but is likely to need help in organizing the data so that relevant information can be isolated and irrelevant data disregarded. By the late phases of the formal operational stage, the individual is able to control the variables in an experiment and to base experiments and interpretations of data on a particular experimental model.

Also in the formal operational stage, the child will, after performing an experiment, be able to determine cause-and-effect relationships. The same child will be unable to do the same thing when he or she is shown an experiment done by another individual. The ability to consider experiments not done personally and to choose those that show a particular factor's effect does not occur until the late formal operational stage.

Table 2–4 includes all of the processes of science that will be considered in this text and the approximate age or grade levels at which the child will be able to work with the process. This table can serve as a guide to when the processes should be introduced into the curriculum and the expectations that the teacher can have for success in the processes at various grade levels.

Table 2–4 The processes of science teaching

PROCESS	LEVEL	PLACEMENT
Communication	1. Oral and pictorial communication.	1. All grade levels, major forms of communication in preschool through second grades.
	2. Reading and writing—no numerical forms other than counting.	2. Third through sixth grades; increasing in complexity as grade level increases.
	3. Numerical forms and computations.	3. Fifth or sixth grades; numerical forms are highly abstract.

Table continues on following page.

Table 2–4 Continued

PROCESS	LEVEL	PLACEMENT
Observation	1. Only one level is considered for classroom practicality.	1. All grade levels should use observation with the main emphasis in the preschool and primary grades.
Using numbers	1. Counting.	1. Counting is most meaningful after the child conserves number; first or second grade level.
	2. Numerical computations.	2. Use of computations is highly abstract and should be delayed until fifth or sixth grade.
	3. Analysis of numerical data.	3. Highly abstract; should be delayed until fifth or sixth grade.
Prediction	1. Only one level considered for classroom practicality.	1. Before seven years of age children are unable to base predictions on observed data. At about seven, children begin to use natural relationships in a logical manner. Predictions should be delayed until about the second grade.
Inference	1. Nonnumerical data.	1. Like prediction, inference should be delayed until about second grade. Second through fourth graders should use nonnumerical information.
	2. Numerical data.	2. Because of the abstractness, delay the drawing of inferences from numerical data until about fifth or sixth grade.
Conclusion	1. Nonnumerical data.	1. Like inference, conclusions should be delayed until about second grade. Second through fourth graders should use nonnumerical information.
	2. Numerical data.	2. Because of the abstractness, delay the drawing of conclusions from numerical data until fifth or sixth grade.
Classification	1. Concrete objects grouped through a single property.	1. Preschool, kindergarten, and many first grade children will be incapable of more than this level; some will find even this difficult.
	2. Concrete objects grouped through more than one property.	2. Second and third graders should be able to group on the basis of sets and subsets using the concepts of all and some; can use more than one property.

Table 2–4 Continued

PROCESS	LEVEL	PLACEMENT
	3. Concrete objects grouped in a hierarchical system.	3. Fourth through sixth graders can use a hierarchical system of classification; by about twelve years of age one-third of all children will still not be able to use this form.
	4. Nonconcrete phenomena used as the material for classification.	4. This should be delayed until fifth or sixth grade because of the abstractness.
Space relations	1. Shapes.	1. Preschool, kindergarten, first grade should be introduced to the common solid shapes; these are more common in the environment than are the plane shapes. 1a. Plane shapes should be introduced at about first or second grade level.
	2. Geometric factors.	2. Direct measurement of objects using meter sticks, liter cylinders, and balances should be introduced first. 2a. Indirect measurements should be considered next. 2b. Measurement by computations should be delayed until fifth or sixth grades. 2c. Approximate age levels for the basic forms of measurement are: (1) length at about eight years; (2) area, conceptually at about eight; through computation at about eleven; (3) weight, conceptually at about nine; through measurement at about ten; (4) volume, conceptually after eleven; by computation after about fourteen.
Interpreting data	1. Nonnumerical, descriptive data.	1. Requires the ability to use logical relationships about the natural world; begin at about the fourth grade.
	2. Numerical data	2. Interpretation of numerical data is highly abstract; delay until fifth or sixth grade.

Table continues on following page.

Table 2–4 Continued

PROCESS	LEVEL	PLACEMENT
Formulating hypotheses	1. Only one level is considered for classroom practicality.	1. This requires the use of causal relations which may not be available before ten years of age. Begin in fourth grade and emphasize in the fifth and sixth grades.
Controlling variables	1. Levels consist of a teaching sequence, as found in Chapter 5.	1. Control of variables is not possible until formal operations. Delay this until about the sixth grade.
Experimenting	1. Only one level is considered for classroom practicality.	1. Experimentation requires the control of variables and the ability to hypothesize. This should be delayed until about the sixth grade level.
Cause and effect	1. Only one level of true causality exists.	1. Preschool through first grade children are unable to use true cause-and-effect relations; they tend to confuse motive with cause. 1a. Second through fourth grade children are making a transition to the use of logical cause-and-effect relations but still have some difficulty in this area. 1b. At about the fifth grade level, children are able to use true, logical causality.
Operational questions	1. Only one level is considered for classroom practicality.	1. Before first grade children should be encouraged to ask any form of question. 2. After, and during, first grade questions should be refined into operational form so that by the intermediate grades most questions asked are operational.
Interaction and systems	1. Concrete objects emphasizing the parts of the system. 2. Concrete objects emphasizing both objects and interactions. 3. Objects and phenomena as system parts.	1. Preschool through second grade should emphasize the concrete aspects of the system. 2. Third and fourth graders are more able to consider the cause and effect of interactions. 3. Fifth and sixth graders, because phenomena are abstract in nature.

Information Processing and the Content of Science

Information processing, a relatively new theory of psychology, attempts to understand the thinking processes of people who are using their ability to think rationally to the fullest possible extent. The information processers have based their work on the notion of a computer program in which different subroutines come into play as needed, depending on the problem which is to be solved.

In attempting to understand the thinking abilities of human beings, the theorist of information processing tries to program a computer to go through a series of procedures which in the most essential ways simulate the thinking of a real person performing a real task. If the computer can solve the programmed problem, it is assumed that the human mind operates in a similar manner. Such computer-based models of human thinking hypothesize within the human mind an array of information processing mechanisms each of which performs a certain activity. These processes or activities are assumed to be organized in a particular way, which can be understood.

This exploration of the human mind has led to confirmation of the idea that the contents of the mind are not an exact replica of the external, so-called real world. Rather, the information stored in the mind is a processed version of reality. This information has been changed for more efficient and effective storage among the rest of the contents of the mind. But, since the information in the mind can be used in a predictable manner, it is assumed that there is a great deal of correspondence between what is stored and what is real.

The study of information processing has led to some understanding of the concerns of many teachers: memory, concept development, and problem solving. Each of these areas will be considered here.

Memory

The Contents of Human Memory. The computer is often held up as the epitome of memory, because once something is stored on a tape or disk it cannot be forgotten unless the storage vehicle is destroyed. Although this storage is a precise replica of what the computer is told and the contents of the human memory are not, the human memory has a distinct advantage over the machine. According to one estimate, the human mind is capable of holding 100 trillion bits of information (Hunt, 1982). This is a great deal more than even the largest research computer can hold in its memory banks. And access to the human memory tends to be a great deal easier than access to the computer memory; even a fuzzy, indistinct, or indirect question can cause correct recall from the human mind.

What is stored in the human memory is not, however, a precise replica of reality. Rather, memory must be viewed as a series of processes that change information from the moment of perception on. The changes which occur may be slight or great, so that the information can be retained in the memory for a short time or for what seems to be forever.

Short-Term Memory. Short-term memory (STM) is able to retain items of information for about eighteen seconds unless that information is rehearsed. In general, STM is used to hold information that must be kept in mind for a moment or that has been recalled from the long-term memory. Short-term memory enables us to focus on what is important and to make decisions quickly. Approximately seven items of information can be held at one time. In considering the capability of short-term memory, try recalling how you remember a telephone number never before called. One says the number over and over until one dials the number, then one promptly forgets it.

Long-Term Memory. Whereas short-term memory can retain only a few pieces of information for a short time, long-term memory (LTM) can retain information, in a highly processed form, theoretically forever. The material in LTM can, however, be returned to short-term memory for use through the processes of retrieval or recognition.

Retrieval is the deliberate, active recall of information. At times this retrieval is direct, operating so rapidly that the answer to a question is out even before the end of the question. A good example of a direct retrieval question is: What is your name? In other cases, information is retrieved from memory through a hierarchical scan which takes about two seconds. In this case, there is a search through a particular category within the memory system until a particular answer is found. A hierarchical scan may be needed to answer a question like: Is a platypus a mammal?

Although a computer can retrieve any bit of information stored in it as an answer to a particular question, the human mind has an advantage over the computer. The computer must search through its memory banks each time a question is asked even if the question is absurd. Consequently, the computer will search through its memory for the answer to a question like: What kind of car did Galileo drive? The human mind recognizes the question as an absurdity and does not scan for an answer.

Recognition is a passive process in which the memory tells the individual what is being experienced. Recognition simply tells the individual that a particular word is "planet" without retrieving any information about the term.

The Processing of Information in the Memory. Nearly everyone has experienced the problem of knowing something or knowing something is known yet being unable to recall the bit of information from the memory. Nearly everyone has had the experience of retrieving the wrong word or the wrong name of a friend from the memory. Both of these problems are experienced because an incorrect cue was used for the recall of the piece of information.

Learning Activity 2–4

Memory

The following is an experiment into memory and learning. In it three groups of individuals are asked to look at and learn a list of words in 60 seconds. Following that time, the participants are given 120 seconds to write as many of the words as possible. The participants are, however, placed in three groups, and each group is given a slightly different set of instructions.

After trying the experiment with a group of people, look at the resulting lists of words that were recalled. Consider the length of the lists (the number of words recalled), the words that were consistently omitted, and the way in which the word lists were organized. How do each of the groups differ?

The word list is:

fork	batter
rose	daisy
slipper	quarterback
bowl	dutch oven
tulip	collie
pitcher	onion
goalie	aster
sauce pan	marigold
poodle	terrier
tackle	frying pan
lotus	retriever
boxer	

The following instructions should be written, and only one set of instructions should be given to each of the participants. Try to have the same number of participants in each of the groups.

Group I: At the start of this experiment you will have 60 seconds to study the accompanying word list. At the end of those 60 seconds, you will have an additional 120 seconds to list all of the words that you can recall from the list in the space below.

Group II: At the start of this experiment you will have 60 seconds to study the accompanying word list. At the end of those 60 seconds, you will have an additional 120 seconds to write down all of the words that you can recall from the list in the space below. The words that you will be learning can be classified into the following groups: flowers, sports, dogs, kitchen items, and miscellaneous.

Group III: At the start of this experiment you will have 60 seconds to study the accompanying word list. At the end of those 60 seconds, you will have an additional 120 seconds to write down all of the words that you can recall from the list in the space below. The words that you are learning begin mainly with consonants. Of the twenty-three words on the list, twenty-one begin with consonants and two with vowels.

After you have analyzed your collected data, the lists of words written by each group, try to decide why the groups differed in the number of words that could be recalled.

Learning Activity 2–5

Memory

Imagine that you are taking a course in geology. Your first assignment is to memorize a list of terms that your instructor has assured you is absolutely vital for your future understanding of the content of the course. Because you intend to earn an "A" in the class, you are going to memorize the words so that you can reproduce them, in any order, on the test which will be given. Consider the following list of words carefully. What strategy would you use to memorize these words in as short a time as possible? Write a detailed description of how you would approach this problem in memorization. You do not need to actually memorize the words.

fumarole	anticline	pedalfer
dripstone	tuff	cirque
conchoidal	drumlin	botryoidal
graben	varve	exfoliation
alluvium	detritus	guyot
facies	pluton	gangue
caliche	batholith	colluvium
ventifact	regolith	dendritic
esker	solifluction	kame
loess	isostasy	vesicle

Now, using a children's science textbook, make a list of about fifteen words. Ask two or three children how they might go about learning (memorizing) all of the words on the list. Compare your strategy for learning a list of words to those of the children whom you interview.

The idea that we need a cue to recall information is based on the theory that the memory system is not a faithful representation of reality. Rather, events that are seen and information that is heard are stored in a processed form. This form may be affected by questions or suggestions and changed by inferences made by the learner that fill in areas that are not heard or understood. In addition, stored memories are continually revised to harmonize with past or ongoing events.

The Process of Storage in Long-Term Memory. All of the information that is taken into the memory comes through the senses. Fortunately, all of that sensory information is neither stored nor even attended to.

Information that is taken in through the senses first arrives at a series of buffers. These buffers allow the individual briefly to notice the sensory information or to retain that information until it is noticed. The buffers allow the individual to select what will be attended to and what will be tuned out.

From the buffers, the information is transformed into a meaningful symbol which is placed in the STM. This allows for awareness of whatever has occurred and permits the information to be processed just deeply enough to be a part of the individual's current mental activity. Unless the information is rehearsed, it is forgotten.

Information from STM that is to be placed in LTM undergoes certain processes, which include looking for patterns, chunking of similar information, extraction of deeper meanings from words, sentences, or images, classification of meanings, and the linking of new information with what has already been incorporated into the long-term memory.

In processing information, LTM appears to be a semantic network in which new material is placed in an appropriate category and then is gradually tied into the network by meaningful connections. The arrangement appears to be in categories, but the categories and the storage of information tend to be redundant. The network is also surrounded by and linked to other networks so that sights, odors, and sounds as well as words may trigger the recall of stored information.

The processing of information permits new material to be included in the memory structure. Recent research into the brain and into the processing of various types of information indicates that the human brain processes different kinds of information in each of the hemispheres.

Figure 2–4 Flow chart of the human memory system

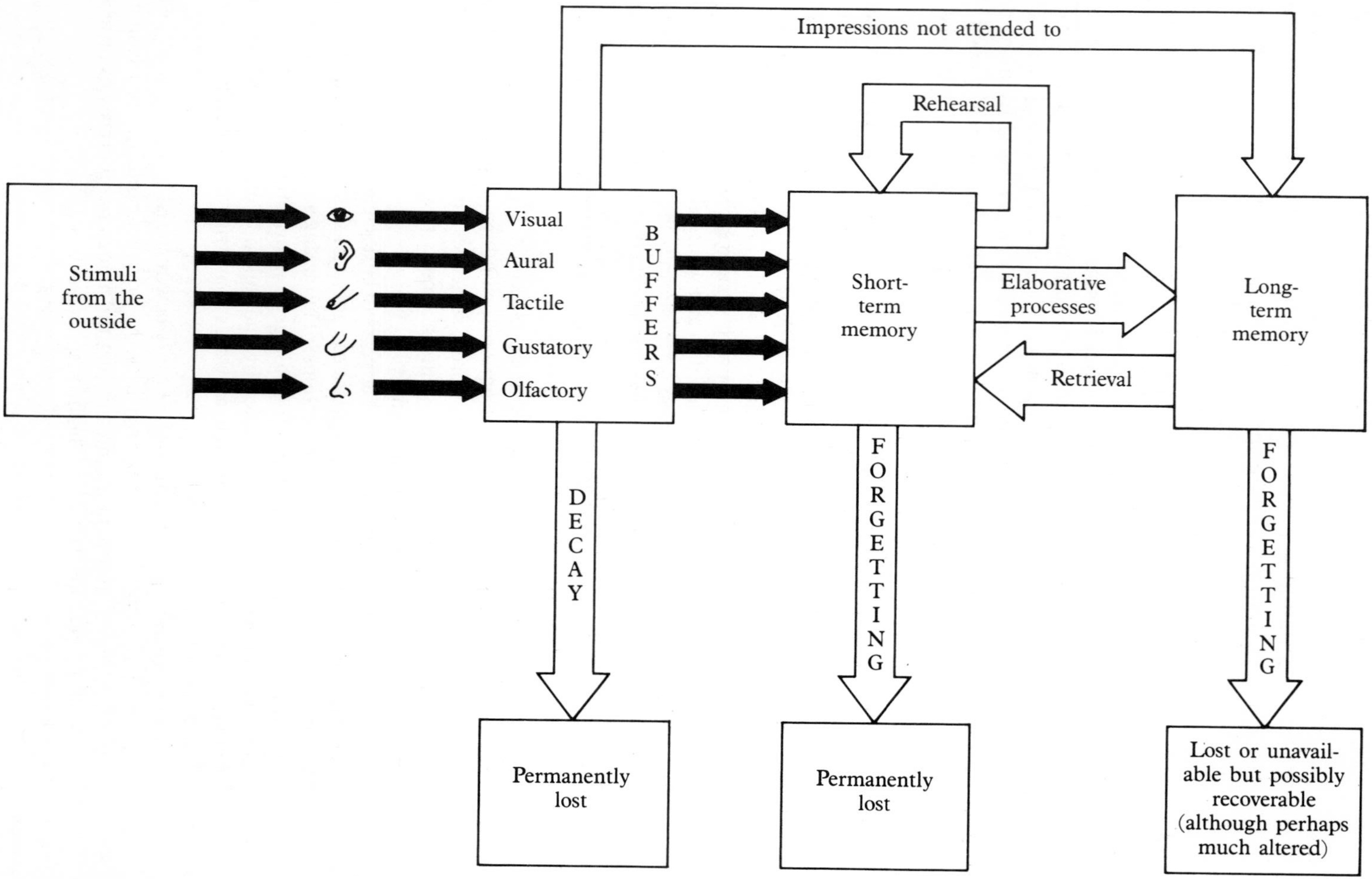

Hunt, M. The Universe Within: A New Science Explores the Human Mind. Simon and Schuster, New York, 1982. p. 103.

Right and Left Brain Processing of Information in the Memory. Physically, the human brain is divided into right and left hemispheres connected by the *corpus callosum,* a bundle of nerve fibers that seems to connect every part of one side of the brain to the corresponding part of the other side of the brain. The function of the *corpus callosum* seems to be to facilitate the interchange of information between the right and the left hemispheres of the brain, so that the nonverbal storage and processing of the right hemisphere can be integrated with the verbal processing of the left hemisphere (Levy, 1983).

Some of the original research into hemispheric processing appeared to indicate that certain types of information were processed in one hemisphere or the other and that certain educational activities were directed toward one hemisphere or the other, but more recent research has shown that although processing is different, the two hemispheres of the brain do operate together to provide meaning. The right hemispheric processes of imaging are as important for the derivation of meaning as are the left hemispheric processes of verbal storage.

Although the right and left hemispheres of the brain do interact, there are differences between the two hemispheres with respect to the processing of information. The right brain tends to be holistic, spatial, pictorial, and nonverbal in its processing of information. In addition, the right hemispheric processes discriminate emotional and humorous overtones important for understanding the full meaning of oral and written communications. The right brain also seems to play a special role in emotion. If students are emotionally engaged in the learning process, both sides of the brain will participate in learning regardless of the subject matter or the type of presentation (Johnson, 1982).

The left hemisphere of the brain has as its province abstract symbols, language, and linear, time-related, or sequential functions. Originally, researchers thought that the left hemisphere was the area in which logical processes were stored. It has recently been shown that thinking, logic, and reasoning are the province of both hemispheres with each contributing its own perspective on a particular problem (Wittrock, 1980).

Helping Children Remember the Content of Science. Recent research has indicated that children, particularly young children, have not yet become aware of their own memory capabilities. Children tend to be better at recognition than they are at recall. It appears to be the demands and procedures of education that develop in children the elementary memory skills of chunking, employing mnemonic devices like rhythm and rhyme, and self-cueing, like visualizing some past event to stir up association or starting at the beginning of an activity and recalling the activity step by step. Even the short-term memory technique of rehearsing is probably learned rather than developed spontaneously. Consequently, children need to be taught the memory skills that they will need in order to be able to recall the science content that they are taught.

If children are to remember the information that is presented to them in the science class, the teacher should make a special effort to teach memory techniques and to sequence information in ways which are likely to help children process this information into long-term memory. Some suggestions for presentation of content are:

1. Teach children to rehearse information that they want to hold in short-term memory. The teacher might suggest that the child say the answer to a question over and over to himself until called upon to give that answer.

2. Teach children mnemonic devices that will aid them in the recall of information. Songs and rhythms are helpful to children as are sentences in which the first letter of each word is the first letter of the information to be recalled. The names of the planets in their correct order can be remembered by the sentence: "*M*y *v*ery *e*legant *m*other *j*ust *s*at *u*pon *n*ine *p*orcupines." Such sentences are particularly good if they are devised by the children.

3. Use classification systems whenever possible to show how one idea in science relates to another. The biological classification system is a ready-made indication that the vertebrate and the invertebrate animals are related to one another and that birds, reptiles, fish, mammals, and amphibians are all types of vertebrate animals. Drawing such systems on the chalkboard or on a chart can be effective in helping children process information for long-term storage.

4. Teach so that children have many concrete and written experiences with the content of science. Involve all of the senses in teaching as well as imagination, drawing skills, and personal experience. The more meaningful a piece of information is, the more likely the content will be remembered. Recall will also be helped because of the extensive number of cues that will be available.

5. Teach so that children develop images of the content as well as a verbal equivalent. The greatest remembering occurs when a word has great imagery; concrete referents are stored as images, which are more resistant to forgetting than are words.

6. Simple, repetitive, uninteresting learning routines result in poor learning, because the entire brain is not engaged in the learning process. The student needs to be emotionally involved in learning; otherwise, there is no interplay between the right and left brain hemispheres. Make the science content personally meaningful to the child.

7. Make your science lessons challenging to the children. Challenges appear to bring the whole brain into function, so that information is fully processed. Challenges seem to generate the excitement that provides for optimal learning.

8. Encourage children to sketch or draw their ideas as well as to write them. This also will facilitate the processing of information into both brain hemispheres.

9. Teach children to use external memory systems as well as internal systems: notes, diagrams, charts, tables, and records of all sorts that will cue the memory.

Concept Development

Much of what is stored in the memory system appears to be in the form of hierarchical classifications, indicating the relationships that exist among the various items in the classification. These hierarchical representations in memory also appear to correspond to the representations of concepts as they are structured by the information processing.

A Definition of Concept. A concept seems to correspond to a category of objects, ideas, or events that have some similar features. In general, a concept is an idea. It tends to be introduced by way of definitions that give the concept's relationships to other, familiar concepts. Concepts may be learned through either concept identification or concept development.

Concept Identification. Concept identification comes about when an individual is given a number of examples of a particular concept and from those examples develops the desired concept. In most cases, this is what is occurring in the science classroom as the teacher gives a number of activities illustrating what it is that the child is to learn for that particular lesson. The concept is already named; it is up to the learner to identify examples of the concept.

Learning Activity 2–6

Concept Identification

The following pictures illustrate a variety of *Crep*. Look at them carefully and try to determine what makes a *Crep* a *Crep*.

The following pictures illustrate creatures that are not *Creps*. Try to determine the characteristics that make these non-*Creps*.

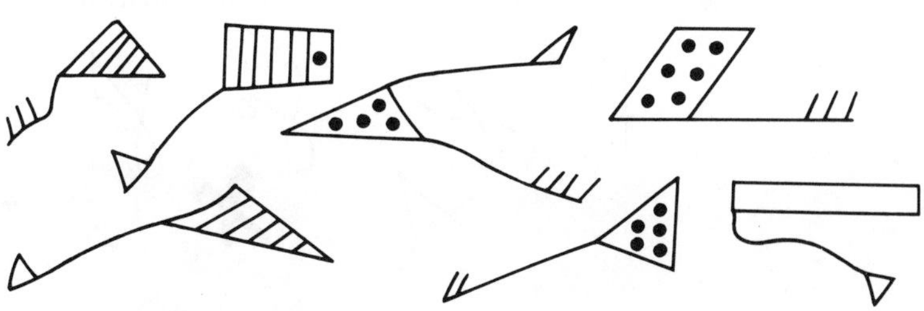

Now, draw a picture of a new *Crep*. What characteristics does your drawing have that make it a *Crep?* How did you go about determining the characteristics that allowed you to label a drawing as a *Crep?*

Learning Activity 2–7

Concept Formation

The following is a simple way of showing how adults form a concept. Required is a set of cards on which are drawn the pictures that follow and three or four subjects.

1. *The Cards*
   Make the following set of cards, one drawing to each card. On the reverse of the card, print the nonsense syllable that is the name of the picture.

   a. *Ope:* The following are illustrations of *Opes.*

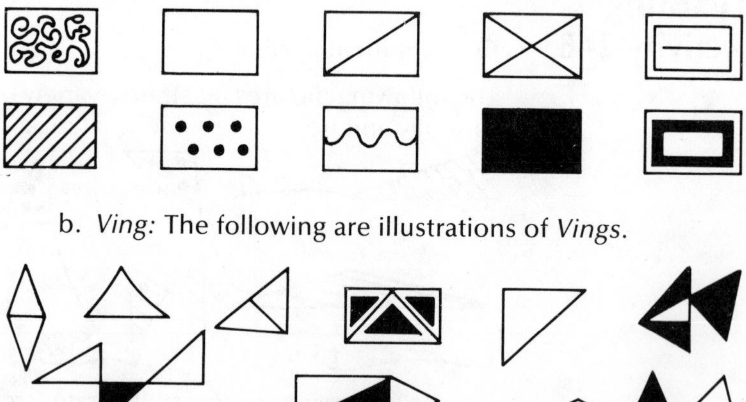

   b. *Ving:* The following are illustrations of *Vings.*

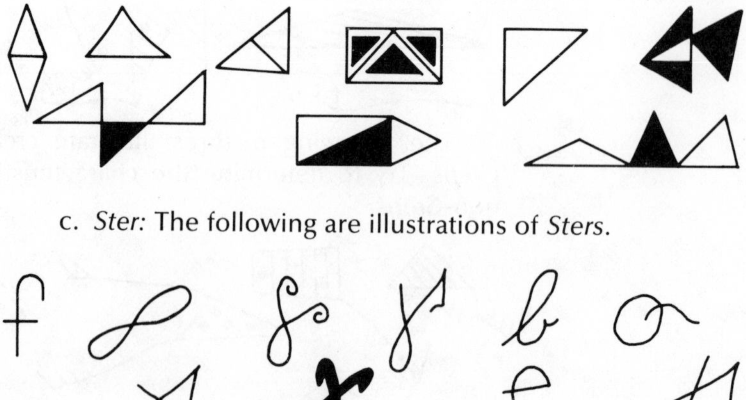

   c. *Ster:* The following are illustrations of *Sters.*

d. *Ranc:* The following are illustrations of *Rancs.*

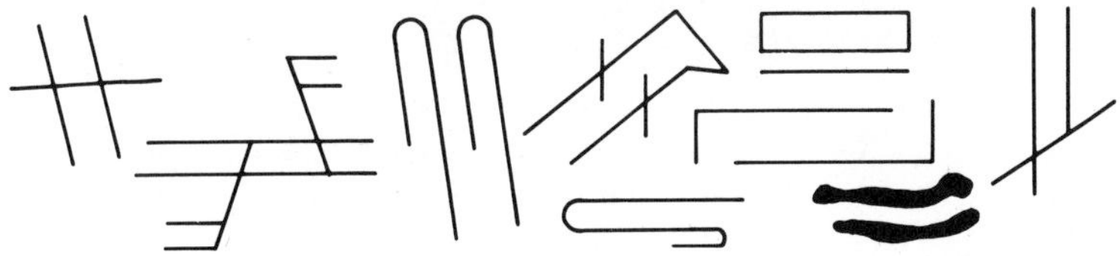

e. *Nole:* The following are illustrations of *Noles.*

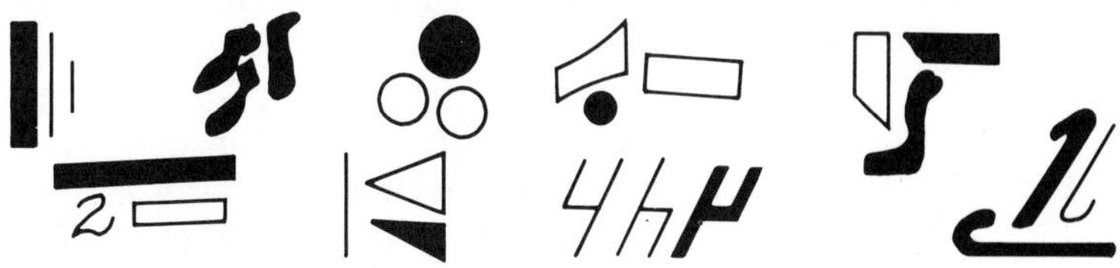

2. *The Directions*
   a. Tell the subject that you will be showing a series of drawings that he or she should try to label with one of the nonsense words.
   b. Tell the subject to call out the name of the picture as soon as he or she knows it. Guessing is permitted. Incorrect names should be corrected.
   c. Shuffle the cards so that the pictures will be in random order.
   d. Show the cards to the subject one at a time at about three-second intervals. Read the name of each picture to the subject.
   e. Continue until the subject can name all of the cards correctly. (This usually takes not more than fifteen minutes.)
   f. After all of the cards have been named:
      (1) Ask the subject for the characteristics of an *Ope, Ving, Ster, Ranc,* and *Nole.*
      (2) Have the subject try to describe how he or she learned the names.

Concept Development. Concept development, on the other hand, occurs when an individual synthesizes a number of experiences and derives a particular concept, although those experiences have not been especially designed to permit the development of any particular concept. Children develop concepts from a very young age as they learn what a dog is as opposed to a cat. There is some evidence to support the idea that children as young as four months of age actually conceptualize (Kagan, 1972; Bornstein, 1979).

Concept Development and the Use of Templates. Concept development seems to begin when a child identifies certain characteristics that are common to a number of examples of a concept. The child extracts two or three characteristics from the examples, then looks for these same characteristics when seeing new information. A very young child, for example, may extract from the animals called "dog" that they have fur, legs, and a tail. On seeing a Great Dane for the first time the child sees those same properties (legs, hair, tail) and is able to correctly categorize the animal as a dog. This same process of concept development occurs when a child learns the meaning of the term "mammal" in the science class.

After being introduced to the concept of a mammal, the child first extracts from the real animals and the pictures of mammals brought into the classroom the fact that animals called mammals are warm and furry. Upon being shown a new animal, the child may look for fur and then touch the animal to find out if it is warm. If both of these characteristics are present, the animal may be categorized under the concept mammal, and the information is stored in the memory system. This use of certain characteristics to which examples are compared is called using a template.

In most cases, the use of a template permits the correct classification of information. But the use of a template can also result in an erroneous classification, if the characteristics chosen are not the most important or if the new object or piece of information merely seems to fit. On the basis of being warm and furry, a penguin might be classified as a mammal. It is warm and its soft, close feathers do look like fur.

Concepts that are formed through the use of templates seem to resemble clusters with a very dense center and indistinct edges where concepts overlap with one another. At the center of the cluster are the most typical examples of the concept; at the edges one finds the more unusual cases of the concept.

For example, the concept *bird* may include at its center examples like robins, sparrows, bluebirds, and chickadees. These tend to be common, typical birds against which other organisms can be compared to determine their birdness. A little further from the center could be the hawks, eagles, and vultures, which, although birds, seem to be more exotic because of their size and their carnivorous tendencies. Still further out may be the birds like the ostrich and emu, which, although feathered, do not fly and which seem too large to really be birds. Finally, at its outer limits the concept may include the penguin, which not only is flightless but also seems to have fur, waddles, and swims in a distinctly nonbird fashion. The central concept tends to be formed out of experience, and each new instance is compared to that concept's template to determine whether or not it fits into the category (Fried and Holyoak, 1981).

Concept Development and the Teaching of Science. Children do begin to develop concepts at an early age. In order to promote concept development in the science classroom, the teacher should present the child with conceptual information in a sequential manner in which the relationships between one concept and another are clearly indicated.

To develop a particular concept, it appears that the child should first be presented with the most concrete and representative examples of the concept. These examples should be thoroughly understood and the most salient characteristics carefully delineated, so that a template can be formed against which other examples of the concept can be matched. The child should have the opportunity to apply the characteristics identified to other examples of the concept in order to reinforce those characteristics. The child should then be presented with examples of the concept that are less ideal in nature but that still have the appropriate characteristics. Finally, the most unusual examples of the concept can be presented, so that the ideal and the unusual can be compared. At this stage examples can also be presented that are not examples of the concept, so that the child becomes able to identify that which is the concept as well as that which is not.

Examples of the concept should be presented to the child in ways which are appropriate to the developmental level of the child. Concrete examples should be shown prior to the actual naming of the concept, but the name should always be presented, for it is through the vocabulary of science that children learn to communicate their ideas and to understand others. The examples presented should also show the concept in a variety of situations moving from the concrete to the abstract.

Conceptual development takes place when children are presented with a wide variety of examples and the relationships between those examples and other information is clearly delineated. The presentation of facts without context, of ideas without examples, and of fragments of the various branches of science without development of their interrelationships do not readily allow for the development of concepts in children.

Changing Concepts Already Held by Children. Unfortunately, what is taught in the science class is not totally new to the child. In many cases, the child comes to science with incorrect concepts already developed. In order to help children develop correct concepts through the science program, the teacher can follow three steps:

1. Help the students realize what their initial concepts are. Before beginning a lesson, try to discover what students already think about a particular topic. As the lesson begins help the children to verbalize their preconceptions, so that they will be more willing to reject those ideas which do not fit the evidence that will result from an activity.

2. Help the students to realize that their ideas are not correct. This should be done in a discussion where the child can talk without fear that he or she will be laughed at for a particular idea.

3. Allow students to experience phenomena which are directly related to

their initial concepts. First-hand observation can help students to realize when an initial idea is not working. Try having students set up experiments or activities to test their ideas.

To construct a new conceptual framework which eliminates the previous, incorrect ideas, students must be helped to confront the discrepancies between their misconceptions and their observations. In some cases such direct experience will be sufficient for students to recognize the need to form new ideas or a new hypothesis. In other cases the children may need to be shown the discrepancy between their ideas and their experiences (Mistrell, 1983).

Problem Solving

The final area to be discussed in this chapter is problem solving. Much of what we do in science class is designed to allow children to solve a particular problem and thereby gain a particular piece of content information. The content selected for teaching in the science program is chosen, in part, because it will have applicability to the real world and to problems that will be encountered there. The development of problem-solving strategies and skills cannot, however, be left to chance. Certain skills can be taught to children as a part of the science program whether it is in a primary or an intermediate grade.

Learning Activity 2–8 Problem Solving

Problem One:

Begin by making six to ten Greek crosses from paper or light cardboard. Three-by-five index cards work well. A Greek cross is made from five equal squares:

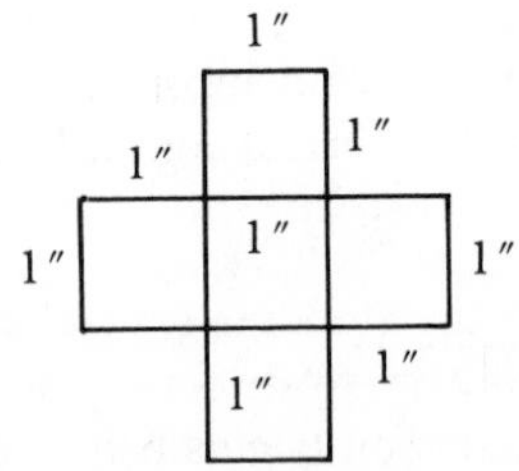

Now, try to solve the following problems:

1. Cut the cross to make *five* pieces which will form a square.
2. Cut the cross to make *four* pieces which will form a square.
3. Make five pieces which will form two Greek crosses of the same size.

4. *Challenge:* Make six pieces which will form an equilateral triangle. (This is extremely difficult, but it can be done.)

Problem Two:

Using each digit from one through nine only once, fill in the blocks in the following diagram so that each of the four problems is correct:

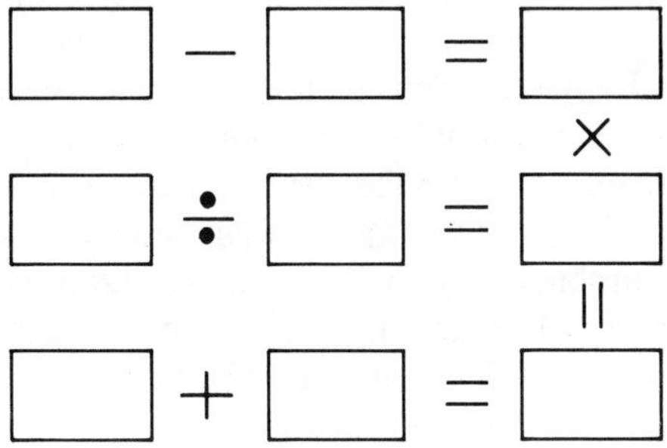

Problem Three:

Draw a circle with a diameter of about six inches or 12.3 centimeters. Using a protractor, scissors, and a ruler, find a method for determining the approximate area of a circle. *You may not use the formula for the area or circumference of a circle.*

Problem Four:

Find a way of arranging four sevens (7, 7, 7, 7), using any arithmetical signs, so that they equal 100. Example: $(5 + 5) \times (5 + 5) = 100$, or $99 + 9/9 = 100$.

As you work with each of these problems, keep a record of your strategies.

Strategies in Problem Solving

Heuristics. Heuristics refers to a means of problem solving that is essentially individually determined. The individual plans a sequence of events that may result in a solution and follows that sequence, modifying it as necessary, until a solution is reached. At times the heuristic approach may take the form of trial and error.

Algorithms. An algorithm, on the other hand, is a programmed strategy which always results in a correct solution. The forms that are used for solving computation problems in arithmetic are forms of algorithms.

Representations in Problem Solving. An individual's choice of a problem-solving strategy generally includes a choice between a verbal representation of a problem and an imagic representation of a problem. Verbalizers tend to memorize words or phrases that help to define and limit the problem; then they use these descriptions as an aid to problem solving. Imagers, on the other hand, tend to generate a picture or image of the problem situation and then to use that image as an aid to problem solving.

Representations that are based on the abstract structures of a problem tend to be powerful problem-solving tools. Fortunately, one of the results of education seems to be the development of problem-solving skill in working with abstract structures rather than simply looking at the surface characteristics of the problem. In some cases, the difference between good and poor students appears to be the amount of information that those students can bring to a problem-solving situation. The better student and the better problem solver is able to see how information that they already possess is relevant to the problem-solving situation and to see how information acquired in one context can be applied to another context (Hunt, 1982).

Science Teaching and Problem Solving. In the teaching of science, inculcation of the ability to use the content of science in a problem-solving situation becomes one of the major goals for the program. In one way, the information that is developed as a part of the elementary science program should be of the sort that can be applied to the solution of such problem-solving situations as operational questions, experiments, demonstrations, hypothesizing, and concluding. Children should have the opportunity to apply the information that they acquire in the solution of one problem to the solution of other types of problems.

Yet, in another way, the content of the science program should be applied to real problem situations, such as consideration of pollution, energy, and discussion of endangered species. In a simpler form children can solve problems in their immediate environment, such as the effect of an ice storm on the trees in the school grounds, the litter in the cafeteria, the nutritional content of school lunches, or health care problems.

Problem Solving in the Primary Grades. By the time children enter the primary grades, they are already accomplished problem solvers (Bruni, 1982; Suydam, 1982). They have solved the major problems of acquiring language and locomotion as well as the minor problems of transporting toys from one place to another or of building sand castles which do not fall over. The primary grade science teacher needs to help these children to refine their problem solving skills so that they become better able to apply those skills to the content of the elementary school science program. Six practical ideas for helping primary grade children use their problem-solving skills in the science classroom follow:

1. Ask open-ended questions during science lessons so that children have the opportunity to use their experiences and their unique knowledge in the solution of the problems presented in the questions.
2. Encourage children to discover patterns in the world around them by showing how the different phenomena considered in the science program are related.
3. Provide opportunities for children to solve problems by setting up their own activities to find out "what will happen if . . ." Provide time for children to discuss the results of activities and particularly to discuss results that are different.
4. Develop scientific vocabulary so that children can talk about the phenomena that they experience.
5. Reward children for finding a variety of solutions to the same problem and for finding creative solutions to problems.
6. Help children to experience science through all of their senses and in a variety of different situations. Show the relationships between the various subject areas in school and how the skills of one area can be useful in another area.

Problem Solving in the Intermediate Grades. The suggestions made for the primary grades are appropriate for the intermediate grades as well. However, the intermediate grade child can be expected to solve problems in a more sophisticated manner, and other suggestions can be made to improve the intermediate grade child's problem-solving skills:

1. Expose the children to many problems, in a variety of situations, so that they develop flexibility in their problem-solving behaviors.
2. Teach children to make a plan for solving problems, such as the experimental method, so that they have a general strategy that can be applied and modified for a variety of situations.
3. Have the children make notes of pertinent information and try to identify inconsistencies. Also, have the children compare the information that they collect with their own ideas about the material and the problem.
4. Have the children generalize across problems, analyzing the features of the problem, looking for analogies, and trying to determine the structure of the problem rather than just looking for details.
5. Provide time for discussion, practice, and reflection on problems and problem-solving strategies.
6. Use dramatization, concrete materials, models, pictures, diagrams, charts, tables, and graphs as aids to problem solving.
7. Whenever possible, have the children try out the solutions they derive for their problems.

8. Use real-world problems, which children can research to gain content knowledge and which will gradually bring them to a greater understanding of the uses of science in daily living.
9. Use small groups in attacking problems rather than individuals, so that brainstorming techniques can be used.

Summary

The science program of the elementary school should develop in children both the content and the process aspects of science. To assist the teacher in finding a more appropriate sequencing of the information from these two areas, psychological theories can be used.

The work of Piaget gives insight into children's capabilities in the use of the processes of science. His detailed descriptions of the child's development of an ability to classify and to work with true experiments as well as to determine causal relationships should help teachers to understand the capabilities of children at various age levels. In addition, the developmental stages for which Piaget is so well known give additional information about the cognitive capabilities of children.

From the theory of information processing, the teacher can gain an understanding of the working of memory, the development of concepts, and the development of problem-solving abilities.

Selected References

Bornstein, M. H., and W. Kessen, eds. *Psychological Development from Infancy.* Hillsdale, New Jersey: Erlbaum, 1979.

Bruni, J. V. Problem solving for the primary grades. *Arithmetic Teacher, 29,* 6, 1982.

Burns, M. How to teach problem solving. *Arithmetic Teacher, 29,* 6, 1982.

Clarke, S. A., and J. Koch. *Children: Development through Adolescence.* New York: Wiley, 1983.

Epstein, H. T. Growth spurts during brain development: Implications for educational policy and practices. In *Education and the Brain.* Chicago: University of Chicago Press, 1979. Eds: Jeanne Chall and Allan W. Mirsky.

Geschwind, N. Specialization of the human brain. *Scientific American,* September 1979.

Hunt, M. *The Universe Within.* New York: Simon and Schuster, 1982.

Inhelder, B., and J. Piaget. *The Early Growth of Logic in the Child.* New York: Harper and Row, 1964.

Johnson, V. R. Myelin and maturation: A fresh look at Piaget. *Science Teacher, 49,* 3, 1982.

Kagan, J. Do infants think? *Scientific American,* March 1972.

———. Jean Piaget's contributions to education. *Kappan, 62,* 4, 1980.

Lawson, A. E. Formal reasoning, achievement, and intelligence: An issue of importance. *Science Education, 66,* 1, 1982.

Lee, K. S. Guiding young children to successful problem solving. *Arithmetic Teacher, 29,* 5, 1982.

Levy, J. Research synthesis on right and left hemispheres: We think with both sides of the brain. *Educational Leadership, 39,* 1, 1983.

Piaget, J. *The Psychology of Intelligence.* Totowa, New Jersey: Littlefield, 1963.

———. *The Child's Conception of Physical Causality.* Totowa, New Jersey: Littlefield, 1972.

———. *Judgment and Reasoning in the Child.* Totowa, New Jersey: Littlefield, 1972.

———. *The Origins of Intelligence in Children.* New York: International Universities Press, Inc., 1974.

———. *The Child's Conception of the World.* Totowa, New Jersey: Littlefield: 1975.

———, and B. Inhelder, *The Child's Conception of Space.* London: Routledge and Kegan Paul, 1956.

Schultz, J. E. *Mathematics for Elementary School Teachers.* Columbus, Ohio: Merrill, 1982.

Shayer, M., and P. Adey. *Towards a Science of Science Teaching.* Exeter, New Hampshire: Heineman, 1981.

Suydam, M. Update on research on problem solving: Implications for classroom teaching. *Arithmetic Teacher, 29,* 6, 1982.

White, E. P. Why self-directed learning? *Science and Children, 19,* 5, 1982.

Wittrock, M. C. *The Brain and Psychology.* New York: Academic, 1980.

Wolfinger, D. M. The effect of science teaching on the young child's concept of Piagetian physical causality: Animism and dynamism. *Journal of Research in Science Teaching, 19,* 7, 1982.

Part II

The Processes of Science

There is no royal road to scientific discovery. The rules for evidence have to be strict, and to imagine that you can come up with important truths in the haphazard and foolish ways that fringe people invariably use is likely to vitiate science and all possibility of human advance.

— Isaac Asimov in F. Kendig, 1983

3 The Basic Processes of Science

Chapter Objectives

Upon completion of this chapter you should be able to

1. use the basic processes of science: observation, classification, communication, operational questions, space relations, and number relations;
2. define each of the basic processes of science: observation, classification, communication, operational questions, space relations, number relations;
3. identify the processes used in a science activity.

By this point, you should have some idea of how children can be expected to work with science experiences, of what they can be expected to do, and of one sequence which can be used to introduce science into the elementary school curriculum. You should have some feel for the processes which are appropriate at the various grade or age levels.

You, the reader, are an adult, to whom these prerequisite concepts can be efficiently communicated in written form along with activities to further illustrate the written material. Children, however, do not effectively learn science or any other subject solely by reading or listening. Rather, children learn best through first-hand experiences with concrete materials — by engaging in the processes of science as a means of learning the content of science. To most effectively help children use the processes of science, you, as a teacher, must be able to use these same processes.

You need to gain an understanding of the processes of observation and classification, of operational questions and space relations. You need to be able to apply number relations and to communicate your findings in an appropriate way. Just as children learn by doing, you should learn by doing. Consequently, this chapter presents both written information and hands-on activities. You will also be carrying out a number of activities to help you gain confidence in your ability to use the basic processes of science, the same processes which you will be using with children.

The six sections in this chapter begin with the definition of a process. The various levels within each process are then examined. Finally, there are three or more activities for you to carry out in order to become more proficient in using the process.

Some of the activities you will be doing to increase your own skill in the processes of science can also be used with few changes in the elementary classroom. Other activities will be most appropriate for adults and useful for children only if extensively modified. It will be helpful to you to try the activities indicated by *** with a small group of children. This not only will give you an occasion for working with children, but also will give you an opportunity to see the difference between adult and child capabilities. Also, your own understanding of how children react to varying situations will increase when you actually work with children.

Observation

Definition

The ability to observe accurately without at first making judgments from those observations is the most basic of all of the science processes. Many of the things we call observations are actually interpretations of what is seen, smelled, tasted, touched, or heard. Consequently, because most individuals almost automatically begin interpreting, making true observations can be difficult at first.

An observation, then, is a piece of information learned directly through the senses. An observation is a fact with which it is nearly impossible to argue, and no interpretation of such a piece of information is required.

Observations can be made through the use of each of the five senses: sight, touch, hearing, taste, smell. Using the sense of sight, one can observe color, luster, relative size, surface markings, and object location. Through the sense of touch, one can observe such things as the texture and the relative temperature of an object. Through the sense of hearing one can observe similarities of sounds, considering pitch and loudness as relative ideas. Through the sense of taste, one can observe such things as the sweetness, sourness, saltiness, or bitterness of an object. Finally, through the sense of smell, one can observe the similarity of one smell to another as well as the relative strength of an odor. When we look at the idea of relative size or temperature or at similarities between or among sounds and smells, we note that an observation is frequently preceded by the phrase, "It smells (tastes, etc.) like . . .". The term "like" immediately indicates that the observation is a comparison.

An Example of Observation

Look at the patterns found in Fig. 3–1. It could be an example of rather poor modern art; it could be a page from a coloring book for children which attempts to teach shapes as well as to provide entertainment. With a good imagination, one could make this figure represent a dozen or more possibilities. But trying to decide what the page could represent is *not* observing. Look at the observations listed below and notice that there are no interpretations involved.

1. There are nine shapes.
2. The shapes have different markings.
3. Three of the shapes are circular.
4. The background is white.
5. There is one striped shape.
6. Each shaded shape has two long parallel sides and two shorter parallel sides.
7. The dotted shape has three sides.
8. The dashed shape is irregular.
9. One cross-hatched shape has four sides whereas the other cross-hatched shape has three sides.
10. All of the shapes are outlined in black.

There are many more observations which can be made of the shapes that appear on the page. No mention has been made of the smell or the texture of the page, nor has mention been made of the proximity of one shape to another.

You should note particularly that the observations listed here require no interpretation; they are simply statements of fact. It would be impossible to argue that the striped shape is not striped or that there are not two cross-hatched shapes, one with four sides and one with three sides. It is unlikely that new

Figure 3–1

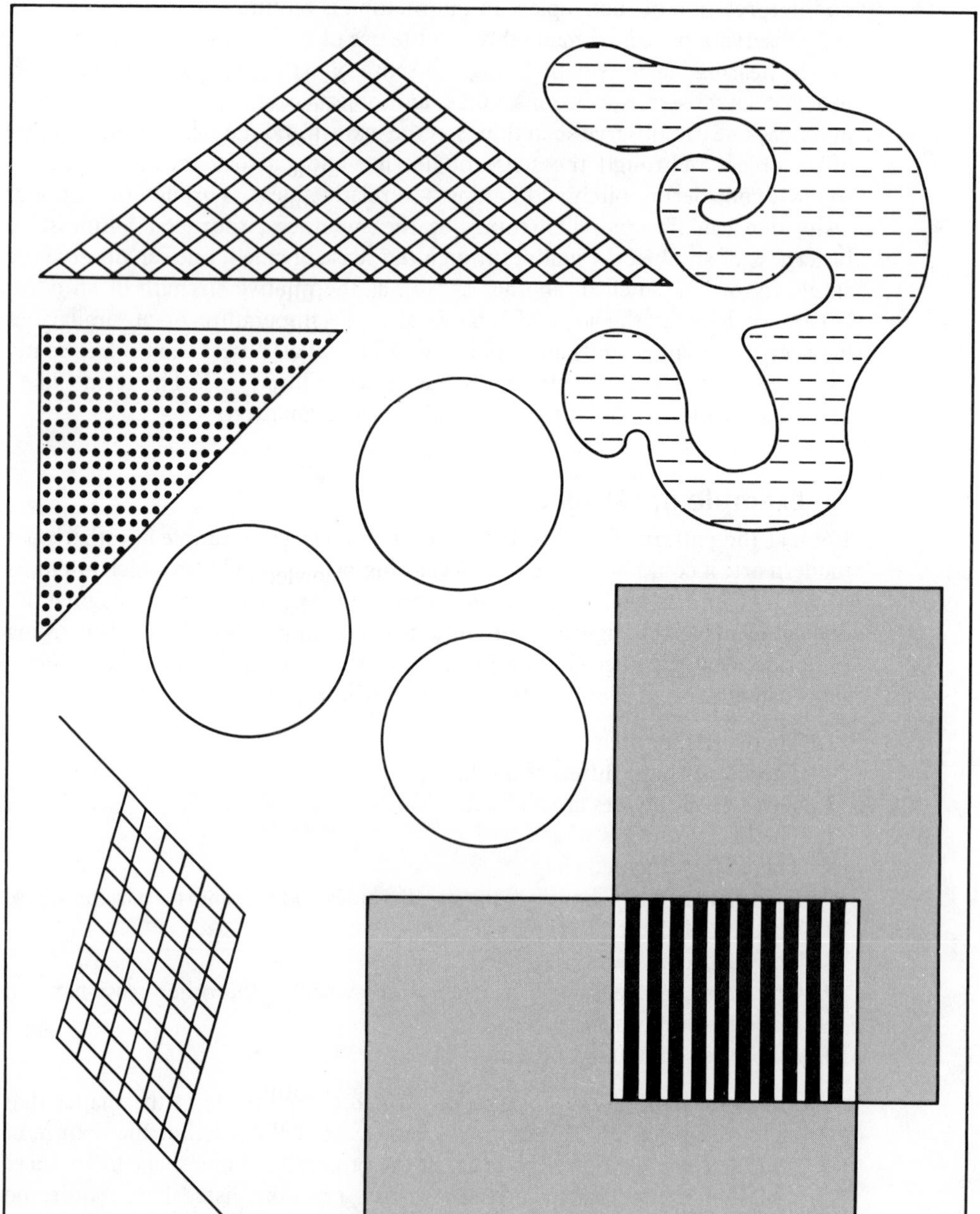

observations will be made that will lead to a change in the observations listed here.

The Use of Observation with Children

As a Process. Children at all grade levels can make observations, but observation is most appropriately emphasized in the preschool, kindergarten, and first grade, since it is the basis for all of the other processes. In grades two through six observations should become a routine part of the total science program. By fourth grade, children should be able to differentiate between observations and inferences.

As a Means for Gaining Content. Once they fully understand and use the process with ease, children should not consider the process of observation in isolation from the content of science. By effectively advocating the process of observation, the teacher is freed from the need to be a constant purveyor of information. Rather than telling the children the characteristics of plants, the teacher can set up an activity in which the children observe and find the characteristics on their own. Rather than hearing a lecture on the kinds of weather brought by various types of clouds, children can observe the daily sky and see which types of weather and clouds are associated. The process of observation should allow the children to develop their own knowledge from situations which are established by the teacher. Once the children have made the observations, the teacher, a textbook, or a film can be used to reinforce what was observed or to determine the accuracy of the observations.

Observation Learning Activities

With this information as a basis, try each of the following activities in observation. You will be using each sense separately, or as separately as possible, then combining them in Learning Activity 3–5. Activity 3–6 can be used as a self-test to determine whether you can differentiate between observations and non-observations.

Learning Activity 3–1

***

Observation

Choose any three of the following objects. Write at least ten observations of each of the objects. *Use only the sense of sight in making your observations.*

1. A chair
2. A book — opened or closed
3. A plant
4. Another person

5. Your own hand
6. A sweater
7. A television set — on or off
8. A musical instrument
9. An automobile
10. An old shoe
11. Any photograph
12. A hamburger
13. A burning candle
14. A bowl of soup
15. Any soft drink can

Learning Activity 3–2
***

Observation

For this activity you will need a crayon, twenty to thirty pieces of paper about 8½ x 5½ inches, and any readily available objects.

Place one sheet of paper over any fairly firm object. Using the side of the crayon, rub the color over the paper hard enough that the texture of the object beneath the paper forms a pattern on the paper.

Repeat the procedure with nine to nineteen other objects — a total of ten to twenty rubbings. Describe the texture of each of the objects, using only observations made from the rubbings and *using only the sense of touch.* You should have a minimum of two observations per rubbing.

Learning Activity 3–3
***

Observation

Different areas of the same building or of the same location may have different sounds. Choose one of the following locations. Then, within that location choose three places. For example, if you choose an apartment building as your location you might choose the basement, just inside the front door, and inside an apartment.

Then, station yourself in each place for ten minutes. *Using only your sense of hearing,* list any sounds that you hear. Remember that you are observing. You cannot list "a bird singing" as an observation, because you would be inferring from the sounds that you hear that it is a bird and not a flute, a truck, or an airplane.

1. An apartment building
2. An elementary school
3. A street in the business section of town
4. A park
5. A supermarket
6. A college dormitory or residence hall
7. A college classroom building
8. A day-care center
9. A playground
10. A parking lot
11. A sports stadium
12. An airport or a bus terminal

Learning Activity 3–4

***

Observation

The one sense that is rarely used during the day is the sense of smell. During one day make a list of the odors that you encounter.

As with the activity dealing with hearing, remember that you cannot list that you smell cabbage or french fries; these would be inferences. Instead, you need to describe the odors that you smell. It is, however, appropriate to say that something "smells like". Although this method is appropriate, it is better to describe the smell in some other way.

Learning Activity 3–5

Observation

Describe in as much detail as possible, *using all of the appropriate senses,* two of the following objects or phenomena. You should describe it so well that, without knowing what the object or phenomenon was, another person could immediately name it.

1. A sunset
2. A sunrise
3. An animal
4. A flowering plant

5. A cake
6. A storm
7. The ocean
8. A pizza place
9. A forest
10. A cup of coffee or tea

Learning Activity 3–6

Observation

From the following list of statements, choose those that are true observations. For those which are not observations, rewrite the statement in the form of an observation.

1. The object is taller than a pencil.
2. The object is a tulip plant.
3. The object is green and white.
4. The object smells like a lemon.
5. The object would float if it were placed in water.
6. The object has five straight sides.
7. The object will dissolve in water.
8. The object melted when it was heated.
9. The object smells like it is beginning to rot.
10. The object has six parts.
11. Each of the six parts of the object has a different function.
12. The pianist is playing a Bach fugue.
13. The turtle ate the mosquito.
14. The cloth is wool.
15. The cup broke because it was dropped on the floor.
16. The tree feels rough when touched.
17. There are six men and fifteen women in the room.
18. The piccolo sounds higher in pitch than the tuba.
19. Potato chips taste salty.
20. A rose smells sweet.

Answers will be found at the end of this chapter.

Classification

Definition

Classification is the ability to place objects into groups on the basis of the characteristics that those objects either do or do not possess. Classification proceeds from placement of objects into two groups on the basis of gross characteristics to the use of a hierarchical system such as that found in the biological classification system.

Concepts Taught Through Simple Classification

We often think of concepts as a means of classifying the phenomena which surround the individual. Below are some of the basic concepts approached through the preschool and primary grade science program that can be taught through classification activities.

1. More–less
2. Over–under
3. On top of–beneath
4. Small–large
5. Small–smaller–smallest
6. Soft–hard
7. Long–short
8. Up–down
9. Solid–liquid–gas
10. Hot–cold–warm
11. Basic primary colors and basic secondary colors
12. Basic plane and solid shapes
13. Vertebrate–invertebrate
14. Element–compound
15. Rock–mineral
16. Chemical change–physical change
17. Matter–energy
18. Mixture–solution
19. Mammal, bird, reptile, amphibian, fish

Using Hierarchical Classification to Teach Content

The hierarchical classification system has such broad application to the teaching of science that children must encounter it at some time. The biological classification system can be used to organize information dealing with plants and animals. Children can, therefore, learn the characteristics of animals in general and the specific characteristics of vertebrate and invertebrate animals. The vertebrate animals can then be divided into the five major classes: fish, amphibians, reptiles, birds, and mammals.

A similar system for the study of rocks and minerals, systems of the human body, astronomical bodies, and forms of matter could be used to enable the child to see the relationships which exist among the various aspects of a single area of study. The use of the hierarchical form of classification as a teaching device thus becomes an aid to conceptual development and to an understanding of the interrelationships that exist within the various parts of science.

Classification Learning Activities

The classification learning activities in this chapter will allow you to

1. develop your own skill at classification,
2. see how children classify,
3. develop a teaching method which uses classification to develop content knowledge.

Learning Activity 3–7

Classification

List the first 30 objects which you see in an elementary school classroom. As you consider the objects on your list, decide on five or more traits which could be used to classify those objects. Classify your objects on the basis of *one* of the traits which you listed. What problems do you encounter?

Then, choose two characteristics different from the first characteristic which you used in classification. Reclassify the objects on the basis of these two characteristics. What additional problems do you encounter when you work with two characteristics rather than with one?

Learning Activity 3–8

***

Classification

Collect eight to ten small, portable, and related objects such as kitchen utensils, school objects, foods, or anything else that is highly familiar to children.

Classify the objects yourself into a hierarchical system. Then, have a child of five, a child of eight, and a child of eleven classify the objects. Question the child to determine the characteristics that the child is using to classify the objects. Also see if the children can form a hierarchical system.

Keep a record of what each child does with the objects and of their answers to the questions that you ask. Compare the classification systems developed by the three children to each other and then to your own system. How are the systems similar to each other? How do the systems differ from each other?

Learning Activity 3–9

Classification

Each of the following concepts can be taught through classification activities. Choose any one of the concepts and develop a means of teaching which involves the use of classification. Prepare all of the materials that you would need in order to teach the concept and try your method with a small group of children.

1. More–less
2. Small–large
3. Matter–energy
4. Element–compound
5. Small–smaller–smallest
6. Vertebrate–invertebrate
7. Soft–hard
8. Smooth–rough
9. Up–down
10. Solid–liquid–gas
11. Plant–animal
12. Living–nonliving
13. Basic primary colors
14. Basic plane figures: square, circle, triangle, rectangle

How successful do you think you were with your teaching? What changes would you make in your method now that you have worked with children?

Learning Activity 3–10

Classification

Classification is used daily in the lives of both children and adults. In order for children to learn classification, they should be able to see it in use in ways that are meaningful to them.

List five ways in which classification could be shown in the daily lives of children at each of the following school levels: preschool-kindergarten, primary grades, intermediate grades. Then list five ways in which classification is used in the science program in the intermediate grade (fourth, fifth, sixth) textbooks of any science program.

Communication

Definition

Communication is any means for passing information from one individual or group of individuals to another. All too frequently, communication is considered to be through words, only through words, and preferably only through words on the printed page of a book. For young children, words and symbols for words are the least appropriate means of communication. This does not mean that oral and written communication should or could be avoided, but it does mean that other types of communication should also be available to the child and teacher.

Types of Communication Used with Children

Pictures. Pictures are a good means of communication for children. Drawings in paint, pencil, crayon, or any other medium can help the child to get across those ideas that he or she wishes to communicate. For very young children, pictures may not convey much because their drawing skills do not allow for realism. However, even the most abstract pictures can serve as a basis for the child to talk about a picture, so that the teacher can write an appropriate caption. Older children can both draw their own pictures and write their own stories to go with those pictures.

Work Sheets. Work sheets that allow the child to circle a picture or to form a cut-and-paste picture from parts that are preformed, or magazines that the child can cut pictures from to illustrate ideas are ways a young child can communicate and demonstrate understanding in science.

Models. Closely tied to using pictures for communication is using models. Models can be made from clay, papier-mâché, paper, boxes, straws, toothpicks, or any other readily available materials. Models allow children not only to communicate ideas but also to explore spatial relationships in three dimensions. Such models also give the child something to talk about if oral communication is being used. For young children, models should be as similar to the modeled object as possible, so that the child is not forced, for example, to pretend that a balloon is a lung and a glass jar is the chest cavity.

Movement. Movement is also an appropriate communication means for children. Forming shapes with their bodies, showing how animals behave by role playing, pretending to be growing plants, or demonstrating different types of motions, all allow children to investigate the common phenomena of their world with their entire bodies, thus involving them in the large muscle activities so appropriate to their physical development. Somewhat less active, yet still involving movement, are fingerplays, which combine science with language and music.

Oral and Written Communication. Children's oral and written skills should also be used and developed. One-to-one conversations with the teacher or with another student allow the child to develop confidence in speaking. Making a tape recording can also help develop confidence, especially when that tape becomes a permanent part of the classroom record of science activity. Experience charts dictated to the teacher can be a way of helping the young child to relate letter and numeral symbols to words. Show-and-tell, the kindergarten tradition, can be extended to allow children to demonstrate activities performed in science.

Songs can help children to relate science to other parts of the curriculum. This activity is especially good if children have the opportunity to write their own words and music. Making instruments as a part of science, decorating them as a part of art, and finally performing the songs written in language arts and music integrate all areas of the curriculum.

Language skills, whether oral or written, should develop naturally from the activities of the science program. In this way, the child is able to see the purpose for learning to read, for learning to write, for learning to interpret the number symbols. A connection can be made between the symbols for words and the ideas conveyed by those symbols.

Usually, the best way to include oral and written communication is to make that communication an integral part of the activity, so that language use follows logically from the first-hand, concrete experiences of the child. Such a sequence — concrete first, language second — allows the child to have something real about which to talk or write rather than trying to rephrase the ideas contained in a text or story. Questions from the teacher that lead the child to talk about the salient points of an activity can be very helpful to the child. Such questions should start with something obvious; in that way all children can answer and all children can experience success. Other questions can then lead the children to make observations they may have missed, to construct inferences, or to draw conclusions about the activity.

Oral forms of communication, as well as written and pictorial forms, can be used throughout the elementary and preschool program in science. Young children, preschool through grade two, should not be expected to make written or even systematic reports of their activities. Even for those children who can write, problems are encountered that cause written work to be troublesome.

Spelling is one of the worst problems, because children frequently want to write words they are unable to spell. Once, I made the mistake of telling second graders to spell the words as they thought they should be spelled. This fiasco resulted in a set of papers incomprehensible to both myself and the writers. Having the teacher rush around the room trying to spell words that the children need is equally unsatisfactory as is limiting them to particular words.

A second problem is the length of time that it takes for children to write anything. With time at a premium, it is best to develop an experience chart as a written record or to tape record children's ideas, if written records are not vital.

As children move into the third and fourth grade, writing is easier. These children can spell somewhat better or can use a dictionary to find words they cannot spell. Written records become possible. These records may not be systematic, so charts of some form may be needed to give structure to the written records. The collection of numerical data is possible at this time but may not be as meaningful to children as other forms of data.

By fifth or sixth grade, children are more able to use numerical forms in their communications, and written reports are much easier. However, alternatives should always be available for those children who find written language difficult.

Finally, written communication includes materials such as textbooks, tradebooks, magazines, and newspapers. Such written materials can effectively enhance the children's experiences with the science program. A good picture book can be used with young children to introduce, reinforce, or sum up an idea. It is best to delay reading a standard textbook until after the children have had some concrete experience with the subject matter. At that point, reading is likely to be more meaningful to children.

Whenever possible, the classroom should have a variety of reading materials on a variety of reading levels sufficient to accommodate as many children as possible. Particularly pertinent material, which all children might not be able to read, can be taped by the teacher or another student so that nonreaders can also obtain the important information.

Communication Learning Activities

The communication learning activities involve you with children on varying grade levels and permit you to develop materials that can be used to help children develop the ability to communicate.

Learning Activity 3–11 Communication

Level One — Preschool or Kindergarten

Collect the following materials: red, yellow, and blue finger paint, white paper, water, sponge, plastic or newspaper to cover a table. Have enough materials so that groups of three or four children can work with the finger paints.

Have the children work freely with the finger paints to create pictures and to find out what happens when the colors are mixed. After the children have had ample time to work with the finger paints and to make a number of pictures, make an experience chart with them. Use large paper with lines about 2.5 centimeters (1 inch) apart placed where all of the children can see the words as they are written. Use the children's exact words on the chart and attempt to have all of the children contribute to the chart.

If the children can read, have them read the chart to you and to the others in the group when it is finished. If the children cannot read, read the chart to them.

What problems did you encounter in developing the chart with the children? What could you do to solve these problems?

Learning Activity 3–12 Communication

Level Two — Kindergarten Through Second Grade

Collect the following materials: ten to fifteen pictures of mammals, a living hamster, guinea pig, or mouse, ten to fifteen pictures of nonmammals.

With a group of five children, use the pictures and the animal to develop the concept of a mammal with the children. Then, have the children draw a picture of a mammal and a picture of an animal that is not a mammal. Collect the children's pictures. You may need to assure the children that you will return their pictures at another time. Review the pictures carefully.

What are some of the problems you encountered with using pictures as a means of communicating? What could you do to overcome these problems?

Learning Activity 3–13 Communication

Level Three — Fourth Through Sixth Grade

Collect the following materials: paper, chalk, yardsticks or meter sticks. Have enough materials for five children. Find a sunny location in a playground or other area where the children can work outdoors in safety. Four or five times during a day, have the children go outdoors to the same location and measure the length of their shadows. This can be done most easily by having one child stand still while a second draws a chalk line the length of the first child's shadow. Each child should measure the length of all the shadows cast: his or her own as well as those cast by the other children. Each child should keep a record of the measurements of each of the shadows. Do not provide the children with a chart to use.

After the last measurements have been made, discuss with the children what they learned about shadows. Collect the papers on which the measurements were recorded.

How well do you think the children understood the idea that shadows change in size during the day? What did the children do or say to indicate understanding or lack of understanding of the concept? Look at the data sheets you collected. How systematic was the collection of the data? What are some of the problems that you see? How could you prevent some of the problems shown by the children?

Learning Activity 3–14 Communication

All Grade Levels

Involve a group of five children from any grade level in an activity that you have developed to alert them to one of the following environmental problems: water pollution, air pollution, the growing shortage of fossil fuels, decreasing natural resources, endangered species.

Following the activity, have the children communicate to you what they learned in a way that is appropriate both to the activity and to the grade level.

1. What level or age children did you choose?
2. What concept did you teach?
3. What was your activity?
4. What method of communication did you try? What reasons did you have for choosing that method?
5. Did the children learn what you expected them to learn?
6. What did they do to indicate that they had learned? What did they learn that you had not expected them to learn?
7. What errors in their learning did you find? How might you account for those errors?
8. What problems did you encounter with the kind of communication you chose to use? What could be done to overcome these problems?

Operational Questions

Questions Asked by Children

Questions frequently seem to make up the bulk of child-to-adult conversation. There is almost no difficulty getting children to ask questions. The problem comes, of course, in answering those questions.

The teacher who tries to answer all of the questions children ask does a disservice both to herself or himself and to the child. Attempting to answer every question asked by a group of children may not lead the teacher to insanity, but it will often lead to feelings of inferiority or, at least, of inadequacy in the area of science. Faced with a question like: "Why aren't there any dinosaurs today?" the teacher has a number of options:

1. Use words the child does not understand and give an answer: "Archaeosaurs became extinct because of macroclimatic variations in the biosphere."
2. Give a simple answer and hope for no further questions: "They died."
3. Tell the truth: "I really don't know." The trick in this response is not to follow it up with a qualifier:
   "I'll try to find out for you."
   "Why don't you find out and let me know."
   "You'll learn about that in seventh grade."
   "We're studying plants *not* dinosaurs."
4. Ignore the question entirely.
5. Refer the child to the librarian to find a book.

In each case, the child has little or no involvement in answering the question. In some cases, there is no answer given, and the child's curiosity is left unsatisfied. The question, "Why aren't there any dinosaurs today?" is a nonproductive question. It is also quite typical of the kinds of questions asked by children encountering new science phenomena. When children ask questions, they frequently begin with "why" or "what."

"Why does a seed sprout?"
"Why is the moon round?"
"What makes a battery work?"
"What makes light turn into a rainbow when it goes through a prism?"
"Why is Tommy taller than Jane?"

Such questions call for highly theoretical or very complex answers. As with the question about dinosaurs, the answers can be found only by reading or by asking an authority. In any case, few children are able to benefit from the answers that they receive, because they simply do not have the cognitive structures or the experiential backgrounds to understand.

A Definition of Operational Questions

Children can be helped to ask productive questions that involve them directly in finding answers and develop the experiential background necessary for later understanding of complex theories. These questions are called operational questions — a term originally coined by Dorothy Alfke of The Pennsylvania State University — and are productive questions.

An operational question is one that either directly or by implication states what must be done with science materials to obtain an answer to the question. An operational question cannot begin with "why," since "why" automatically implies a theoretical answer. Some examples of operational questions are:

1. What would happen to the number of times the pendulum swings if the length of the string were changed?
2. How does the kind of liquid you use change the shape of the drops you get?
3. How does the surface affect the height to which a ball will bounce?
4. What happens to light when it goes through liquids other than water?
5. How does the weight of a paper airplane affect the distance it flies?
6. In what kind of soil will radish seeds grow best?

Developing Children's Ability to Use Operational Questions

Children do not automatically use operational questions, but they can learn to ask them with some ease. Activities can be planned to elicit questions from students. Some unusual or interesting phenomenon can be shown and the children given the opportunity to ask any questions that they have. These questions can be recorded on the chalkboard then reworded as operational questions that the children can investigate through the use of concrete objects.

Once children understand the basic idea of an operational question, whenever they ask questions they can be helped to rephrase those questions as operational questions that can be investigated.

Of course, other kinds of questions can be asked and investigated. Some questions and topics do not lend themselves to rewording as operational questions. It would be very difficult to ask an operational question about dinosaurs, moon trips, nuclear energy, or endangered species. Consequently, operational questions are only one of the many ways to gain information that children should be encouraged to use.

Operational Question Learning Activities

These activities are designed to enable you to describe the kinds of questions children ask, to discriminate between operational questions and nonoperational questions, and to develop and investigate your own operational questions.

Learning Activity 3–14 Operational Questions

Preschool, Kindergarten, First Grade

Collect the following materials so that each child in a group of five or six children has a set with which to work: liquid detergent or commercial "bubble stuff," straws, paper tubes, bubble pipes, and other objects that can be used to blow bubbles, paper towels, newspaper or plastic, paper cups, water.

Pour about an inch of detergent or bubble liquid into paper cups so that each child has a cup. Use the straws or bubble pipes to blow some bubbles while the children watch. Talk about bubbles for a few minutes, then have the children blow bubbles. Use the newspaper or plastic to cover the area and contain the resulting mess.

While the children blow bubbles, as they talk to one another, and following the activity, keep a record of the questions which the children ask. Write the questions just as the children phrase them. You might also ask, after the activity, what questions about bubbles the children have.

Review the list of children's questions. Classify the questions as operational or nonoperational and rewrite as operational questions any of the questions that are nonoperational.

Learning Activity 3–15 Operational Questions

First, Second, Third Grade

Collect the following materials: clear plastic cups, warm water, ice, red, blue, and yellow food coloring, water at room temperature. Have an assortment of these materials with more than enough for a group of five children.

Collect the following materials for *your* use: two quart glass jars, hot water (near boiling), ice water, blue food coloring. Fill one jar about half full of hot water and the other half full of cold water.

Place both of the jars on the table in full view of the children. Have the children touch the outside of the jar with the *cold* water, to establish with the children the fact that the water is cold. Do not allow the children to handle the jar with the hot water, but establish with them the idea that it is hot. While the children watch place a few drops of food coloring in each of the jars. Discuss with the children the differences in the rate at which the color spreads through the two jars of water.

Ask if they have any questions about what happened. Collect the questions. With the children, rewrite some of the questions into operational questions. Allow the children to use the materials to find the answers to their own questions.

What problems did you encounter in working with the children using this method? How might you overcome these problems?

Learning Activity 3–16 Operational Questions

Fourth, Fifth, Sixth Grades

Collect the following materials: two quart jars with lids, rubbing alcohol (three pints), ice cubes, marker. Prior to working with the children, fill one jar about two-thirds full of alcohol and label it *A*. Fill the other jar about two-thirds full of water and label it *B*. Put the lids tightly on the jars. Have the ice ready.

Place the jars on a table in front of a group of five or six students. Have the children observe the two jars and write down their observations. Discuss the observations. Then, as the children watch, place two or three ice cubes in each of the two jars, quickly replacing the lids so that the odor of alcohol does not reach the students.*

Have the students make observations again. Then, have them ask questions about what happened. As each question is asked, have the students reword them until you, or one of them, can do something with the jars, the ice, or other materials to find the answer. Try to draw some conclusion about the activity.

What questions were asked by the children? What questions were asked that were operational? Did the operational questions help the children to draw some conclusion as to the cause of floating in one case and sinking in the second?

* The ice will float in the water and sink in the alcohol, because the ice is less dense than the water and more dense than the alcohol.

Learning Activity 3–17

Operational Questions

Read each of the following questions. Decide which are operational questions and which are nonoperational questions. Then, rewrite each of the nonoperational questions as an operational question. Remember, some questions cannot be asked operationally.

1. What kinds of objects will float in water?
2. Why does light pass through some objects and not through others?
3. What causes a light bulb to light?
4. Does food coloring spread through warm and cold cooking oil in the same way that it spreads through warm and cold water?
5. How do birds fly?
6. When does salt dissolve best in water?
7. Why is grass green?
8. What is a molecule?
9. What kind of paper makes the best paper airplane?
10. On what kind of surface will a ball bounce the highest?
11. When is the temperature the highest during a school day?
12. Why does a lever make it easier to pick up objects?

Answers to this activity are found at the end of this chapter.

Space Relations

Definition

Space relations, as a process, uses three major geometric concepts: solid geometric forms, plane geometric forms, and measurement as a part of data collection.

Solid Geometric Forms. The first of the three geometric concepts is that of common solid geometric forms. The preschool, kindergarten, and first grade child should already have experiences with those solid shapes that are common to their environment: sphere, cube, rectangular solid, pyramid, prism, cylinder, and cone. Such shapes are commonly seen in the child's environment as balls, boxes, blocks, tents, ice cream cones, and cans.

Plane Geometric Forms. As children gain familiarity with the solid shapes, and beginning about the first grade, the second concept, that of plane geometric shapes, can be introduced. The plane shapes may first be considered in relation to the already known solid shapes: cylinders show circles as their bases, the sides of rectangular solids are rectangles, a pyramid has triangular sides. Other common shapes like the pentagon, hexagon, and octagon as well as the parallelogram and rhombus can be introduced in terms of objects in the environment. Snow flakes are hexagons. A stop sign is an octagon while some of the tables found in classrooms are trapezoids. By the end of the third grade, the child should be familiar enough with both plane and solid shapes so that he or she can use them in making observations.

Teaching Young Children Geometric Forms. The following procedure for teaching both plane and solid geometric forms tends to work very well. It is particularly designed for introducing young children to the various shapes.

Step 1. Introduce only one shape at a time using familiar concrete objects.

Step 2. Allow the children to work with the shape until they have developed a concept of the shape and can recognize it in the environment. The objects should be freely handled by the children.

Step 3. Through questions, concrete objects, and semiconcrete examples, help the children to discover the characteristics of the shape. Have the children use observation rather than telling the children the characteristics.

Step 4. After a concept of the shape has been developed, have the class compare it with other shapes in the environment, so that the children begin to know what the shape is as well as what it is not.

Step 5. Each time a new shape is introduced, preface the lesson with a review of each of the previously learned shapes.

Measurement. The third concept used in the study of the process of space relations is measurement. Length, area, weight, and volume are all a part of space relations. These concepts, however, require more complex cognitive understandings than does the recognition of plane or solid shapes. For a true understanding of these measurement concepts, the child needs to have attained conservation. According to Piaget, conservation of each of these measurement concepts is attained at approximately the following ages:

conservation of length — about eight years,
conservation of area — conceptually after eight years and computationally at about eleven years,
conservation of weight — about ten years,
conservation of volume — conceptually after eleven years and computationally after fifteen years.

Consequently, in working with space relations, those relations that involve measurement should be introduced at about the third grade level. Prior to the third grade level, informal means of measurement can be used to develop needed background information.

Informal Measurement. Children can measure by placing shoes end to end and counting how many shoes long a room is or by pacing off the length of the room and counting the number of steps taken, or measurements can be made using hands, body lengths, paper clips, strings, or any other uniform objects that the children can lay end to end and count. At first, it is a good idea to have enough objects so that the entire length or width under consideration can be covered; this will eliminate the problem of moving the object and remembering not only the original position but the number of times the object was used. After using such informal means of measurement, children should be conceptually ready to develop the more formal concepts of measurement consistently used in the sciences.

Formal Measurement. Formal measurement uses a particular standard as well as specific devices for measuring. Because of its simplicity and common usage in science, the metric system is probably the best formal measurement system to use in the elementary science program.

An appropriate sequence in teaching the metric system is to begin with the meter, using the meter stick to teach not only how to measure length but also the standard prefixes of the system. Once the children are able to use the meter and to comprehend the use of the prefixes, move to the use of the liter as a measure of liquid volume. Finally, work with the gram and kilogram as measurements of mass. Practice with measuring devices and with direct measurement of length, mass, and volume should occur before the children are expected to use the metric system in their science classes.

If both the metric system and the English system are known to the children or are being taught simultaneously, use one system consistently in the science program rather than both. Consistency in the choice and use of a method of formal measurement may help to prevent confusion of units.

Using Space Relations

Children should be encouraged to describe objects in terms of the various solid and plane shapes, as soon as they are familiar enough with those shapes for them to be meaningful. Measurements, both formal and informal, should also be taken as soon as children are able to understand them.

Space Relations Learning Activities

The activities using the process of space relations will allow you to develop a set of materials that can be used in the classroom to help children learn the various geometric shapes. In addition you will be involved in informal measurement and in formal measurement using the metric system.

Learning Activity 3–18

Space Relations

Observe the environment in a preschool, kindergarten, or primary grade classroom. What common objects are found in the classroom that could be used to illustrate each of the following plane and solid shapes?

1. circle
2. square
3. rectangle
4. triangle
5. ellipse
6. parallelogram
7. trapezoid
8. octagon
9. pentagon
10. cube
11. solid rectangle
12. sphere
13. ovoid
14. prism
15. pyramid
16. cylinder
17. cone
18. hexagon

What common objects outside of the classroom could be used to illustrate those shapes not found among the classroom objects?

Learning Activity 3–19

Space Relations

Children learn through more than one sense at a time just as adults learn through more than one sense at a time. For many children, particularly those who are visually handicapped, the sense of touch is of great importance in learning.

Construct a set of plane shapes such as those suggested below that which will allow the child to use more than one sense in learning the shapes. Be certain to include the sense of touch as one of those used.

1. circle
2. square
3. rectangle
4. triangle
5. ellipse
6. parallelogram
7. trapezoid
8. octagon
9. hexagon
10. pentagon

Learning Activity 3–20

Space Relations

Try the following activity with a group of five or six children in kindergarten, first, or second grade. Have the children name as many ways as they can to measure the following objects without using a ruler.

1. length of their classroom
2. height of the classroom
3. width of a desk
4. their own heights
5. the width of a book
6. the length of their own feet

After making a list of all of the possible ways, have the children measure each object using one of the methods. Observe the children as they measure. What problems do they encounter? How could you help the children overcome these problems?

Learning Activity 3–21

Space Relations

For this activity you will need a meter stick, a 3 in. × 5 in. card, a paper clip, a penny, a sheet of notebook paper, a new pencil, a chalkboard eraser, a new piece of chalk, and the room you are in.

In the room, locate three or more objects that are approximately the length of a meter, three that are approximately the length of a decimeter, and three that are approximately the length of a centimeter. Knowing some objects that are approximately these lengths will give you something to use with children so that they can relate common lengths to metric measurements.

Then, measure each of the following objects using the metric system of linear measurements. Be certain to use the most appropriate measurement unit. In other words, you would not want to use the meter as the unit of measurement of the letter *t* in the word meter.

1. this page's length
2. the width of the door
3. the height of the doorway

4. the width of a sheet of notebook paper
5. the height of the space between the lines on a sheet of paper
6. the height of a chalkboard eraser
7. the width of a 3 in. × 5 in. card
8. the diameter and circumference of a penny
9. the width of a paper clip
10. the length and diameter of a new piece of chalk
11. the height of the ceiling
12. your own height
13. the length of your foot
14. the width of your little finger
15. the distance around your head at the forehead

Learning Activity 3–22

Space Relations

For this activity you will need a simple balance, a set of metric masses, a paper clip, a penny, a new piece of chalk, a chalkboard eraser, a can of soda, a wooden block, two teaspoonfuls of salt, a candy bar, 100 milliliters of oil, 100 milliliters of water, two plastic cups.

Using the balance, find the mass of each of the following objects.

1. a paperclip
2. a penny
3. a new piece of chalk
4. a chalkboard eraser
5. a can of soda
6. a wooden block
7. two level teaspoonfuls of salt
8. a candy bar
9. 100 milliliters of cooking oil
10. 100 milliliters of water
11. any five objects that are commonly found in the early childhood or elementary grade classroom

---

Number Relations

Definition

Using number relations involves more abstract concepts than do any of the previously considered processes. Number relations is the process of using numbers to describe the outcome or ongoing occurrences of an activity. This includes the use of graphs. Since, according to Piaget, children do not typically conserve number until approximately six years of age, the process of number relations should probably be delayed until the first grade.

Sequencing the Use of Number Relations: Numerical Forms

The child who does not conserve number can use numbers, but generally this use is meaningless and involves rote learning. Some nonconservers will even consider the same two numerals (5 for example) as differing in quantity if one symbol is smaller in size than the other.

Counting. Counting, both ordinal and cardinal, should be the first use of number relations encountered by children. Responses to questions like the following can form the child's first encounter with quantification in science activities:

1. How many seeds did you plant?
2. How many ways did you find to classify the stones?
3. How many children like vanilla ice cream best?

Questions like these ask the child to count concrete objects; that is, to give a cardinal number to a set of objects. For that cardinal number to have meaning, the child needs to have a great deal of experience with sets of concrete objects. Such experience permits the development of the concept of a number before an actual name for the number is used.

The concept of five, for example, can be developed by making sets of five objects, counting sets of five objects, drawing sets of five objects, and finally by adding the symbol 5 to the concept. Remember, symbols are abstractions which should only be applied to developed concepts.

Computations. Once children are capable of using the basic counting skill to describe activities and experiments, other forms of numerical usage should be added. Children can use addition, subtraction, multiplication, and division to quantify science activities as soon as they understand these computational skills through their mathematics program. The use of arithmetic skills in the science program can make arithmetic more meaningful by showing that arithmetic can be used outside of the daily arithmetic class to solve real problems. The use of computations should follow from the activity and be a direct, integral part of the activity rather than an artificial something added to include the process of number relations.

Numerical Relationships. Finding the average height of a group of fifth graders while studying the human body or determining the growth rates of various plants while investigating various fertilizers are science activities that naturally use numbers. Such computations use the numbers derived from these activities, and the end-point of the calculation is a number that can be used to describe the activity results or to compare different aspects of the activity — as when rates of growth for two plants are calculated and compared.

There is, however, still another step in the use of number relations: finding a relationship that exists within collected data for purposes of developing a law or extrapolating from the data.

For example, the data in Table 3–1 were collected during an activity using a first-class lever and various masses. Students placed blocks of differing masses on either side of the fulcrum and moved the blocks until the lever balanced. The distance from the fulcrum to the center of each of the blocks was then measured.

Through questions, the children were guided to see that the heavier mass is always closer to the fulcrum. With this rule developed, students were guided, through attention to trials one, three, and four, to derive the relationship that exists between mass and distance to the fulcrum: if one side is twice as heavy as the other, then the heavier mass is half as far from the fulcrum. Finally, the formula, mass × distance = mass × distance, was developed. With this formula, students can determine that trial six is not accurate and can also calculate placement of other masses on the lever. Rather than simply calculating a number, children have developed a relationship between numbers that they can use in other situations.

The Hand Calculator. As children use their arithmetical abilities to determine relationships within data and to apply the formulas they derive to other situations, the hand calculator becomes a useful learning device. By using the calculator children can concentrate on the data rather than on how to do division. When numbers grow larger than those found in their books, children find that the calculator can provide an extra edge of confidence. In particular, the calculator can help the nonmathematical child to compete on an equal basis in science with the child whose main ability is in mathematics.

Formulas. The final step in the use of numerical forms involves the use of formulas. The discovery of a formula is a highly abstract use of number rela-

Table 3–1 Levers

	LEFT SIDE		RIGHT SIDE	
TRIAL	MASS	DISTANCE	MASS	DISTANCE
1	1 g	50 cm	2 g	25 cm
2	5 g	17 cm	9 g	10 cm
3	20 g	9 cm	60 g	3 cm
4	100 g	10 cm	500 g	2 cm
5	15 g	27 cm	45 g	9 cm
6	27 g	31 cm	54 g	70 cm

tions. This degree of abstraction would not be appropriate before the fifth or sixth grade level, when children begin to make the transition to formal operational thought processes. All children cannot be expected to reach this level of abstraction, so formulas should be used only sparingly.

Sequencing the Use of Number Relations: Charts

A second aspect of the use of number relations involves the use of charts for the collection and organization of data. In general, charts provide children with an easy way to record information that they collect during an activity. A chart also allows for systematic collection of data, so that children can easily find their data for later discussion. Problems arise, however, when children are suddenly confronted with an activity and told to collect certain pieces of information, yet do not know how to go about the actual collection. To help children develop their ability systematically to collect information, the teacher can follow five steps. These steps assume that the child has had no previous experience with data collection; however, it is not necessary to begin at step one if children do have some experience.

Step 1. Rather than giving each child a chart, use the chalkboard or an overhead projector and collect the data for the entire class. Children can either fill in a section of the chart themselves or can call out information to the teacher. In this step children must be informed of exactly what information they will need to collect as they work, and they must be guided as they fill in the chart.

Step 2. In this step, each child is given an individual data chart to use in data collection, but a similar chart is displayed either on the chalkboard or overhead projector. The students watch as the teacher fills in a sample section of the data chart, fill in the corresponding section of their own charts, then work on their own with the rest of the data collected.

Step 3. By this step, children should be well acquainted with the use of a chart and can simply be given a chart, with some general instructions; they should be able to use it on their own during the activity.

Step 4. In step four, the class develops its own data-collection chart with the aid of the teacher. It is important that the children thoroughly understand the activity before the chart is constructed. The teacher should give a quick demonstration of what is to be done.

Step 5. Finally, the students should be able to develop their own data-collection charts, without the teacher's aid.

Sequencing the Use of Number Relations: Graphing

Number relations as a process also includes a third aspect — graphing. Graphing, like all other aspects of science teaching, moves most appropriately from concrete to abstract forms.

Concrete Object Graphs. In their most concrete form — the form most appropriate for young children — graphs can be formed from real, concrete objects to show concepts like *most, least,* and *none.*

Preschoolers can make *people graphs* — two or more lines of children showing traits of the children themselves. Hair color, clothing color or type, shoe style, favorite foods, or favorite television programs can be graphed by placing children in the various categories and having them form straight lines that can be compared. Discussion can then focus on questions like:

1. Which line has the most children?
2. Which line has the least children?
3. Which food do most people call their favorite?
4. Which color are the fewest children wearing?

Similar to people graphs are graphs formed by placing actual toys, blocks, or other objects in columns. From this step, children can begin to make bar graphs.

Bar Graphs and Cartesian Coordinate Graphs. Two kinds of bar graphs can be formed from object graphs. In the first case, children can cut strips of paper the length of each column of the object graph and paste them onto another sheet of paper to form a bar graph. In the second case, children can be given crayons and graph paper with large blocks. The child can then count the objects and color one block on the sheet of graph paper for each of the objects in the object graph.

The bar graph can then be divorced from concrete objects by having the children either count or measure objects and graph them directly as a bar graph. Measurements such as height of plants over a number of days, temperature during a day, length of shadows, or the results of other activities can be graphed using the bar graph.

Once they can use the bar graph with some ease, children can be introduced to the use of Cartesian coordinates in graphing. The same sequence of steps as used with charts can be followed in introducing children to the use of coordinate graphing.

Interpreting Graphs. In all cases, when teaching graphing, it is best to coordinate the development of graphs with the child's ability to read or interpret the information contained in the graph. Constructing a graph is fairly easy; interpreting a graph can be difficult. Interpreting a graph may involve:

1. reading data directly from a graph;
2. identifying trends in the data shown by the graph;
3. interpolating, that is, reading between the actual collected data in order to gain more information;

4. extrapolating, that is, going beyond the data to make predictions as to what could occur in the future or what occurred in the past before the start of the data collection.

Children will need help in all four of these graph interpretation skills, as well as in the construction of graphs from the data that they collect. Coordination with the mathematics program in teaching graphing can be very helpful.

Learning Activities for Number Relations

Number relations, as a process, is actually the quantification of an activity. The learning activities for number relations will help you to develop skill in this area and show you how children can work with the various number relation skills.

Learning Activity 3–23 Number Relations

Counting

Prior to writing numerals, children need to develop the concept of number. Only after the concept has been developed should children be expected to use numbers in a science activity. In general, an appropriate sequence for teaching numbers follows from concrete to semiconcrete and finally to abstract, that is, from objects to pictures or drawings to numerals.

1. Develop a method for teaching the numbers zero through nine to a group of kindergarten or first grade children. Prepare all of the necessary materials.
2. Identify a group of about six children who do not yet count well and who cannot yet match numerals to sets.
3. Using your materials, work with the children teaching the concept of the numbers from zero through nine. Do not try to teach the symbols and do not try to teach all ten numbers at one session. Matching of a symbol that is already written to a set of objects should be the last step.
4. Following your teaching, assess how well the children learned the concepts and numeral symbols.
   a. What problems did you encounter?
   b. What changes would you make in your teaching method?
   c. What changes would you make in your teaching materials?
   d. What factors other than method or materials could have affected how well the children learned?

Learning Activity 3–24 Number Relations

Graphing

For this activity you will need five paper cups, soil, water, a few small stones, and twenty to twenty-five radish or popcorn seeds. Plant the seeds by

1. punching a hole in the bottom of each cup;
2. placing a few stones in the bottom of each cup;
3. filling each cup with soil to within one centimeter of the top;
4. placing about five seeds on the top of the soil;
5. filling the cup with soil and pressing it firmly over the seeds;
6. watering each cup until a little water runs out the bottom hole. Keep the soil moist during the entire activity.

As the seeds in each cup begin to grow, measure the height of each seedling. Find the average height for all of the seedlings in each of the cups each day until you have ten to twelve measurements. Prepare a bar graph of the average data. Then, prepare a graph using Cartesian coordinates.

Learning Activity 3–25 Number Relations

Graphing

Review a set of science textbooks for first through sixth grade. Make a listing of twelve to eighteen activities in which graphs could be used. The use of graphs may not be a part of the activity as it is written in the text but could be included by the teacher to enhance the activity.

Classify the activities according to the type of graph which would be most appropriate: people graph, object graph, strip graph, bar graph, or Cartesian coordinate graph. Some might be appropriate for more than one type of graph. Keep in mind the level of the children. For example, a Cartesian coordinate graph would not be appropriate for first grade children.

Learning Activity 3–26 Number Relations

Charts

Develop a chart that would allow individual children to collect the data from the following activity. Try the activity yourself, then make the chart duplicating enough for each child to be able to have one.

Collect the following materials so that you have enough for a group of five children: a bucket of garden soil, magnifiers, paper towels, charts, tweezers, newspaper. Place the newspapers on the floor or a table and seat the children around them. Empty the bucket of soil on the newspaper.

Have the children use any appropriate senses as well as the magnifiers and the tweezers to determine what materials make up soil. Have the children use your chart to collect the data for this activity, that is, to record the materials that they find in the soil. At the conclusion of the activity, collect the charts completed by the children.

What problems did the children encounter in using the chart? How would you modify the chart to reduce those problems?

Learning Activity 3–27 Number Relations

Charts

Using either a textbook or science program for the fourth, fifth, or sixth grade level find an activity that requires the collection of data in numerical form. Topics dealing with magnets, electricity, light, sound, simple machines, and weather are the most likely to have this kind of activity.

Collect the materials needed for the activity and try it yourself. Develop a chart that could be used by children to collect the data from the activity. With a group of five or six children on a grade level appropriate to the activity, try the activity and your chart.

What problems did the children encounter with the activity? What problems did they encounter with the use of the chart? What changes could you make in the chart in order to make it easier for children to use? What suggestions did the children have that might make data collection easier?

Learning Activity 3–28 Number Relations

Number Relations in Activities

Review a textbook for any grade level from first through sixth. Choose one of the units or chapters in the textbook and read it carefully including the teacher's manual suggestions. Make a list of those places in the unit or chapter where number relations are used.

Reread each of the activities. Indicate those places where number relations could be used but where they have not been suggested by the text. Be as specific as possible about what number relation could be used at each identified place.

Learning Activity 3–29 Number Relations

Graphing and Rates

Obtain the following materials: pyrex beaker (400 milliliters), alcohol burner and stand or hotplate, 200 milliliters of water, Celsius thermometer, timer, graph paper, pad, potholder or tongs.

Place the 200 milliliters of water into the beaker and determine the starting temperature by placing the thermometer in the water for about two minutes or until the mercury or alcohol in the thermometer no longer moves.

Place the beaker over the heat source and heat until the water boils. While it is heating, take and record the temperature of the water each minute. Be careful that the thermometer is not resting on the bottom of the beaker. If it does touch the bottom you will not get an accurate measurement. After the water boils, carefully remove the beaker from the heat and again record the temperature every minute for the next ten minutes. Make a graph of each set of data, one for heating and one for cooling, using the Cartesian coordinate form.

Calculate the rate at which the water heated to boiling using the following formula:

$$\text{rate} = \frac{\text{change in temperature}}{\text{elapsed time}}$$

Calculate the rate at which the water cooled using the same formula.

Using the appropriate graph of data, determine the approximate temperature of the water after heating 2.5, 3.5, and 5.5 minutes. Using the appropriate graph of data determine the approximate number of minutes that would need to pass before the water returned to its starting temperature.

Describe, in words, each of the graphs that resulted from the data.

Summary

The processes of observation, classification, communication, operational questions, space relations, and number relations can be used by children beginning at the preschool level and progressing to the sixth grade level and beyond.

The degree of difficulty changes depending upon the age and ability of the children and is directly tied to the degree of abstractness of the process. Particularly in the case of space relations and number relations, the level needs to be carefully controlled so that it meets both the cognitive and skill-level abilities of the children. Both space relations and number relations can be highly abstract, involving numerical calculations and the interpretation of numerical data.

The teacher's introduction of the basic processes should move from concrete to abstract, with the highest levels of abstraction postponed until the highest levels of the elementary school.

The final learning activities of this chapter combine all of the primary processes.

Learning Activity 3–30 Summary

The Basic Processes

Collect the following materials: five or more different types of papers including at least two types of paper towels, glass jars, watch with a second hand, centimeter ruler, graduated cylinder, oil, vinegar, water.

Cut each of the pieces of paper into strips 3 centimeters by 20 centimeters. List five or more observations of each of the paper strips. Fold the strips in half lengthwise and then crosswise forming a folded item 1.5 centimeters wide and 10 centimeters long from each paper strip. Pour 150 milliliters of water into a jar. Place a paper strip in the jar with the narrow folded edge out of the water. Time for 30 seconds. Remove the paper, place it on the table, quickly measure the height to which the water rose. After another 30 seconds, again measure the height to which the water rose. Record both measurements. Develop a chart that would be used to collect the same data for each type of paper.

Repeat the activity with each type of paper and graph the data using the most appropriate form of graph. From the graphs that you develop, and your chart, write three operational questions that could be investigated by children. Finally, use two methods to communicate the results of the activity you have just completed to others.

Learning Activity 3–31 Summary

The Basic Processes

Choose a textbook for the grade level between first and sixth grade that you would most prefer to teach. Carefully read a single chapter and the suggestions for that chapter contained in the teacher's edition. Review the activities and the teaching suggestions to determine the processes used. Prepare a chart showing the suggested activity and the processes used in that activity.

Answer each of the following questions:

1. What processes are most frequently included?
2. What processes are omitted?
3. What suggestions would you make in order to provide for a better balance of processes in the unit?
4. What processes, if any, did you find that might not be appropriate for the grade level being considered?

Answers to Learning Activity 3–6

Observation

Observations

1, 3, 4, 6, 7, 9, 10, 16, 17, 18, 19, 20

Inferences

The sentences below illustrate possible restatements. They are not the only possibilities.

1. The object is red and green. The object has no odor.
5. When placed in water the object does not fall to the bottom of the container.
8. The object could be poured from the container after it was heated.
11. The object has six parts. The ends of the first of the parts are pointed.
12. The pianist is pushing the keys. A sound can be heard.
13. The turtle took the mosquito into its mouth.
14. The cloth is smooth to the touch. The cloth is yellow.
15. The cup on the floor is made up of seven pieces.

Answers to Learning Activity 3–17

Operational Questions

Questions 1, 3, 4, 6, 9, 10, and 11 are operational. Possible rewordings of nonoperational questions are:

2. Through what kinds of objects will light pass most easily.
5. What are some of the things birds do as they fly?
7. This would be impossible to operationalize because of the nature of the concept.
8. This would be impossible to operationalize because of the nature of the concept.
12. How much easier is it to pick up an object with a lever than without a lever?

Selected References

Baust, J. A. Spatial relationships and young children. *Arithmetic Teacher, 29,* 1, 1981.

———. Teaching spatial relationships using language arts and physical education. *School Science and Mathematics, 82,* 7, 1982.

Craig, R. P. The child's construction of space and time. *Science and Children, 19,* 3, 1981.

Damarin, S. K. What makes a triangle. *Arithmetic Teacher, 29,* 1, 1981.

Finley, F. N. Science processes. *Journal of Research in Science Teaching, 20,* 1, 1983.

Floriani, B. P., and J. C. Cairns. Assessing combining forms in science. *Science and Children, 19,* 4, 1982.

Ginsburg, H., and S. Opper. *Piaget's Theory of Intellectual Development: An Introduction.* Englewood Cliffs, New Jersey: Prentice-Hall, 1979.

Kendig, F. A conversation with Isaac Asimov. *Psychology Today, 17,* 1, 1983.

McAnarney, H. How much space does an object take up? *Science and Children, 19,* 4, 1982.

Schlichter, C. L. The answer is in the question. *Science and Children, 20,* 5, 1983.

Shaw, J. M., and M. Cliatt. Searching and researching. *Science and Children, 19,* 3, 1981.

Tobin, K. G., and W. Capie. Lessons with an emphasis on process skills. *Science and Children, 19,* 6, 1982.

Causality or explanations of physical phenomena are central to the work of scientists, and the resulting theories and models that turn up in various forms in public school curricula assume causal rather than precausal thinking.

— Good, 1977

4 The Causal Processes of Science

Chapter Objectives

Upon completion of this chapter, you should be able to

1. discuss why children have greater difficulty in using the causal processes than in using the basic processes;
2. sequence the causal processes for optimal teaching;
3. define each of the causal processes: interaction and systems, cause and effect, inference, prediction, and conclusion;
4. use each of the causal processes: interaction and systems, cause and effect, inference, prediction, and conclusion.

The child's ability to use logical causal relationships develops during the elementary school years as the child moves from precausal to logical causal reasoning. Although science texts and programs consider the processes of inference, prediction, and conclusion to be vital to the understanding of science, little is done in science classes to develop two skills that are necessary if children are to make good inferences, testable predictions, and logical conclusions. The skills that underly prediction, inference, and conclusion are (1) the ability to determine cause and effect and (2) the ability to recognize a system and its interactions.

Although cause and effect and interaction and systems are not usually listed as processes, each does fit the criteria for a process:

1. Each process is a specific intellectual skill used by all scientists and applicable to the understanding of any phenomenon.
2. Each process is an identifiable behavior of scientists and can be learned by any student.
3. The processes are generalizable across content domains and contribute to rational thinking in everyday affairs. (Finley, 1983, p. 48)

The causal processes are more difficult for children to learn than are the basic processes. The first reason for this, the slow development of logical causality, was discussed in Chapter 2. The second reason for the difficulty experienced by children lies in the nature of the phenomena being considered.

Although some causal relationships are concrete in nature and can be demonstrated easily, many are nonconcrete and must be inferred from the actions of objects or from the actions of inferred phenomena. The necessity for abstract thought, and for the management of those inferences, makes these processes more difficult to learn and use.

Finally, the causal processes tend to be more difficult because we give little attention to developing the child's ability to recognize those parts of a system that are important to the results and those that are not. We all too frequently assume that children can make such determinations without systematic instruction. Most children cannot.

By sequencing the causal processes appropriately, we can help children develop the ability to look logically at the results of an activity. A suggested sequence for the introduction of the causal processes is:

1. interaction and systems,
2. cause and effect,
3. inference,
4. prediction,
5. conclusion.

This sequence attempts (1) to provide a foundation by considering interaction and systems and cause and effect as prerequisite skills and (2) to move the child from a relatively concrete foundation through a series of steps to the more abstract causal process of conclusion.

Each of these processes is discussed in this chapter, including the sequence in which the various types of systems and predictions should be introduced to the children in a science class.

Following the discussion of each process are six activities, which will both illustrate the causal processes and develop your ability to use these processes.

Interaction and Systems

Definition

A system is a group of objects and phenomena that act together. The relationships between and among the various parts of the system are known as interactions. A very simple system, for example, is a paper fan being used to move air to cool a person's face. The parts of this system are the paper fan, the hand and arm, the air, and the face being cooled. Within this simple system three major interactions take place: the hand and arm interact with the fan; the fan interacts with the air; the air interacts with the face.

Introducing the Process of Interaction and Systems

The process of interaction and systems, because understanding it is a cognitive skill that lays the foundation for the other cause-and-effect processes, should be the first of the cause-and-effect process concepts introduced to the child. The child has the opportunity to look at a system, to choose the parts actually functioning to cause the phenomenon, and to relate the objects to the phenomenon.

For example, imagine a child working with a pendulum attached to a support rod. The purpose is to determine what affects the number of times the pendulum swings in one minute. The child's first task is to determine what parts of the activity actually make up the system being studied. The bob, string, support, and the hand that pulls back the pendulum are identified as the system. The table on which the support stands is not an interacting part of the system. Neither are the lights in the room, the timing device used, the person writing down the number of swings, or the pencil with which she is writing. Certainly all of these are important, but they do not directly contribute to the pendulum.

Once the directly contributing aspects of the system are determined, the child can be helped to search out those parts of the system that interact with one another. The string interacts with the support, the string interacts with the bob, and the hand interacts with the bob.

Types of Systems

Within the process of interaction and systems are three types of systems, classified according to their concreteness and implying a sequence for their presentation.

Concrete Systems. Children should work with systems in which the components are all easily visible or easily sensed concrete objects. Examples of this type of system would be the pendulum, the lever, a pinwheel, a paper airplane, and a bouncing ball.

Partially Concrete Systems. Systems in which the components are both concrete objects and inferred phenomena should be considered second. Some examples would be magnets, gravity, bulbs and batteries, and tuning forks. In each of these cases, the system includes not only objects but also a form of energy. Because the energy form is not visible and must be inferred from its action on objects, these systems are more abstract than the concrete systems considered first.

Nonconcrete Systems. Finally, systems in which the major components are phenomena should be considered. It is not possible to divorce such phenomena from concrete objects, but the major effects are due to something unseen. Examples might be the effect of a current-carrying wire on a magnetic compass or the effect of light on a radiometer.

Children who can pick out the important parts of a system and can show how those parts interact will be better able to move to the next of the cause-and-effect processes: cause and effect itself.

Cause and Effect

Definition

Mastering the concept of interaction is the first step toward an understanding of the concept of cause and effect. If a child can say that the string and the bob of the pendulum interact as a part of a system, then it is a fairly easy step to determine that lengthening the string causes the number of swings of the pendulum to decrease. The child can rule out the table as a cause (a phenomenistic explanation) because the table is not a part of the system and because the table and the pendulum do not interact.

Imputing cause and effect, then, requires three actual steps. First, the system and its parts are identified. Second, the interactions in the system are determined. Finally, the effects of the interactions are determined. Assigning cause and effect is the ability correctly to attribute a certain effect to a certain occurrence or cause.

Introducing the Process of Cause and Effect

As with interaction and systems, cause and effect, as a process, should follow a sequence of development from concrete to abstract. The interaction that occurs when a block is hit by a marble and moved is easy to see. Therefore, the child can state that the marble caused the block to move. This is cause and effect at the concrete level.

At the next level, white light may be passed through a prism so that the child can see the colors of the spectrum. This stage uses a form of energy and a concrete object. The interaction needs to be inferred although the effect of that interaction can be easily seen. Finally, on an abstract level, students may be asked to determine the cause of a rise of temperature as the result of a chemical reaction. Temperature is a measurement, not a concrete object. The result of a chemical reaction may be seen, but not the reaction itself. This level of cause-and-effect determination tends to be highly abstract.

The ability to say that one thing causes another is the beginning of the ability to make inferences.

Inferences

Definition

An inference is an interpretation of the observations one makes during an activity or experiment. An inference may also be thought of as a statement showing a relationship among the parts of a system and frequently detailing a cause-and-effect relationship. Usually, an inference is a highly tenuous interpretation subject to change and modification as more and more data are collected. It is also likely that multiple inferences can be made from the same set of data.

Multiple Inferences

The idea of multiple inferences is illustrated by the example of a group of sixth grade students shown the "collapsing can" demonstration. A gallon metal can containing a little water is heated until the water boils and steam emerges from the opening at the top. Then, the cap is screwed on tightly and the sealed can is removed from the heat. As the can cools, it collapses, crumples almost magically. A little cool water poured over the can causes it to crumple even more. After seeing this demonstration, sixth graders inferred some possible causes for the collapse:

1. The heat made the metal soft and it melted.
2. The metal absorbed the water and it got soft.
3. The water was heavy and when you poured it over the can it smashed the can.
4. The water turned into steam and chased out some of the air. The outside air pushed on the can and collapsed it.
5. The water turned to steam and left the can kind of empty. The metal was too heavy for the air inside and it squashed.
6. You switched cans!

Faced with so many inferences, the teacher and the class are put in the position of having ideas to test: some through reading, one through careful observation of the teacher, and some through further activity. Testing inferences allows the child to emulate the scientist, but less formally than the true experiment of the scientist. Testing inferences also allows the child to become involved in all of the primary processes, particularly with the asking of operational questions. The testing of inferences also leads to the cause-and-effect process of prediction.

Prediction

Definition

A prediction is a special form of inference that attempts to determine, on the basis of data collected, what will happen in the future. A prediction is not a guess. A guess is strictly that: it has no basis in data; it can be pulled out of a hat. A prediction, on the other hand, must have a sound foundation in data that has been collected or in background experience. Thus, one may predict with confidence that four inches of water will evaporate from a particular container in eight days, because the rate of evaporation has been shown to be, for that container, one-half inch per day.

The Two Types of Predictions

Concrete Predictions. For the first type of prediction they make, children should use concrete materials, so that they can predict directly from the data they have collected. In this case, there should be no need for children to read supplementary material for background information or for additional information on which to base their predictions.

Theoretical Predictions. Theoretical predictions are based either (1) on a combination of data drawn from concrete experiences and reading matter or (2) on reading matter alone. In the first case, children are using the written material to supplement what they have gained through concrete experience. For example, students could work with levers, then go to the textbook to obtain more information before they tried to predict what could occur if the placement of the fulcrum were changed. In the second case, students make predictions on the basis of theoretical material they acquire from reading or other verbal sources. For example, children can read about the requirements for good nutrition in mice and predict what type of diet will cause mice to gain the greatest weight over a period of time.

Testing Inferences Through Prediction

When we test inferences, predictions become highly important. For example, if the students who watched the collapsing can demonstration were to test the inference that the water poured over the can was heavy and smashed the can, their first step would be to predict what would happen if

1. less water were used,
2. more water were used,

3. a different kind of liquid were used,
4. no water were used.

Predictions, then, are made on the basis of data. But, once made, predictions must be tested to determine their validity. At times, students' predictions will need to be tested through reading. More often, however, predictions should be tested through the use of concrete materials. Once the predictions have been tested, students can change or modify inferences on the basis of the new data and, finally, when all of the evidence is in, they can draw conclusions.

Conclusion

Definition

A conclusion, like a prediction, is a special form of inference. Many inferences can be drawn from the evidence of a single activity. As each inference is tested by means of predictions and activities, a particular inference may be revised or eliminated. Inferences have that property; they can be changed. But, finally, after predictions have been tested and various inferences discarded or revised, there should still be a single inference left that fits all of the data and to which all of the predictions point. The end-product of the prediction and the testing phases is a conclusion.

Because conclusions are based on a greater amount of evidence than are inferences, conclusions are less likely than inferences to change. However, in the face of new, solid evidence even a conclusion may need revision.

Abstraction and the Causal Processes

The causal processes tend to be more difficult for children to use than the basic processes previously discussed. Although the causal processes are developed through the use of concrete objects, they still require a further cognitive step. The objects are visible, touchable, smellable entities, but the relationships among those objects must be inferred from the results of the interactions taking place. These inferences are not concrete in nature; they are the beginnings of abstraction.

A child can measure the length of a string as 20 centimeters and can count 60 swings of a pendulum in a minute. That same child can increase the length to 60 centimeters and can count 30 swings in a minute. The child directly measures length and number of swings. However, the child must infer from those measurements the relationship of string length to number of swings. An inference is not a concrete object but the result of a cognitive process. As such, it is an abstraction. But, determination of cause and effect, although unlike the other processes in that it is a cognitive skill, is necessary for development of the child's ability to use the experimental processes, which require a determination of cause and effect prior to the writing of an hypothesis.

Because of the abstract nature of the cause-and-effect processes, children will find their use difficult. The key is to move from the most concrete cases to the most abstract cases, allowing time for children to develop their abilities at each of the levels of concreteness.

Content Teaching and the Causal Processes

The use of the causal processes forms the heart of the scientific enterprise. It is through inference, prediction, and the determination of cause and effect that scientific knowledge is gained.

Children should use these processes for the same purpose they are used in the scientific enterprise: to gain knowledge. Rather than reading which animals are classified as mammals, students could:

1. observe the overt characteristics of real, small mammals;
2. infer the major characteristics of mammals;
3. read to find the characteristics of mammals not observed directly;
4. predict which of the animals from a list would be classified as mammals;
5. test their predictions by classifying the animals and then researching the correct classification in textbooks, tradebooks, and films;
6. draw conclusions detailing the characteristics used to classify mammals;
7. test their conclusions by classifying other animals and testing their classifications.

Or, in studying about magnetism, students could:

1. observe the interaction which occurs between a magnet and various metallic and nonmetallic objects;
2. identify the parts of the system that interact;
3. predict what will happen if layers of cardboard are placed between the magnet and the objects;
4. test their predictions through concrete materials;
5. draw inferences dealing with the interaction through cardboard of magnets with metallic objects;
6. read to determine if the inferences are valid;
7. draw a conclusion about the effect of magnets through cardboard and test that conclusion to be certain of its validity.

Students using the causal processes to learn content should be involved directly with concrete materials, so that they will develop a conceptual basis. They should then move to written materials in order to develop a more thorough understanding of the content information. Moreover, the child's development of an understanding of cause and effect will permit his or her development of a more thorough understanding of the true experiment and its role in science.

The use of the causal processes to teach content allows the student to structure his or her knowledge in a way that will be personally meaningful. In this way, the information will be consistent with his or her previous knowledge and developmental level.

Causal Process Learning Activities

Each of the learning activities included here demonstrates one or more of the causal processes. Try each activity in order to increase your ability to use these processes and to develop your understanding of the particular process examined.

Learning Activity 4–1

Causal Processes

Interaction and Systems

Research any two of the following topics. After completing your research answer each of the following questions:

1. What are the parts of the system?
2. What interactions occur?
3. Which parts of the system are directly involved in the interactions?

The topics are:

1. How does an automobile engine work?
2. How does a television set work?
3. How does a radio work?
4. What causes a thunderstorm?
5. What causes a hurricane?
6. What causes a rainbow?
7. How does a human being hear sounds?
8. How does a human being digest food?
9. How does a camera work?
10. What causes a volcano to erupt?
11. What causes an earthquake?

Learning Activity 4–2

Causal Processes

Inference

Collect the following materials to use with a group of five third or fourth grade children: one pyrex beaker (400 milliliters), one-half cup of granulated sugar, hot plate, potholder or tongs, wire hot pad or second potholder.

Without telling the children what the white material is, pour it into the beaker and place the beaker on the hot plate until the sugar has carbonized (turned black) and begins to rise to the top of the beaker. Remove the beaker from the heat using the tongs or potholder.

Have the children make inferences about what they have seen. Questions like the following will help them to infer:

1. What could the white "stuff" have been?
2. What do you think happened that made the white material turn black and get larger?
3. What could the black "stuff" in the beaker be?

Remember, even if the first child answering the first question says that the material was sugar, get other ideas. Ask what else the material could be. And, above all, do not tell the child who answers correctly the first time, "that's right." Your response should be as neutral as possible, so that children feel free to propose their own ideas. Try to get multiple inferences.

Learning Activity 4–3

Causal Processes

Prediction

Try any of the following situations with a group of third, fourth, or fifth graders. The first questions or statements are to recall the children's background or previous experiences. Record the predictions made by the students. How well do you think these children were able to predict? What evidence do you have from your interviews that children are not able to use cause-and-effect relationships easily?

Situation One:

What is it like when the sun is behind a lot of clouds? What is it like at night? The planet Pluto is very far away from the sun and so gets very little light. What do you think it is like on Pluto?

Situation Two:

A few years ago there was not enough gasoline for everyone to get as much as they wanted. Some people could not drive their cars as much as they wanted. Some trucks carrying things to stores could not get to those stores as quickly. Buses, airplanes, tractors, and all kinds of farm machines also use gasoline. What would happen if there were no gasoline at all?

Situation Three:

In order to keep insects from eating food crops like corn, wheat, rye, and various vegetables, farmers spray pesticides — poisons — that will kill the insects. But, scientists are now finding that some insects are becoming resistant to the poisons being used. The insects are no longer killed by the pesticides. What could happen if all of the insects that eat food crops are no longer killed by pesticides?

Learning Activity 4–4 Causal Processes

Conclusion

Collect the following materials having enough both for your demonstration and for the use of four pairs of children: red, blue, yellow, and green food coloring; various sized jars; various clear liquids; timer; chalkboard or large sheet of paper with marker. Jar sizes should range from baby-food jars to gallon jars. Liquids may include oil, vinegar, tonic water, club soda, clear brand-name soda, or alcohol.

Do the following. No attempt should be made to keep all conditions the same. Choose a pint jar and a gallon jar. Fill the pint jar about one-quarter full of cold water and the gallon jar about half full of warm water. Do not tell the children about the difference in temperature. Into the pint jar place about ten drops of blue food coloring. Time how long it takes for the food coloring to spread throughout the water, stopping after five minutes if it takes longer than that. After recording that time, place two or three drops of red coloring into the gallon jar. Time how long it takes for the coloring to spread throughout the water. Do not stir or shake the containers and be certain that the water is still before adding the coloring.

After the demonstration ask: "What could be some reasons why the coloring spread faster in this jar than in this jar?" Record all of the inferences the children make in response to this question. Encourage the children to make as many inferences as possible.

Allow the children to select one of the inferences, or more if time permits, and test it using the materials. Collect the observations made as the children work and help them come to a conclusion that reflects this data.

Learning Activity 4–5

Causal Processes

Interaction and Systems, and Conclusion

Collect the following materials: round balloon, cylindrical balloon, drinking straw, masking tape, vinegar, baking soda, test tube, cork to fit the test tube, four or five crayons, tissue, fine string.

Blow up the round balloon and let it go. Describe what happens using as many of the basic processes as are appropriate.

Cut about ten feet of string. Thread the string through the straw. Tie each end of the string to a doorknob or chair so the string is stretched taut. Blow up the cylindrical balloon and tape it to the straw. Release the balloon. Describe what happens using as many of the basic processes as are appropriate.

Put a half teaspoon of baking soda on a small, single thickness of tissue, wrap it. Place the four crayons in a row on a table top with about a half inch between them. Holding the test tube upright, pour about an inch of vinegar into the test tube and insert the tissue and baking soda to within half an inch of the vinegar. Place the cork in the test tube loosely. Quickly lay the test tube on its side across the crayons. Describe what happens using as many of the basic processes as are appropriate.

For each of the above activities:

1. List the directly contributing parts of the system.
2. Describe the interactions that occur.
3. List any inferences you can as to the cause of what you observed.

Now, using all of your observations and inferences, write one conclusion as to the common cause of each of the events you observed.

Learning Activity 4–6

Causal Processes

Concluding

Look at each of the following tables of data or graphs. What conclusions can you draw from each of the sets of data?

1. A chemist mixed two solutions together causing a yellow color to form. The experiment was repeated several times at different temperatures. What conclusion can be drawn from the table of data below?

Temperature in Degrees Celsius	Reaction Time in Seconds
10	96
20	73
30	69
40	50
50	10
60	9
70	10
80	10

2. The following table shows the results of an experiment in which different amounts of zinc metal are added to 20 milliliters of acid causing the temperature of the acid to rise varying amounts. What conclusion can be drawn from this data?

Grams of Zinc	Final Temperature in Degrees Celsius
1	16
2	20
3	30
4	42
5	60
6	102

3. The following graph shows the mass of an object plotted against its momentum. The line generated represents the velocity. What does the graph show about the relationship of momentum to mass?

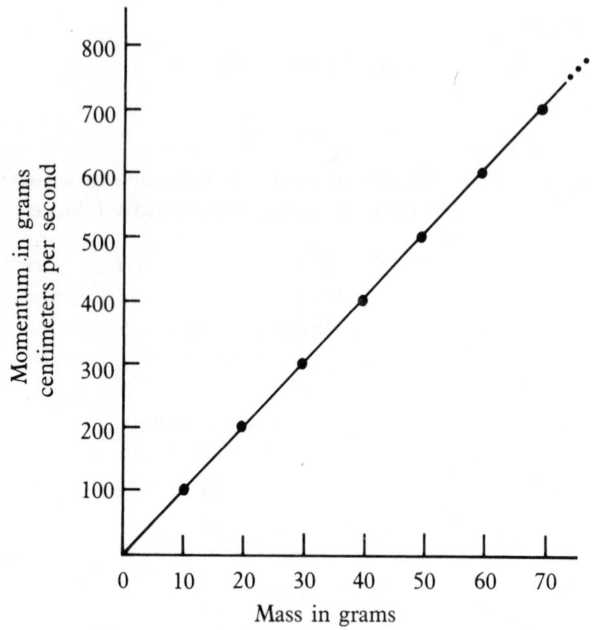

Summary

The causal processes are the first of the scientific processes with which we move the child from the use of concrete objects to the use of abstractions. Because of this use of abstraction, the child needs to have attained a certain level of maturity in his or her thinking. Piaget has placed the beginning of this level of maturity at approximately ten years of age. Prior to that age level, children may supply precausal relations, that is, they may think of all things as being alive, man-made, or magical. Later, once they discard the tendency to use precausal relations, children may have difficulty in seeing that objects must directly interact for an effect to occur. Exposure to the causal processes should help children to develop their ability to use more logical thought processes when it comes to the identification of causal relations in science activities.

As with most of science teaching and learning, presentation of the causal processes should move from the concrete to the abstract, so that the child has objects with which to work at first and thoughts or phenomena with which to work at the end.

The teacher can then couple causal processes with the primary processes in order to teach content material through the use of activity. Development of their ability to use the causal processes should also permit children more fully to use and understand the experiment as a means for learning in science.

Selected References

American Association for the Advancement of Science. *Science — A Process Approach.* Lexington, Mass.: Ginn, 1975.

Bellamy, M. L. What is your theory? *Science Teacher, 50,* 2, 1983.

Finley, F. N. Science processes. *Journal of Research in Science Teaching, 20,* 1, 1983.

Good, R. G. *How Children Learn Science: Conceptual Development and Implications for Teaching.* New York: Macmillan, 1977.

Rice, D. R., and W. P. Dunlap. Introducing the ways and means of scientific inquiry. *Science Teacher, 49,* 3, 1982.

Science — A Process Approach, Materials. Lexington, Mass.: Ginn, 1979.

SCIIS Materials. Chicago: Rand-McNally, 1980.

SCIS Sampler Guide. Chicago: Rand-McNally, 1970.

Shaw, J. M., and M. Cliatt. Searching and researching. *Science and Children, 19,* 3, 1981.

Tobin, K. G. and W. Capie. Lessons with an emphasis on process skills. *Science and Children, 19,* 6, 1982.

Science is based on experiment, on a willingness to challenge old dogma, on an openness to see the universe as it really is. Accordingly, science sometimes requires courage — at the very least to question the conventional wisdom.

— Sagan, 1974

5 The Experimental Processes of Science

Chapter Objectives:

Upon completion of this chapter, you should be able to

1. define each of the experimental processes: controlling variables, formulating hypotheses, interpreting data, defining operationally, and experimenting;
2. use each of the experimental processes: controlling variables, formulating hypotheses, interpreting data, defining operationally, and experimenting;
3. describe the development of experimental abilities as identified by Piaget.

The experimental processes are welded into a single powerful tool for research in science: the experiment is the powerful tool used by the scientist to gain the evidence that will prove or disprove a given hypothesis. The experiment is also the means by which the scientist gains the information that will support or refute a scientific theory. Because the experiment is the basis for the factual knowledge of science, its structure and conditions are rigidly prescribed. Only by adherence to the rigorous conditions of the experimental method can the scientist be certain that the results he or she obtains are due to one particular factor and not to something else, which the scientist may not have considered important.

Once the scientist has obtained the results of an experiment, he or she is ready for a second vital step in the scientific process. One set of results is not enough to convince the scientific community that a hypothesis is correct. Rather, the results of an experiment must be replicated in order to provide further certainty that the conditions of experimental rigor have been maintained. Normally, the results of an experiment are published or circulated, so that others in the scientific community can read the results and can attempt to provide the necessary replication. At times the results are replicated, and the new ideas developed through the experiment become a part of accepted knowledge, which is science. At other times, the results cannot be duplicated and the results are discarded or modified. Another scientist frequently discovers some variable or some condition that was not considered in the original experiment and affected the outcome.

The Experiment as a Research Tool

The experiment is the ultimate means for the development of scientific knowledge. To insure certainty that a cause is correctly attributed to a particular effect within the experiment, the experimental procedure must rigidly control variables.

Variables

Definition. Variables are all of the factors within an experiment that may be changed by the experimenter, that may change because of a change made by the experimenter, or that are kept the same because the experimenter wishes to rule them out as the cause of a change. Three types of variables are identifiable within an experimental procedure.

Types of Variables. The variable that the experimenter purposely changes in order to determine its effect on the rest of the experimental system is called the independent variable. The experimenter expects the purposeful manipulation of the independent variable to result in a change in some other part of the system. The changed variable, resulting from the manipulation of the independent variable, is termed the dependent variable, that is, it depends upon the independent variable in order to change. A change in the independent variable usually results in a change in the dependent variable. If this change is to be correctly attributed to the change in the independent variable then all other aspects of the system must remain the same. The factors that are kept the same are referred to as constants.

Types of Variables — an Illustration. As an illustration of these three types of variables, consider an activity in which a child tries to determine whether a magnet will act through cardboard as strongly as it does through air. The child is given a bar magnet, a box of steel pins, and five sheets of cardboard cut from a shoebox. First, the child sticks the magnet into the pile of pins, pulls it out, and counts the number of pins stuck to the magnet. All of the pins are then taken off the magnet and returned to the pile. Now, a single layer of cardboard is placed on top of the pins and the magnet touched to the cardboard. The magnet and the cardboard are carefully raised together, and the number of pins attracted counted. Additional pieces of cardboard are added one at a time, and the activity is repeated.

In this activity, the child uses the same magnet, the same pins, the same pile for the pins, and the same type of cardboard cut to the same size for each of the trials. These are the parts of the system which are being held constant. The five sheets of cardboard are used to find out what will happen to the strength of the magnet. The amount of cardboard placed between the magnet and the pins is purposely changed by the child. Therefore, the amount of cardboard is the independent variable. And, finally, a part of the system changes because of the change in the thickness of the cardboard: the number of pins attracted continuously decreases. The number of pins, then, is the dependent variable. The number of pins held by the magnet depends upon the thickness of the cardboard.

The Control Group. Although rigid control of variables is an attempt to be certain that the results of an experiment can be attributed to the independent variable, a second safeguard is employed by the scientist in order to be even more certain of the results. This second safeguard is the use of a control group.

A control group is a comparison group that receives no experimental manipulation but otherwise has the same characteristics as the experimental group. For example, if research is being done into the optimum amount of fertilizer to use to produce the greatest number of tomatoes per acre of land, the scientist will plant a number of identical fields. Each field would have the same amount of seed, the same type of soil, receive the same amount of water, and be planted using the same type of equipment and at approximately the same time. One of the fields would be left to grow with the application of the usual amount of fertilizer, that is, whatever the farmer normally uses. Each of the other fields would be treated with varying amounts of fertilizer. After the harvest, the yield of the experimental fields would be compared with one another as well as with the typically fertilized field. In this case, the typically fertilized field acts as a control, so that other factors which might have increased yield can be ruled out. This control field gives additional assurances that the amount of fertilizer designated for optimum production was the actual cause of that production.

Children and Control of Variables

Control of variables is a process that only becomes possible when an individual has reached the level of formal operational thought, the final stage of development hypothesized by Piaget. It may also be the one stage of development identified by Piaget that is not reached by all normal human beings. Chiapetta (1976) showed that as many as 85 percent of adolescents and young adults do not reach the stage of formal operations. This high percentage has been shown by other researchers as well.

According to Lawson (1974), performance on certain tasks can be used to determine whether or not an individual has reached the level of formal operational thought. Some of these tasks are included here in order to illustrate the type of thought processes used by the formal operations thinker. Try them yourself. You must be able to give a correct solution to the task and to demonstrate your reasoning for the task in order to give a complete answer. The solutions are found at the end of this chapter.

Learning Activity 5–1

Piagetian Tasks

The Height of a Liquid

The following diagram shows two containers and a liquid. Container *B* is wider than container *A*. Container *B* originally has 8 units of water in it. Container *A* has no water.

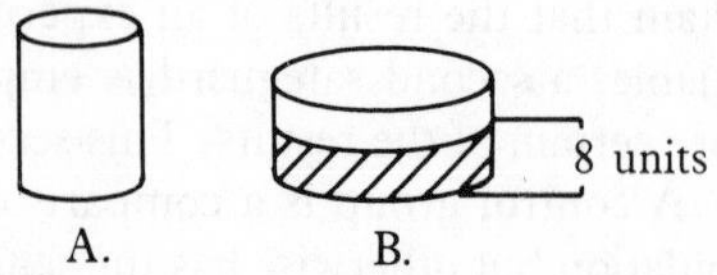

All of the water in container *B* is poured into container *A*, and the level is seen to be 12 units in container *A*.

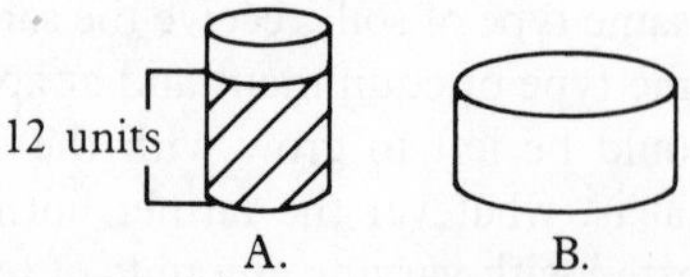

1. Now, all water is removed and container *B* is refilled with 6 units of water. If that water is poured into container *A*, to what level will the water reach?

2. Now, suppose 11 units of water are poured into an empty container *A*. If all 11 units are poured from container *A* into empty container *B*, to what level will the water reach?

Be certain to give a verbal explanation of how you reached your answers. A numerical formula is not enough.

Learning Activity 5–2

Piagetian Tasks

The Balance Problem

The following is a drawing of a simple balance showing a mass of 8 grams suspended on the beam at a distance of 10 centimeters from the center. The 8-gram mass is on the left side of the balance.

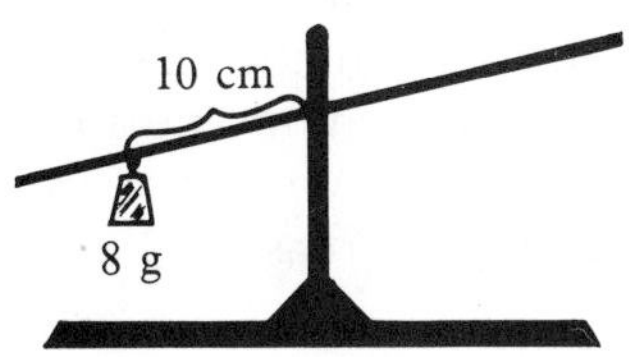

1. Where on the right side of this beam should a 4-gram mass be placed in order to cause the beam to balance?
2. Now, suppose that a 3-gram mass is placed 15 centimeters from the center on the left side of the balance. Where on the right side of the beam should an 11-gram mass be placed in order for the beam to balance?

Be certain to give both a numerical answer and an explanation of how you arrived at the answer. A numerical formula alone is not sufficient.

Learning Activity 5–3

Piagetian Tasks

The Pendulum Problem

You have been provided with three pendula:

1. Pendulum *A* is 50 centimeters long and has a mass of 100 grams.

2. Pendulum *B* is 100 centimeters long and has a mass of 50 grams.
3. Pendulum *C* is 50 centimeters long and has a mass of 50 grams.

Which of these pendula would you choose in order to determine the effect of *mass* on the number of times a pendulum will swing in one minute? Explain your reasoning.

Learning Activity 5–4

Piagetian Tasks

The Problem of the Stores

Four stores are to be put into a shopping center: a shoe store, a dress shop, a candy store, and a basket shop. List all of the possible ways in which these stores could be arranged side-by-side in the mall. They cannot be placed one above the other, behind one another, or around corners.

After you have listed all possible combinations, explain how you reasoned through this problem.

Learning Activity 5–5

Piagetian Tasks

The Problem of Choice

The following shapes are placed in a basket, and the basket is then shaken to assure that the shapes are completely mixed: eight green squares, six purple squares, five yellow squares, four green triangles, six purple triangles, and five yellow triangles.

1. What are your chances of drawing out a purple triangle on your first try? Explain how you reasoned out your response.
2. Now, the purple triangle is returned to the basket and the basket is again shaken. What are your chances of drawing out a yellow or a green square on your first try? Explain how you arrived at your response.

In general the ability to use formal operational thought does not begin until the child reaches about eleven or twelve years of age. The experimental processes are, therefore, best left until the sixth grade level. At this point, the first of the experimental processes that children should work with would be the process of controlling variables.

Stages in the Process of Controlling Variables. According to Piaget and Inhelder (1958) the ability to control variables develops in four stages. During the first stage, the individual is unable to differentiate between the action of the variables and his or her own actions. The child at this stage may, when working with the pendulum, be unable to determine that how hard he or she pushes the pendulum has no bearing on the number of swings which the pendulum will make in a minute. In the second stage, the individual is able to rule out himself or herself as the cause of a change but has difficulty distinguishing between relevant and irrelevant variables. In this case, the child may discover that the length of the pendulum affects the number of swings but will remain unconvinced that other factors do not cause changes. In stage three, the individual is able to isolate one variable and keep others constant. The individual may, however, state that one variable is going to be manipulated, then actually manipulate another. Consequently, the child may state that he or she is going to test for the effect of weight on the pendulum and actually test for the effect of string length. The child does this without realization. Finally, in stage four, the individual becomes able correctly to manipulate and control variables, the same as the scientist does.

Relationship of the Stages in Controlling Variables to Teaching. Children at stage one are not yet cognitively ready to work with the control of variables except in a situation that is highly structured by the teacher. Even then, it is unlikely that children will be able to learn meaningfully. Rather than force the child to perform a meaningless experiment, the teacher should return to the cause-and-effect processes to develop more fully the child's ability to identify the relevant parts of a system and to attribute correctly cause and effect in simple, nonexperimental situations. Once children are able to identify relevant factors and to rule out their own participation, the teacher can move to stage two.

The stage two child is able to rule out himself or herself as a cause but may not be able to rule out all variables other than the relevant one. In this case, children should be encouraged to identify all the factors they consider possible causes of an effect, to develop experiments in which each of the factors is tested in turn, and to produce a chart which indicates which variables are direct causes of a phenomenon and which are not. Time will probably not permit each child to test each factor, or even each small group of children to test each factor. However, each small group could be assigned one factor to test and the results pooled to provide the total picture. Final conclusions can then be drawn on the basis of the testing of all identified possibilities rather than only one.

In stage three, when children are able to identify factors independently and to rule out some, the problem is to be certain that the identified factor is actually being tested. This stage is easy for the teacher, who needs only to check experimental procedure against intention to see if there is a correct match.

The last stage should be one of independent work, so that children who have developed the ability to use the experiment appropriately are able to do so. At this point the child is able to gain content information and to generate ideas which can be tested through further experimentation or through the use of other sources of information.

The Other Experimental Processes

Control of variables is a vital aspect of experimentation, but it is not the only part of an experiment. The scientist cannot know which variables to control or manipulate without the guidance of a hypothesis. Without an interpretation of the data collected as the variables are manipulated, the scientist actually has learned nothing. And without the use of operational definitions the phenomenon under consideration may not be correctly identified by others who are replicating the experimental procedure. These other experimental processes will be considered below.

Formulating Hypotheses

Definition. A hypothesis brings order to an experiment by determining what is being tested and what is expected as a result.

The idea of a hypothesis has been defined in a variety of ways. It is sometimes called an "educated guess." In other cases the hypothesis is called "an if . . . then statement" or a "statement to be proven wrong." In essence, a hypothesis is a prediction of cause and effect in which the independent and dependent variables are clearly stated. For the previously described experiment with the cardboard, pins, and magnet, an appropriate hypothesis could be:

> If the thickness of the cardboard is increased then the number of pins picked up by the magnet will decrease.

From this statement, the experimenter can tell that the thickness of the cardboard is to be purposely changed. It is the independent variable. From this change in the thickness of the cardboard, the experimenter expects a change in the number of pins. The number of pins will depend on the thickness and is the dependent variable. The hypothesis imposes order on the experiment.

Purpose of the Hypothesis. A hypothesis focuses an experiment so that the data collected by the experimenter are useful and organized. The hypothesis also gives an indication of the experimental procedure to be used in doing the experiment. The hypothesis is the starting point for the development of the procedure. Finally, the hypothesis indicates the kind of relationship that should be evident in the data collected as a result of the procedure.

Interpreting Data

Definition. The interpretation of data is the ability to perceive patterns in the information collected from an experiment and to express those patterns as a conclusion which either supports or refutes the hypothesis of the experiment. In interpreting data two basic processes are combined: using numbers and drawing conclusions.

In the activity with the magnets and the pins, the following data were collected:

PIECES OF CARDBOARD	NUMBER OF PINS
0	22
1	20
2	15
3	10
4	8
5	5
6	2

It is easy to see from this set of data that the number of pins decreases with the number of pieces — the thickness — of the cardboard. Returning to the hypothesis that an increase in the thickness of the cardboard will result in a decrease in the number of pins, the data indicate that the hypothesis is supported. However, if one were to draw the general conclusion that the thickness of any material determines the number of pins that will be picked up by a magnet, a great deal of additional testing would need to be done. The only information collected deals with cardboard. To conclude that all materials will act in the same manner would be to draw a conclusion not warranted by the data.

Supported and Nonsupported Hypotheses. At times, the interpretation of data will indicate that the hypothesis proposed by the experimenter was not supported. In this case, it is important to realize that the processes of hypothesizing and data interpretation were not incorrect nor did they fail. The fact that the data did not support the hypothesis does not make the hypothesis any less an hypothesis nor does it invalidate the way in which the data were interpreted. In fact, the development and testing of nonsupported hypotheses are important to the practice of science. The amount of knowledge is increased by showing that a factor does not cause a change in a system. Experiments are successful even if the prediction made by the hypothesis is found to be not supported by the data. The child who is developing his or her ability to experiment cannot experience failure, if he or she understands this feature of experimental method.

Defining Operationally

Definition. Defining operationally is the last aspect of experimenting. Operational definitions are those developed by the experimenter to satisfy a need experienced during the planning and carrying out of an experiment. For an experiment that is to be replicated by another individual, the operational definitions assure that the second researcher will identify same phenomena as representative of what the original researcher had considered.

An Example of Operational Definitions. Once, doing a demonstration for a sixth grade class as a starting point for later experimentation by the children, I asked four different children to time how long it took for a candle placed under a gallon jar to go out. They all used the same clock, but the numbers the children gave for the time the candle took to go out were 63, 74, 97, and 128 seconds. Some variation is to be expected, but not 55 seconds. Why the difference? Each child had a different, mental definition of "out."

63 seconds — It was out when I couldn't see the yellow flame.
74 seconds — It was out when I couldn't see any flame at all.
69 seconds — It was out when the little red spot on the flame was gone.
128 seconds — It was out when there was no more smoke coming from the wick.

In order to solve the problem of what was meant by the term "out," I proposed an operational definition. The operational definition stated that the candle would be called "out" when there was no flame but a red spot or smoke could still be seen. This operational definition was appropriate for this class, at this time, and for this experiment. At another time or with another class a different operational definition might be needed. It is important that the children create their own operational definitions rather than accepting definitions created for them by the teacher.

Teaching Children to Experiment

In working with the experimental processes, the teacher needs to keep in mind that experimenting, which requires control of variables, is a particularly difficult task for children. It is the first of the science processes that requires the use of formal thought processes. Even the first step in an experiment, the development of a hypothesis, is difficult because it necessitates the use of logical cause-and-effect relationships.

As children in the intermediate grades begin to conduct experiments, they will need a great deal of guidance. Children who have had the opportunity to write and to answer their own operational questions as well as to determine cause-and-effect relationships will probably have less difficulty developing the ability to experiment than will those children who have had little experience in these processes. The ability to experiment is the culmination of the ability to use the processes of science.

Timing the Teaching of the Experiment

Teacher Structured Experiments. Because of their difficulty in using experimental processes, the first exposure children should have should be highly structured, with the teacher giving the hypothesis, the procedure, and the means for collecting the data. This structured step is designed to allow the children to see how an experiment is constructed with a hypothesis, procedure, and data collection procedures. After the children are able to carry out the instructions of a preplanned experiment, they can be given a hypothesis and can develop as a group a procedure to test the hypothesis. At this time the teacher can emphasize the variables under consideration and define, through use, each of the types of variables, while guiding children in their use and in their control.

Group Structured Experiments. The second step in the development of the ability to experiment would be to have individuals or small groups develop the procedure used to determine the validity of a predetermined hypothesis. At this stage children should be encouraged to find a variety of ways of testing an hypothesis, both to encourage creative approaches and to allow them to attempt a variety of conditions for testing. Children can be given the starting hypothesis through an interesting or challenging demonstration done by the teacher.

Student Structured Experiments. Finally, children can be given background information and a problem to solve from which they can develop an experiment. In this stage children should be developing their own procedures and their own hypotheses rather than being provided with a ready-made problem and a ready-made hypothesis. Another possibility at this final stage is to have children develop experiments from operational questions.

However, because of the need for formal levels of thought, many children will be unable to carry out a true experiment without extensive teacher direction. For these children, the teacher should make available the opportunity to investigate scientific phenomena through the use of operational questions and noncontrolled activities. The use of the process skills of science has been shown to be strongly correlated with the development of formal operational thought processes (Padilla, Okey, and Dellashaw, 1983).

But even those children who are unable to work individually with the experimental processes should be exposed to the processes of controlling variables, hypothesizing, and experimenting so that the concepts will not be entirely new to them when they make the transition to formal operations.

Content Teaching and the Experiment

The use of the experiment brings the child to a level of activity equal to that of the research scientist. Just as the scientist does not carry out an experiment solely for the purpose of experimenting, the child should not experiment just to learn the parts of an experiment or the general experimental process.

The purpose of the experiment is also to gain content information. The key to using the experiment with children is to give them only enough background information to carry out the experiment and no more. In this way the child generates knowledge on his or her own rather than simply verifying what he or she has already been told.

Any content area in which students can do experiments should be used. Experiment to find the effect of water on plant growth. Experiment to find the advantage gained through the use of an inclined plane. Experiment to find the relative learning abilities of mice and beetles. Experiment to find the effect of cooling rate on the size of crystals. Then, when the experiment through the use of concrete materials has helped the child develop the content being studied, use textbooks, tradebooks, magazines, or other sources to determine the validity of the results or to add content information which the children could not obtain experimentally. The experiment should begin to teach the content, the verbal material should extend the content. But, because of the advanced nature of the thought processes required by the experiment, be certain that you make it possible for children who need to do so to use operational questions rather than hypotheses and to engage in noncontrolled activities rather than controlled experimental procedures. Although the controlled experiment is a vital tool of the researcher, it is more important to let the child learn in an effective manner than it is to push for the child to reach the level of process embodied in the experiment.

A good textbook abounds with activities that children can carry out to verify the content of that textbook. These activities generally not only provide the answers through pictures or through the written text but also do not ask the child to undertake true experiments. The teacher can derive experiments from these activities by determining the content to be demonstrated through the activity, turning the content into a hypothesis, and having the students develop a procedure which will determine the validity of the hypothesis. This is best done prior to the students' review of the material in the text or the activity. To make the classroom more interesting, the teacher could present more than one hypothesis for the textbook activity and have various groups determine which of the hypotheses has the greatest amount of supporting data.

The experiment is a powerful means for teaching content to children and should be used as fully as possible to teach children in the sixth grade.

Experimental Process Learning Activities

In order to develop your own skills at experimentation, try the experimental process learning activities. Each of the activities combines all of the experimental processes rather than isolating them from one another in an artificial manner.

Learning Activity 5–6

Experimental Processes

Collect the following materials: ruler with a groove, small marble (1.5 centimeters), large marble (2.5 centimeters), white paper, block (see directions), salt or sand, balance, masking tape, 3 inch × 5 inch card, books.

Make a 2.5 centimeter cube by marking 2.5 centimeter lines on the 3 inch × 5 inch card forming a grid then cutting out the following pattern:

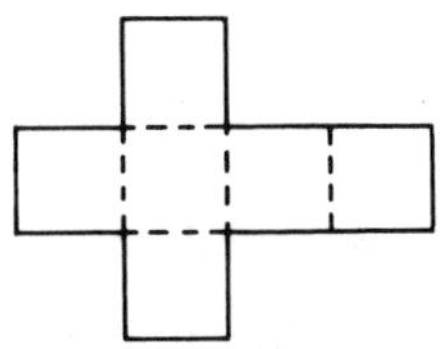

Fold along the dotted lines and tape edges to form a block with a top that can be opened and resealed.

Tape the white paper to a tabletop. Place one end of the ruler so that it just touches the midpoint of one edge of the paper and prop the other end up on a book so that it is at approximately a 45 degree angle. Place the block at the base of the ruler.

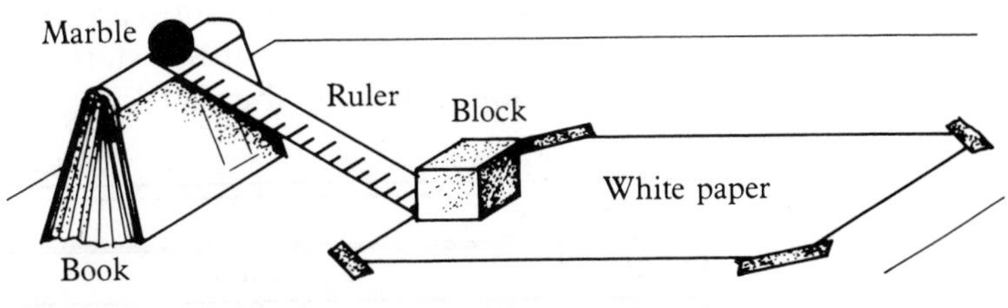

Mark the position of the block by drawing a line around it then finding the center point by drawing two diagonal lines.

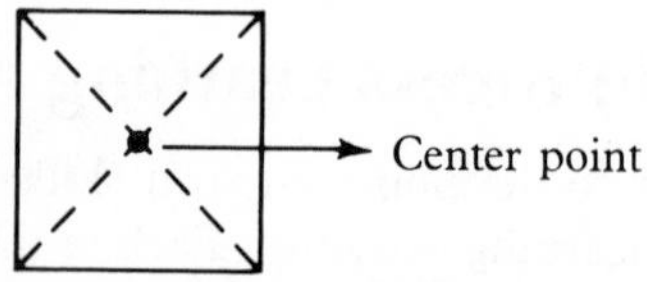

Hold the marble at the top of the ruler. Release the marble. Mark the new position of the block by finding the center point. Measure the distance which the block moved by measuring from center point to center point. Repeat three times and find the average distance traveled by the block.

List five or more variables that could affect the distance the block moves. Choose one of the five variables that you listed and write an hypothesis to test. (The salt or sand listed in the materials can be used to change mass or surface.)

Develop and carry out an experiment to test your hypothesis. List your independent and dependent variables as well as those factors which you held constant. Be certain to collect the appropriate data and to draw a conclusion as to the validity of your hypothesis.

Learning Activity 5–7

Experimental Processes

Obtain the following materials: small toy truck, four meter sticks, pulley, set of gram masses (5 grams through 500 grams), stopwatch or other timer, masking tape and other materials as needed.

On a flat table top tape the meter sticks to form a track a little wider than the width of the toy truck and two meters long. Tie a string to the front of the truck and make a loop in the other end. The string should be long enough to reach to the end of the table and hang over 10 to 15 centimeters. Tape the pulley to the end of the table so that the wheel is perpendicular to the table and can move freely. Stretch the string out so the truck is at the start of the meter stick track and the loop is through the pulley.

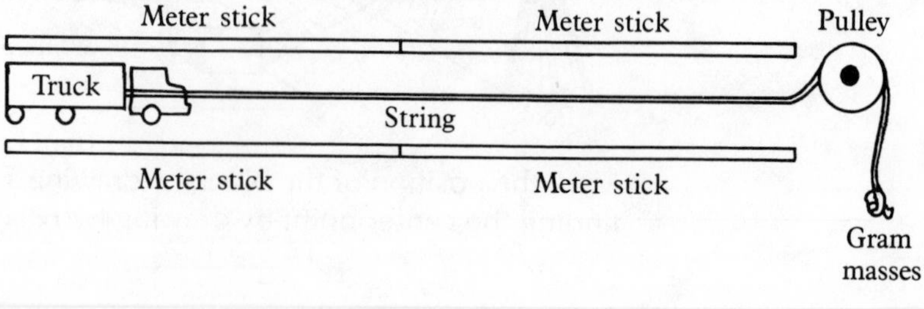

Using gram masses, try each one until you find a single mass which will cause the truck to move slowly down the track when it is tied to the looped end of the string. Time how long it takes for the truck to move the two meters. Repeat the timing twice and find the average length of time for the truck to move the two meters.

List five or more factors which could affect the speed at which the truck travels. Write an hypothesis to test one of the variables listed previously, then design an experiment to test the hypothesis.

Learning Activity 5–8

Experimental Processes

Collect the following materials: two meter sticks, graph paper, tennis ball, rubber ball, ping-pong ball, soccer ball, and any other types of balls that you can find, and masking tape. You will also need a partner.

Tape the two meter sticks vertically to a wall so that they are end to end and form a continuous length of two meters. Starting with any ball, drop it from a height of 100 centimeters and measure the height of the resulting bounce. Try this three times for each of the balls finding an average height of bounce for each. Graph the results.

List five or more variables that could affect the height to which a ball bounces. Write an hypothesis to test one of your variables. List your independent and dependent variables as well as those factors which you held constant. Design and carry out an experiment to test your hypothesis. Graph your results.

Learning Activity 5–9

Experimental Processes

For each of the following hypotheses (1) identify the independent variable, (2) identify the dependent variable, and (3) list and write an operational definition for any terms which may need such a definition. Then, choose *one* of the hypotheses and write an experimental procedure which could be followed by another person. Finally, give your procedure to a classmate and, without giving any help, have that person try your experiment. Revise your written procedure as necessary.

The hypotheses are:

1. If a heavy object is dropped from a height, then it will fall faster than a light object dropped from the same height.
2. If the surface area of a container is increased, then water will evaporate from the container more quickly.
3. If a marble is dropped into a basin of water, then the distance the water splashes will depend on the height of the drop.
4. If the stretch on a rubber band is increased, then the pitch of the sound produced when the rubber band is plucked will be higher.
5. If the area of a parachute is increased, then an object suspended from that parachute will fall more slowly.
6. If the temperature of water is increased, then the amount of salt which will dissolve in the water will increase.
7. If the number of coils of wire around the core of an electromagnet is increased, then the strength of the magnet will increase.

Learning Activity 5–10

Experimental Processes

Most of the activities contained in elementary science textbooks are not true experiments. However, many of those in fifth and sixth grade level texts can be changed into true experiments in which control of variables is required.

Choose a fifth or sixth grade level textbook from any elementary science textbook program. Find three activities in the text which can be changed from an activity to an experiment that requires the control of variables.

Write a procedure for each of the experiments that could be followed by a fifth or sixth grade student. Be certain to include the hypothesis to be tested and the materials needed, as well as a step-by-step procedure.

Answers to Learning Activities 5–1 to 5–5

Piagetian Tasks

5–1: The Height of a Liquid

1. The height of the liquid in container *A* will be nine units.
2. The height of the liquid in container *B* will be seven and one-third units.

Reasoning: From the first two paragraphs it is known that 8 units in container *B* is equal to 12 units in container *A*. Therefore, each unit in *B* rises 1½ units in container *A*. So, if container *B* has 6 units and that is poured into container *A*, each of those 6 units will rise 1½ units in container *A*. Six times 1½ is equal to 9 units. In problem two, if A has 11 units, each of those units will be ⅔ of a container *B* unit (the ratio of 8 to 12 is ⅔). Eleven times ⅔ is equal to 7⅓.

5–2: The Balance Problem

1. The 4-gram mass should be placed 20 centimeters from the center.
2. The 11-gram mass should be placed 4.09 centimeters from the center.

Reasoning: If something is balanced, the amount of force on each side of the balance must be the same. On a lever the amount of force is determined by the product of the mass of the object times the distance to the fulcrum. Since a balance is a form of lever, the same principle should hold. So, in the first case, the force on the left side is 8 grams times the distance to the center 10 centimeters or 80 gram/centimeters. With a 4-gram mass the distance must be 20 centimeters, because 4 times 20 is equal to 80. This same procedure can be used for the second problem. Three grams is 15 centimeters from the center. This is equal to 45 gram/centimeters of force. An 11 gram mass must therefore be placed 4.09 centimeters from the center since 11 times 4.09 is equal to 45.

5–3: The Pendulum Problem

Use pendula *A* and *C* to determine the effect of mass.

Reasoning: Since mass is the factor being investigated, it needs to be different for each trial. In order to be certain that it is mass that causes or does not cause an effect, everything else must be kept the same. Pendulum *B* is twice as long as the others, and length could not be ruled out as a factor.

5–4: The Problem of the Stores

Let *S* be the shoe store, *D* be the dress shop, *C* be the candy store, and *B* be the basket shop. There are four stores. Each store can appear in first, second, third, or fourth place in a row of stores. It is possible for the other stores to be arranged so that six patterns appear with each of the four stores first:

$S-D-C-B$	$S-D-B-C$
$S-C-D-B$	$S-C-D-B$
$S-B-D-C$	$S-B-C-D$

Since there are four possible first stores and six combinations with each of the stores appearing first in the row, a total of twenty-four possible combinations can be shown:

$S-D-C-B$	$D-S-C-B$
$S-C-B-D$	$D-C-B-S$
$S-B-D-C$	$D-B-S-C$
$S-D-B-C$	$D-S-B-C$
$S-C-D-B$	$D-C-S-B$
$S-B-C-D$	$D-B-C-S$
$C-D-B-S$	$B-D-C-S$
$C-B-D-S$	$B-C-S-D$
$C-S-B-D$	$B-S-D-C$
$C-D-S-B$	$B-D-S-C$
$C-B-S-D$	$B-C-D-S$
$C-S-D-B$	$B-S-C-D$

5–5: The Problem of Choice

1. The probability of getting a purple triangle on the first try is one in six.
2. The probability of getting a yellow or a green square on the first chance is thirteen out of thirty-six.

Reasoning: There are a total of thirty-six colored shapes in the basket. Out of those thirty-six shapes, six are purple triangles. Each time a shape is chosen there are six possible chances of getting a purple triangle: six out of thirty-six shapes or one out of six chances. The total number of green or yellow squares is thirteen. So thirteen of the thirty-six possible shapes to be drawn out are green or yellow squares. The probability of drawing out a yellow or green square is, therefore, thirteen out of thirty-six.

Summary

The experiment, which is composed of the individual experimental processes, constitutes the most powerful means which science has for gaining information. It is also the most difficult of the scientific processes for children to learn because it presupposes the ability to use formal thought processes.

Because the student must use formal operational thought processes, the experimental processes are best left until the upper intermediate grades, particularly the sixth grade. Even then, the child should be able to fall back on operational questions and noncontrolled activities when it is necessary for his or her understanding.

In general, teaching the experimental processes moves from highly structured situations to situations which the student structures alone. In this way the child gains more and more independence in the use of the experiment to enlarge his or her knowledge of the content of science.

Selected References

Chiapetta, E. L. A review of Piagetian studies relevant to science instruction at the secondary and college levels. *Science Education, 60,* 1967.

Epstein, H. T. Growth spurts during brain development: Implications for educational policy and practices. *Education and the Brain.* Eds. Chall, Jeanne and Mirskey, Allan W. Chicago: University of Chicago Press, 1979.

Johnson, V. R. Myelin and maturation: A fresh look at Piaget. *Science Teacher, 49,* 3, 1982.

Lawson, A. E. The development and validation of a classroom test of formal reasoning. *Journal of Research in Science Teaching, 15,* 1, 1978.

———. Formal reasoning, achievement, and intelligence: An issue of importance. *Science Education, 66,* 1, 1982.

Padilla, M. J., J. R. Okey, and F. G. Dellashaw. The relationship between science process skill and formal thinking abilities. *Journal of Research in Science Teaching, 20,* 3, 1983.

Pallrand, G. J. The transition to formal thought. *Journal of Research in Science Teaching, 16,* 5, 1979.

Piaget, J., and B. Inhelder. *The Growth of Logical Thinking from Childhood to Adolescence.* New York: Basic, 1958.

Mistrell, J. Conceptual development research in the natural setting of the classroom. In Mary Budd Rowe, ed., *Education in the 80's: Science.* Washington, D.C.: National Education Association, 1982.

Part III

Teaching Science

Because even the most commonplace event is ultimately related to the laws that govern the entire physical universe, one is often drawn, in thinking about that event, to questions of the deepest intellectual content.

— Trefil, 1983

6 Developing Questioning Skills

Chapter Objectives

Upon completion of this chapter you should be able to

1. classify the questions asked during a science lesson as either convergent or divergent;
2. write examples of convergent and divergent questions that could be used in an elementary science lesson;
3. define each of the following levels of Bloom's Taxonomy: knowledge, comprehension, application, analysis, synthesis, and evaluation;
4. write examples of questions for each of the following levels of Bloom's Taxonomy: knowledge, comprehension, application, analysis, synthesis, and evaluation;
5. describe effective and ineffective ways of asking questions during a science class;
6. define wait time I and wait time II;
7. list the major benefits of the use of wait time in asking questions.

An observer sitting in almost any elementary school classroom immediately notices one fact that many teachers do not recognize themselves: questions make up the predominant form of interaction in the classroom. For the most part, these questions are asked by the teacher and are answered by a student designated by the teacher. Because so much time is spent in asking and answering questions and because questions can make or break a science lesson, the teacher needs to be especially careful with the kinds of questions that are asked and the way in which they are asked. In addition the teacher needs to be aware of the kinds of questions that cause children to investigate science using concrete materials rather than recall.

Rapid-fire questions accompanied by a pointing finger can cause even the most secure individual to forget a simple fact. Unclear questions can result in confusion, and questions calling for a single, specific answer can make children guess, as they try to determine exactly what word or words the teacher is expecting.

Questions should enhance a science lesson. They should allow children to think critically, to go beyond the simple regurgitation of words they have read or heard. Responses to questions should also provide the teacher with some measure of how children stand in ability to recall science facts, apply science concepts, and evaluate the results of their experimental activities. The questions the teacher asks during a science lesson should require children to recall material as well as to evaluate information or to use information creatively. Better achievement in science seems to result when teachers ask questions on a variety of different levels (Tisher, 1971). The teacher needs to ask simple questions during science lessons so that slower children in the class can experience success, just as he or she should ask more complex questions for those children who are able to answer such questions (Sanders, 1966). There is satisfaction in having an answer to a question, particularly when such answers allow for creativity on the part of the respondent.

Only when the teacher plans questioning strategies can he or she have any assurance that they will be appropriate to a particular science lesson. The type of question asked will depend on the result desired. Questions that ask students to recall the information in their science textbooks are phrased differently and are asked in a different manner than questions that ask students to infer the cause-and-effect relationships they have observed in an experiment.

In order to develop your ability to ask questions during a science lesson, you will be considering three aspects of questioning in this chapter:

1. ways of classifying questions,
2. ways of asking and responding to questions,
3. the use of wait time in asking questions.

The Two General Categories of Questions

In the simplest classification, one finds two kinds of questions in the science classroom. Based upon the latitude allowed the student in answering the questions, this classification divides questions into either convergent or divergent.

Convergent Questions

Definition. A convergent question is one in which a single answer is the correct answer to the question. Although there is a single answer, that answer may be phrased in many ways depending on the child's ability to respond and on the child's background experiences.

Examples of Convergent Questions. Each of the following questions represents the kind of content found in the elementary school science program and is a convergent question.

1. How many legs does an insect have?
2. What is your textbook's definition of the word "environment"?
3. Of what three minerals is the rock granite composed?
4. If a Celsius thermometer reads 100 degress, what would the temperature be in Fahrenheit?
5. Measured in centimeters, how long is the chalkboard?

The Use of Convergent Questions. Each of these questions has a single, rather specific answer that the child can memorize or find with a measuring device. The important point, however, is that convergent questions focus on a single, correct answer, that is, they converge on the answer. Because of these characteristics, the teacher can use convergent questions in the elementary science class to:

1. review previously learned information in order to increase retention through use;
2. review observations made during an activity or an experiment in order to permit more accurate inferences and conclusions;
3. recall needed background information prior to an activity, demonstration, or experiment;
4. define vocabulary that will be encountered in reading material or that was previously defined through the use of materials.

Divergent Questions

Definition. A divergent question is one in which the student is asked to use background material as well as personal experiences to answer a question that may have many equally valid answers. Divergent questions promote divergent thought and promote the creative use of information in science.

Examples of Divergent Questions. The following questions are all divergent. As you read through these examples, compare them with the examples of convergent questions, which were previously given. Once again, the content of the questions is typical of the content in an elementary school science textbook.

1. A box of bricks is too heavy for a single person to move from one place to another. What methods could be used to move the box?
2. Your favorite beach has been eroding away each winter until only a strip of sand three feet wide is left. What could be done to keep the rest of the sand from disappearing as well?
3. Nuclear energy, wind energy, solar energy, and energy from the Earth have all been suggested as ways of supplying energy that do not use up our petroleum supplies. Which of these do you think would be best for our community?
4. You are one of the first colonists on the planet Mars. What is it like there?
5. What are some possible alternatives to a zoo for keeping rare animals like the Giant Panda, the California Condor, and the Whooping Crane?

Each of these divergent questions has a number of answers. Because of the variety of possible answers, students can think more creatively and can apply material already known to new problems or situations. In the case of question four, students can put their imaginations to work to create something new. For the most part, divergent questions do not have answers that can be memorized. They diverge from one question to many equally appropriate answers.

Uses of Divergent Questions. Divergent questions, unlike convergent questions, can be used during problem solving situations or during process activities. Operational questions are divergent, because they do not focus on a single, specific answer. Questions that allow children to use their imaginations — say, to describe life on another planet or life in a period of time long past — are also divergent. Questions that make children create their own experiments to solve a particular problem are also divergent. A general key to the use of divergent questions is that they are used whenever children are to be involved in problem solving situations or in situations where they are able to use their knowledge creatively.

The following learning activities will allow you to practice recognizing and writing convergent and divergent questions.

Learning Activity 6–1

Investigating Classroom Questions

Observe a teacher during two thirty-minute periods as he or she teaches a science lesson. During the first period, make a tally of the number of divergent and convergent questions the teacher asks. Then, on the basis of your tally and your observations answer the following questions:

1. What is the ratio of convergent questions to divergent questions?
2. How did the students react to the questions? Consider both verbal responses and body language.
3. What opportunities did you observe for the teacher to ask divergent questions rather than convergent questions?

During the second thirty-minute period observe the students while the questions are asked. Then answer the following questions:

1. What pattern of response and question emerges as you watch?
2. How many of the students are involved in answering?
3. What seems to be the cause of the patterns that you observe?

Learning Activity 6–2

Classifying Convergent and Dívergent Questions

Consider each of the following convergent questions. Rewrite each of them to allow for divergent thought.

1. How many legs does an insect have?
2. What three minerals are found in granite?
3. Find the examples of energy being used in each of the pictures on page 34 of your textbook.
4. According to your textbook, why are some animals in danger of becoming extinct?
5. What does NASA list as three conditions for becoming an astronaut?
6. Classify each of the following animals according to whether they are fish, amphibians, birds, reptiles, or mammals.
7. How long is your classroom in meters and centimeters?
8. What example of friction did you see in class yesterday?
9. Use the glossary of your book to find the definitions of each of the following words: corpuscle, vein, artery, capillary, plasma, platelet.
10. What definition did the film you saw give for the word magma?

11. Your book listed four materials that are elements. What were they?
12. Which of the following is an observation and which is an inference?
13. What is the boiling point of water on the Celsius temperature scale?

Classifying Questions in the Cognitive Domain

Although questions can be classified simply as either convergent or divergent, this system does not assist the teacher to ask questions that elicit the variety of thought processes that should be seen in the elementary science classroom. To allow for more variety, questions can be classified using Bloom's Taxonomy.

Bloom's Taxonomy was originally developed in 1956 to provide a system for the classification of educational goals. It has since been extended to the classification of questions like those asked during elementary science lessons.

Bloom designated the cognitive domain as that which includes such activities as remembering and recalling knowledge, thinking, applying material, solving problems, creating new ideas, and evaluating information. With all of these activities, the student can operate on the content material of the elementary science program. The range of these activities, moreover, suggests that much more can be done with the content of science than the simple recall of factual information on a test or a quiz.

In classifying the questions asked in the science class, we may use Bloom's six categories of the cognitive domain:

1. knowledge,
2. comprehension,
3. application,
4. analysis,
5. synthesis,
6. evaluation.

This listing moves from the simplest use of content information to its most complex use. We must keep in mind that this classification system is hierarchical, so that the student can attain a given evaluation level only if he or she has factual knowledge, understanding of that knowledge, and the ability to apply, analyze, and synthesize that knowledge. One cannot be expected to apply science content that one does not comprehend. One cannot be expected to evaluate science content or to make science-related decisions without a knowledge of relevant facts or the ability to analyze a situation and determine its component parts. The arrangement of the levels of this taxonomy is not only from the simple to the complex but also from the concrete to the abstract. Moreover, questions on one level of the hierarchy make use of or build upon the content elicited by questions on the previous levels.

With this information as background, let us consider each of the categories of the cognitive taxonomy in terms of questions for the elementary science classroom.

Levels of the Cognitive Taxonomy

Knowledge Level. The knowledge level of the taxonomy includes behaviors that emphasize the student's recall or recognition of factual information. The student stores certain science content in his or her memory and later recalls that information as it is needed. The knowledge level consists of three major subdivisions: knowledge of specifics, knowledge of ways and means of dealing with specifics, and knowledge of the universals in a field.

Knowledge of Specifics. This sublevel deals with the recall of specific bits of information such as terms, dates, persons, places, events, or sources of information. This can be called the hard core of facts or information which make up the content of science. Without mastery of this level of knowledge, the student may be unable to think about or to discuss many of the phenomena of science. Although the content at this level is in the form of words or symbols, they all have concrete referents.

Knowledge of Ways and Means of Dealing with Specifics. This sublevel consists of a knowledge of how information is organized, studied, judged, and criticized. Although it is somewhat more abstract than the previous level, it still depends on recall. This level includes a knowledge of trends, sequences, classifications, criteria, and methods. Although this level requires knowledge of each of these items, we do not expect the student to be able to use them; the student is still working with the recall of information.

Knowledge of the Universals and Abstractions in a Field. This sublevel deals with the principles, generalizations, and theories which are used to organize the content of science. These are the broad concepts that dominate science and are generally used in studying its phenomena or in solving its problems. Once again, students are only expected to recall memorized information and not to use that information in any way.

Examples of Knowledge Level Questions. The following questions represent knowledge level questions. Each uses the kind of content found in elementary science textbooks.

1. Who was the first person into space?
2. What is the name of the largest planet in our solar system?
3. What is the system of measurement most commonly used in science?
4. What names are usually given to the poles of a magnet?
5. What is the order of stages in the development of a butterfly?

6. What are the three major groups of rocks found on the Earth?
7. What example of a chemical change is found in your textbook?

Questions at the knowledge level are useful when the teacher wishes to recall information that the student has previously read or heard. At this level, we do not expect the students to comprehend that information in any way. The understanding of information arises at the second level of the taxonomy.

Comprehension Level. The comprehension level includes those questions asked during a science lesson that determine whether or not the student understands information. The three sublevels of comprehension are translation, interpretation, and extrapolation.

Translation. This sublevel provides a transition between the behaviors classified as knowledge level and the higher cognitive levels of the taxonomy. Working at the translation level, the student must be able to tell what a word, definition, or concept means in his or her own words. This can also mean a translation of symbols into a written statement which gives the meaning of the symbols.

Interpretation. This sublevel asks the student not only to translate each of the major parts of a particular segment of content into his or her words but also to go beyond those parts and give a total view of the essential meaning of the content.

Extrapolation. This sublevel requires that the student go beyond the limits set by the information and apply some of the ideas to situations or problems not actually included in the original material. Extrapolations are actually inferences made from the information. Drawing conclusions from various written or concrete materials comes under the category of extrapolation.

Examples of Comprehension Level Questions. The following questions illustrate the comprehension level of the taxonomy. As you read through them, compare them with the previous knowledge level questions. Once again, the questions are representative of the typical textbook.

1. What is meant by the term "food web"?
2. Rewrite the following symbol in words: H_2O.
3. Look at the graph showing the rate at which various plants grow. Which of the conclusions following the graph are not supported?
4. Compare animals from the Age of Dinosaurs to the animals of today.
5. Which of the following terms does not belong in this sequence: lever, pulley, screw, truck, inclined plane, wedge?
6. From the three experiments with magnets and electricity, what conclusion can you draw as to the relationship between electricity and magnetism?

When they attain comprehension, students are showing more than the ability to memorize. They are demonstrating the beginnings of an understanding of the science content they have been studying. On the next level, students begin to work with the information in settings that require more than memorization or simple understanding.

Application Level. At the application level the student needs to use science content correctly in a situation where no method of solution for the problem is given. This differs from comprehension, because at the comprehension level the student can use information only when specifically asked to use it. At the application level, however, the student does not need to be told what material to use. Since much of what is learned in elementary science should have applicability to real-life situations, the application level is of particular importance. Possession of knowledge and application of knowledge cannot be considered synonymous. It is possible to know something, yet not be able to use it in a problem solving situation.

Examples of Application Level Questions. The application level of the taxonomy is exemplified in each of the following questions. Although the content may be found in the elementary science program, the activity these questions should elicit from the students is not necessarily found in the pages of the text. At the application level students must go beyond the bounds of the textbook and use information in new settings.

1. Classify the twelve rocks on the table using the most appropriate method.
2. If a bean plant grows at the rate of two centimeters per day, how tall will the plant be after fifteen days?
3. Compare the conditions on the planet Mars to those found on Mercury.
4. Study the pictures of the Grand Canyon. What could have caused the features that you see in the pictures?
5. Using what you know about simple machines, design a machine that could be used to move a giant Sequoia tree from California to Pennsylvania.

Application level questions use the knowledge of science content as well as the comprehension of that content in new situations. The key term at the application level is the *use* of information. At the fourth level of the taxonomy analysis, the individual begins to consider material in a more critical manner than previously.

Analysis Level. The analysis level emphasizes separation of material into its constituent parts and detection of the relationships between those parts. The analysis level can aid in a fuller comprehension of science content and can lead in to the evaluation level.

The analysis level is of particular importance to the elementary science curriculum. Through analysis students learn to distinguish between inference and observation, between facts and hypotheses, and between conclusions and supporting statements. At this level, students also learn to distinguish between relevant and extraneous material. Each of these skills is important in science, as students gather data, draw conclusions from that data, and determine cause-and-effect relationships.

Analysis of elements, analysis of relationships, and analysis of organizational principles are the three sublevels of analysis.

Analysis of Elements. At this sublevel the student should be able to identify both the clearly stated facts of a written piece and the underlying assumptions of the author. Analysis of elements may include recognizing the assumptions on which a theory is based, distinguishing between fact and theory, and differentiating between conclusions and supporting statements.

Analysis of Relationships. Once the various parts of a piece of writing have been identified, the student must still determine the relationships among those parts. Analysis of relationships can include determining the relationships between an hypothesis and the evidence gathered during an experiment, seeing the relationships within the data collected, as well as determining cause-and-effect relationships.

Analysis of Organizational Principles. This sublevel is the most complex level of analysis, because it includes the task of analyzing the organization of a piece of written material. Students are asked to read in order to determine the author's purpose, point of view, or attitude.

Examples of Analysis Level Questions. At the analysis level, questions like the following could be asked during the science class. Once again, although the content is considered in the elementary science program, the answers to questions like these can only come when the children use that content and their problem solving skills.

1. Look at the following table. Which of the conclusions listed below it are supported by the data in the table?

Swings of a pendulum (one-minute period)

LENGTH (CENTIMETERS)	NUMBER OF SWINGS	MASS (GRAMS)
50	57	10
45	64	10
75	39	25
75	39	30
100	26	30
25	80	15
25	80	50

Neither the length nor the mass of a pendulum affects the number of swings.
The shorter the pendulum, the greater the number of swings.
The longer the pendulum, the greater the number of swings.
The mass of the pendulum does not affect the number of swings.

2. Read the following paragraph. What is the writer's hypothesis? What evidence is given to support that hypothesis? [Use a paragraph appropriate to the grade level.]
3. From studying the three experimental procedures used in class, the data collected, and the conclusions drawn, list the cause-and-effect relationships that were illustrated [in a given experiment].
4. Listen to a tape recording of television commercials. What inferences do you think people are supposed to make about the product advertised? What observations can actually be made from the information given?
5. Read a newspaper article on using solar energy to produce electricity. Do you think the writer is for or against using solar energy? What evidence do you have for your decision?

As you can see from these five questions, at the analysis level students must use a higher level of reasoning than at any of the previous levels. Once again, however, the student cannot attain the analysis level unless he or she has the ability to recall and comprehend factual information pertinent to the question as well as to use that information in various situations. This need for higher reasoning abilities is also apparent at the next level — synthesis.

Synthesis Level. The synthesis level requires an even higher level of reasoning ability than the analysis level and involves the putting together of parts to form a whole. Generally the parts are both previously learned science content and newly encountered material. At the synthesis level, the student is for the first time involved in the creative use of information. This is not the completely free creativity experienced by the author writing a novel or the artist creating a painting, but creativity in which the student must act within the limits established by a particular problem or a certain set of materials.

Performing a synthesis, the student must draw upon material from many sources and put that material together in a product that did not obviously exist before.

The synthesis level provides the science teacher with an opportunity not present on the other levels of the taxonomy. At the synthesis level, the student can use information and skills from a variety of subject areas to aid in the solution of a science oriented problem. Art, music, language, math, and social science can all be brought into play at the synthesis level. It provides the teacher with an appropriate arena for developing relationships among subject areas and allows the student to use skills gained in varying subjects. The synthesis level also allows for problem solving in real situations.

The synthesis level consists of three sublevels: production of a unique communication, production of a plan, and derivation of a set of abstract relations.

Production of a Unique Communication. This sublevel has as its primary emphasis communication: getting ideas, feelings, or experiences across to others. Although the communication is unique, that does not mean that pure creativity is required of the student. Rather, the student is constrained by limitations placed by the teacher, by the medium used, and by the experiential content from which the student is able to draw. Very different types of communications are produced, if the child is writing a creative story rather than a report of an experiment or activity. The content of the final product is selected by the student rather than by the teacher, but it must fall within minimum standards set by the teacher.

Production of a Plan. At this sublevel the primary emphasis is on development of a particular plan of operation such as an experimental procedure or a procedure used to answer an operational question. The child's product at this level must satisfy the requirements established by the science teacher, but there is a great deal of room for creative variation within those requirements. Even devising an experiment or activity to test a specific hypothesis gives the student the leeway to approach that hypothesis from his or her own perspective and background.

Derivation of a Set of Abstract Relations. At this sublevel the student has to derive from either concrete data or phenomena some type of statement to explain or classify that data. This particular type of synthesis is of great importance to science, because it is through such a synthesis that students interpret the data they collect and draw conclusions from that data.

Examples of Synthesis Level Questions. At the synthesis level the teacher can ask the following kinds of questions to permit the student to use science content in a more creative manner.

1. Develop your own experiment to determine what effect talking to a plant has on its growth.
2. Pretend that you are the first person to land on the planet Venus. You meet a Venusian. What is he or she like? What kind of life does he or she live on Venus?
3. Draw a mural showing what it would be like to live for one day as a cave man.
4. Suppose that you caught the Loch Ness Monster or Big Foot. What would you do with it?
5. Design a place that could be used to house the last pair of Bald Eagles in the world.

6. You live in a place where there is no way to keep track of time. What system could you invent that could be used by your fellow countrymen?

The Importance of the Synthesis Level to Science Teaching. The synthesis level is an important one for science teaching for a variety of reasons. For the first time, the student is able to work creatively with the content material he or she has acquired through reading and activity. For the first time the student is engaged in problem solving processes that bring diverse subjects together: the child sees that science is related to other subject areas and to everyday life. At the synthesis level, the elementary school child has the opportunity to emulate the scientist as he or she attempts to solve a real problem.

Second, at the synthesis level the child has for the first time the opportunity to put his or her own ideas, feelings, and experiences into a response. The inclusion of such affective elements in the child's response may trigger full-brain learning. The inclusion of the affective has been shown to allow the coordination of both brain hemispheres in learning.

Third, the synthesis level permits the child who has talents and abilities outside of science to apply those talents or abilities to the solution of a science-oriented problem. Consequently, the synthesis level provides the child with an opportunity to succeed in a subject area which may not fall high on his or her list of success-oriented situations. The artistic child can create a painting or sculpture, and the child who writes well can create a story.

Last, at the synthesis level the teacher finally leaves the control of the situation to the child and can watch how the students respond to the various situations presented. The child finally has the opportunity to show what he or she can really do in science.

Once the synthesis level has been attained, only one further level remains. At the evaluation level, the student is faced with one final cognitive task: making a judgment.

Evaluation Level. At the evaluation level, the student is asked to make judgments according to some established criteria about the value of ideas, solutions, methods or materials. The criteria may be determined by the student or may be provided by the teacher.

Evaluation is placed at the highest level of the taxonomy because it involves a combination of all of the other behaviors: knowledge, comprehension, application, analysis, and synthesis. The evaluation level also provides a link between the cognitive and affective areas of behavior, because values, likes and dislikes, and enjoyment are all involved in the process of evaluation. Once again the full-brain use rather than hemispheric use is possible.

The evaluation level, however, presents a difficulty not found at the other levels of the taxonomy: evaluation involves a judgment. This necessity causes difficulty because individuals tend to make judgments in relation to themselves.

Adults tend to make judgments in terms of personal usefulness; useful ideas are rated highly, whereas those not perceived as useful are rated low. Children have an additional difficulty in making judgments.

Some children may find the use of objective criteria for evaluation close to impossible, because of the egocentricity characteristic of the child during the preoperational stage of development. However, one of the goals of the elementary science program should be to develop in children the ability to evaluate on an objective basis rather than a subjective basis.

Although performance at the evaluation level is difficult for both children and adults, children can learn to evaluate material. The teacher should insure that questions at the evaluation level, however, are suited to the child's background, level or ability, age, and level of knowledge.

The evaluation level has two sublevels: judgment in terms of internal evidence and judgment in terms of external evidence.

Judgment in Terms of Internal Evidence. At this sublevel students have to analyze data or conclusions from the standpoint of logical accuracy or consistency or some other criteria inherent in the material. For the most part, at this sublevel evaluation involves determining the accuracy of particular statements.

Judgment in Terms of External Evidence. At this sublevel students must evaluate material with reference to certain selected or recalled criteria. Usually this is accomplished by comparing a set of materials to a set of standards designed for the evaluation of such materials.

Examples of Evaluation Level Questions. Evaluation level questions require that students use high levels of thinking and have the prerequisite knowledge implied by the question. The teacher should not pose such questions unless the students have sufficient contact with the topic to be able to comprehend the questions and to recall the material necessary to answer.

1. You have done three experiments showing the effect of water on the growth of green plants. Which of these experiments do you think yielded the most accurate results? On what are you basing your answer?
2. Think about the cartoon "The Flintstones" and about what you have learned about prehistoric times. Which do you think presents the most accurate picture of life in prehistoric times? What reasons do you have for selecting one over the other?
3. We have four ideas about what to do with the Loch Ness monster if it is found. Which of these ideas do you think would be best and why?

    Kill it and stuff it for a museum.
    Put it in a zoo.
    Keep it in a big cage which is a part of the loch.

Keep it in a cage that is a part of the loch while everything possible is learned about it then let it return to the loch.

4. How important do you think it is for scientists to explore planets like Venus, Mars, Saturn, and Jupiter?
5. Each of you has received a copy of a classification system made by a group of fifth grade students. Using the criteria for a good classification system which you learned in science, would you rank this as an excellent, good, fair, or poor system for classification?

The teacher attempting to work with evaluation level has to keep in mind the caveat that students must have the necessary prerequisite information as well as the fact that children are egocentric. One additional factor should be kept in mind when we work at the evaluation level. Because the evaluation level can include an individual's values and feelings, the teacher must be careful to show a respect for those values and feelings different from his or her own. The evaluation level should permit such differences to come through, but it may not be an appropriate time to evaluate those differences on the basis of which is purportedly best. Ours is a multicultural society, and the word "best" has little meaning in this area; we agree, however, that all must be respected.

Learning Activity 6–3

Classifying Questions

Read each of the following questions then classify them in two ways: first as either convergent or divergent, second according to the level of the taxonomy represented by the question.

1. Looking at the graph [presented to the student], how far did the marble cause the block to move on the third try?
2. [After reading information on the use of nuclear energy for electrical production], what assumptions are being used to defend the safety of this method of energy production?
3. Who were the first two astronauts to step on the Moon?
4. Two methods have been considered [in a given textbook] for determining the number of stars visible on any given night. Which is the better method? Why?
5. What are the three types of variables in an experiment?
6. Knowing how the three varieties of rocks are formed, in which type of rock would it be best to search for fossils?
7. Devise a plan that you feel would keep the California Condor from becoming extinct.
8. How many categories of rock are generally used by geologists?

9. Using the definition you have of a simple machine, classify the following as simple or nonsimple machines: tweezers, wheelbarrow, bicycle, staircase, truck, can opener, seesaw.
10. What were some of the experiments leading to our present understanding of the atom?
11. Using the ten criteria for a true hierarchical classification system, determine which of these classification systems is best.
12. What do geologists mean by the term "fault"?
13. A penny is placed on a stiff card and balanced over a glass; when the card is suddenly flicked away the penny will fall into the glass. What principle is illustrated in this example?
14. In your opinion, how applicable is the study of science to everyday life?
15. Write a story in which you describe the first encounter with a creature from another planet.
16. Develop an experiment to test the effect of sunlight on the growth of a green plant.
17. If each degree on the Celsius thermometer is three-fifths of a degree on the Fahrenheit thermometer, what would the boiling point of alcohol be in degrees Celsius if it is 179 degrees Fahrenheit?
18. What is the Earth's average distance from the sun?
19. In your own words, what is meant by the term "Pyramid of Life?"
20. What could happen to the Earth if it were to collide with a comet?

Learning Activity 6–4

Writing Questions

Read a section or chapter from a fourth, fifth, or sixth grade textbook. For that section or chapter, write the following types of questions:

1. five knowledge level questions,
2. three comprehension level questions,
3. three application level questions,
4. two analysis level questions,
5. two synthesis level questions,
6. two evaluation level questions.

Remember: the analysis, synthesis, and evaluation levels of questions will not have answers that can be found directly in the reading material of the textbook, but they must be based on that material.

Using Questions Effectively

Factors in Effective Questioning

It is not enough to know that there are various types of questions we, as teachers, can ask in order to enhance content learning in science. Such knowledge does not insure that those questions will be asked appropriately.

To ask questions appropriately, we must take three factors into consideration. First, the question should be on a level that will elicit the kind of information desired. Second, the questions should be asked in an appropriate sequence. And, third, the questions should be asked in an appropriate manner, so that the student knows what is being asked and has the time to consider a response. We have already considered the level of question along with the kinds of information that can be elicited at each of the levels. The second step in appropriately asking questions requires sequencing.

Sequencing Questions. Suppose that the ultimate question for a particular lesson is at the application level: How could we move a box that weighs 700 pounds from the floor to the top of a table without using more than one person to do it?

In order to prepare the students for this application level question, it may be a good idea to prime their thoughts with some knowledge level questions:

1. Name five kinds of simple machines.
2. Draw a diagram of at least one of the kinds of simple machines.
3. What does your textbook say is the advantage of using a simple machine rather than only muscle power?

Similarly, the final question of a particular lesson might ask students to work on the synthesis level: Design an experiment to test the hypothesis that if the temperature of water increases then the amount of a solid which can be dissolved in that water will also increase.

Students can be primed with questions from lower levels of the taxonomy such as:

1. What is the purpose of an experiment?
2. What parts are generally included in an experiment?

3. What is the purpose of the hypothesis of an experiment?
4. What should be done in the procedure of an experiment to be certain that the results are actually caused by the change introduced into the experiment?

Such sequences of questions prime the student for success by reviewing the prerequisites, then calling for the use of information. In this way, students move from simple to complex behaviors and have more possibility for success.

Asking Questions Appropriately

Finally we should consider the manner in which questions are put to the students. Nearly every student has been subjected to rapid-fire questions, to unclear questions, to "tooth-pulling" questions, or to statements which suddenly become questions; none of these give the student a chance to arrive at the correct answer. Certain principles, however, do help the teacher to ask questions in a way that will allow students to answer correctly.

1. *Ask only one question at a time.* Asking, "What are three characteristics of green plants?" is more appropriate than asking: "What are the characteristics of green plants? Do you think all plants have these same characteristics? If all plants don't have the same characteristics what do they have?" Asking three questions at once only confuses the student by permitting him or her no time to think, and because there are three questions requiring different responses, the student has no idea which question to answer.

2. *Phrase questions as questions, rather than starting with a statement and finishing with a question.* Rather than, "Dinosaurs ruled the Earth for millions of years during what eras?" ask: "During what eras did dinosaurs rule the Earth?" By beginning with a statement and ending with a question, you cause the students to have to switch gears midsentence, because different listening skills are used for statements and questions.

3. *Ask a question before designating who is to answer the question.* "John, what instrument is used to measure mass?" immediately tells the other students in the class that there is no need to listen further; John is going to answer so no one else must be concerned. A better form is: "What instrument is used to measure mass? John?"

4. *Ask questions suited to all of the students in the class.* Some questions should be easy and some difficult so that all children have a chance to respond correctly.

5. *Ask questions that students can answer.* Questions that students cannot be expected to answer because they lack experience are frustrating to the teacher and simply unfair to the students. Children who are just beginning a unit of work dealing with matter cannot be expected to answer a question like: "What is the difference between an element and a compound?" The teacher who asks this as a lead-in to a lesson on elements and compounds can be successful only

in giving the students a message that they are stupid — they do not know the answer to a question the teacher seems to think they should know.

6. *Ask questions that elicit a variety of responses.* Such questions can be used even when a certain answer is desired since it is always possible to go back to the desired response. When many answers are given to a question, it is helpful to use the chalkboard or an overhead projector to make a record of the answers. Then, even if the first child to reply had the desired answer, it will still be there to review.

7. *Ask questions that have been carefully planned to lead to the objectives of the lesson.* Planning questions in advance not only permits the teacher to be certain they will be appropriate to the lesson and will address a variety of levels, but also provides a jog for the teacher's memory during a lesson.

Listening to Children's Responses

Asking questions requires certain strategies of sequencing and of presentation. But once the question is asked the teacher's role in questioning does not end. As children respond the teacher should practice good listening skills:

1. *Listen to the answers that the children give.* A nod, a smile, or just standing near the responding individual, all help that child know that you are listening and interested in what he or she is saying.

2. *Ask for clarification from the child when the answer is not clear.* Rather than trying yourself to tell the child what he or she said, have the child tell you more about the answer and try to clarify the material. Only then should the teacher try to clarify. An opening statement like, "I think this is what you are saying. Tell me if I'm right," is a good way of indicating that you value the child's answer but are not quite certain of its meaning.

3. *Provide equipment, materials, or drawings, which are referred to in the question.* Some children find it much easier to talk about materials if they have those materials in their hands.

4. *Reward student answers with discretion.* Every answer does not need to be rewarded. When you give a reward be certain that the student understands what is being rewarded. Is that word "good" expressed for effort, creativity, a correct answer, or for being the first to respond?

5. *Try to find the cause of incorrect answers.* Ask the student how he or she came to a certain answer. Only by determining the reason for an incorrect response can the teacher provide an explanation that will allow the student to change it to a correct one.

6. *Try not to reject an answer out of hand.* Some of the answers children give may not seem to have any bearing on the questions, but they may have bearing in the mind of the child. Rather than reject an answer or admonish the child to listen more carefully or not be silly, ask the child for further information. The child may see a direct connection to the question.

Questions from Children

On the other side of the firing line, the teacher is often asked questions by the children in a class. When those questions lend themselves to concrete investigation with materials, children should be encouraged to try to use those materials to find their own answers. When students can be guided to sources of information where they can find information for themselves, they should be given such guidance. Teaching is not telling, even if the teacher knows the exact answer to a question.

But, there are bound to be many questions the teacher cannot answer. When this occurs, a simple, "I really don't know," followed by, "How could we find out?" usually works very well. This strategy also provides the teacher with a real situation in which to have the students apply problem solving skills.

Questioning, then, involves not only knowing the most appropriate way to ask and reply to a question but also knowing how to get children to reply at their maximum level. This last skill, getting children to reply at a high level, deserves a great deal of attention from teachers. A particularly powerful strategy for eliciting high-level responses is called "wait time."

Wait Time

Definition

Children need time to think, time to ponder the answers they will give to the questions asked during a lesson in science. During a recently observed science lesson, the teacher sat on a stool in the front of the class and asked sixty-four questions during a fifteen-minute period. At a rate of more than four questions per minute, the questions came so quickly that the children began to look glassy-eyed. The first four minutes of the lesson proceeded according to the following script:

TEACHER: How many body parts does an insect have?
STUDENT: Three.
TEACHER: How many legs does an insect have?
STUDENT: Six.
TEACHER: What are the names of the three body parts?
STUDENT: Head, thorax, abdomen.
TEACHER: What name is given to the outer skeleton of an insect?
STUDENT: Exoskeleton.
TEACHER: What is the exoskeleton made from?
STUDENT: Chitin.
TEACHER: What are three helpful insects?
STUDENT: Bee, praying mantis, ladybug.
TEACHER: What are three harmful insects?
STUDENT: Locusts, termites, mosquitoes.

TEACHER: What can be used in a garden to kill harmful insects?
STUDENT: A pesticide.
TEACHER: What harm can a pesticide do?
STUDENT: It can get into the food chain.
TEACHER: What is a food chain?
STUDENT: It shows which animals eat plants and which eat other animals.
TEACHER: Name one insect that eats other insects.
STUDENT: Praying mantis.
TEACHER: Name one insect that eats plants.
STUDENT: Aphid.

This question-and-answer period continued for another eleven minutes. Only once did the teacher depart from the knowledge level questions illustrated here. She asked one application question, but when an answer did not come immediately, the teacher supplied the answer herself.

The pattern of this questioning is all too typical in the elementary school classroom:

Teacher——————→Student *A*
Teacher——————→Student *B*
Teacher——————→Student *C*

Other students do not have the opportunity to comment or to ask questions. In most cases, the answers given to the teacher consist of only one or two words, not even sentence fragments. The questions asked are at the knowledge level. Higher level questions cannot be asked when the set-up requires four or more questions and their answers every minute.

A much better way of asking questions gives students time to think, provides time for answering, and even provides time for other students to comment. This time provided for students to think and for students to respond to one another is called "wait time." Generally we describe it as five seconds between when a question is asked and when a child is called on to respond. In addition, wait time includes a few seconds after the child answers, so that the teacher can be certain the child is finished talking and can allow other children to comment.

Lead-ins that Provide Wait Time. Wait time should follow a question asked by the teacher. Since most children are not used to being given time to think, lead-ins to questions are helpful. These lead-ins alert students to the fact that they will actually have time to consider their answers. Some possible lead-ins include:

1. I want each of you to think about what you are going to answer, so I'm not going to call on anyone right away.
2. Think about this question. When you have an idea raise your hand. As soon as I see you, put your hand down until others have some ideas as well.

3. Think about what you have just seen happen and decide on one reason you think it happened. I'll give you some time to think before you answer.
4. Johnny said:______________. Think about that for a few minutes. Do you agree or disagree with his idea? Why?
5. Think about this question, and as you are thinking, write down some ideas that come to mind. Be ready to share your ideas with others.

Once children realize that they will actually have time to think, they tend to use that time effectively. One thing that the teacher must keep in mind, however, is that the first child to put up a hand should not always be called on to respond. Rewards should go to the children who really think about their answers as well as to the child who is fast about getting a hand raised.

Results of Using Wait Time

The Changing Pattern of Response. A period of wait time following a question can change the sequence of response from:

Teacher ——————→ Student
Teacher ——————→ Student

to

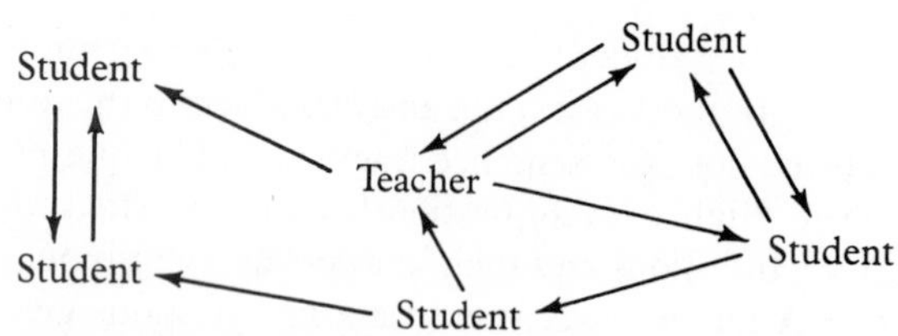

Rather than a question-answer session, the lesson becomes a discussion. Students comment on answers given by other students, ask each other questions, turn to the teacher for a response (not a question), then continue from there.

The use of wait time is a powerful technique; one teacher developed her technique to the extent that she changed her class of twenty-five students only one of whom gave a desultory answer to a single question to a class where all of the students commented eagerly.

Benefits of Wait Time to Children. A number of benefits result from the use of a period of wait time both after a question is asked and after a student responds:

1. Teacher-centered questioning periods decrease, while child-to-child interaction increases.
2. Children show more indications of listening to one another rather than listening for the next question.

3. Fewer questions remain unanswered or receive an "I don't know" answer.
4. Students give longer responses to questions and use phrases and sentences rather than single words.
5. More students give evidence to support their responses or make inferences from data that they collect.
6. Rather than simply replying with memorized, factual information, students engage in speculative thinking.
7. More students contribute unsolicited, but appropriate, responses. The lesson, therefore, becomes more student oriented.
8. The number of questions the children ask increases, and the number of experiments the children propose increases as well.
9. The number of students who respond to questions increases. Rather than eliciting answers from a few facile thinkers, wait time allows the class ponderers and the so-called slow children time to think and develop answers.
10. Confidence in expressing ideas increases. Use of the vocal inflection that asks "is that right" decreases.
11. Children become more frequent inquirers into science rather than readers of science.

Benefits of Wait Time to Teachers. The effect of wait time on children is impressive, but wait time also has effects on the teacher. First, the teacher tends to respond to students with a more flexibile attitude and is more flexible in the range of acceptable answers; rather than a single correct answer, a variety of answers are permissible.

Second, the number and kinds of questions change. The number of questions decreases. It is simply impossible for the teacher to ask the same number of questions, when he or she allows time for thought, and student responses become more complex. Also, the kind of question changes as the teacher asks more high-level cognitive questions rather than simple knowledge level questions. High-level questions such as those on the analysis and synthesis levels require more time for thought and response.

Finally, the teacher's expectations of students change. Children who were thought to be slow or nonverbal are seen as capable. Not only do more children become bright and verbal in the eyes of their peers, but those who appeared to be average and perhaps unable to handle high-level thinking become more capable. Children come to be viewed as learners rather than as memorizers.

Using Rewards with Wait Time

The benefits of wait time can be negated by inappropriate and constant application of rewards. Rewards are those encouragements the teacher gives to students as the result of some behavior. Words like "good," "super," "what a great idea," etc., are all rewards.

Although some rewards are good, the too frequent application of rewards can negate the good effects of wait time. Wait time is designed to allow many children to answer, to encourage speculative thinking, and to enhance inquiry behaviors. If the teacher rewards children early in the answering sequence, other children may decide not to respond because they fear their answers could not be as good as the first response. Consider the following:

TEACHER: What are some of the ways of telling what kind of weather is headed our way?
STUDENTS: (A dozen children raise their hands.)
TEACHER: Tommy?
TOMMY: The kinds of clouds and the way the wind is blowing.
TEACHER: Excellent answer! That's exactly right!
STUDENTS: (Eleven hands go down.)

Although these students had a number of answers, they no longer had the inclination to answer. After all, Tommy's was so good they could not possibly compete. And, if Tommy's answer was "exactly right," it was quite possible that their answers were "exactly wrong." Rather than rewarding Tommy so profusely, the teacher should have had as many children as possible answer, rewarded all of them, then returned to Tommy's answer as the best way to get into the lesson.

Wait time is also designed to allow children to exercise their inquiry skills. The idea of inquiry carries with it the connotation that all ideas are of equal value until evidence to the contrary is gathered. Such evidence enables the individual to differentiate between those ideas with supporting evidence and those without such evidence. A reward immediately designates one idea as correct and implies that another is incorrect. Therefore, says the child, if a particular idea is correct there is no need for further inquiry.

The key to the exploitation of wait time and the acquisition of all of its benefits is to use rewards sparingly. Reward all answers at the same time, then return to the answer that will best help children to understand the concepts being considered in the science lesson.

Summary

Asking good questions in a science lesson involves more than simply phrasing a question clearly. First, the teacher needs to determine the purpose of the question. Is the question to determine whether the child holds certain information in his or her memory or is the question to determine whether the child can use that knowledge in some way? Second, the teacher needs to ask questions which will elicit a variety of cognitive behaviors, ranging from knowledge level recall, to the creativity of synthesis, to the judgmental behaviors of evaluation. Third, the teacher needs to allow time for thought processes, as well as for a student to finish a response. Remember, it can take two seconds or more for a student to do a hierarchical search through his or her memory. The child needs time to recall information and to shape that information into a response. Finally, the teacher needs to know how to respond effectively to questions, both to stimulate discussion and to reward ideas. Two keys here are to listen carefully and to reward sparingly.

Learning Activity 6–5

Investigating Wait Time

Find an activity that you could use with a small group of elementary grade children. Make a list of questions that you could ask before and after the activity.

Present your activity to two small groups of children on the same grade level. With the first group, ask the questions without allowing wait time. With the second group, ask the questions using wait time.

Record both of the lessons on audio or video tape. Listen to or view each of the tapes. What effect did wait time have on the activity and on the way the children responded to the questions?

Learning Activity 6–6

Investigating Textbook Questions

Choose a textbook for any grade level first through sixth that has an accompanying teacher's manual. Choose one unit within that textbook and analyze the questions contained in the student text and the questions suggested by the teacher's edition. Include in your analysis any tests, quizzes, or review sections.

What types of questions are most frequently used: convergent or divergent? Into which levels of Bloom's Taxonomy do the questions fall? What suggestions would you make to a teacher about the use of the textbook to improve questioning strategies?

Learning Activity 6–7

Analyzing Classroom Questions

Read each of the following questioning scripts. Using the information in this chapter, analyze each of the scripts for the questioning techniques being used. What suggestions for improvement would you offer to each of the teachers in the scripts?

Questioning Script One (time — two minutes):

TEACHER: Adam, what word is used for all of the air around the Earth?

ADAM: Atmosphere.

TEACHER: Carol, what happens to the atmosphere as you get higher up?

CAROL: It gets thinner.

TEACHER: Ed, is the atmosphere a mixture or a solution?

ED: A mixture.

TEACHER: Gina, what holds the air to the Earth's surface?

GINA: Gravity.

TEACHER: Inez, what is the most abundant gas in the atmosphere?

INEZ: Nitrogen.

TEACHER: Ken, what percentage of the atmosphere is nitrogen?

KEN: About 78 percent.

TEACHER: Mark, do we breathe nitrogen?

MARK: No.

TEACHER: Oscar, what gas do we breathe?

OSCAR: Oxygen.

TEACHER: Patsy, what percentage of the atmosphere is oxygen?

PATSY: About 21 percent.

TEACHER: Ricky, what is the next important gas in the atmosphere?

RICKY: Carbon monoxide.

TEACHER: That's carbon *di*oxide. Tom, what percentage of the atmosphere is carbon dioxide?

TOM: About .03 percent.

TEACHER: Vic, what makes carbon dioxide so important?

VIC: Plants use it to make food.

TEACHER: What gas do plants release when they make food, Joan?

JOAN: Oxygen.

TEACHER: Is nitrogen the most plentiful gas in the solar system, Tony?

TONY: No.

TEACHER: Frank, what is the most plentiful gas in the solar system?

FRANK: Hydrogen.

Questioning Script Two

TEACHER: What is the most important characteristic of a mammal? Tom?

TOM: It has fur.

TEACHER: No. I want the most important characteristic. Maria?

MARIA: It has live babies?

TEACHER: Let's not guess! What is the most important characteristic? Todd?

TODD: It has warm blood?

TEACHER: So do birds, Todd. What is the *most important* characteristic? Janice?

JANICE: It feeds milk to its babies?

TEACHER: Good. I'm glad to see someone read the homework assignment.

End of questioning. The teacher began to use expository teaching.

Questioning Script Three:

TEACHER: In this demonstration, the amount of matter in the container before the steel wool rusted should be the same as the amount of matter in the container after the steel wool rusted. But our container weighed more before the steel wool rusted than it did after. What could be some of the reasons why ours weighed more before rusting than it did after rusting? Betsy?

BETSY: There could be a leak around the edge of the plastic wrap on top of the jar so some of the water evaporated.

TEACHER: What an excellent answer! That really shows you were observing and thinking! Now, what could be some other reasons?

[No one else answered.]

Questioning Script Four:

TEACHER: Your book talks about some things that plants have. Who can name some? Susan?

SUSAN: Flowers.

TEACHER: Good. Plants have flowers. Flowers are used by plants to . . . what? What do flowers do for plants? Are flowers important to plants? John?

JOHN: Flowers are used to make seeds.

TEACHER: Listen to the question. Are flowers important? Now, John?

JOHN: Yes.

TEACHER: Flowers are important because they make seeds, and they also do what else? Terrie?

TERRIE: They make the garden pretty.

TEACHER: Yes, they do make a garden look pretty. What other things do flowers have? Think about that. What are some of the other parts of a plant? Is the whole plant made up of the flower? What other parts are there? Ray?

RAY: Leaves, stems, roots, flowers. . . .

TEACHER: [Interrupting] That's enough. Leave some for others. Ray said leaves, roots, stems, and flowers. What is the other part? We already know that there are leaves, roots, stems, and flowers. What else? Elsie?

ELSIE: Aren't there *two* more parts? Seeds and fruit?

TEACHER: Yes, Elsie, you're absolutely right. There were two more parts rather than just one more part. Now, how many parts does a plant have all together? Terrie?

TERRIE: Six.

Questioning Script Five:

TEACHER: In this demonstration, the egg was supposed to go into the bottle. Ours didn't do that. What happened instead? [Pause] Joey?

JOEY: The egg split in half and a little of the white fell into the bottle and got burned. The rest just stayed on top.

TEACHER: That's exactly what happened. What could be some of the reasons why the entire egg didn't go into the bottle the way it was supposed to? [Pause] Jean?

JEAN: Maybe the egg was too big.

TEACHER: Carlos?

CARLOS: Maybe the fire in the bottom of the bottle went out too fast so you didn't get a vacuum.

TEACHER: We've got two possibilities. What else? [Pause] Lee?

LEE: Maybe the bottle got too hot and made the egg hot and the egg got bigger than the top of the bottle and so it wouldn't fit through.

TOM: But the bottle would get hot, too, and expand so the egg should fall in. Maybe the egg was . . . or the jar . . . was sticky.

CATHY: Maybe the air pressure outside isn't high enough today to push the egg into the bottle.

MARIA: Maybe the egg needs to have the shell left on.
JACK: Maybe you shouldn't burn the paper in the bottle. Just put the egg on top.
TEACHER: Let's get one last answer. Mark?
MARK: Maybe you need a bottle with a different shape.
TEACHER: All of you have fine ideas. Let's look in our textbooks and see which of them was right. Open to page 212.

Questioning Script Six:

TEACHER: According to the film that we just saw, what characteristics most distinguish birds from other animals? Jason?
JASON: They have feathers.
TEACHER: What were the three functions of feathers mentioned in the film? Martha?
MARTHA: For warmth, for flying, and. . . .
TEACHER: The third one is to shed water. What did the film mean when it used the word "Camouflage"? [Pause] Tony?
TONY: I think it meant that some kinds of birds hide.
TEACHER: OK. What else does it mean?
WILL: They hide without really hiding. It's like you can't see them, but they're really there.
TEACHER: Good, but please remember to raise your hand. Joe?
JOE: I know what he means. It's like they blend into the ground or the grass.
TEACHER: Sandra?
SANDRA: Like a white . . . uh. . . . I don't remember the bird's name . . . but that white. . . .
TEACHER: What was the name of the bird? Paul?
PAUL: Ptarmigan.
TEACHER: Good. Go on, Sandra.
SANDRA: I forgot.
TEACHER: Jason?
JASON: Camouflage means something can hide because it has coloring like the place where it lives. It blends into the background so you can't see it.
TEACHER: Very good, Jason. I know I can always count on you. What were some of the birds in the film that used camouflage? Let's get someone other than Jason.

Selected References

Bloom, B. S., ed. *Taxonomy of Educational Objectives: The Classification of Educational Goals. Handbook I: The Cognitive Domain.* New York: McCay, 1956.

Blosser, P. E. *How to Ask the Right Questions.* Washington, D.C.: National Science Teacher's Association, 1975.

Rowe, M. B. Wait-time and rewards as instructional variables, their influence on language, logic, and fate control: Part one, wait-time. *Journal of Research in Science Teaching, 11,* 2, 1974.

———. Relation of wait-time and rewards to the development of language, logic, and fate control: Part two, rewards. *Journal of Research in Science Teaching, 11,* 4, 1974.

———. Pausing phenomena: Influence on the quality of instruction. *Journal of Psycholinguistic Research, 3,* 3, 1974.

Sanders, N. M. *Classroom Questions: What Kinds?* New York: Harper, 1966.

Tisher, R. R. Verbal interaction in science classes. *Journal of Research in Science Teaching, 8,* 1, 1971.

Trefil, J. S. *The Unexpected Vista: A Physicist's View of Nature.* New York: Scribner, 1983.

> As a teacher he is not concerned with adding new facts to the science he teaches; in propounding new hypotheses or in verifying them. He is concerned with the subject-matter of the science as representing a given stage and phase of the development of experience. His problem is that of inducing a vital and personal experiencing.
>
> — Dewey, 1961

7 Methods of Teaching Science

Chapter Objectives:

Upon completion of this chapter you should be able to

1. list the eight most common methods of science teaching: exposition, exposition with interaction, discussion, Socratic, ordinary demonstration, problem solving demonstration, guided discovery, and open inquiry;
2. identify the common problems that may be encountered in using each of the common methods of science teaching;
3. identify the most appropriate use of each of the common methods of science teaching;
4. write a lesson plan illustrating good science teaching;
5. demonstrate how a textbook can be enhanced through a variety of teaching methods.

Throughout this text you have worked with children and have read descriptions of how children react in various situations. Teaching an effective science lesson, however, involves a good deal more than simply presenting materials and waiting to see what happens. A science lesson should be a teacher's organized attempt to accomplish an objective in a way appropriate to both the children and the material being taught. Teachers are not engaged in teaching either science *or* children but in teaching science to children. For a lesson to be effective, the teacher must insure compatibility between the child and the subject matter.

Because any form of presentation becomes tiresome, because all children do not learn in the same way, because all subject matter cannot be presented effectively in the same way, and because the teacher is frequently constrained by time, eight different teaching methods are offered in this chapter. Before the specific methods are considered, let us consider some general suggestions on planning.

Planning for Teaching

Common Factors in Science Lessons

Whether the choice for a lesson is strict exposition (lecture) or open inquiry, all lessons have three common factors:

1. Some objective or objectives are to be attained by the learner.
2. A logical means of presentation is evident.
3. Some means for evaluating the effectiveness of the lesson for the learner and for the teacher is present.

The simplest way to assure organization is to plan the lesson according to an organized form — a lesson plan. There are, of course, many different strategies for planning lessons. Many teachers develop their own personal style for planning lessons, but it is helpful for the new teacher to have some starting point from which he or she can later individualize.

Long-Range Planning

Planning for the Total Program. Before actually starting to write a lesson plan, review all of the material to be covered in a particular unit of work. Determine the goals of a particular section or unit of science, then plan individual lessons to lead to those goals. Always plan according to the total program rather than for an isolated lesson. Be prepared as lessons are taught to make changes, to adjust the lesson to fit the students, and to add or delete lessons when it becomes evident that a particular content area or a certain process will require a different amount of teaching time.

Long-Range Plans. As you make long-range plans, you must consider a number of questions. First, what are the final outcomes for the unit? Second, what should children be able to do if they have learned the material? Third, what skills or content must children learn in order to accomplish the object? Fourth, what order would be most logical for presentation of the new skills or content? Fifth, how much time will be needed to teach each skill or content segment? And, finally, how can you determine whether the children have actually learned the material?

An Example of Long-Range Planning. As an example, consider the following section of work, planned for a sixth grade class, dealing with the process of controlling variables. The final outcome of the unit would be to have the children control variables in an experimental setting.

Skills. To be able to identify variables and constants in a system the children will need to acquire various skills. They need to be able to:

1. define independent variable, dependent variable, and constant;
2. recognize independent variables, dependent variables, and constants in an experiment;
3. identify the components of a system;
4. define a system;
5. define variable and constant;
6. recognize variables and constants in a system;
7. list the characteristics of an experiment;
8. control variables during an experiment.

Ordering the Skills. Once the teacher identifies the skills leading to the objective, by studying the information given by the textbook or program, his or her next step is to order those points in a logical teaching sequence. Skills must be learned before they can be applied. One possible way of organizing these eight skills is:

1. define a system;
2. identify the components of a system;
3. list the characteristics of an experiment;
4. define variable and constant;
5. recognize variables and constants in a system;
6. define independent variable, dependent variable, and constant;
7. recognize independent variables, dependent variables, and constants in an experiment;
8. control variables in an experiment.

Time Planning. The next step in long-range planning is for the teacher to determine how much time will be devoted to each of the skills. The time allocation should be appropriate to the total amount of time to be spent on the topic as well as to the importance of each specific skill to the topic as a whole.

Supposing that three weeks are to be allowed for teaching control of variables — fifteen teaching days — charting the concepts to be taught, as in Table 7–1, can help you to determine a time frame. The total of only twelve classes allows extra time for review, reteaching, extra practice, or pursuit of special interests.

Writing Objectives. Finally, for each of the skills you list you should identify a means by which it may be determined if the child has reached the skill. One effective way to show what a child will be able to do as a result of learning a particular concept is to define a behavioral objective.

Again consider the eight skills one needs in order to control variables in an experimental situation. This time each is shown with its corresponding objective.

SKILL 1 — DEFINE A SYSTEM:

OBJECTIVE: After listening to a review presented by the teacher each child will be able to define in writing the term "system."

SKILL 2 — IDENTIFY THE COMPONENTS OF A SYSTEM:

OBJECTIVE: After watching the "collapsing can" demonstration each child will be able to identify five of the six parts of the system: can, hot plate, can lid, electricity, water, air.

SKILL 3 — LIST THE CHARACTERISTICS OF AN EXPERIMENT:

OBJECTIVE: After following the directions given for a teacher planned experiment on the effect of temperature on the solubility of salt in water, each student will be able to list four of the five characteristics of an experiment: hypothesis, control of variables, set procedure, data collection, conclusion drawn from the data.

SKILL 4 — DEFINE VARIABLE AND CONSTANT:

OBJECTIVE: After participating in a group activity dealing with pulse rate and exercise, each student will be able orally to define the terms variable and constant.

Table 7–1 Determining a time frame (control of variables)

CONCEPT	TEACHING ACTIVITY	TIME
1. define system	review	½ class period
2. identify system components	review	½ class period
3. list experiment characteristics	review	1 class period
4. define variable and constant	introduce	1 class period
5. recognize variables and constants in a system	develop previous concept	2 class periods
6. define independent and dependent variables, constants	introduce	2 class periods
7. recognize variables and constants in an experiment	develop previous concept	2 class periods
8. control variables in an experiment	develop previous concept	3 class periods

SKILL 5 — RECOGNIZE THE VARIABLES AND CONSTANTS IN A SYSTEM:

OBJECTIVE: After watching four demonstrations, each student will be able to list the two main variables and three of the constants present in any three of the demonstrations.

SKILL 6 — DEFINE INDEPENDENT VARIABLE, DEPENDENT VARIABLE, AND CONSTANT:

OBJECTIVE: After reviewing the activity dealing with pulse rate and exercise, each student will be able to define orally the terms independent variable, dependent variable, and constant.

SKILL 7 — RECOGNIZE THE INDEPENDENT VARIABLE, DEPENDENT VARIABLE, AND THE CONSTANTS IN AN EXPERIMENT:

OBJECTIVE: (a) Given the procedure for an experiment, each child will be able to carry out the experiment and in a class discussion, identify the independent variable, the dependent variable, and four factors held constant.

(b) Given the procedure for an experiment, each child will be able to carry out the experiment and then identify in writing the independent variable, dependent variable, and at least four factors held constant.

SKILL 8 — CONTROL THE VARIABLES IN AN EXPERIMENT:

OBJECTIVE: (a) Given an hypothesis each child will develop an experiment in which a single variable is manipulated and all others are held constant.

(b) Following an open-ended activity each child will be able to (1) write three operational questions, (2) devise a procedure in which variables are controlled to answer one of the operational questions, and (3) carry out the procedure.

In reviewing these objectives, notice that they not only describe what the child will be able to do, but also imply how the teacher will teach the lesson and how the teacher will evaluate the lesson.

The objective for Skill 1 states: after listening to a review presented by the teacher, each child will be able to define in writing the term "system." The teacher is, obviously, going to be the center of attention as he or she reviews the previously learned concept of system. No new material will be included. In order to determine if children know this definition, the teacher will ask them to write it. The teacher can then review the written statements to determine whether the objective has been met. This is a knowledge level objective: the children are asked to recall information presented by the teacher.

In contrast, the objective for Skill 8 states: following an open-ended activity each child will be able to (1) write three operational questions, (2) develop a procedure using control of variables which will answer one of the questions, and (3) carry out the procedure. In this case, the child's own activity is the focal point of the lesson. The teacher provides the starting activity, support, advice, and encouragement, but no definite information. Instead of recalling information the child must apply the concepts of variables, constants, and experiments to the development of a new experiment. The child is working at both the application and synthesis levels. One would evaluate this objective by determining the answers to these questions:

1. Did the child write three operational questions?
2. Are the questions truly operational?
3. Did the child develop a procedure to answer one of the questions?
4. Does the child's procedure control variables?
5. Did the child carry out the experimental procedure?

An Example of Long-Range Planning for Content Teaching. Processes are only one aspect of science teaching. In planning a total science program in the elementary school, it is also necessary to make long-range plans for the teaching of content. Consider the following section of a lesson from a fourth grade science textbook. The final outcome of the section is that children will understand that the Earth has changed over its billions of years of history.

The concepts to which children are introduced in the Figure 7–1 science lesson include:

1. Rocks can be dated using radioactivity.
2. Radioactivity tests have been used on both earth rocks and moon rocks.
3. Any evidence of a plant or animal that once lived on earth is called a fossil.
4. Fossils are found in sedimentary rocks.
5. Most fossils are of plants and animals that lived in or near water.
6. Geologic history is a record of what has happened on earth from the beginning of time to the present.
7. Geologic history is written in rocks and fossils.
8. A mold fossil is a print of something that lived.
9. A cast fossil is made when animal or plant parts decay in sediments and the resulting space is filled with other sediments or materials.
10. A mummy results when an entire body is trapped and does not decay.
11. Incomplete fossils can be made more complete by comparing the fossil with modern animals and then filling in the missing pieces.
12. Fossils can reveal what happened on earth a long time ago.
13. Petrified wood is fossil wood made by minerals acting on the wood.

Ordering the Concepts. Once the teacher has identified the concepts that will lead to the general concept for the section, by reading the textbook and the teacher's manual, the next step is to order those concepts in a manner appropriate to the class. During this ordering procedure it may become evident that some of the concepts are actually subconcepts that will contribute to an understanding of the more general, major concepts. One way of ordering these concepts and subconcepts is as follows:

1. Geologic history is a record of what has happened on earth from the beginning of time to the present.
   a. Rocks can be dated using radioactivity.
   b. Radioactivity tests have been used on both earth rocks and moon rocks.

Figure 7–1 Sample science textbook lesson

FOSSILS AND ROCKS

You have learned that sediments can be pressed into rocks. But sand and mud aren't the only materials that have changed into rocks. Some materials were whole plants and animals that died long ago. More often, they were only parts of living things. Examples of these are leaves, pollen, shells, teeth, and bones. Any evidence of a plant or an animal that once lived on the earth is called a **fossil.**

Billions of plants and animals have lived on earth. But only a few have left fossils. Most fossils formed from shells and bones and from the woody parts of plants. But some animals, such as jellyfish and earthworms, do not have hard parts. So fossils of soft-bodied animals are rarely found. Their bodies either decayed rapidly or they were destroyed by pressure.

Most fossils are of plants and animals that lived in or near the water. Why is this true? A few land animals were trapped in the mud of rivers and swamps. Fossils of those animals formed if their bodies were quickly covered with sediments. The sediments kept air from the bodies. Nearly all bacteria (bak tir ē ə) that cause decay need oxygen. So bacteria did not change the remains.

Most fossils are found in sedimentary rocks. Look at the pictures on page 22. Can you describe the steps in the formation of this fossil? In the third picture, the water from the lake has disappeared. Plants are growing where the water once was. Forces deep in the earth have pushed the layer with the fossil up to the surface. It took a very long time for all this to happen.

Have you ever visited a museum? If you have, you have seen many things that were collected from the past. Often, different things were grouped according to how old they are. This is what happens in the earth. Some layers of rock are older than others. Fossils found in the same layer were probably formed about the same time. Sedimentary rocks are like museums. By studying the fossils in different layers, scientists can write a history of life on earth. They can tell how living things have changed through time.

GEOLOGIC TIME

The study of the earth is called **geology** (jē ol′ ə jē). The record of what has happened on the earth is called **geologic** (jē ə loj′ik) **history.** It begins with the beginning of the earth. It continues right up to the present time.

SOURCE: Mallinson, G.G., et al. *Science: Understanding Your Environment, Book 4, Teacher's Edition.* Silver Burdett Company, 1981, pp. 22–23. Reprinted by permission.

2. Geologic history is written in rocks and fossils.
   a. Fossils can reveal what happened on earth long ago.
3. Any evidence of a plant or animal that once lived on earth is called a fossil.
   a. Fossils are found in sedimentary rocks.
   b. Most fossils are of plants and animals that lived in or near water.
   c. A mold fossil is a print of something that once lived.
   d. A cast fossil is made when animal or plant parts decay in sediments and the resulting space is filled with other sediments or materials.
   e. A mummy results when an entire body is trapped and does not decay.
   f. Petrified wood is fossil wood made by minerals acting on the wood.
   g. Incomplete fossils can be made more complete by comparing them with modern animals and then filling in the missing pieces.

Time Planning. The third step in long-range planning for content teaching is to determine how much time will be devoted to each concept and subconcept. The time frame should suit the total amount of time to be spent on the topic, as well as the importance of each concept and subconcept to the topic as a whole.

Considering that the concepts used in this example are a small part of a textbook section dealing with the earth and its history, only two weeks will be allotted to the material: ten teaching days. Table 7–2 shows how to plan teaching the ordered concepts.

Writing Objectives. Finally, for each of the concepts and subconcepts listed, a means of determining if the child has grasped the concept should be identified.

Again consider the concepts which have been developed for this particular section of the unit on earth history. This time each of the major concepts and three subconcepts is shown with the corresponding objective. In actual planning for teaching all of the concepts and subconcepts would be translated into the objective form.

CONCEPT 1: GEOLOGIC HISTORY IS A RECORD OF WHAT HAS HAPPENED ON EARTH FROM THE BEGINNING OF TIME TO THE PRESENT.

OBJECTIVE: After viewing a filmstrip dealing with the concept of geologic history and reading the text section, each child will be able to define the term "geologic history" in his or her own words.

CONCEPT 2: GEOLOGIC HISTORY IS WRITTEN IN ROCKS AND FOSSILS.

OBJECTIVE: Following a field trip to a local area where fossils are found, each student will be able to draw a picture showing how fossils indicate the geologic history of an area.

CONCEPT 3: ANY EVIDENCE OF A PLANT OR ANIMAL THAT ONCE LIVED ON THE EARTH IS CALLED A FOSSIL.

OBJECTIVE: After reviewing the field trip and the fossils found, each child will be able to define the term "fossil" in writing and then compare his or her definition with that found in the textbook.

Table 7–2 Determining a time frame (content teaching)

CONCEPT	TEACHING ACTIVITY	TIME
1. Geologic history is a record of what happened from the beginning of time to the present.	introduce	1 class period
a. Rocks can be dated using radioactivity.	introduce	½ class period
b. Radioactivity tests have been used on both earth rocks and moon rocks.	develop previous concept	½ class period
2. Geologic history is written in rocks and fossils.	develop concept one	1 class period
a. Fossils can reveal what happened on earth long ago.	develop concept two	1 class period
3. Any evidence of a plant or animal that once lived on earth is a fossil.	review (from previous grade)	½ class period
a. Fossils are found in sedimentary rocks.	review (from previous grade)	½ class period
b. Most fossils are of plants and animals that lived in or near water.	introduce	1 class period
c. A mold fossil is a print of something that lived.	introduce	1 class period
d. A cast fossil is made when animal or plant parts decay in sediments and the resulting space is filled with other sediments or materials.	introduce	1 class period
e. A mummy results when an entire body is trapped and does not decay.	introduce	½ class period
f. Petrified wood is fossil wood made by minerals acting on the wood.	introduce	½ class period
g. Incomplete fossils can be made more complete by comparing them with modern animals and then filling in the missing pieces.	introduce	1 class period

CONCEPT 3B: MOST FOSSILS ARE OF PLANTS AND ANIMALS THAT LIVED IN OR NEAR WATER.

OBJECTIVE: Following a research project in which each student is given a fossil to research and then shares with the class findings about where the organism lived, each student will be able to generalize that most fossil organisms lived in or near water.

CONCEPT 3F: PETRIFIED WOOD IS FOSSIL WOOD MADE BY MINERALS ACTING ON THE WOOD.

OBJECTIVE: After observing natural wood and petrified wood, each child will be able to make an inference about how petrified wood forms, and then check that inference against the textbook material.

CONCEPT 3G: INCOMPLETE FOSSILS CAN BE MADE MORE COMPLETE BY COMPARING THEM WITH MODERN ANIMALS AND THEN FILLING IN THE MISSING PIECES.

OBJECTIVE: Given a partial skeleton of an unknown animal, each small group of children will decide (a) how the bones might go together, (b) how the group could determine what the animal was, and (3) how they could reconstruct the rest of the animal. The results for each group will be presented to the class.

Once the time planning has been done and the objectives written, working with content involves the same tasks as developing process: writing the lesson plans or doing the short-range planning.

Short-Range Planning

Once the objectives for the lessons to be taught have been written, long-range planning is completed. The teacher, at this point, has an overview of the entire unit. Now, it is up to the teacher to plan individual, daily lessons: this is termed short-range planning.

Objectives can be written to elicit a variety of behaviors. The method the teacher uses to help children reach the behavior specified by the objective should match the objective as well as possible. Objective b for Skill 8 could not be accomplished through a lecture. It could, however, be accomplished through an open-inquiry lesson.

So that you will become better able to match objectives to methods, we will discuss a variety of teaching techniques in this chapter. A lesson plan, an example of short-range planning, is included with each method as an illustration of how the lesson would appear at the planning stage.

Method I: Exposition

Definition

Exposition includes those verbal methods in which some authority — textbook, teacher, speaker, film, or filmstrip — presents information without overt interaction taking place between the authority and the students. Most often the expository method is encountered as a lecture or a textbook reading.

Uses of Exposition

Although the expository teaching method is not highly recommended for extensive use in teaching science to children, it does have its place in the repertoire of the elementary teacher. Exposition can be effectively used in three ways:

1. to present background information that children will need in order to understand or be able to carry out an activity or an experiment;
2. to give directions for an activity, experiment, or other classroom procedure;
3. to wrap up an activity, experiment, or other classroom procedure.

Exposition for Providing Background Information. Before you show a film or filmstrip, an expository lesson can be effective. In this case, the brief exposition should indicate the important points the students should attend to during the film or filmstrip. Also, before you ask them to carry out an activity, you can offer an exposition to refresh the memories of children on necessary content or the use of equipment.

Exposition for Giving Directions. When giving directions for an activity, the teacher always uses the expository method. Certain *do not's* should be observed when giving directions as well as certain *do's*. First, do not give out materials before you give directions. The materials will be much more interesting than anything you can say. Second, do not expect children to follow written directions without your review of those directions. Third, do not expect children to understand directions without a myriad of questions, before they start the activity as well as during the activity. With all of the *do not's* in mind, do follow the following sequence for giving directions; it is effective when both written instructions and materials are to be used:

1. Read the instructions to the students.
2. Review the instructions by asking various students what should be done first, second, third, etc.
3. Give out the written instructions and have the children read them silently.
4. Ask for questions.
5. Have students get their materials.
6. Tell them to get to work. But, be prepared for questions once students start and circulate around the room to be certain students are following the instructions.

Exposition as a Wrap-Up to an Activity. Exposition can be used to wrap up a just completed activity. In this case, the follow-up lecture serves as a review of the salient points learned that day. It helps children to develop concepts by presenting the review of the activity in the same order as they met the points in the activity and by tying the material into what they already know.

Planning an Expository Lesson

For an expository lesson to be meaningful to the learner, David Ausubel (1963) has suggested that new information be related to the knowledge already possessed by the learner. The learner, therefore, should have encountered the material previously in some form. To assure that this encounter has occurred, the teacher should use an advance organizer as the first step in preparing an expository lesson.

Advance Organizers. An advance organizer is a verbal device, first suggested by Ausubel, that provides relevant introductory material, so that the learner has at least heard about the material to be presented in the lesson. The organizer presents a broad survey of the information to be covered in more detail during the exposition to follow. Advance organizers may be either expository or comparative.

Expository Organizers. When presenting completely unfamiliar material to the learner, the lecturer can use an expository organizer at the start of the lesson. Basically, the expository organizer presents several broad generalizations to which detail will be added. The speaker, in essence, states that he or she will consider certain points and lists those points in the order of their subsequent presentation.

For example, students in a fifth grade class are about to begin a unit on ecology. An advance organizer could take the following form: "Today, class, we'll be going on a field trip to the park. Before we go, there are three definitions that you need to know so that the activity will be easy to do. The first word is the topic of the new unit: *ecology*. The other two terms are words used to describe the way plants, animals, and the rest of the environment are related. The terms are *food web* and *food chain*."

With this brief bit of information as a starting point, the student is alerted to the fact that the important information in the lecture to come deals with the definitions of three terms. The listener is also alerted to the fact that those terms will help him to complete the activity in the park that day. This organizer tells the students what to listen for and why.

Comparative Organizers. The expository organizer is useful when the information to come is new to the listener. Many times, however, the listener possesses some knowledge similar to the new material. In that case, the lecturer can use a comparative organizer. A comparative organizer compares the new material to that already known in a way that will highlight the similarities between the two and will indicate, as well, what information is to come. A teacher could use the following organizer with children who are about to classify rocks for the first time and who have experience in classifying other objects.

"Last week we classified shells that we collected into a number of different groups. Some of the groups that we used were based on color, shine, weight, and even how hard they were. Today, we are going to be classifying rocks according to some of the characteristics used by geologists. Just like the shells, rocks can be classified by their color, their shine, their weight, and their hardness. There are some other characteristics that we can use as well, but first, we'll look at the same characteristics as we used for shells."

In this organizer, the students are reminded of something familiar: classifying shells. The shells' characteristics are reviewed. Then, the lecturer introduces the idea that rocks can be classified in the same way as shells are classified. Students are told that they will be using those same traits for rocks. This type of organizer is reassuring: the new material is not really new; it is just something familiar in a new guise.

Sequencing a Lesson. Once he or she has presented an organizer, the teacher must follow the sequence presented in the expository or comparative organizer. Following the presentation of the new material, the teacher should complete the lecture by once more pointing out the important points.

In developing background information through the use of the expository method remember to:

1. use an advance organizer;
2. follow up with the information you intend to present to your listeners;
3. be brief — children do not give attention to verbal presentations for long periods;
4. use pictures, drawings, charts, and models to add another dimension to the presentation.

Problems in Using the Expository Method

The expository method of teaching has inherent in it a number of problems, all of which stem from its strictly verbal nature:

1. Verbal presentations are difficult for children in the elementary grades to follow. Elementary grade children tend to need concrete materials in order to understand concepts and ideas.

2. Verbal presentations are limited by the child's attention span. Pictures, slides, and other visual aids help to maintain a high level of attention, but the total time is still short.

3. Verbal learning tends to be passive learning. Only the teacher is active in the learning process, whereas the child should be active.

4. Any verbal presentation is organized according to the teacher's idea of a logical order. That order may not be equally logical to the students.

5. What is said is not always what is heard. People interpret what they hear in terms of their own backgrounds. Consequently, the reception of something that seems to be clearly presented can be muddled by preconceptions, misconceptions, and previous experiences.

Lesson Plan 7–1
Exposition (Sixth Grade Level)

Topic: Introduction to the ecology of a field.

Objective: After listening to the material presented by the teacher, each student will be able to define in writing each of the following terms: mini-environment, food chain, food web.

Materials: chalkboard, chalk, masking tape, slides of field trip site, pictures of a rabbit, a dandelion, a stream, a hawk, a grasshopper, a deer, and a human.

Procedure:

1. *Advance Organizer:* Today we will be visiting a field not too far from the school in order to learn about the kinds of plants and animals that live there. More important, we will be considering how those plants and animals are related to one another. So that you will have a better understanding of the activity, there are some words you need to be able to define. These words are: mini-environment, food chain, and food web. First, we'll look at what is meant by a mini-environment. Second, we'll consider the idea of a food chain. And, finally, we'll consider the food web.
2. *Exposition:*
   a. Show slides of the area that will be visited, beginning with the broadest possible picture and ending with a marked section of one square meter.
   b. Point out the most important features of each slide using the term environment as it is appropriate. At the final slide indicate that the square meter section is a mini-environment: a small part of a larger area, which can be conveniently studied.
   c. Tape on the chalkboard the following pattern of pictures:

      stream←—dandelion←—rabbit←—human

      Draw chalk arrows between to show how one uses another for food in a linear chain.
   d. Using the sequence of pictures, define a food chain as the relationship between organisms and their environment that shows where food is obtained.
   e. Add to the linear chain the other pictures:

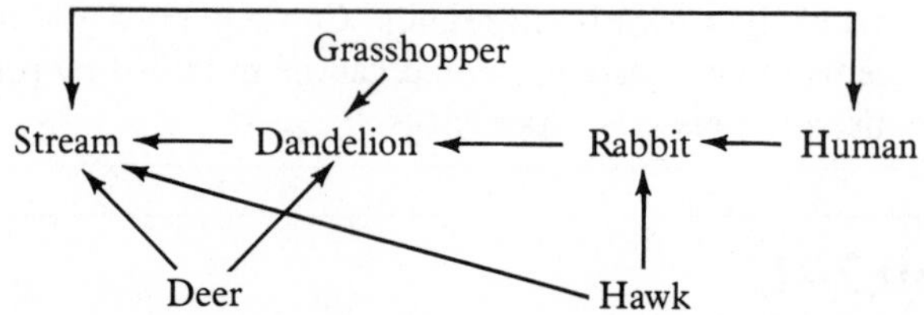

   f. Using the pictures, define a food web as the relationships that exist among food chains.
3. *Ending:*
   Review each of the three definitions by writing the term on the board and then orally defining it once again.

Evaluation: Give each student a sheet of paper with the terms mini-environment, food chain, and food web. Have each student define the terms in writing.

The purpose of this plan is to define the three terms in preparation for the activity to follow. The definitions are sufficient only as a basis. The activity that follows — a first-hand investigation of a field through isolation of a mini-environment outdoors — will more fully develop these concepts. However, with the basic ideas already implanted, students should better understand and retain the concepts of ecology developed during the activity.

Learning Activity 7–1

The Expository Teaching Method

Choose a unit or section from any textbook for grades one through six. Read the section thoroughly to determine the major thrust of the information. After determining the major thrust, write either an expository or a comparative advance organizer for the section of information.

Follow the organizer with a brief — ten- to fifteen-minute — lecture written in either paragraph or outline form. Be certain that the vocabulary you use is appropriate to the grade level of the material.

Prepare any visual aids you would need for the lecture.

Method II: Exposition with Interaction

Definition

Exposition with interaction is a method of teaching in which the teacher both presents information verbally and asks questions to determine whether that information is understood. The questions provide interaction between teacher and students.

Uses of Exposition with Interaction

The teacher can use exposition with interaction in two ways during the teaching of science. Similar to the ways in which exposition alone is used, exposition with interaction can be used to:

1. review previously learned content material,
2. present new content material.

Reviewing Old Content Material. Exposition with interaction permits the teacher both to present old material in a review session and to ask questions of students that will enable him or her to determine how well students have retained that information. By asking questions, the teacher can, in fact, permit the children to do the review session themselves.

Presenting New Content Material. In this application, the teacher uses exposition with interaction exactly as he or she uses expository teaching. The only difference between the two methods is the addition of questions by which the teacher will be able to determine whether the class understands the information presented.

Planning an Exposition with Interaction Lesson

One plans an exposition with interaction lesson in much the same way as an expository lesson. The lesson should begin with an advance organizer. If the lesson is to provide for a review, the organizer should remind children about the previously studied area. If the lesson is to present new material, then the organizer should provide general information about the topic to be studied.

Once he or she has written the organizer, the teacher should plan the lesson to include both content information and questions.

Content Information. The content information contained in exposition with interaction lessons should be presented in the same order as the generalizations were presented in the advance organizer. Once again, pictures, slides, diagrams, models, and drawings will be helpful in capturing student attention and in making the exposition clearer.

Questions. One of the purposes of the questions we ask during an exposition with interaction lesson is to determine the understanding of the children. Questions can, of course, be answered either correctly or incorrectly. Correct responses permit the teacher to continue with the planned lesson; there is no apparent need to repeat or expand on the information already presented. However, when the students give incorrect responses, the teacher must return to the point that is not understood and clarify it through further information or examples.

Because one of the advantages of exposition with interaction is the teacher's use of questions to determine understanding, the questions are better placed throughout the lecture rather than lumped together at the end. Major points can be developed, questions asked, and necessary clarification given before the lecture continues along its preplanned route.

Summary. Finally, in planning an exposition with interaction lesson, the teacher should expect to present a summary in which children respond to questions that will allow them to highlight the most important points of the lesson.

Planning for a Review Lesson. In using exposition with interaction for review, the lecturer's advance organizer need be little more than a reminder that the material is something previously learned. The teacher then reviews the major points of previous learning and asks questions after each of the reviewed points, both to determine understanding of those points and to recall previously learned material.

Problems in Using the Exposition with Interaction Method

As with any teaching method, exposition with interaction has certain problems:

1. It is a verbal method. The use of visual materials does help to clarify the words used as well as to focus attention, but the method is still verbal.
2. It is a passive method of teaching. Although the students do have some opportunity to be active through the questions, it is not the kind of interaction that permits students to develop their own ideas. Instead, the students need only return to the teacher what he or she has said.
3. The teacher does begin to learn how effective the lecture has been because of the students' responses to questions. However, not all of the students can answer all questions, so the teacher's determination of understanding will be sketchy at best.
4. For the teacher, this method has an additional problem: planning for non-understanding. When answers to questions are erroneous, the teacher needs to be able quickly to review the material and to present new examples and clarifications. This means that the teacher must have a thorough knowledge of the subject matter.

Both exposition and exposition with interaction are methods that we can use effectively to teach content. Because they are both verbal methods and do not utilize materials, we cannot use them to teach the processes of science. These two verbal methods can, however, provide introductory material that will enable children to understand more effectively the processes of science. By introducing basic vocabulary, expository methods also give children words they can use to describe and discuss their activities.

Lesson Plan 7–2
Exposition with Interaction (Fifth Grade Level)

Topic: Simple Machines

Objective: After listening to the material presented by the teacher each student will be able to define in writing each of the following terms: balanced, unbalanced, lever, fulcrum.

Materials: meter stick, triangular block, two 20 gram masses, a one-fifth gram mass, drawings of inclined plane, wheel and axle, pulley, wedge, lever, screw, and picture of a seesaw with children

Procedure:

1. *Advance Organizer:* Today we are going to begin to study simple machines. Simple machines are used to make work easier to do. They include such things as wheelbarrows, tweezers, axes, ramps, screws, and crowbars. Each of these falls into a particular category of simple machines. We will be studying each of these categories in this unit. They are wheel and axle, inclined plane, lever, screw, pulley, and wedge. The first of the simple machines we will be studying is the lever.
   a. As each type of machine is named display a drawing of the machine.

2. *Exposition with Interaction:*
   a. Show the picture of children on a seesaw.
   b. Tell the class that a seesaw is a kind of lever.
      (1) Ask: What are the parts of the seesaw that you see in the picture?
   c. Present the class with the idea that each of them is going to play on the seesaw with the smallest child in the class.
      (1) Ask the children where each of them will have to sit.
   d. Set up a lever using the meter stick and the triangular block.
      (1) Ask the children to compare this meter stick and block lever to the seesaw.
   e. Tell the class that a lever has a fulcrum and a bar of some sort. On the seesaw, the wood board that you sit on is the bar. In the lever on the table the meter stick is the bar. Point out the fulcrum in both levers. Define fulcrum as the place where the lever moves.
      (1) Ask: What are the two parts of a lever?
   f. Tell them that if you put a block on one side of the lever and a block of the same weight on the other side of the lever, the lever will be balanced.
      (1) Place weights on the meter stick so it is balanced.
      (2) Ask: How can I get a seesaw to balance?
      (3) Remove one block. Ask: Is the lever still balanced? How can you tell the lever is no longer balanced?
   g. Say: When one side of the lever is higher or lower than the other side, the lever is unbalanced. It is no longer even. One side is heavier than the other side.
      (1) Ask: What are some other ways that I could make the lever unbalanced?
      (2) Ask: What are some of the ways that a seesaw can be made unbalanced?

h. Say: A lever, then, is made up of a bar that rests on a fulcrum. It is balanced when the weight on one side of the lever is the same as the weight on the other side of the lever. The lever is unbalanced when one side of the lever is heavier than the other side of the lever.
   (1) Ask: What are the two parts of a lever?
   (2) Ask: What does it mean when we say a lever is balanced?
   (3) Ask: How can a lever be made unbalanced?

Evaluation: Write on the chalkboard the terms lever, fulcrum, balanced, and unbalanced. Have each child write a definition of each of the words.

Learning Activity 7–2

Exposition with Interaction

Choose a unit or section from any textbook for grades one through six. Read through the section thoroughly, determining the major thrust of the information. After reading and determining the major thrust, write either an expository or a comparative organizer for the unit.

Follow the organizer with a brief — no more than fifteen-minute — expository presentation in either outline or paragraph form. Include in your exposition ten to fifteen questions you could ask to determine the effectiveness of the expository material. Try to have at least four levels of Bloom's Taxonomy represented in the questions.

In all parts — organizer, questions, and lecture — keep in mind the grade level of the material. Be certain that the vocabulary you use is appropriate.

Prepare any visual aids you would use with the expository information.

Method III: Discussion

Definition

All too frequently what passes for discussion is really a lecture with periodic breaks for students to ask questions. In a true discussion, however, the students should talk as much as and preferably more than the teacher. A discussion is an open forum in which students can express their opinions as well as review factual material. In addition, the discussion is a natural opportunity for students to exercise their command of the processes of communication, inference, and conclusion.

Types of Discussions and Their Uses

The Open Discussion. Consider first the following discussion which took place in a fifth grade class. A picture alleged to be of the Loch Ness Monster appeared in the daily newspaper. The dark, shadowy object in the picture could have been anything from a rock to a tree to an unknown creature from the depths of the loch. The children were, however, firmly convinced that it was the Loch Ness Monster and wanted to talk about it. One part of the article that accompanied the picture mentioned that the expedition that had taken the photograph hoped to capture the monster. A natural question evolved from that statement: What should be done with the Loch Ness Monster if the team does capture it?

The first two responses were to be expected: stuff it and put it in a museum or put it in a zoo. At first the rest of the group agreed, but as the children considered these two alternatives, they decided that neither alternative was satisfactory. In the first case, you might be killing the only Loch Ness Monster in existence. In the second case, a zoo is like a cage and the animal would need a cage as big as a lake to be "happy." The idea of a cage the size of a lake presented obvious problems.

At that point the teacher posed a second question: What else could be done? We don't want to kill "Nessie" and a cage in a zoo would be difficult. What other possibilities are there?

The children came up with a variety of ideas, from turning the entire loch into a cage to just leaving the animal alone. By the end of the forty-minute period, the children had come to their own conclusion. The best thing, they decided, would be to capture the monster, keep it in a huge cage in the loch, study it, then let it go back to the loch and leave it alone.

From this description, we can see that an open discussion is one in which the children determine the topic and the role of the teacher is to ask those questions that will lead the children to consider various ideas. The teacher might also be responsible for defining unfamiliar terms and for taking the opposite point of view in order to show the other side of an issue. There can be no planning because the open discussion is spontaneous by definition.

Uses of the Open Discussion. Open discussions can be extremely effective in getting children to make inferences, draw conclusions, and communicate. The open discussion is always on a topic of interest to the children, because they initiate the discussion. Besides its utility in promoting the use of processes, the open discussion can also be used to alleviate fears children have because of a severe storm, frightening television program, or nightmare. Last, the open discussion is a way of determining student attitudes and of assessing their interests and ideas.

The Planned Discussion. Not all discussions are or should be open. Most of the discussions that take place in the science classroom should be planned, and planning is one factor affecting the degree of success. In a planned discussion, the teacher determines the content of the discussion, plans the questions, and guides the students toward some predetermined goal.

Uses of the Planned Discussion. We use the planned discussion to introduce a unit by providing an opportunity for children to voice their thoughts on a particular topic. The planned discussion is also a way of introducing and teaching content to the children in a way that will involve them cognitively.

The Formal Debate. The discussion may be taken one step further and evolve into a formal debate. The debate can be used in the science classroom to stimulate critical thinking by the presentation of opposing viewpoints.

Uses of the Formal Debate. We can use the formal debate whenever we want to approach controversial information in the science class. The debate can then stimulate critical thinking, give students the opportunity to present supporting evidence for a controversial viewpoint, encourage research, clarify values, and increase awareness of various problems that exist in the world today.

Planning for a Discussion Lesson

Planning for a Preplanned Discussion. A discussion needs some starting point: a question is good, but an object or other device is better. Secondly, a discussion needs someone (usually the teacher) who will present the opposite point of view. This is the "devil's advocate" role: taking the opposite point of view whether you believe that point of view or not.

The following discussion began with these statements, posted on the door of the classroom as the sixth grade arrived:

> Be it known to all who enter this realm that the following statements are true and have been verified by much observation:
>
> Snakes are born from wet grass.
> Flies come from rotten meat.
> Witches turn milk sour.
> Frogs are born out of mud.
> Mice come from wheat wrapped in a wet cloth.
>
> These statements are held to be true. Anyone who does not believe will be punished by banishment from the realm.
>
> — By Order of the Chief Scientist

Naturally, seeing something new the children stopped and read the sign. A few laughed. A few looked oddly at the teacher and said: "That's not true! Is it?" The teacher's reply was: "Of course it's true."

The children's challenge then became to convince the teacher that the assertions on the chart were not true. Verbal attempts to convince the teacher were all met with countercomments: nothing was acceptable. Finally, a child left the room, went to the cafeteria, returned with a chunk of raw meat, put it in the teacher's hand and said: "Prove it." This, of course, was the outcome the teacher desired from this discussion: the idea that it is necessary to prove or disprove a theory through experimentation, rather than through discussion.

Although these children came to this conclusion on their own, such is not always the result. Discussion can fizzle unless the teacher is ready with questions which will lead the class to the desired outcome.

When you plan a discussion, then, you should first have a starting point: a picture, chart, or challenging question. Second, you should plan a series of questions that will lead to the end-point or objective of the discussion. These questions will not be on the knowledge or comprehension levels. Rather, children should be working on the analysis, synthesis, and evaluation levels during the discussion. As the teacher, you should keep one point in mind: a discussion is neither a lecture nor a question-and-answer session. You, as the teacher, should say less than the students — much, much less.

Planning for a Formal Debate. The teacher should begin a formal debate in the classroom by teaching the procedure for a debate. The general steps are:

1. a brief speech for the affirmative side;
2. a brief period to allow the negative side time to formulate a rebuttal to the affirmative speech, followed by the rebuttal;
3. a brief speech for the negative side;
4. a brief period to allow the positive side to prepare a rebuttal to the negative speech, followed by the rebuttal;
5. a second affirmative speech;
6. a brief period to allow the second negative speaker time to prepare a rebuttal, followed by the rebuttal;
7. a second negative speech;
8. a brief period to allow the second positive speaker time to prepare a rebuttal, followed by the rebuttal;
9. rebuttal by the negative side's team captain;
10. rebuttal by the positive side's team captain;
11. questions from the audience.

Once they have learned the format for a debate, students who are to participate in the debate should be given time to do their research into the topic. Only after they complete the research should the students present their debate.

This type of discussion is rather complex and requires a great deal of research by the student. It is better left to the upper elementary grades. Even at the upper elementary grades, the debate will require a great deal of formal teaching, so that students can understand the purpose of each of the rebuttal speeches and the necessity for the presentation of evidence in each case. The debate format provides students with a fine opportunity to combine language arts with science.

Problems in Using the Discussion Method

The problems of the discussion method are three: it is verbal, it can be controversial, and it can become dominated by one individual.

The major problem of the discussion method lies in its verbal nature. Once again, verbal techniques are not the most appropriate for children.

Second, the teacher must make certain that the students have enough information at hand so that any discussion contains accurate information rather than hearsay or opinions only. The teacher must be certain that the students respect differing viewpoints. This is particularly important where those viewpoints represent the teaching of the home or the church. A discussion should never deteriorate into a verbal attack on one child's beliefs or values. If this seems to be happening, the teacher needs either to stop the discussion or to suggest that both sides do some research into the opposing viewpoint before continuing.

Finally, the last problem of the discussion lies in who does the talking. The most common pitfall is for the teacher to take over the discussion and begin to lecture students. This is most likely to occur when the students begin to challenge the teacher's own beliefs, and he or she feels compelled to set the students straight on a particular issue. Rather than taking over the discussion, you should try asking questions, presenting your point of view as a simple part of the discussion, and preparing yourself to be overruled once in awhile.

But the teacher is not the only individual who can dominate a discussion. A child can try to dominate the discussion, either because he or she has superior knowledge or a dominant personality. The child with superior knowledge could be asked to play the role of moderator, while the dominant personality could be given the attention he or she needs by asking other children to decide what evidence could be used to support or refute what the dominant child has said.

Last, there is also the child who does not overtly participate. In many cases, this child is listening to the discussion and may be participating nonverbally through eye contact, body posture, or facial expressions. The right of a child not to participate in a particular discussion should be respected. The child may be choosing not to participate because the ideas expressed conflict with his or her value system. The child may be silent because of a lack of knowledge in a particular area. To try to force a child who does not wish to participate to do so can lead to increasing discomfort for the child and a power struggle for the teacher. Respect the right of the child to be silent on occasion, just as you respect the right of an adult to be silent on occasion.

Lesson Plan 7–3
Discussion (Sixth Grade Level)

Topic: Experimenting is a way of proving or disproving a theory.

Objectives:

1. As a participant in the discussion each child will be able to make one or more contributions.
2. After participating in the discussion each student will be able to state in writing that experiments are an effective means for proving or disproving a theory.

Materials: chart, glass, water, soil, three similar containers, jar lid, gauze, tape or rubber band.

Procedure:

1. Prominently display a chart, similar to the one presented on page 213, just prior to the beginning of the lesson. Place all other materials out of sight.
2. If no one questions the statements ask:
   a. Do you think these statements are true?
   b. What could you do to convince me that these statements are not true?
   c. Be ready to contradict every verbal attempt no matter how ridiculous the contradiction.
3. Additional questions, if necessary, to lead to the desired objectives:
   a. What could you do to prove that the statements are wrong?
   b. What are some possibilities other than words and arguments to convince me that these statements are wrong?
   c. How could we use these materials (display the hidden materials) to prove these statements are wrong?

Evaluation:

1. Mentally note which children have participated in the discussion.
2. Have each child write one effective way to prove an idea right or wrong.

Learning Activity 7–3

Discussion Method

With a group of three or four classmates brainstorm a list of possible discussion topics. Once the list has been developed, decide on an opening question or starting idea for each of the topics on the list.

Remember, brainstorming is a technique in which we try to develop as many ideas as possible. We do not attempt to make a judgment as to the quality of the ideas.

Finally, after you and your classmates have developed the topics and possible starting questions or ideas, determine which of the brainstormed discussion topics would be most appropriate for use in an elementary science class.

Method IV: The Socratic Method

Definition

The Socratic method receives its name from its traditionally ascribed adherent: Socrates. It is a way of asking questions designed to draw information out of the students rather than pouring it into them. The Socratic method is purely verbal. It is an interesting change of pace for students used to expository methods of teaching.

Uses of the Socratic Method

Teachers use the Socratic method to develop content information. It is particularly effective in helping children develop a definition or a simple concept, where the children already have some concrete experience with the definition or concept.

Planning a Socratic Lesson

In developing a Socratic lesson, the teacher needs to consider five factors:

1. the concept or definition to be taught during the lesson,
2. the backgrounds of the children in the class,
3. the sequence to be used in the questioning,
4. alternate questions in case those planned do not elicit the expected answers,
5. alternative procedures for the same concept should the questioning strategy fail.

The Concept or Definition to Be Taught. The teacher should first determine whether the children have had any experience with the concept. The concept name may not be known, but examples of the concept may be known. For example, children know that all things fall to the ground unless held up in some way but they may not know the term gravity. This concept can be approached through the Socratic method.

The Backgrounds of the Children. The teacher should next consider the backgrounds of the children in the class. The teacher should know the experiential backgrounds of the children so that the questions he or she plans can be answered and the experiences of the children played upon as the strategy unfolds. By knowing the backgrounds of the children, the teacher can better anticipate answers and more logically word follow-up questions.

The Sequence to Be Used in Questioning. In general, questions in the Socratic method follow a general pattern:

1. A broad, general question that any child can answer is first.
2. The second question begins to narrow the range of response and focus the students onto the topic of the questioning strategy.
3. Review statements are interspersed among the questions in order to keep the salient points in the forefront.
4. A final concluding question brings the students to the desired end-point.

This does not mean that there are only four questions asked; the narrowing questions and review statements are repeated, so that a number of examples are developed before any conclusion is drawn. Table 7–3 shows a Socratic questioning strategy that worked well with a group of first grade children.

Alternate Questions. No matter how well planned a Socratic teaching strategy may be, the questions will not always elicit the answers desired. To permit the lesson to continue, the teacher should always have a few extra questions that

Table 7–3 Socratic method and the concept, mammal (first grade level)

QUESTION	ANSWER
1. How many of you have a pet?	1. [hands raised]
2. What kinds of pets do you have?	2. dog, kitten, cat, gerbil, hamster, horse, fish, turtle
3. Pretend that you're holding Mary's kitten. What does it feel like?	3. soft, warm, furry, squirmy, purring, scratchy
4. Pretend that you're petting Johnny's horse. What does it feel like?	4. warm, smooth, hairy, hard, moves, makes noise, smells
5. The kitten and the horse are both warm and furry or hairy.	5. [review statement]
6. What are some other animals that are warm and furry?	6. dogs, rabbits, squirrels, lions and tigers, ponies, my Daddy—he has a beard that is kind of furry
7. What word do scientists use for an animal that is warm and furry?	7. [no response—word was not known]
8. Scientists call these animals mammals.	8. [introduction of the word]
9. What are some animals that are mammals?	9. kittens, dogs, bears, lions and tigers, horses
10. What word do scientists use for animals that are warm and furry?	10. mammal

will lead the children in the same direction as the original questions but will require slightly different answers.

Alternate Procedures for Teaching the Same Concept. Although the Socratic method tends to work well when we teach a concept or definition, it is possible for the strategy simply not to work. The questions may be too difficult for the class or the class may not have the background necessary to answer the questions. The teacher should always have a back-up activity, preferably one that uses materials, to teach the desired concept or definition.

Problems in Using the Socratic Method

Like all teaching methods, the Socratic method has certain problems. Some of these we have already discussed under planning and we will repeat them. We will discuss two illustrations of questioning techniques that did not work. The major problems of the Socratic method are:

1. You must know your audience thoroughly.
2. Questions must be well planned and sequenced.
3. You may suddenly need to change a question or sequence of questions because no answer is offered or because the answer is strange or unanticipated.
4. You must be able to keep students from presenting lengthy monologues which stop the flow of information.
5. You must be prepared to present the final point, if the students are not able to reach the precise end-point desired.
6. You must have some alternative planned in case the questioning strategy does not work with a particular group of children.

With these points in mind, consider the two illustrations of Socratic lessons presented in Tables 7–4 and 7–5. The first indicates the same strategy as Table 7–3, but with a different set of children. The result was total disaster. Had the teacher known that these children came from apartment buildings where pets

Table 7–4 Socratic method and the concept, mammal (first grade level)

QUESTION	ANSWER
1. How many of you have pets?	1. [hands raised by seven of the children]
2. What kinds of pets do you have?	2. turtle, fish, garter snake, chameleon, parakeet, tarantula
3. What other kinds of pets might you have?	3. My neighbor has a *big* snake.
4. I have a dog for a pet. How many of you have ever petted a dog?	4. I'm scared of dogs. My mother said never to touch a dog. My brother got bit by a dog once.

were not permitted and from housing projects where dogs could be dangerous, the first questions could have been changed to better reflect the lives of the children. The teacher could have played upon the trip to the zoo that had occurred a week earlier. By the third question, the teacher should have realized the impossibility of teaching the definition of a mammal in this way and taken a sudden change in teaching strategy. A back-up plan should have been ready for the teacher to turn to as an alternative.

Table 7–5 shows an additional problem stemming from not knowing the students well. In this case, the students simply did not know the answers to the questions that the teacher asked. Following the revelation that brownies were made from potatoes, the teacher should simply have given up and gone on to reading.

Table 7–5 Socratic method and depèndence of life on green plants (fifth grade level)

QUESTION	ANSWER
1. What is your favorite food?	1. pizza, spaghetti, hamburgers, french fries, brownies, peanut butter sandwiches, ice cream, chocolate milk, soda, chicken
2. Pretend that we're having lunch: a hamburger, french fries, and brownies.	2. frozen french fries
3. But where do frozen french fries come from?	3. the store, the freezer
4. What plant do french fries come from?	4. Aren't they made from potatoes?
5. Good, french fries are made from potatoes. What are brownies made from?	5. Potatoes?
6. No, not potatoes. What are brownies made from?	6. [after much hesitation] Brownie mix!
7. True, but what is brownie mix made from?	7. [no response]
8. Let's look at the hamburger instead. What do you like on your hamburgers?	8. catsup, pickles, onions, cheese, meat, a bun, relish
9. What is catsup made from?	9. tomatoes
10. Are tomatoes plants or animals?	10. plants
11. What about the onions? Plants or animals?	11. plants
12. Where does the meat come from?	12. a cow
13. Good. What do cows eat?	13. [again, a long period of hesitation and silence until one child tentatively said: rabbits—at which a half-dozen others nodded solemnly]

A better strategy would have been to begin some research into where certain foods originate, what those foods are made from, and what preparation goes into the foods we eat. These children were sorely lacking in background knowledge about the foods that they commonly ate. Before any questioning strategy could be developed, these children needed background. In this case the Socratic technique gave the teacher an understanding of the children's lack of knowledge, so that the science program could be modified to meet their needs.

Lesson Plan 7–4
Socratic Technique (Second Grade Level)

Topic: A force is a push or a pull.

Objectives:

1. As a participant in this lesson each child will answer one or more questions.
2. After participating in this lesson each child will be able orally to define the term force as a push or a pull.

Materials: cardboard box filled with books and placed on the floor in front of the room

Procedure:

QUESTION	ANTICIPATED RESPONSE
1. This box is filled with books. Do you think it would be heavy or light?	1. heavy [Should someone say light, have the person try to push it.]
2. How could I move this box from here to the back of the room?	2. carry it, slide it, roll it, put it on a wagon, get someone strong to move it, put a rope around it and drag it
3. If I decide to slide the box, where would I stand?	3. behind it
4. What would I have to do to get the box to move?	4. push it
5. What would I need to do to get the box to roll?	5. push it
6. What if I put the box on a wagon. What would I do to get it to move?	6. push it or pull it

7. So, to slide the box or to roll it, I have to give the box a push. To move the box on a wagon, I can either push it or pull it.	7. [review — no response]
8. What are some other things I need to pull to get them to move?	8. some toys, sometimes my puppy — I have to pull its leash, that box when you have a rope
9. What are some things I need to push to get them to move?	9. toy car, sled, swing
10. Some things need to have either a push or a pull to make them move. What word is used to mean a push or a pull?	10. [Some children may know the word force from reading. If not, introduce the word.]
11. What is a force?	11. a push or a pull

Evaluation:

1. Mentally note those children who answer questions during the lesson.
2. Ask several children to tell the meaning of the word *force*.

One final note about the Socratic lesson: Each time examples are called for (as in questions eight and nine of the Lesson Plan 7–4) have as many children answer as possible. This provides more cognitive activity for the students and allows the teacher to determine how effective the lesson has been to that point.

Learning Activity 7–4

The Socratic Teaching Method

Choose any two of the following concepts taken from elementary science textbooks. Develop a Socratic questioning strategy for the two concepts. Be prepared to try one of your strategies with your class.

1. A mammal is a warm blooded animal with fur.
2. A reptile is a cold blooded animal with scaly skin.
3. Pulse rate increases with exercise.
4. The farther away an object is the smaller it looks.
5. There are four seasons.
6. Precipitation is any form of water falling from the sky.

7. Energy is a push or a pull.
8. An endangered species is one which may become extinct.
9. All things depend on one another for survival.
10. Living things grow and change.
11. Matter is anything which has mass and takes up space.
12. What goes up must come down.
13. For every action there is an equal and opposite reaction.
14. Plants need sunlight and water to grow.
15. In a physical change there is a change in the state or appearance of an object but not in its chemical composition.
16. Molds grow in warm, dark, damp places.
17. A rock is made up of more than one kind of mineral.
18. There are five senses.
19. The higher up in the atmosphere you go the colder it becomes.
20. Animals which have backbones are called vertebrates.

Method V: The Ordinary Demonstration

Definition

The ordinary demonstration is the type with which most people are familiar. In this case the teacher, or other designated individual, stands before the class, shows something, then tells what happened. The only individual actually involved with materials is the individual doing the demonstration. Depending on the interest generated by the demonstration, the reaction of the students watching can range from sleepy apathy to wide-eyed excitement.

Uses of the Ordinary Demonstration

There are a number of reasons for doing a demonstration. Like the demonstrations themselves, these reasons range from poor to excellent. Possibly the worst reason for demonstrating was given by the teacher who said that she demonstrated "because it keeps the room neater than if you let children do the activities." A neat room may be commendable, but it should not be a reason for preventing children from interacting with materials. Running a close second for worst reason for demonstrating is: "Give these kids materials and they'll tear the place apart." In general, it is the child who only watches or listens without any interaction who causes the problems, not the child who is actively involved. Moreover, those children who do not use materials well may not know how to work with materials because they have never had the opportunity to learn to work competently.

Those two reasons for demonstrating, although sometimes used, are always poor, but there are eight times when it is appropriate to do a demonstration for the children.

1. The teacher should demonstrate when there is some danger involved. This includes the use of open flames, open coil heating units, and some dangerous or toxic materials.
2. The teacher should demonstrate how to use a piece of equipment properly: microscope, thermometer, balance, graduated cylinder, etc.
3. The teacher should demonstrate when there is some spectacular effect that can initiate or end a unit of study: a volcano erupting, a dramatic chemical change.
4. The teacher should demonstrate when the action needs to be stopped periodically to show important changes or to point out specific points. In decomposing sugar, the teacher can stop the action by periodically removing the sugar from the heat, so that the various changes can be shown.
5. The teacher should demonstrate when there is not enough equipment, substitutions cannot be made, and the activity is particularly appropriate for illustrating a concept.
6. A student should demonstrate when he or she has developed an activity that will help the rest of the class understand a particular concept.
7. A student should demonstrate when it will help her or him to get a point across that he or she cannot easily express in words.
8. A student should demonstrate to develop communication skills and self-confidence in speaking before a group.

Planning an Ordinary Demonstration

Using an Advance Organizer. A good demonstration begins with an advance organizer that indicates what the children are to look for and, perhaps, defines terms the teacher will use as she demonstrates. The organizer should not, however, detail what is going to occur or tell the final outcome; otherwise, the suspense is destroyed. By giving an organizer, the teacher lets the students know on what to focus their attention, thus making the purpose of the demonstration clearer.

The Demonstration. Following the organizer, the teacher should do the demonstration. If equipment is being demonstrated that the students will later use, the teacher should demonstrate exactly how that piece of equipment is to be used in the correct, step-by-step order. If the demonstration is of an activity, the teacher should do it, stopping action as necessary and holding any comments to a minimum, because listening may interfere with the students' observation of what occurs. The demonstration can even be done silently the first time and repeated a second time with explanations.

Cautions. The teacher should first try the demonstration to be certain that it works and that it works in a reasonable amount of time. The teacher should be certain of the cause of the phenomenon being demonstrated, so that he or she can answer questions from the students. The teacher should also position the students and the demonstration so that they can see it clearly and easily. Finally, it is a good idea to have enough materials to be able to repeat the demonstration one or more times. This is particularly true for the more spectacular sort of demonstration, which children tend to want to see again and again.

Following the Demonstration. After the demonstration, the class can use either the exposition with interaction method or the Socratic method to determine the effectiveness of the demonstration. Whichever method is chosen for a follow-up to the demonstration, it should follow the advance organizer and focus on the most important aspects of the demonstration.

Problems in Using the Ordinary Demonstration

The ordinary demonstration tends to present four major problems. Fortunately, the teacher can easily handle each of these problems, so that the demonstration can be a success.

Failure of the Demonstration to Work. Even foolproof demonstrations have been known to fail: the egg that does not get sucked into the bottle, the can that does not collapse, the balloon that does not get bigger as the bottle is heated. No matter how frequently a teacher demonstrates or how carefully he or she does the demonstration, there are times when a demonstration will not work. The first feeling one experiences is panic. Rather than causing panic, however, the failure should be turned into a success and a better lesson. The best course of action when confronted with a failed demonstration is to tell what usually happens and to challenge the children to try to determine why the demonstration did not work as expected. Be prepared to try out their ideas, to have some of the children show their ideas, and finally to find out what went wrong. Even if the demonstration never does work, the students will still have gained a valuable experience in using problem solving techniques, making inferences and observations, analyzing a system, and determining cause and effect.

Restlessness or Inattentiveness. During a demonstration, children can tend to become restless or inattentive. In most cases, this problem can be solved by presenting demonstrations that are exciting or by being certain that the demonstration is on a level the children can understand. During the course of a demonstration, the teacher can regain wandering attention by asking questions that insist on a greater application of the processes of observation, inferences, interaction and systems, and cause and effect.

Visibility. With large classes children may not be able to see the demonstration. Seating the children in a semicircle around the demonstration table can be a solution. If the class is too large for this approach, the teacher could divide the class into two or more smaller groups and conduct the demonstration for each group.

Models. Teachers frequently use models in demonstrating. A model volcano can be made to erupt. A model of the heart can be shown. A model of the human body can be used to illustrate the digestive processes. For these models successfully to teach the desired information, they should be as close to real as possible. The best types of models are those in which the objects represent only themselves and not some part of the human body or a cell of some kind, or anything else that the child must use his or her imagination to understand. The objects should look like the real thing.

Lesson Plan 7–5
Ordinary Demonstration (Fifth Grade Level)

Topic: Chemical changes

Objective: After watching the demonstration dealing with chemical changes, each child will be able to define in writing the term chemical change.

Materials: sugar, pyrex beaker, hot plate, tongs, hot pad or potholder

Procedure:

1. *Advance Organizer*
   Teacher to class: For the past few days we have been looking at the idea of change. One of the kinds of changes was a physical change. At that time we defined a physical change as one that caused a difference in the appearance of an object but not in the material that an object was made from. Some of the physical changes that we saw were breaking chalk, tearing paper, adding sugar to water, and melting chocolate. Watch today's demonstration carefully because it shows another type of change. Try to find out the answers to these questions: What happens to the white material as it is heated? What do you see happen? What do you smell? How does the change in the white powder differ from the change in the chocolate we melted?
2. *Demonstration*
   a. Turn the hot plate to high.
   b. Place four tablespoons of sugar into the beaker. Do not tell what the material is.
   c. Place the beaker on the hot plate and allow the sugar to melt.
   d. Using the tongs, remove the beaker and sugar from the heat at

each of the following points so that the children can observe the changes:
(1) just beginning to melt;
(2) as a brownish-red liquid;
(3) as it begins to turn black and bubble;
(4) as the black material begins to climb the sides of the beaker;
(5) after the beaker is filled with a black, foamy material, *stop*.

e. Turn off the hot plate.
f. Place the beaker on the hot pad where it can be easily seen. Place a small amount of sugar next to the beaker for comparison.

3. *Socratic Method*
Interrogate the children as follows:
a. Look at the white material. What observations can you make? [List them on the chalkboard.]
b. What do you think the white material is?
c. We started with white, granular sugar. What do you see now? Collect the observations on the chalkboard.
d. As the sugar was heating, what did you smell?
e. As the sugar was heating, what did you hear?
f. Review the characteristics of the original sugar and the resulting material as listed on the board.
g. Do you think that the material left in the beaker is still sugar?
h. How does what you've just seen differ from the physical changes that we've seen previously?
i. What name is given to the kind of change that happened to the sugar?

An ordinary demonstration, then, is a means of teaching using materials, but the teacher is the only person to handle those materials. The teacher closely plans the final result of the demonstration and guides the students through questions and through the materials to the desired end-point. The teacher also plans the second type of demonstration, but the end-point is problem solving skills rather than a particular bit of content selected by the teacher.

Learning Activity 7–5

Ordinary Demonstration

Develop a lesson plan for an ordinary demonstration. Remember to include the objective or objectives for the lesson as well as an advance organizer and a follow-up for the demonstration.

List any questions you would ask children during the demonstration as well as during your follow-up. Be prepared to present your demonstration to your peers as a lesson.

Method VI: Discovery Demonstration

Definition

A discovery demonstration is a method of teaching the processes of science or problem solving in which the teacher silently conducts the demonstration and the students attempt to determine why what is shown occurs.

The Basis for the Discovery Demonstration

The discovery demonstration is based on the inquiry training model of J. Richard Suchman (1962). The inquiry training program was designed around three broad objectives: (1) development of the skills of searching and of data processing, which would allow children to solve problems autonomously, (2) development of a means for learning that would allow children to develop concepts through analysis of concrete problems, and (3) development of intrinsic forms of motivation.

In order to attain these objectives, children were shown motion pictures depicting short demonstrations taken from physics. The title of each of the filmed demonstrations asked why the outcome of the demonstration occurred. The program developers used physics problems in the training because the number of variables could be limited.

The films were designed to present a problem. The teacher's role was to develop an environment where inquiry could take place. Rather than telling the students about the phenomena they had seen, the teacher was to help the children to structure concepts and develop reasoning.

The inquiry training model focused on the process by which information was acquired rather than on the final information. This problem solving strategy took place in three steps.

Phase I: Episode Analysis. In Phase I, children asked questions in order to learn everything possible about the properties of the objects shown in the film. They also determined the conditions of each object and system at the beginning of the event and at each change throughout the entire episode. Finally, by the end of Phase I, children developed a chart posted on the board on which they listed the data found. All questions the children asked during Phase I had to be worded so that the teacher could answer only yes or no.

Phase II: Determination of Relevance. In Phase II, children attempted to isolate relevant variables. The questions they asked during this phase had to be phrased as tests of the identified variables: If the temperature had been kept the same would the material have melted? Also during Phase II, children attempted to determine what conditions were necessary for the final outcome to come about.

Phase III: Induction of Relational Constructs. In Phase III, children attempted to discover why the conditions identified in Phase II were necessary to the final outcome. In this final phase children attempted to determine the cause of the phenomenon.

Inquiry training was shown, through trials with fifth and sixth grade students, to help children develop conceptually. Children who participated in inquiry sessions developed the physics concepts to a higher level than did similar students who were taught those same concepts directly by teachers. Moreover, children who were taught to inquire in this way also developed greater ability to ask questions and so developed greater verbal fluency. In addition, they were better able to make use of the information that they had gained through questions. Children who learned to inquire also showed significant increases in learning autonomy and in motivation to learn.

Differences Between Discovery Demonstrations and Inquiry Training. The discovery demonstration differs from Suchman's model in two ways. First, the episode to be considered is shown directly through materials rather than through films. Second, the students receive more guidance from the teacher than did the students in inquiry training. The purpose of the guidance is not, however, to limit inquiry but to help the teacher conform to the time limits set by the elementary school curriculum.

Differences Between Discovery Demonstrations and Ordinary Demonstrations. The discovery demonstration differs from an ordinary demonstration in four ways:

1. The discovery demonstration is oriented toward problem solving and processes rather than toward presentation of a single content item.
2. The discovery demonstration has more student participation than the ordinary demonstration. Students guide the teacher toward the solution to the problem presented in the demonstration rather than simply being shown the solution.
3. The discovery demonstration allows students to draw their own conclusions rather than listening to the conclusions drawn by the teacher.
4. The discovery demonstration may never reach closure. The children may not solve the problem presented to them.

The Use of the Discovery Demonstration

The discovery demonstration is used for a single purpose: to develop problem solving skills. Children are presented with a problem in the form of a demonstration and are challenged to determine the cause of the phenomenon. One type of demonstration is particularly effective. This is the discrepant event — something which goes against common sense, such as a rock that floats (pumice) or two clear liquids that when mixed turn magenta (phenolphthalein in ammonia water).

Planning a Discovery Demonstration

The discovery demonstration has a six-step teaching sequence, which enables the children to solve the problem presented or to use problem solving skills to attempt to solve the problem:

1. Silently show the demonstration after telling the group to watch carefully and challenging them to try to determine why what they see occurs.
2. Collect observations on the chalkboard.
3. Have the class ask questions that can be answered by yes or no in order to obtain information to supplement their observations.
4. Ask if there are any operational questions that could be investigated or other demonstrations that need to be done in order to supply more information. Allow time to investigate or to perform the desired demonstrations.
5. Collect on the chalkboard those points or factors that the class deems important to the problem solution.
6. Call for a solution, or multiple solutions, to the problem. Children should not only present their solutions but also present supporting evidence from the problem solving session.

Problems in Using the Discovery Demonstration

1. It is frequently difficult to locate demonstrations that are both difficult enough to challenge the children yet easy enough to allow for a possible solution.
2. Because the class asks questions to obtain more information, the demonstrating teacher needs to know precisely what happened and the cause so that he or she can give correct answers.
3. Two difficulties for many teachers are the silence and the "no-telling" aspects of the discovery demonstration. The teacher must try not to make comments while doing the demonstration and must try not to show those factors that are important or those that are extraneous. Determination of relevance is the role of the students.
4. For many teachers the lack of closure in the discovery demonstration is a problem. A discovery demonstration is a way to encourage problem solving strategies. Therefore, if students have used the processes of science appropriately and have deployed problem solving strategies appropriately, the lesson is a success even if closure is not reached. The discovery demonstration is a no-fail means of teaching.

5. The discovery demonstration, because it encourages children to suggest other demonstrations or to investigate operational questions, may be difficult to manage in terms of materials and time. The teacher may overcome this by having the science area well stocked with the kinds of materials children can use safely and easily. Although they cannot be heated, baby-food jars can substitute for test tubes and other kinds of containers. Ice can be kept in a picnic cooler. Straws make fine stirring rods and can be made into simple balances. You can anticipate some needs and provide for them. You can alleviate the time problem by either allowing a longer than usual time period for science or by imposing a time limit on investigations. The imposition of a time limit is not entirely satisfactory, but may have to be considered because of the structure of the elementary school.

Lesson Plan 7–6
Discovery Demonstration (Sixth Grade Level)

Lesson Plan 7–6 is much shorter than that for the other teaching methods already considered. In general it is a reminder to the teacher of the steps to be followed in the discovery demonstration.

Topic: Problem Solving

Objective: Each child will participate in the problem solving session by doing one or more of the following:

1. providing one or more observations,
2. asking one or more questions,
3. offering ideas for one or more follow-up demonstrations,
4. asking and investigating an operational question,
5. providing a possible solution to the problem.

Materials: four or five empty ditto fluid cans (well aired and rinsed), caps for the cans, hot plate, cookie sheet or tray, potholder or tongs, water; other materials as needed

Procedure:

1. Tell the class that they are to watch the demonstration carefully. Challenge them to try to explain what caused the change in the can.
   a. If the children are new to discovery demonstrations review the steps that they should follow.
2. Do the following demonstration silently:
   a. Turn the hot plate to high.
   b. Show that the can is empty.

c. Pour a small amount of water into the can. Do not put the cap on the can.
d. Place the can on the hot plate and heat it until steam begins to escape.
e. Screw the cap tightly on the container and remove the can from the heat. Place the can on the tray.
f. Wait for one minute.
g. Pour a little cold water over the can so it will quickly collapse.

3. Ask for observations from the class including the materials used, how the materials were used, and what occurred.
4. Ask for questions from the children that can be answered by yes or no.
5. Ask if there are any other demonstrations needed or if anyone has an operational question that could be used to get more information.
6. Ask for any solutions to the problem, encouraging the students to support their solutions with evidence from the demonstration or from other sources.

Evaluation: Using a check list, indicate which students accomplished the stated objective.

The discovery demonstration is a way to promote problem solving skills in a no-fail situation. It allows students to interact with materials, with one another, and with the teacher in a scene that permits the student to direct his or her own learning. The teacher who uses this method must keep in mind that content is not the goal of the discovery demonstration.

Learning Activity 7–6

The Discovery Demonstration

Develop a card file of fifteen to twenty ideas for discovery demonstrations. Include on the file card the materials needed, the specific directions for the demonstration, and an explanation of the occurrences in the demonstration.

Choose one of the discovery demonstrations from your file. Plan a lesson around it including your objectives. Be prepared to conduct the discovery demonstration for your peers.

Method VII: Guided Discovery

Definition

Guided discovery is a means by which children use the processes of science to develop information. The students are totally involved with materials, using those materials to develop concepts and facts without reading or listening to verbal information from the teacher.

The Uses of Guided Discovery

The teacher can use guided discovery any time the content of the science program lends itself to exploration through the use of concrete materials. The major consideration in deciding whether to use guided discovery should be the safety of the materials. If the planned activity is safe for children then the teacher should use guided discovery. If the materials are not safe for children, the teacher should choose either the discovery demonstration (if problem solving skills are to be developed) or the ordinary demonstration (if content is to be developed). Guided discovery should predominate in the elementary science classroom.

Teaching Strategies for Guided Discovery

In order to facilitate the learning that occurs during a guided discovery lesson, the teacher should employ certain teaching strategies.

The Use of Process. The activity developed for the guided discovery lesson should permit the students to use as many of the science processes as they are able. The teacher should allow the children to develop the desired content by using those processes, rather than presenting the content to them through expository teaching.

Supporting Evidence. The conclusions drawn and the inferences made by the children should always have supporting evidence obtained through the materials they use. The teacher should consistently ask students to support their statements. In order to help the children develop their skills in providing supporting evidence, the teacher should ask questions like (1) How do you know? (2) What did you see that tells you what you've said is true? and (3) Show us, using your materials, what you have found.

Wait Time. When asking questions, the teacher should use wait time. Wait time will give students time to formulate answers to questions, to decide on the evidence they will use to support their answers, and to clarify their responses. Wait time will also allow other students to add to what has been said or to challenge the conclusions made by other students.

Accepting Answers. Any conclusion based on evidence gleaned from activity with materials should be accepted. This sometimes means that the teacher has to accept a scientifically incorrect conclusion. In such a case, it is the teacher's responsibility to guide students into another activity or into a repetition of the current activity that will enable the students to reach scientifically correct conclusions. It is not the teacher's role to lecture on the correct conclusion or to require that the student read the correct solution from a textbook.

Guidance and Open-Endedness. A teaching strategy allowing for open-ended activities means that students are given the freedom to investigate questions arising spontaneously during the activity. It should also allow students the leeway to develop similar activities along slightly different lines. The variety of approaches children use in guided discovery allows each child to learn the information in the way most appropriate for him or her. It also provides results obtained in a variety of ways so that evaluation level questions become a natural part of the lesson. By developing their own activities to reach a particular end-point, children are working in a problem solving situation and on a synthesis level. The teacher's role is to provide the guidance the children will need to carry out their plans successfully.

The Benefits of Guided Discovery

Guided discovery is appropriate to the developmental level of children in the elementary school. In addition it provides a teaching method that will allow children to develop their own knowledge from first-hand experience. And guided discovery has three benefits not found in the previous teaching methods.

Use of Processes. Guided discovery allows children to use the processes of science to generate content information: a procedure very similar to that of the research scientist attempting to solve some problem in the laboratory. The child can engage in operational questioning, observing, measuring, recording data, drawing conclusions, and all other processes during guided discovery. But the activity is purposeful. There is reason for the activity other than to allow the child to practice the process skill. There is a final point at which the child gains information that will further his or her understanding of the physical world.

Motivation. Guided discovery also has the benefit of switching motivation from extrinsic to intrinsic sources. In verbal teaching methods, the motivation to learn and the reward for learning both come from the teacher's comments made after the student's contributions to a discussion or answers to questions or from grades received on written assignments. In guided discovery, the rewards come from the activity: from the excitement of learning and discovering on one's own. This excitement tends to be self-sustaining, so is intrinsically rewarding.

The Role of the Teacher. Guided discovery releases the teacher from a continuous position of authority. Instead the teacher becomes a guide and a fellow investigator. Although the teacher in guided discovery must be well versed in science, there is no need to know all of the answers. Answers come from materials in guided discovery and not from a particular authority. The teacher can check the validity of the answers obtained when he or she is uncertain. Consequently, the teacher can become a part of the discovery experience.

Planning a Guided Discovery Lesson

The guided discovery lesson consists of three sections, in which three or more different teaching methods may be included. The final outcome of the combination of all of the methods is a guided discovery lesson.

Introduction to the Lesson. A guided discovery lesson begins with background information and preliminary instructions, both of which can be presented through expository teaching. At times, students need definitions before an activity can be accomplished easily. The teacher can develop these definitions through the Socratic method. And, if a new piece of equipment is to be used, an ordinary demonstration can show how that piece of equipment is correctly used.

The Activity and the Challenge. In guided discovery, the teacher develops a laboratory experience designed to reach a particular end-point. The starting activity is highly structured, but the total lesson allows students freedom to develop their own activities once that starting activity has been completed. For example, students are given the instructions for constructing a complete circuit out of wire, bulb, socket, and battery. Once they have completed that circuit, the students are challenged to answer one or more questions like:

1. How many bulbs will one battery light?
2. What materials could you use instead of a wire and still have the bulb light?
3. What effect does the size of the battery have on the number of bulbs which will light?

Summary and Conclusions. Following the activity section of the lesson, the teacher should use Socratic questioning or a discussion to synthesize the findings from the activity and the challenge activities that the children complete. In this final section, the teacher should be careful to ask questions and draw out the conclusions rather than providing those conclusions for the children.

Problems in Using Guided Discovery

Guided discovery, because of its orientation toward materials and children, presents some problems that are not found in more teacher directed and structured methods of teaching. These problems can, however, be overcome by good planning and classroom management skills.

Problem One. Children are not inherently good investigators nor do they automatically know how to work appropriately with materials.

Solution. Rules on use, acquisition, and clean-up of materials should be established early. Even first and second grade children can learn to get, clean, and return materials to a central source. The more practice children have with using materials the more competent they become in using those materials.

Problem Two. Because children are investigating independently, time is the greatest problem of guided discovery. Children who are in the midst of activity do not want to stop even if the schedule does say it is time for reading. But, although some do not want to end, others are quick to finish. Consequently, time is a dual problem.

Solution. For those who are still actively involved when time is up, a place in the classroom should be provided where partly finished activities can be stored and worked at during free time. A windowsill, table, closet, or learning center will work well for a storage space. For those who finish early, a new question or a new challenge from the teacher can often renew investigation. However, when children have gone as far as their understanding will allow, there should be alternatives: other activities, books to read, a film or filmstrip to view, or some other learning experience.

Problem Three. Because children are developing their own activities, one frequently finds differing answers and incorrect answers. But because the final outcome of guided discovery is the teaching of content, such differences and deviations can cause confusion.

Solution. When students obtain differing answers for the same question, all of the possible answers should be listed on the chalkboard and the evidence for each of them presented. Children can then evaluate the various answers and try to determine which is the most probable. When scientifically incorrect answers are obtained, the children should be directed back to their materials whenever possible and to reading materials when this is not possible, so that they can determine correct answers.

Problem Four. As children develop guided discovery activities, those activities may bear no resemblance to the problem at hand. These are known as tangents or offshoots of the original problem.

Solution. When tangents occur, the teacher should first determine whether the activity is really a tangent or if it is actually relevant to the problem being investigated. Those children coating the table top with mud may appear to be making a mess but a question like, "What are you trying to find out?" may reveal that the mess is being used to determine how fast water evaporates from soil of varying thicknesses. A real tangent activity needs to be evaluated. If the direction of the tangent is valid and the activity contributes to the topic being studied, the teacher should probably not interfere. In cases where the activity has become purposeless, the children will need to be drawn back into an appropriate path. Questions that help to clarify the purpose of the activity or that provide a problem for investigation are usually all that is needed to return children to purposeful activity.

Problem Five. Guided discovery is a time consuming method. Investigation, activity development, and the drawing of conclusions all take time.

Solution. To solve the problem of the time consuming nature of guided discovery, the teacher can assign some activities as homework. A second possibility is to decrease the amount of material that is covered in a particular unit of work so that enough time will be available.

Problem Six. Guided discovery can become chaotic as children begin to investigate the challenge questions.

Solution. Although this is presented as a problem, it usually is not. Children who are involved tend to be less of a discipline problem than children who are not involved. However, if children tend to become unruly, stop the children's work, review the ground rules, and have the children pick up where they left off.

Lesson Plan 7–7
Guided Discovery (Sixth Grade Level)

The following lesson plan illustrates the way in which a guided discovery lesson is planned. Unlike the other lesson plans, this one is designed for a period of time longer than a single class—probably a two-week period of time would be needed to consider the topic adequately.

Topic: Evaporation

Objective: As a result of the activities, each student will be able to:

1. name two factors that affect the rate of evaporation of water,
2. design and carry out an experiment or activity to test the effect of some factor on the rate of evaporation of water,

3. graph the data from the experiment or activity dealing with rate of evaporation.

Materials: jars, cans, bottles, glasses of various sizes and shapes, water, rulers, measuring cups or graduated cylinders, marking pens or grease pencils, food coloring, salt, sugar, other materials as needed.

Procedure:

1. *Introductory Review*
   a. Review the idea of an experiment including writing an hypothesis, controlling variables, collecting data, and drawing a conclusion.
   b. Review how to make a graph of collected data.
   c. Review how to determine rate.
2. *Original Activity Instructions*
   a. Divide into groups of three.
   b. Collect the following materials: jar, water, marking pencil, ruler, measuring cup or graduated cylinder.
   c. Measure 250 milliliters (one-half cup) of water and pour it into the jar.
   d. Mark the level of the water in the jar, measure the height, and record it in your data chart.
   e. Place the jar where it will not be disturbed for four days.
   f. Each day measure the height of the water and record.
   g. Find the rate of evaporation.
3. *Challenge*
   a. After the original activity has been set up by each group, have the groups once again meet together to do the following:
      (1) make a list of as many variables as possible that could affect how fast the water will evaporate;
      (2) choose one of the variables in the list to investigate;
      (3) design an experiment to test the actual effect of the variable.
   b. Have children who are unable to control variables investigate an operational question.
4. *Conclusion*
   a. After the class has completed the experiments and presented the results, develop as a group any possible conclusions about the evaporation of water warranted by the data collected.
   b. Compare the conclusions drawn with the written text material.
      (1) Differences in the two sources of material should be investigated through new activities.

Evaluation: Through a written record of the experiments and operational questions determine whether:

1. two factors affecting evaporation can be named,
2. activities or experiments have been designed and carried out to test the effect of some factor on evaporation,
3. data has been appropriately graphed.

In Lesson Plan 7–7, the class used the textbook as a source of information after the students had discovered all that they could about evaporation. The class investigated differences between the text and the conclusions drawn by the students, so that the textbook was not blindly accepted as correct. In no instance should the students read the textbook before their activities. The book provides the answers students should be trying to discover for themselves. In essence, reading the textbook before doing the activity is like reading the end of a mystery novel before reading the beginning: anticlimactic.

Learning Activity 7–7

Guided Discovery

Develop a guided discovery lesson plan for one of the following topics. Be certain to include the objectives for the lesson, an introduction, and a means for concluding the lesson with the children, as well as an activity and a challenge:

1. simple machines: lever, pulley, inclined plane, wheel and axle, wedge, screw;
2. electricity: simple circuit, series circuit, parallel circuit, conductors, nonconductors;
3. magnets: permanent magnets, compasses, electromagnets;
4. chemical changes;
5. physical changes;
6. light: lenses, reflection, refraction, shadows, transparency;
7. sound;
8. collisions.

Method VIII: Open Inquiry

Definition

Open inquiry provides a degree of freedom not found in any of the previous teaching methods. In open inquiry, the teacher presents a starting problem and provides materials that could be used to solve the problem, then allows the students to use any method they wish to arrive at a solution.

Uses of Open Inquiry

Open inquiry cannot be used to teach specific content. It is too unstructured to assure that all children or even a majority of children will reach a certain endpoint or concept. Instead, the teacher should use open inquiry as a way of developing process and problem solving skills. Because of the emphasis on process and problem solving, the open inquiry lesson can be fun and can be used to develop positive attitudes toward science. Paper airplanes, soap bubbles, soil, watermelons, and rubber bands can all provide a starting point for open inquiry. In this teaching method it is particularly important for students to feel at ease and certain of success. The prerequisites for open inquiry are a lively curiosity and a willingness to share what has been found.

The Benefits of Open Inquiry

Benefits to the Teacher. In open inquiry, the teacher's role is to provide materials and encouragement. Consequently, the teacher is no longer an authority figure who must know all of the answers. The teacher is able to investigate with the students, thus providing a model of inquiry behaviors. Finally, the teacher can see the students in a different type of learning situation and perhaps can determine a learning style for some students that will be more effective than the typical classroom procedures.

Benefits to the Students. The open inquiry method of teaching benefits the student in a number of unique ways.

Creativity. The open inquiry method allows students an opportunity to develop creative solutions to the problems presented. There are no rigid guidelines, so imagination as well as process skills can be used. In addition, students can, without penalty, go off on tangents eventually having little to do with the original problem. The investigations can be as original as the student's own imagination.

Freedom. The freedom of open inquiry allows children to solve a problem in any way they can. The only constraints on the children are those of safety and materials.

Process. Open inquiry allows children to use the processes of science in a genuine problem solving situation. Open inquiry allows children to investigate a problem to the limits of their abilities without being penalized for a lack of content information. Students who are capable of experimentation are able to use that skill, whereas those who are not can fall back on the processes that they are most able to use.

Success. Because of the process orientation and the individuality possible in the development of problem solving methods, it is impossible to fail in an open inquiry lesson. A child can carry an activity to the furthest of his or her ability, then stop without being penalized for not reaching a particular end-point. In this way, the no-fail characteristic of open inquiry allows children's self-confidence to develop.

Planning an Open Inquiry Lesson

In planning for an open inquiry lesson, the teacher follows four general steps:

1. Decide which of the processes you would most like to emphasize in the lesson.
2. Locate a starting activity that you can use as a basis for the lesson.
3. Plan the opening question, which children will use as a basis for their activities.
4. Collect any materials that the children could use in their activities. Try to anticipate some of the ideas that children might have so that a variety of materials is available.

Problems with Open Inquiry

The problems the teacher may encounter using the open inquiry technique are a result of the very openness of the method. Each of those problems may, however, be easily solved.

Problem One. Open inquiry tends to look, and sometimes to be, chaotic.

Solution. It is quite possible during open inquiry for a class of thirty children to be carrying out thirty different investigations. This can appear to be chaotic. Fortunately, the teacher can easily maintain control during an open inquiry lesson. Children who are actively involved tend to cause few problems. In order to prevent problems, however, be certain that children know the rules established for classroom behavior and that you have a technique for gaining the attention of all the children in the class, so that behavior problems can be quickly corrected.

Problem Two. Open inquiry can be very noisy as children discuss their findings and demonstrate their activities for one another.

Solution. Children should be free to discuss their activities with one another, because communication is one of the basic processes of science. However, should the noise level become high enough to be disruptive to the learning process, the teacher should ask for a reduction in noise level. Turn out the lights, ring a bell, play a chord on the piano, whistle, or clap to get the children's attention. Silence them, then tell them they may continue, but more quietly.

Problem Three. Anticipating and locating enough materials can be a major problem of open inquiry. It is impossible to anticipate everything that children will need.

Solution. Although you cannot anticipate everything that children will need to conduct their activities, it is possible to select open inquiry activities that can be accomplished with easily obtainable materials: junk and common household or school materials. When an open inquiry lesson continues for more than one day, children should be encouraged to bring in the other kinds of materials they may require. Then, keep a record of the kinds of materials the children actually use, so that you may obtain them the next time the activity is done.

Problem Four. As with guided discovery, a problem with open inquiry is time. Because children can investigate up to their own limits some will finish quickly while others will not want to stop at all. In addition, open inquiry is, like guided discovery, time consuming.

Solution. The teacher can solve the problem of children finishing at different rates in the same way it was solved in guided discovery. The problem of time consumption can be addressed by establishing a time limit during which particular activities can take place.

Problem Five. A problem unique to open inquiry is evaluation. Because schools must insure accountability and provide grades, we need some means of evaluation that takes into account more than the gleam in the eye of the children.

Solution. Students engaged in open inquiry can be encouraged to keep a diary or record book of their investigations, either in a formal lab report or in an informal descriptive system. Young children can dictate their reports to the teacher or into a tape recorder: a method also helpful for older children who have reading or writing difficulties. From such records, the teacher can determine the child's progress in understanding and using processes, the direction of the child's investigations, and the child's ability to communicate.

Lesson Plan 7–8
Open Inquiry (Third Grade Level)

Like a plan for guided discovery, a lesson plan for open inquiry is not a lesson plan for a single class period. Actually, an open inquiry lesson plan is unlike other plans in that it is mainly an objective, a challenging problem, and a list of materials that the teacher should collect.

Topic: Problem Solving

Objective: As a result of this lesson each child will be able to use the processes of science to solve a problem.

Materials: electric fan; various types of paper such as construction paper, onion skin, magazine pages, newspaper, waxed paper, aluminum foil, paper bags; scissors, masking tape, cellophane tape, glue, stapler, paper clips, meter sticks, ruler, crayons, pencils, paint and paint brushes

Procedure:

1. Review with the children the need for keeping a diary or log of their investigations.
2. While the children watch, make a paper airplane and fly it across the room. Measure how far it flew.
3. *Challenge:* My airplane flew in a straight line for ______ centimeters. What could you do to get a paper airplane to fly further than that? What could you do to get an airplane to fly in some other way than in a straight line?

Evaluation: Read each child's log or diary.

The open inquiry method of teaching provides students with a way of sharpening their problem solving and process skills. However, it also provides something equally important, if the major thrust of the science curriculum is content. Children who have investigated paper airplanes in an open inquiry situation will have developed some background understanding that will help them more fully to comprehend principles of flight. Children who have investigated bubbles may be able to understand ideas of pressure more fully and children who have investigated liquids may understand concepts of density, fluidity, and viscosity more fully, because they have experienced those ideas in an unstructured situation. New information on the content of the science program will not be totally new to the child who has experienced the ideas in the unstructured setting of open inquiry.

Learning Activity 7–8

Open Inquiry

Develop an open inquiry lesson plan that will allow children to use three or more of the following processes. Be certain to indicate which of the processes you would be most likely to develop in your lesson:

1. observation
2. inference
3. concluding
4. prediction
5. space relations
6. collecting data
7. classification
8. cause and effect
9. number relations
10. interaction and systems
11. experimenting

Plan to present your starting activity to your peers.

Choosing an Appropriate Method for Teaching

Factors That Should Be Considered in Choosing a Method

Basic Questions for Consideration. The teacher should choose the method used for a particular lesson because it is the most effective method for accomplishing the lesson objectives. In selecting a teaching method, the teacher should ask himself or herself four questions:

1. What is the major purpose of the lesson: content, process, or problem solving?
2. Is this an area in which students have a great deal of background knowledge or only a small amount of background knowledge?
3. Can materials be effectively used to develop the concept? Should these materials be used by the teacher or by the students?
4. How much time should be devoted to the concept or process? The amount of time should be determined, in part, by the importance of the concept to the total program of science as well as by the difficulty of the concept.

Basic Uses of the Teaching Methods. Once the teacher has evaluated the lesson to be taught in terms of the questions, he or she should compare the answers to those questions to the uses that can be made of the various teaching methods.

Content, Process, or Problem Solving. If the major purpose of the lesson is to teach content the teacher can effectively use exposition, exposition with interaction, closed discussion, Socratic, ordinary demonstration, and guided discovery methods. For teaching the use of processes, open discussion, guided discovery, discovery demonstration, and open inquiry methods are all possibilities. For lessons with a primary purpose of teaching problem solving, the discovery demonstration and the open inquiry methods are the best choices.

Background of the Students. Students with little background in a particular area could be helped to attain that background through the use of exposition, exposition with interaction, or open inquiry, whereas those with a great deal of background could be offered the Socratic method, discovery demonstration, or guided discovery methods very effectively.

Use of Materials. Methods requiring materials range from the ordinary demonstration and discovery demonstrations, which require few materials, to guided discovery and open inquiry, which require many materials. All other techniques do not require the use of concrete materials.

Amount of Time Required. Time-efficient methods are exposition, exposition with interaction, closed discussion, ordinary demonstration, and Socratic. The teacher can carefully control all of these so that the lesson fits neatly into a certain time period. Methods requiring a great deal of time to be most effective are those that require materials or lean heavily on problem solving: open discussions, discovery demonstrations, guided discovery, and open inquiry.

Examples of Method Choice

Example One. A lesson is to be presented that has as its major objective to nurture the sixth grade student's ability to develop an experiment. This is a process oriented lesson. Because the lesson is process oriented, the main teaching methods would be open discussion, discovery demonstration, guided discovery, or open inquiry. All four of these methods can develop process skills.

The students in this class have background in what an experiment is, but have not done a great deal of actual experimenting. In this case, discovery demonstrations and guided discovery are equally appropriate.

Because the lesson deals with the process of experimenting, and students are to develop the skill themselves, they should be working with materials rather than watching the teacher use materials. The discovery demonstration does not put materials into the hands of the children unless they have an operational question to investigate. The guided discovery method is based on direct interaction with materials.

Finally, this process is important to the understanding of science as a means of investigating the environment. It is therefore one on which the students can spend a good deal of time, so that they thoroughly understand the process of experimentation. Guided discovery, the only method not eliminated by other considerations, does not violate time constraints because sufficient time is available.

For teaching children to develop and experiment, the most effective teaching method appears to be guided discovery.

Example Two. The lesson under consideration is a part of an astronomy unit in which fifth graders are learning the concept that the hotter a star is the closer to white the color of the star becomes. Because this is a concept, we can immediately eliminate the three methods that teach process or problem solving only: discovery demonstration, open inquiry, open discussion.

Although students have probably seen objects glow as they become hot, they probably have not related this to the idea that stars might have different colors due to differing temperatures. Little background is, therefore, present in these students. Methods that are suitable both to content teaching and to little background are exposition, exposition with interaction, and ordinary demonstration.

Although it is tempting to lecture or to have children read about coloration in stars, children tend to learn more effectively when they can see the concepts in a realistic situation. The idea that color changes as temperature increases can be shown using materials, but because of the high heat involved, students should not work directly with those materials. The best choice here is an ordinary demonstration in which the teacher shows the color changes perhaps by heating a piece of wire in a gas flame.

For this lesson, the best choice would be an ordinary demonstration.

Example Three. In this lesson, children in the fourth grade are to be taught the concept that vitamins are necessary for human health. This is strictly a content centered lesson and is only one of a series of lessons dealing with nutrition. Although this is important to human health, it is not an important part of the entire unit. For the most part, the children in the class are familiar with vitamins only as a pill taken at breakfast.

Because this lesson deals with content, the teaching methods which are most effective would be exposition, exposition with interaction, Socratic, ordinary demonstration, or guided discovery.

The students have little background in this area of knowledge. Those methods which are consistent with both content teaching and little knowledge are exposition and exposition with interaction.

Materials are difficult to use for this particular concept. Although experiments can be done with white rats, mice, or gerbils, the relative unimportance of the concept to the total unit does not really permit the use of a great deal of teaching time. The expository method and the exposition with interaction method are the final choices.

The exact method the teacher chooses for the lesson can be selected on the basis of the characteristics of the two methods. Exposition is very time efficient and with the use of pictures or drawings can be effective with children. The problem is that the teacher receives no feedback from the children, so he or she cannot review points that are not understood or immediately correct misconceptions. By adding questions to the expository method the teacher changes it to exposition with interaction and provides for feedback from the students. Exposition with interaction is probably the better method for this lesson.

Example Four. This lesson is an introduction to a fifth grade unit on flight. The unit is designed for maximum involvement with materials, so the children will develop process and problem solving skills. It is also the first unit on flight in the textbook series. Although many of the children in the class have flown in airplanes, seen the launch of the space shuttle on television, and viewed a blimp or hot air balloons, they really have little knowledge of how such aircraft fly.

The major thrust of the unit is developing process skills with the addition of problem solving. Content is included, but the content is secondary to the other outcomes. The most logical methods for the teaching of process and problem solving include the open discussion, guided discovery, discovery demonstration, and open inquiry methods.

Students do have a certain degree of familiarity with the area of flight, but have not used problem solving skills frequently. Because these children have a minimum of background information, the open discussion should be eliminated from the list of possible methods.

Materials seem, at first glance, to be difficult to use. The logistics of bringing airplanes, rockets, dirigibles, and hot air balloons to the students seem to rule out the use of concrete experiences. But, there are many possibilities: paper airplanes, balloons, model airplanes, and rockets, parachutes, and kites. Children can readily get involved with all of these items, so the discovery demonstration can be eliminated as a method leaving guided discovery and open inquiry as choices.

Both of these methods are time consuming, but at the start of a unit this should not be too much of a problem.

Which method, then, should be chosen? Guided discovery is a process oriented method, but it leans heavily toward the development of content. An introduction generally tries to present a broad overview of the entire unit, to develop interest, and to show the variety of things to come. In the open inquiry methods, students are free to pursue their own interests in a process oriented situation. The best choice in this case would be open inquiry.

Learning Activity 7–9

Selecting a Teaching Method

For each of the following descriptions, choose the teaching method that will most appropriately teach the lesson. Once you have chosen the method, give your reasoning for your choice.

Situation One:

This third grade class is in the middle of a unit dealing with matter. They have already considered a definition for "matter" and have studied the differences between elements and compounds, compounds and mixtures. The remainder of the unit is concerned with chemical and physical changes: topics never before considered. The next lesson is to teach the following definition: a physical change is a change in the physical properties of matter but not in its chemical composition. You would want to simplify this definition so that the children could understand it more easily. Which method would you choose for this lesson?

Situation Two:

This sixth grade unit deals with sources of energy. Students have already studied fossil fuels, renewable energy sources, solar energy, geothermal energy, and nuclear energy. The unit is coming to a close. At this point, you want the students to weigh the pros and cons of each source of energy. Which method would you choose for this lesson?

Situation Three:

You are half way through a unit dealing with chemistry and have begun to realize that your fifth grade students are unable to gather information from an activity or an experiment and to draw conclusions from that data. Something must be done to help the students learn the skills of using processes and of solving problems through the use of those processes. You want to make this a part of the chemistry unit. Which teaching method would you choose?

Situation Four:

This class of second graders is going to be making a field trip to a museum that has a particularly good exhibition of dinosaur fossils. The children studied dinosaurs in the first grade but have not considered the topic in more than a year. Which method would you use to review the information previously studied on dinosaurs prior to the trip to the museum?

Situation Five:

A fourth grade unit on rocks and minerals contains directions for an activity to show why some rock crystals are larger in some rocks than in others. The activity requires melting of sulfur over an alcohol lamp. The melted sulfur is then poured onto a glass plate to cool slowly or into a cup of cool water to cool quickly. You feel that this shows the effect of cooling rate on crystal growth very well. Which teaching method would you choose for this lesson?

Situation Six:

The next information to be studied by this second grade class deals with soil. The children are indifferent to the topic. You want to introduce this unit in a way that will generate interest and questions for study. Which method would you choose to use?

Situation Seven:

As always, green plants are included as a unit in your fifth grade textbook. You know that students have studied this area in previous grades, but are not certain what they can recall. Which teaching method would you use to determine what material has been retained by the students?

Situation Eight:

The unit you have been teaching on ecology deals with the basic concepts of ecology: food webs and food chains. In earlier grades, the students studied the various groups of plants and animals. Which teaching method would you use to teach the concepts of food webs and food chains?

Situation Nine:

These third grade students are very good at making observations and are gaining in ability to make reasonable inferences and conclusions. Now you want them to begin to work with operational questions, a new process. Which teaching method would you use for this topic?

Learning Activity 7–10

Organizing for Teaching

Choose a textbook or program for any grade from one through six. From that textbook choose a single unit or chapter depending on how the text or program is organized. Read the material from the chapter or unit carefully. Determine the major content and process points which are to be taught in the unit.

Write behavioral objectives that the children would accomplish during the unit in order to learn the major points. Then indicate the teaching method you would use for each of the objectives. Briefly describe your reason for choosing each of the methods.

Summary

The major points of this chapter can be easily summarized. First, there are many ways of teaching science to children. Each of those ways has appropriate and inappropriate uses. Second, the choice of the method to be used should depend on the objective of the lesson, the background of the students, and the area of science to be emphasized, content or process. Third, a well-equipped teacher of science has a wide variety of teaching methods from which to choose. And, last, when in doubt about a teaching method, the teacher should choose the method that provides for the most interaction between children and materials.

Selected References

Anderson, C., and D. Butts. A comparison of individualized and group instruction in a sixth grade electricity unit. *Journal of Research in Science Teaching, 17*, 2, 1980.

Susubel, D. P. *Psychology of Meaningful Verbal Learning*. New York: Greene and Stratton, 1963.

Barrow, L. H. The basics — communicating, thinking, and valuing. *School Science and Mathematics, 70*, 8, 1979.

Blankenship, T. Is anyone listening? *Science Teacher, 49*, 9, 1982.

Boulanger, F. D. Instruction and science learning: A quantitative synthesis. *Journal of Research in Science Teaching, 18*, 4, 1980.

Bruni, J. V. Problem solving for the primary grades. *Arithmetic Teacher, 29*, 6, 1982.

Burns, M. How to teach problem solving. *Arithmetic Teacher, 29*, 6, 1982.

Dewey, J. *The Child and Curriculum and the School and Society*. Chicago: University of Chicago Press, 1961.

Gallagher, J. J. Basic skills common to science and mathematics. *School Science and Mathematics, 79*, 8, 1979.

Minstrell, J. Getting the facts straight. *Science Teacher, 50*, 1, 1983.

Palmer, G. A. Teaching the nature of scientific enterprise. *School Science and Mathematics, 70*, 1, 1979.

Pepir, M. K. A science activity teaching plan. *School Science and Mathematics, 80*, 5, 1980.

Schneider, L., and J. W. Renner. Concrete and formal teaching. *Journal of Research in Science Teaching, 17*, 6, 1980.

Smith, W. S. Engineering a classroom discussion. *Science and Children. 20*, 5, 1983.

Suchman, J. R. *The Elementary School Training Program in Scientific Inquiry*. Champaign/Urbana: University of Illinois, 1962.

Suydam, M. Update on research on problem solving: Implications for classroom teaching. *Arithmetic Teacher, 29*, 6, 1982.

Victor, E. The inquiry approach to teaching and learning: A primer for the teacher. *Science and Children, 12*, 2, 1974.

Welch, W. W. Inquiry in school science. In M. B. Rowe, ed., *What Research Says to the Science Teacher*, vol. 3. Washington, D.C.: National Science Teachers Association, 1981.

White, E. P. Why self-directed learning? *Science and Children, 19*, 5, 1982.

The most successful scientists are capable of the zeal of the fanatic but are disciplined by objective judgment of their results and by the need to meet criticism from others. Love of science is likely to be accompanied by scientific taste and also is necessary to enable one to persist in the face of frustration.

— Beveridge, 1950

8 Attitudes and Science Teaching

Chapter Objectives

Upon completion of this chapter you should be able to

1. define each of the following terms: affective, attitude, scientific attitude, and classroom climate;
2. describe five factors which contribute to a positive learning environment;
3. describe the effect of attitudes on student achievement;
4. define each of the following scientific attitudes: curiosity, willingness to suspend judgment, skepticism, objectivity, and positive approach to failure;
5. list three means a teacher can use to develop each of the scientific attitudes.

"Johnny has such a good attitude. I could teach him anything."

"Mary just won't learn. Her attitude is terrible."

"I hate science."

"My favorite subjects are science, reading, and music."

"I'm too dumb to get good grades."

"This book says insects are bad. I think we should kill every insect in the world."

"I don't want to work with her. She talks funny."

As teachers, we daily confront these kinds of statements both from teachers and from students. Although some attitudes reflect a positive approach to school, to the environment, and toward people, other attitudes that students bring with them to school, or develop while in school, are negative. Still others, such as deep-seated prejudices, can even be debilitating to the individual.

Children tend to begin with a positive attitude toward school. Most children arrive for kindergarten or first grade with an enthusiasm and a desire to learn. Unfortunately, these positive attitudes do not continue throughout the typical child's elementary school career. From grade one through grade eight, general attitude toward school declines: positive attitudes become progressively less positive until many children view school as an unhappy experience. We can attribute this decline in positive attitude toward school, in part, to the failure that children so frequently experience.

The general decline in favorable attitude toward school is paralleled by a similar decline in attitude toward science. Although children often investigate "science things" at home and outside of school (rocks, insects, plants, stars, animals, and motions) and tend to enjoy science fiction movies, they often have a negative view of science in school.

What happens to the eager, enthusiastic, first-grader to turn him or her into a receptive, but apathetic, sixth grader? The cause of this change appears to lie in the complex interaction of a variety of factors. Among these factors are parental attitudes, interpersonal relations with teachers and other students, interactions with materials, and general classroom climate. To deal with attitudes is to deal with the affective domain rather than with the cognitive domain in learning.

The Affective Domain

Affective learning deals with the emotional aspects of behavior. It includes likes and dislikes, attitudes, values, and beliefs, all of which influence the individual's choice of goals and the means that person chooses for attaining those goals. Because human beings are a totality and cannot separate their emotion from their knowledge, there is an affective component to every school situation. Indeed, this affective component must come into play if full-brain rather than hemispheric processing of information is to occur.

Teachers do not, however, tend to plan effectively for affective learning experiences. Rather, much of learning in the affective domain is incidental or is concomitant to other learning. Through this incidental curriculum, students learn self-confidence or self-doubt, ease or anxiety, superiority or inferiority, success or failure, acceptance or rejection of others or themselves.

The Affective Domain of Bloom's Taxonomy

In order to develop a more systematic approach to affective learning, a taxonomy of educational objectives for the affective domain (Bloom, 1964) has been developed. Like his cognitive taxonomy, Bloom's affective taxonomy has a hierarchy of behaviors ascending in five levels from a simple to a complex form of affective behavior.

Level One: Receiving. At this level, the teacher places the individual in a situation where he or she is made cognizant of a particular phenomenon. This is the first and crucial step if the student is to be oriented to learn what the teacher intends for the student to learn. The student who is receiving is said to be "paying attention" to what is taking place in the classroom. The receiving level is divided into three sublevels: awareness, willingness to receive, and controlled or selected attention.

Awareness. At the awareness level we simply want the student to be conscious of a particular situation, phenomenon, or state of affairs in the science classroom. An object or phenomenon is simply noticed but does not need to be of any real concern to the learner. At this level of the affective domain, the student may:

1. show an awareness of the importance of controlling,
2. show a sensitivity to the existence of other viewpoints,
3. show a realization of the importance of science to a well-balanced adult.

Willingness to Receive. At this level, the student is expected not only to be aware of a stimulus but also to tolerate rather than avoid that stimulus. At worst the student will not actively avoid a particular situation or idea; at best the student will be willing to give the situation his or her attention. At this level a student may be expected to:

1. listen to an opposing viewpoint,
2. appreciate the contributions to science of women and minorities,
3. accept challenges to his or her data.

Controlled or Selected Attention. At this stage the student can separate the desired phenomenon from a background of many phenomena. The student still makes no judgment, but he or she is finally in control of the situation. At this point the student may be expected to:

1. appreciate the contribution science has made to the quality of life,
2. listen to an argument with some discrimination as to its logic and clarity,
3. show a preference for factual science books over fictionalized science books.

At the lowest level of the affective domain, we simply make the student aware of certain phenomena. There is no need for the individual to make judgments about the phenomena or to accept or reject what is said. Rather, it is enough for the student to be aware that something has occurred. To achieve this awareness, the learner may have to view unacceptable material for a longer period than acceptable material. But, the leaner often distorts the unacceptable, making it more acceptable through additions, deletions, and substitutions.

Level Two: Responding. At the responding level of the affective domain, the student is not simply attending but is actively attending. The student now commits himself or herself to what is going on in the classroom but at a very low level. The responding level, like the receiving level, is divided into three sublevels: acquiescence in responding, satisfaction in response, and willingness to respond.

Acquiescence in Responding. At this first level, we expect the learner actively to respond to some classroom situation. However, the student does not respond willingly but only to comply with a particular request. Although objectives are rarely stated at this level since compliance and obedience are expected in the classroom, a student may be expected to:

1. work with a particular student during an activity because the teacher requests it,
2. complete an experiment,
3. follow the rules for the safe use of science equipment.

Willingness to Respond. Action taken by the learner at this level is voluntary rather than compliant. The learner's response is not prompted by the teacher but results from the learner's desire to respond. The implication is that the learner is sufficiently committed to the behavior to want to act as he or she does. At this level a student may:

1. voluntarily look for books dealing with science,
2. engage on his or her own in a variety of science experiments or activities,
3. practice recycling of glass and paper on a voluntary basis,
4. accept the need for data to support a conclusion.

Satisfaction in Response. By this level the individual has gone beyond simply responding voluntarily to feeling satisfaction in responding. The student achieves a feeling of pleasure or enjoyment in making a particular response, so the particular behavior is reinforced. The student at this level can be expected to:

1. find pleasure in reading science books,
2. show enjoyment in science activities,
3. develop a keen interest in his or her physical environment.

Level Three: Valuing. At this level, the learner sees a thing, a behavior, or a phenomenon as having some worth. Attribution of worth is a result of both the individual's own assessment and the influence of society. A value is only slowly internalized or accepted; eventually an individual's behavior becomes consistent with the particular value. At the lowest level, the individual is willing to be perceived as sharing a particular value. At the highest level, the individual actively furthers the acceptance by others of the value. Three subdivisions of the valuing level exist: acceptance of a value, preference for a value, and commitment.

Acceptance of a Value. At this level, the individual imputes worth to a phenomenon, behavior, object, or idea. He or she holds a belief, but that belief is somewhat tentative. The student still tends to re-evaluate a position. However, there is enough stability and consistency to the learner's belief that others perceive the individual to be holding that value. A student may evidence at this level:

1. a continuing desire to learn more about a particular area of science,
2. an increasing recognition of the role of scientific thought in life,
3. recognition of the interrelations between man and the rest of the environment.

Preference for a Value. At this point not only does an individual accept a value and show a willingness to be identified with it, but also the individual is committed to the value. The individual actually wants to be associated with believing in a particular way. At this level the student may:

1. initiate a program to inform the class about the benefits of nuclear energy,
2. deliberately seek out a variety of viewpoints on a controversial issue before forming opinions,
3. write a letter to a Congressman about a particular issue.

Commitment. The notion of commitment brings with it a high level of certainty; there is conviction or certainty about a particular value. In some cases, the individual's commitment may border on faith, because he or she shows a firm and emotional acceptance. The individual's behavior at this level is such that he or she tries actively to develop his commitment, to forward the cause, or to win others to the cause. At this level the individual may:

1. show faith in the power of reason and in the method of experimentation,
2. show devotion to the ideals held by a particular organization,
3. try to advance the role of the scientist, the lay person, and the politician in decision making on scientific issues.

Level Four: Organization. In many situations more than one value is relevant. In such cases an individual needs to develop a system through which he or she can relate the applicable values to one another. Such a system represents not only an organization of values, but also the determination of the interrelationships which exist among those values, as well as the establishment of dominant or pervasive values. The organization level is divided into two sublevels: conceptualization of a value and organization of a value system.

Conceptualization of a Value. This is an abstract process; it is symbolic in nature and may be verbal or nonverbal depending on the inclinations of the individual. At this level, the learner manipulates sensory impressions and draws from them generalizations. The individual may:

1. attempt to identify the characteristics of an individual he or she admires,
2. form a judgment as to the responsibility of society for protecting endangered plant and animal species,
3. derive ideas about the mind set of the successful scientist by reading biographies of famous scientists.

Organization of a Value System. At this level, the learner must put a complex of often opposing values into an ordered relationship with one another. The resulting system of values usually is in a state of dynamic equilibrium dependent upon the environment at a particular time. On this level the individual may:

1. weigh alternative sources of energy against a set of standards of environmental quality,
2. attempt to determine how the concept of scientific thought can be related to the problems of society,
3. begin to form judgments as to the directions scientific progress should take.

Level Five: Characterization by a Value or Value Complex. At this level an individual has organized his or her values into a consistent system and has acted in accordance with these values for some time. In essence, the individual has developed a philosophy of life that governs his or her behavior. Formal education cannot, realistically, reach this level; for most of us this is a personal integration we do not reach until some years after the completion of formal education. Time and experience must interact with both affective and cognitive learning before an individual is able to answer a question like: What do I stand for in life?

The Relevance of the Affective Domain to Science Teaching

The affective domain provides a pattern the teacher can use as he or she considers the scientific attitudes that are a part of the total elementary school science curriculum. It also indicates that we cannot expect children quickly to develop scientific attitudes. Children can only do so through a general, slow process by which they not only gain an understanding of the attitude but also begin to consider that attitude as a part of a personal philosophy.

The affective domain taxonomy indicates that in teaching the scientific attitudes we must first make the student aware that the attitude exists, then help him or her to develop an ability to respond in a way consistent with the attitude and behave in a way that indicates that he or she actually values the particular attitude. This entire sequence takes time, and the teacher must be willing not only to take that time but also to act as a model of the particular behavior in the classroom.

An additional consideration for teachers working with scientific attitudes and with the values which form the foundation for scientific thought is that the society in which we live is multicultural. Children of varying backgrounds can be expected to bring to school varying attitudes and values. At times, the values and attitudes of science can touch upon areas that conflict with a child's beliefs. At this point, the teacher must tread lightly. The teacher must be a model of the scientific attitude of open-mindedness in these situations.

Also, attitudes and behavior, particularly in children, are not always consistent with one another. One set of values may override another in a particular situation. Because peer pressure is strong upon children from the upper primary grades onward, the child may give lip service to the attitudes or values of the majority of the class, although the child's true values are very different. In this situation, the teacher needs to provide a forum in which children may discuss, without fear of ridicule, various viewpoints. A number of social issues can form the basis for this type of discussion in the science classroom: environmental quality, the effects of various types of power plants, science in medicine, and drugs, alcohol, and tobacco.

As a final point, when considering the affective domain and the development of attitudes and values, the teacher must be careful to act as a model of appropriate scientific behaviors, because modeling is a particularly strong way to develop attitudes. The teacher cannot try to force particular attitudes on children or to preach particular attitudes — especially his or her own — to children. Attitudes develop gradually and change even more gradually. The scientific attitudes should be developed on a gradual, experiential basis.

Developing Scientific Attitudes

The scientist is said to have a particular outlook or attitude toward the world that colors his or her work. This attitude is actually a composite of a number of scientific attitudes, all of which should be considered as a part of the elementary school science program. Students can develop a true understanding of the nature of science only if they develop an understanding of the scientist's attitudes as well as an understanding of his or her concepts and methods. The component attitudes that form the total outlook of the scientist are:

1. curiosity,
2. a willingness to suspend judgment,
3. open-mindedness,

4. skepticism,
5. objectivity,
6. a positive approach to failure.

Curiosity

The scientific attitude of curiosity is the basis for science itself. It is a spontaneous desire to explore the environment and to learn about its phenomena. It is the only one of the scientific attitudes teachers can expect to find naturally in children.

Maintaining Curiosity in Children. To maintain a child's curiosity, the teacher must maintain a classroom atmosphere where a child feels free to be curious. The teacher must consider questions rather than ignoring or answering them in an authoritarian manner. Students need to be able to investigate educationally valid tangents as well as the topics directly under consideration. Maintaining curiosity also means that the child has an opportunity to investigate those things that are interesting at a particular time. Teachers should take advantage of what we call "teachable moments" and "spontaneous events" when they occur and not wait three months until the question finally comes back as a part of the standard curriculum in science. A cocoon, a bunch of berries, a cement truck pouring a new sidewalk, all may generate a great deal of curiosity and often provide for a more effective lesson than the one we planned for the day. Finally, the teacher must demonstrate curiosity about the environment so that the children see it as a desirable behavior.

Techniques for Maintaining Curiosity. The teacher can maintain curiosity through a variety of techniques:

1. You can answer and investigate spontaneous questions from students. This is particularly effective when the class develops operational questions to be used in determining answers.
2. You should consider spontaneous events as a part of the curriculum rather than as an irritation. The noise from a cement truck should be an invitation to investigate rather than a reason to close all the windows and forge ahead with the unit on heat.
3. You can use mystery boxes or other puzzling objects to permit the child to investigate an unknown quantity.
4. You can insert discrepant events, that is, demonstrations or activities that have an unexpected result can generate curiosity. These provide a puzzle for which the class must find a reason.
5. You can provide for open-ended, process-oriented activities, which the child may investigate in a no-fail setting.
6. You can maintain curiosity with discussion questions that children ask, pictures that are unusual, motion pictures with science content, and television programs that have science content.

7. You should provide books, magazines, and other sources of information on topics in which children have demonstrated some curiosity.

Curiosity helps the child develop interest in a particular area of science. Once the child is interested in an area, there is little that the teacher cannot accomplish with the child.

Willingness to Suspend Judgment

This attitude requires that the individual wait until all of the facts are in before he or she makes a judgment or draws a conclusion. At times, it asks the individual to set aside a strongly held belief and to consider conflicting evidence. Children do not take up this scientific attitude spontaneously.

Developing a Willingness to Suspend Judgment. This scientific attitude is difficult to develop when the class considers only a single source of information. The ability to withhold judgment is developed when the student is able to consider a number of sources of information, to determine the value and accuracy of the sources, and only after much consideration to draw a conclusion that reflects the information. In the science classroom, this means that the students should have access to a wide variety of printed sources of information rather than just a single textbook. It also means that the teacher should use more than a single activity to teach a particular concept. One activity allows children to "jump to conclusions," whereas a number of activities require that the students weigh and consider a variety of sources of evidence. The classroom atmosphere should be such that children feel comfortable presenting evidence that may conflict with that of other children.

Techniques for Developing a Willingness to Suspend Judgment. In a classroom where willingness to suspend judgment is fostered, one would expect to see:

1. a variety of different sources of information including books, magazines, newspapers, films, tapes, filmstrips, and resource people;
2. children learning which criteria can be used to judge the validity and/or bias of a source of information;
3. consideration of differing results of an activity or experiment with a view toward determining the causes of such differences as well as the validity of the varying results;
4. debate and discussion of controversial issues in which all sides are considered no matter how popular or unpopular the view;
5. the use of more than a single activity to show a particular concept;
6. displays of newspaper and/or magazine articles that show the development of a theory over time;
7. questions from teachers or students like:
   a. What was your source of information?
   b. What evidence do you have to support that idea?

c. Did you consider the other side of the issue?
d. How valid do you think that source of information is?

Willingness to suspend judgment, as a scientific attitude, asks the individual to consider a variety of viewpoints. It also asks the teacher to model the attitude by using a variety of resources in teaching, by being familiar with a variety of viewpoints, and by not jumping to conclusions himself or herself until all of the facts are in. If your students are to think for themselves, you cannot let your personal viewpoints and prejudices surface.

Skepticism

A skeptic is an individual who questions the validity of something that is supposedly accepted factual knowledge. The scientific attitude of skepticism is one in which the individual maintains a doubting attitude. Willingness to suspend judgment and skepticism are closely related scientific attitudes.

Developing Skepticism as a Scientific Attitude. The skeptic is going to seek out information in order to resolve the doubt that he or she has. Such a resolution does not come easily, and the seeker may need to consider a variety of sources before his or her skepticism is satisfied.

This kind of attitude cannot flourish in a situation where it is not considered proper to question authority. Rather, children should be taught that it is not only all right to ask questions but desirable to do so, even when those questions challenge what is presented as fact. Errors do occur in textbooks, tradebooks, and newspaper or magazine articles. At times, new information is discovered after a text or book goes to press. When material is presented as fact without support, or when conclusions are drawn where additional evidence could cause a different conclusion, the information should be open to the skeptic's questioning.

Techniques for Developing Skepticism. You can encourage the development of an attitude of skepticism through:

1. consideration of sources of information by study of biased versus unbiased approaches;
2. presentation of a variety of differing sources of information during any unit of study;
3. consideration of a variety of activities in which a principle is clearly shown in the majority, but its opposite is indicated in some;
4. displays and reading of new advances in science, which may conflict with text or program material;
5. interviews in which the interviewer must probe for the reasoning and information sources of the interviewee;

6. comparison of fictional materials — books, comics, cartoons — with factual materials and a discussion of the differences in a "which is more accurate" framework.

The teacher who would encourage the scientific attitude of skepticism on the part of students must be willing not only to model that behavior but also to be subjected to student doubt. When this attitude has developed it may be transferred to other areas through questions like:

What's the purpose for learning this?
Why can't I try it this way?
But I got the same answer. What's wrong with my method?
How do you know that's true?

Objectivity

To be objective is to look at many sides of an issue without prejudice. Objectivity asks us to start with a neutral position and attempt to determine what will happen in a particular situation or which position on a topic is most valid.

Problems in Working with the Scientific Attitude of Objectivity. A major problem in working with the attitude of objectivity is that a wide variety of the topics tackled under the heading of science have emotional overtones. Interests, tastes, attitudes, values, and morality, a class will touch upon them all at one time or another.

Consider the following topics. When we study insects in the elementary science program, the insects are usually butterflies, bees, and ants. Generally, these types of insects do not arouse highly negative feelings. But if the insects are roaches, lice, or flies, the teacher has a hard time convincing anyone that these creatures have a place in the food web. The latter group tends to arouse feelings of disgust.

A study of dinosaurs in which the class names the various types, describes what they might have eaten, and where they lived is a fascinating topic for almost any grade level. But a study of evolution if it touches on man can be highly emotional, because it may impinge on the religious beliefs of students.

Factors Influencing Objectivity. Objectivity asks that an individual bring into a situation a nonbiased approach. But topics like those previously indicated show that science subjects are not devoid of attitudes, values, emotions, and previous learning. If the information presented in the science program is consistent with one's value system it is easily attended to and assimilated. Information that is not consistent may be shut out or negatively processed. The first factor influencing objectivity is the individual's personal value system.

Working with children the teacher must also consider a second factor influencing objectivity. Children in the preoperational stage of development tend to be highly egocentric. The egocentric child finds it difficult, if not impossible, to consider any viewpoint other than his or her own. Consequently, the egocentric child may reject, out of hand, anything that does not agree with his or her own viewpoint.

Finally, the teacher may have difficulty developing the scientific attitude of objectivity in children because of his or her own difficulty in permitting children to draw differing conclusions from those he or she holds. In order for children to learn to be objective, they must see objectivity on the part of the teacher.

Techniques for Developing Objectivity. Developing the child's ability to look objectively at the content of the science program means that the teacher must change the customary pattern of teaching science in the elementary school.

Using a Textbook. Most textbook activities for teaching content are presented so as to illustrate the principle being discussed in the textbook. Figure 8–1 illustrates this strategy.

As we can see from this illustration, the student was told the purpose of the activity not once but twice. There could be no doubt in anyone's mind that a chemical change is to occur. This activity is illustrative rather than instructive. In many cases, even if the activity does not work as it is supposed to work, the children will still see or say they see exactly what they were supposed to see, because they have been told to see it.

Rather than illustrating what is already known, activities designed to develop objectivity should be presented in such a way that the students will not know the precise outcome. The activity should be presented so that the learner is asked to determine what is being illustrated. Foregone conclusions are closely allied to biases and have no place in the objective world of science. Teaching that uses activities in which the students determine what is being shown allows students to develop concepts rather than to check the accuracy of the textbook.

Use of Operational Questions. A second way to develop the scientific attitude of objectivity is to ask operational questions. The teacher should pose such questions in a neutral form so that students must base their answers to the questions on the data collected rather than on the thrust of the question. Neutral operational questions are phrased like the following:

What is the effect of sunlight on plant growth?
What factors affect the amount of force needed to use a lever to lift an object?
How can the rate of evaporation of a liquid be increased?

Evaluation Level Questions. A third possibility for the development of objectivity in children is for the teacher to propose evaluation level questions, particularly when the student is asked to judge against a set of established

Figure 8–1 A textbook illustration—chemical changes

A chemical change occurs when two or more materials are combined to form a new material. We have already seen that when sulfur and iron are mixed together we can still recognize both of these elements. If we bring a magnet into contact with the mixture of iron and sulfur, we can collect all of the iron. If we heat the mixture, there is a new material. A chemical change has occurred.

Now try this:

Needed: 1 tablespoon powdered sulfur
1 tablespoon iron filings
aluminum pie pan
hot plate
magnet

Procedure: Place the sulfur powder on the pie plate.
Test it with the magnet.
Is it magnetic?
Place the iron filings in a different place on the pie plate.
Test the filings with the magnet.
Are the filings magnetic?
Mix the iron and sulfur together.
Heat the mixture until the iron and the sulfur are no longer separate.
Let the new material cool.
Test the material with a magnet.
Is the new material magnetic?

When iron and sulfur are heated together, a new material is formed. Iron and sulfur form a new compound called iron sulfide. A chemical change has occurred.

criteria. Thus, two theories can be compared using appropriate criteria developed either by the teacher or by the students in large- or small-group settings.

For example, a list of criteria for evaluation of one theory against another might include the fact to be considered by each theory followed by an unbiased outline of each theory, and a list of questions to be considered:

1. Which theory is best able to explain the facts? Why?
2. Which theory has the most scientific research to support it?
3. Which theory is best able to make predictions about what will be found or learned in the future?

4. Which theory can best be determined through experimentation?
5. What problems exist with each of the theories? How serious are these problems?
6. What data would be needed to strengthen each theory?
7. What facts might cause scientists to abandon each theory?

Use of Modeling. Finally, the teacher must act as a model of the scientific attitude of objectivity. Even when the teacher's values cause him or her to reject a certain point of view, the teacher must provide a model committed to the consideration of a variety of viewpoints. The teacher who strongly objects to the use of nuclear power, for example, should still present unbiased material that considers both sides of the issue.

The development of objectivity is important to an understanding of the nature of science, but it is a particularly difficult area to develop because it is influenced by the individual's attitudes and biases. Probably the best means for fostering objectivity in the classroom is for the teacher to embody that attitude.

Positive Approach to Failure

Having a positive approach to failure means that each testing of an hypothesis, whether positive or negative, yields some new information that the scientist can incorporate into further experimentation. If the hypothesis is proven to be correct, the experiment is viewed as a success. If the hypothesis is proven incorrect, the experiment is still successful. In the latter case, the scientist has still gained information, which he will use to construct new hypotheses for further experimentation. Consequently, even the experiment that fails to prove an hypothesis provides new information.

As an example of this orientation, consider this hypothesis and the data collected when the experiment was done: The smaller the candle the longer it will take for it to go out in a quart jar.

These data show that the height of the candle has no real effect on the length of time that the candle burned. In one sense, the child who carried out this experiment failed: the hypothesis was incorrect. However, the child enjoyed a great deal of success in this case. The child has, of course, successfully used a great many of the science processes. But the child has also learned one

HEIGHT OF CANDLE	TRIAL 1	TRIAL 2	TRIAL 3	AVERAGE
10cm	75s	73s	76s	74.7s
8cm	74s	74s	75s	74.3s
6cm	69s	78s	74s	73.7s
4cm	75s	75s	73s	74.3s
2cm	77s	71s	74s	74.0s
1cm	75s	76s	73s	74.7s

factor which does not need to be controlled in further experiments dealing with this topic.

A Positive Approach to Failure in the World of Science. The failure to prove an hypothesis may be unusual in a school science program where the activities are specifically designed to illustrate particular hypotheses. In the actual world of science, however, so-called failure is much more common than success. Many years of cancer research are only now beginning to lead to cures for certain specific types of cancer. Thousands of failures have occurred in thousands of laboratories, yet although that elusive cure has not been discovered each of the failures has increased knowledge of causes, cures, and possible paths for further research. The elimination one by one of causal factors means the search for a cause is progressing.

The school science program that has a content orientation cannot allow students to develop the same attitude toward failure as is developed in the research scientist. A content-oriented program is generally directed toward a single, predetermined correct answer. This viewpoint is misleading in a number of ways. It, first of all, shows science as an enterprise in which all things are known and in which answers can be memorized because they do not change. Second, the content-only orientation gives the impression that the scientist always knows precisely what he or she will find as a result of an experiment or other form of research. And, third, the content-only orientation tends to treat theory and fact as equivalent rather than dealing with the tentative nature of a theory. Showing that scientists do fail, that they do not know everything, and that what they can learn from their failures is important can alert children to a more realistic view of science.

A Positive Approach to Failure and the Reduction of Anxiety. The attitude that allows a positive approach to failure also has the side benefit of reducing anxiety in those children who have become anxious about the work they do in school. Extreme anxiety can cause a decrease in the quality of a student's work. A particularly clear example of anxiety's effect on students is test anxiety in which a student's test grade is lower than anticipated as a result of fear.

Highly anxious students tend to lack self-confidence, curiosity, and adventurousness, all qualities of great importance to exploratory science. Building student trust both in themselves and in others may reduce anxiety and promote learning. Trust tends to increase when the threat of failure is reduced.

By developing in students the ability to learn from their incorrect hypotheses and incorrect predictions of operational questions, the teacher can help the child who has constantly experienced failure to begin to experience success and to see that one can learn from failure as well as from success.

Techniques for Developing a Positive Approach to Failure. In general the best technique for developing a positive approach toward failure is to institute a process-oriented science program in which the content of the program is developed through the use of the processes of science. Within this general orientation, certain techniques are particularly appropriate:

1. In the lower elementary grades develop operational questions to which the children respond by making predictions of the outcome and testing their predictions.
2. In the upper elementary grades present experimentation in which students develop hypotheses that predict the outcome of the experiment.
3. Discuss the data collected from both operational questions and experiments in which incorrect predictions were made, trying to show what has been learned from that data.
4. Encourage children to make multiple inferences from their data and to develop ways of testing to determine the validity of those inferences.
5. Display magazine and newspaper articles in which research is discussed that did not produce the expected results. These are fairly common in topics dealing with medical research and with research in space.
6. Accept answers that are based on evidence, even when scientifically incorrect, and have the child develop a means for retesting an hypothesis.
7. Rewrite textbook activities and experiments so that the outcome is not known. Have the children do the activities and experiments before they read the information in the textbook.

Each of the scientific attitudes brings the child into closer contact with the viewpoint of the scientist and into greater understanding of the nature of science. By working with the scientific attitudes, the teacher can make the elementary science program a true reflection of the scientific enterprise: a combination of content, process, and attitudes.

Affect and Learning

The affective domain and the scientific attitudes provide an important link between the content learned in the science program and the behavior of the child.

We can, for example, train anyone to write an hypothesis, control variables, carry out an experiment, and draw a conclusion from the data that he or she collects. But unless that individual also comes to value the experiment for itself, as a powerful means for gaining knowledge, it is unlikely that the experiment or even the objectivity inherent in the experiment will be effective. Unless affective learning takes place the content that teachers so carefully teach in the science program may never be used by the children.

Affect, then, should permeate all that we do in the classroom. It is both an aid to internalization and an aid to the processing of information into memory. A pleasant learning environment with a knowledgeable teacher who embodies models of appropriate behaviors works positively to develop both content and attitude. Research indicates that the affective aspects of the curriculum are most strongly influenced by:

1. the attitude of the teacher,
2. the enthusiasm shown by the teacher,
3. the personality of the teacher,
4. interrelationships between the teacher and the students,
5. the teacher's knowledge of the subject matter,
6. the participation of students in active learning,
7. a classroom that is low on anxiety.

From this listing, you can see that the teacher is probably the most important classroom influence on the development of attitudes in children. Because he or she is influential, the teacher must be careful to maintain a neutral position in the face of controversy and to be a model of the attitudes that she or he intends for the children to develop.

Summary

The teacher in the elementary science classroom may have a great deal of knowledge of the content of science, may be able to use the processes of science, and may be able to plan an appropriate science lesson, yet that teacher may be ineffective in working with science. The teacher who ignores the affective aspects of science education is not likely to produce lasting changes in the behavior of the students. For every content topic, there is a corresponding affective component.

The teacher's first concern is with the development of a range of attitudes: from simply attending to the information presented to actually valuing the information and attempting to demonstrate that value to others. This sequence of development, outlined in Bloom's taxonomy, grows only slowly but can be started in the elementary school.

The teacher's second concern should be with the development of scientific attitudes as they illustrate the mind set of the research scientist. Curiosity, willingness to suspend judgment, objectivity, skepticism, and a positive approach to failure should all be a part of the total science curriculum for the elementary school. Specific teaching techniques can help the teacher develop these scientific attitudes, but the teacher also needs to be a model for the students.

Selected References

Aspy, D. N., and F. N. Roebuck. Affective education: Sound investment. *Educational Leadership, 39*, 7, 1982.

Beane, J. A. Self-concept and self-esteem as curriculum issues. *Educational Leadership, 39*, 7, 1982.

Beveridge, W. *The Art of Scientific Investigation.* New York: Vintage, 1950.

Bloom, B. S., (ed.) *Taxonomy of Educational Objectives. The Classification of Educational Goals. Handbook II: Affective Domain.* New York: McCay, 1964.

Coble, C. R., and D. R. Rice. Rekindling scientific curiosity. *Science Teacher, 50,* 2, 1983.

Dunfee, J. Investigating children's science learning. *The Education Digest, 36,* 5, 1971.

Farley, J. R. Raising student achievement through the affective domain. *Educational Leadership, 39,* 7, 1982.

Gaudry, E., and C. D. Spielberger. *Anxiety and Educational Achievement.* New York: Wiley and Sons Australasia, 1971.

Gauld, G. The scientific attitude and science education: A critical reappraisal. *Science Education, 66,* 1, 1982.

Hoffman, H. H. An assessment of eight-year-old children's attitudes toward science. *School Science and Mathematics, 77,* 8, 1977.

Kurzwell, Z. E. *Anxiety and Education.* New York: Yorseloff, 1968.

Lawrenz, F. The relationship between science teacher characteristics and student achievement and attitude. *Journal of Research in Science Teaching, 12,* 10, 1975.

Lloyd, S. E., and I. D. Brown. Investigation of children's attitudes toward science fostered by a field-based science methods course. *Science Education, 63,* 5, 1979.

Markle, G. Generating good vibrations for science. *Science and Children, 49,* 4, 1982.

McMillian, J. H., and M. J. May. A study of factors influencing attitudes of fifth grade students toward science. *School Science and Mathematics, 67,* 1967.

Moore, R. W. Open-mindedness and proof. *School Science and Mathematics, 82,* 6, 1982.

Ringness, T. A. *The Affective Domain in Education.* Boston: Little, Brown, 1975.

Robinson, M. L. Attitudes and achievement: A complex relationship. March 1975. ERIC Document 111 678.

Wager, W. Instructional design and attitude learning. *Educational Technology, 19,* 2, 1979.

A handicapped person functions at his or her optimum level in an environment and lifestyle as close to normal as possible. Science is a vital part of that environment and lifestyle.

— Hoffman and Ricker, 1979

9 Teaching Children with Special Needs

Chapter Objectives:

Upon completion of this chapter you should be able to

1. define mainstreaming and discuss its purpose;
2. discuss the characteristics of the following groups of children with special needs: children with visual handicaps, children with auditory handicaps, children with intellectual handicaps, children with orthopedic handicaps, children who are culturally different, gifted children, and girls in science;
3. discuss the role of science in the education of each group of children with special needs;
4. discuss teaching techniques for teaching science to the various groups of children with special needs;
5. adapt a textbook or program to the needs of special children in the regular classroom.

Traditionally, the child with special learning needs has been considered so different from the typical child that he or she has been isolated from the mainstream of education and placed in special classes. Such classes were established so that children with similar needs could be collected into a single setting with a teacher trained to work effectively with a specific type of child. Classes for the visually handicapped, the hearing handicapped, the mentally retarded, the orthopedically handicapped, and the gifted were established. Unfortunately, special classes for these children resulted not in the best possible education but in the greatest possible isolation. Within the public schools, mentally handicapped children were so effectively separated from other children that the two groups rarely met. In other cases, the public schools did not provide education for all children. Blind and partially sighted children frequently had to be sent to private schools, but the costs kept many parents from sending their children to school at all. Many handicapped children received no significant education even though the public schools were supposedly established to provide a free education for all children.

But the handicapped child was not the only child to suffer from group isolation. The gifted child, placed into academically challenged classes had little chance to interact with average children, thus perpetuating the stereotype of the aloof and physically incompetent gifted child. In many of those classes, girls were a minority, because social stereotypes prevented their identification as gifted. Isolation arising from grouping for a homogeneous classroom led to a lack of interaction among all kinds of children.

In the 1970s two federal laws were passed to deal with the needs of special children. Public Law (PL) 95-561, the Gifted and Talented Children's Act of 1978, attempted to define "gifted"; Public Law (PL) 94-142 of 1975 considered the various classes of handicapped individuals. In both laws, the emphasis was on providing an appropriate education for all children within the framework of the public school system.

These laws, particularly PL 94-142, emphasized the concepts of mainstreaming and of the least restrictive environment. No longer were children to be isolated from their average peers because of their special needs. Instead, whenever possible, the special child was to be educated in the regular public school setting. This placement was made with the assumption that the regular classroom would be the best place for the handicapped child to learn.

For purposes of this textbook, we will discuss seven groups of children with special learning needs:

1. visually handicapped,
2. auditorially handicapped,
3. intellectually handicapped,
4. orthopedically handicapped,
5. culturally different,
6. gifted,
7. girls in science.

Science and the Handicapped Child

General Suggestions

Some general suggestions are pertinent to working with all children who have special needs. These suggestions were complied by Bybee (1979) and are of particular help to the teacher working with special children for the first time:

1. Obtain and read any background information available on the special student. Talk with teachers who have previously worked with the child.
2. Learn about the nature of the child's difference and how that difference affects the student's potential for learning.
3. Determine if there is special help you can obtain through resources of a special education expert.
4. Determine whether the child will need any special equipment in order to be able to function at an optimum level.
5. Talk with the handicapped student to learn about the child's limitations and about any particular needs.
6. Be aware of barriers, both physical and psychological, to the student's fullest possible functioning.
7. Consider how to modify or adapt the curriculum and your teaching strategies to allow the child's fullest possible participation.
8. Do not underestimate the capabilities of the special student.
9. Use the same standards for grading and disciplining the handicapped student as you use for the rest of the class.
10. Provide for as much individualization of the curriculum as possible.

The Role of Science in the Education of the Handicapped Child

Science has as much of a place in the elementary school education of the visually handicapped, hearing handicapped, orthopedically handicapped, or intellectually handicapped child as it does in the education of the average child. These children will be citizens of a scientifically oriented society just as much as their nonhandicapped peers. But, in addition to the general preparation of children for adult life, science education can play a specific role in the education of the handicapped child.

Conceptual Development. Children with such sensory deprivations as visual, hearing, or motor problems frequently have a poorer concept of the environment and particularly of causal relations than do their nonhandicapped peers. The cause of this deficiency lies not in the child's intellectual capacity but in the child's inability to gain information through all senses. Because science education attends to the development of observational skills, which allow the child to use all available senses, science in the elementary school can provide the child with experiences that will allow for greater conceptual development.

Working with the processes of inference, conclusion, data interpretation, spatial relations, cause and effect, and interaction and systems contributes to the development of a causal sense in the child who has had little opportunity to develop that sense.

Vocabulary Development. With the exception of the orthopedically handicapped child, other handicapped children may be deficient in vocabulary. This is particularly true for the hearing impaired or deaf child. Access to a vocabulary based upon concrete experiences can aid the hearing impaired child to develop the vocabulary skills needed for an understanding of the environment. The intellectually handicapped child also benefits greatly from concrete development of a scientific vocabulary. In addition to developing the vocabulary one needs for a discussion of the phenomena of the world, the visually handicapped child can be aided, through the use of equipment and models, to develop a vocabulary dealing with familiar scientific objects in the environment and with the more technical names for various parts of plants and animals.

Problem Solving Skills. The handicapped child has few opportunities to participate in problem solving situations that are commonplace for nonhandicapped peers. Even the simple situation of deciding who might be at the door after a knock is denied to the child with a hearing handicap. The orthopedically handicapped child, like the intellectually handicapped child, is often barred from problem solving situations by overly helpful adults, who feel these children might be unable to cope with such situations. In reality, all children need the experience of solving problems. The teacher can use operational questions, experimentation, and participation in discovery demonstration and open inquiry lessons to allow all children to participate in and learn to solve practical problems. These skills can then be transferred to the world outside the classroom.

Career Choice. Traditionally the visually, hearing, and orthopedically handicapped have been guided away from careers in science. Today the emphasis is on recruiting such individuals for careers in chemistry, physics, astronomy, geology, and biology. There are no compelling reasons why the handicapped individual who has no intellectual impairment should not be a candidate for a science career. The visually handicapped individual can plan for experimentation as well as the nonhandicapped and can guide laboratory assistants in the conduct of that experiment. The hearing handicapped individual has no difficulty even in the laboratory. The hearing handicapped individual who is able to speak can effectively communicate with others, and by employing an interpreter the nonoral individual can communicate as well. The orthopedically handicapped individual is barred from a laboratory situation only by physical barriers, which can be removed. Ramps with platforms give access to high lab tables and laboratory assistants who can, if needed, act as the scientist's hands are examples of aids that can enable the interested individual to pursue a career in science. The handicapped individual who is enthusiastic and capable in science should be encouraged to take up that career option.

In order for the handicapped individual to receive the various benefits of science in the elementary school program, the school and the teacher may have to adapt the program or the teaching methods to the needs of the child. For the most part the regular classroom teacher can easily make these adaptations and will not have to give more attention to the handicapped student than he or she gives to any student.

Science and the Visually Handicapped Student

Adapting Teaching Methods. For the visually handicapped child, research has indicated that the most effective teaching methods are those that involve the child in hands-on experiences. Discovery and open inquiry are, therefore, the most appropriate teaching methods for these children. When the teacher has to use exposition and exposition with interaction, he or she should be careful to explain clearly and in detail, being certain not to write or draw anything on the chalkboard or overhead projector without providing a verbal description and/or a model for the student to touch during the exposition. If the child has some residual sight, large projections with great contrast may permit him or her to see what the teacher is describing. When conducting an ordinary demonstration, the teacher should permit the visually handicapped child to touch each of the items prior to its use and should describe everything that happens during the demonstration in detail. The discussion method and the Socratic method should need no adaptations, whereas the discovery demonstration will be unsuitable to the visually handicapped child.

Adapting Activities. The visually handicapped child should fully participate in the activities of the science program. There is no evidence that the visually handicapped child is more prone to accidents or to breaking things than are other children in the classroom. Instructions for the activities should be tape recorded so that the child can listen to them or provided in Braille or in magnified print if the child can make use of either of them. The materials that are used in the activities should be large enough so that the visually handicapped child can manipulate them easily. This may mean provision for alligator clips in a circuit rather than screws or a large dry cell with screw type terminals rather than smaller "D" batteries. In some cases, materials especially adapted to the visually impaired child are available, including rulers and measuring cups with raised graduations, beeper scales rather than those which use a pointer, and plastic rather than glass containers, which will not shatter if dropped. The teacher may also have to substitute materials or activities if the predominant sense needed by the observing student is sight. This may entail something as simple as exchanging a buzzer for a light bulb in a circuit, or it may mean the use of a different activity if no adaptation can be made to let the child use other senses. Also, be certain to orient the child to the location of the materials in the classroom as well as to a source of water if needed and to the location of each of the materials that will be used in an activity carried out at the child's desk. Finally, only when it is necessary should the visually handicapped child be assigned a partner. And the partner assigned should be one who will do what the child directs or describe what the child has done rather than one who will do everything for the child.

Adapting Content. For the most part no adaptation of content should be needed for the visually handicapped child because there is no intellectual impairment. However, be certain that the visually handicapped child has the same background and experiences as his or her sighted peers. You may establish this through a formal pretest or through a one-to-one discussion with the child. Only if you find a deficiency in background should you adapt the curriculum. Or you may institute additional enrichment activities, which may also be suitable for some of the nonhandicapped in the class.

Adapting Verbal Material. The use of written material with the visually impaired student will require the greatest adaptation. For the child who understands Braille, textbooks and tradebooks may be available. Television-like devices which magnify the print of a text or other written document may be appropriate for some children. In other cases, it may be necessary for the teacher to make a tape recording of the written material or ask another student to make one. A reader may also be assigned to the child. A scribe or a tape recorder should also be available to the visually handicapped child, so that he or she can make records of activities and experiments. Always keep in mind that it will take longer for the visually handicapped child to work with written material than it will most nonhandicapped children. And, remember that the visually handicapped child is unable to see your body language; in this case you should express verbal rewards.

Science and the Hearing Handicapped Student

Adapting Teaching Methods. For the hearing handicapped child, research has shown that the most effective teaching methods are those which allow direct, hands-on contact with materials. The methods that permit this kind of contact are guided discovery, open inquiry, and ordinary demonstration or discovery demonstrations. Although the latter methods do not allow direct contact, the inclusion of materials provides the visual experience that hearing handicapped children need. In using exposition or exposition with interaction, the teacher should be certain to use illustrations, pictures, drawings, and models extensively. The teacher should screen films prior to showing to determine whether the hearing handicapped child will be able to gain the concepts from the visual portion of the film. Older children could be given written material prior to the film that will orient them to the major concepts shown. In the discussion, the child who can speak adequately should be encouraged to participate orally, and the teacher should repeat comments that may not be clear enough for other children to understand. If an interpreter is in the classroom with the child, the interpreter should convey the child's comments orally. Children with difficulty in speaking should also be encouraged to write comments or questions, which could be read by another student.

Adapting Activities. For the most part, the hearing handicapped child should be able to participate in the same activities as his or her peers. Adaptations will be needed only when the activity calls for hearing as the major way to gain information. In this case, adaptation may mean replacing a buzzer with a light in a circuit, using a probe box rather than a mystery box, or determining information about sound by feeling vibrations rather than listening to pitch or duration. Written instructions should be provided for the child including an extensive use of diagrams. In addition, when oral directions are given, the teacher should demonstrate using the actual materials. It will be rare for the hearing handicapped child to be unable to participate in an activity. However, if that should occur, an alternative should be found to illustrate the concept in a more appropriate manner.

Adapting Content. The teacher should not have to adapt the content of the elementary science program for the hearing handicapped child. However, you should be certain that the child does have the required background information through a pretest or a one-on-one discussion.

Adapting Verbal Material. As with the visually handicapped individual, the greatest problem to the science teacher will be the adaptation of verbal material. Be certain that written material is on the level of the child. Because there may be some retardation in the development of language ability, the hearing handicapped child may need to have written material on a grade level below that of the average children in the class. The child should be encouraged to participate in discussions and other verbal activities of the classroom using whatever speech is available. Moreover, drawings, demonstrations, mime, and written communications can help the child to communicate with the nonhandicapped in the classroom. Always be certain during verbal work that the child's hearing aid is functioning properly, that the volume is loud enough, and that the battery does not need to be replaced. The teacher should always place himself or herself so that his or her face is well lighted and so that the child is not looking into a bright light. In addition, when speaking to the hearing handicapped child do not speak louder than usual or draw words out into distorted versions. The child who has some hearing will be able to understand the teacher more easily if he or she speaks in an ordinary tone of voice. Lastly, the child who is learning to use oral speech will have a professional to help in developing that speech.

You should convey new vocabulary terms developed in the science class to that professional so that the child can learn to pronounce them correctly. If there is an interpreter in the classroom who aids the child with sign language, that person may also appreciate a list of such vocabulary.

Science and the Orthopedically Handicapped Student

Adapting Teaching Methods. The orthopedically handicapped student, unless other handicaps are also present, generally suffers from no impairments that would require changes in your usual teaching methods. The only change might be for the child who is unable to move his or her head; he or she would need to be positioned so that demonstrations would be easily visible. In a case like this, the teacher should also be aware that his or her pacing or moving around the classroom while teaching could hinder the child's ability to learn.

Adapting Activities. For the most part, the adaptations needed for the orthopedically handicapped child will be ones to accommodate to the child's level of mobility. If desks are too low or too high to permit the child in a wheelchair to use the surface for an activity, a tray could be provided. If science is taught in a special classroom with high lab tables, the child could be accommodated with a ramp and an elevated platform that raises him or her to the height of the table. Access to materials should be made easy for the handicapped child. To more easily obtain materials, the child who uses canes or a walker could be provided with a bag or plastic bucket that could be carried over the shoulder. If the class goes outdoors, an area that is inaccessible to a wheelchair or canes can be made accessible with a wagon or by carrying the child. Weakness or spasticity in the hands or arms that might prevent the child from participating in an activity can be overcome through a lab partner. Once again, it is important for the teacher to assign as a partner a child who will work at the handicapped student's instruction rather than doing everything for the handicapped child.

Adapting Content. The content of the typical elementary school science program should be appropriate to the orthopedically handicapped child without adaptation.

Adapting Verbal Material. The orthopedically handicapped child should need no adaptation of verbal material other than that needed by any child to place him or her on a proper reading level. It may be necessary, however, to provide a book holder or scanning device if the child is unable to hold a book or to turn pages. A pencil or pen holder, an electric typewriter, or a tape recorder may also be needed for the child who has problems with hand coordination or hand use. The handicapped child who is able to use a pen or pencil holder may still find writing a difficult and physically tiring task. Provide enough time for the child to be able to complete written assignments.

Science and the Intellectually Handicapped Student

Adapting Teaching Methods. For the intellectually handicapped, or mentally retarded, child, the most appropriate teaching methods are those that allow the child to work directly with materials. The guided discovery and open inquiry methods are, therefore, the most appropriate. Because open inquiry permits children to investigate up to their capacities, open inquiry is the most desirable of the process oriented methods. Ordinary demonstration and guided discovery are successful methods for teaching content because of their structured approach. When using verbal methods, however, the teacher should be certain that the content is well sequenced and presented in small steps with much repetition and practice. Verbal presentations should be based on the child's concrete experiences. In the discovery demonstration, the intellectually handicapped child can be expected to watch, to offer observations, and to develop simple questions, but not to come to a final conclusion about the demonstration. Films should have an advance organizer to alert the intellectually handicapped child to the important points prior to showing. In addition, it is helpful to show a film in small segments with an organizer prior to each segment and a brief discussion following. This viewing technique is also highly effective with the average child.

Adapting Activities. For the most part the retarded child can do the activities of the science program. Some ideas that will enable you to help the retarded child work more effectively include making activities open ended so that the child will be able to work on an appropriate level while other children in the class carry the activity to more complex levels, using very familiar materials to illustrate new concepts, breaking activities of some length into smaller steps, having many activities which show the same concept, and providing the child with easy-to-read instructions. You should not expect the retarded child to develop and carry out an experiment involving control of variables. For the most part, the intellectually handicapped individual will not reach the formal operations level of thought where experimentation becomes possible.

Adapting Content. The content of the elementary science program may need some adaptation to be appropriate for the intellectually handicapped child. Information should be presented in small, sequential steps with much repetition and with much opportunity for the child to use the information in appropriate situations. In addition, the regular curriculum of the science program should be adapted to emphasize the practical aspects of science. For the intellectually handicapped child, science should contribute to the child's ability to function nearly normally in society. Topics most appropriate for the intellectually handicapped child include: electricity, energy, matter, weather, health (including alcohol, drugs, and tobacco), plant and animal care, the human body and high interest topics of the day that will allow the child to interact with peers. Today this topic might include space and space travel.

Adapting Verbal Material. The major adaptation in this area will be in written materials. The intellectually handicapped child can be expected to function at a reading level from two to four years below his or her peers. Consequently, the classroom should have books and other written materials on a grade level that the child will be able to read. High-interest, low-level materials are available through a number of companies. In addition, most textbook series no longer display the grade level prominently but do continue to include much of the same material at varying grade levels. The teacher can, therefore, provide a lower level textbook from the same series for the child. If materials are not available, the teacher should rewrite materials on an appropriate level. The retarded child will also need more time than the average to complete written assignments and reading assignments.

Learning Activity 9–1

Adapting Science Activities to the Visually Handicapped

Choose any science textbook series for grades one through six. Scan one chapter in a primary grade textbook from the series and one chapter from an intermediate level textbook. Determine which of the suggested activities would need to be modified for use with the visually handicapped child.

For those activities needing modification, discuss ways in which they could be easily changed by the classroom teacher to permit the visually handicapped child to participate effectively.

Should an activity be totally inappropriate, suggest an alternate activity that would get across the same concept as the original activity.

Learning Activity 9–2

Science Materials for the Visually Handicapped

Investigate one of the following programs or sources of materials for the visually handicapped:

1. Science Activities for the Visually Impaired (SAVI),
2. Adapting Science Materials for the Blind (ASMB),

3. Concept Development for Visually Handicapped Children (William T. Lyndon and Loretta McGraw),
4. American Printing House for the Blind.

Learning Activity 9–3

Adapting Science Activities to the Hearing Impaired

For the most part you will not have to adapt science activities for use with hearing impaired children. There are, however, two areas where the teacher may need to consider the capabilities of the hearing handicapped child: in giving directions and in having the child report the results of an activity.

In any textbook for grades one through six, find two activities. First, adapt the directions so that they can be given to the hearing impaired or deaf child in a way that the child can understand. If you have ability in signing, demonstrate the use of that language. Second, consider the child who has difficulties with oral language. Describe some ways the child could communicate to the rest of the class the results of the activity.

Learning Activity 9–4

Working with the Orthopedically Handicapped Child in Science

Visit any first through sixth grade classroom in which science is taught. Imagine a situation in which this classroom will receive a mainstreamed orthopedically handicapped child in a wheelchair.

What adaptations would be necessary to permit the child to work effectively in the classroom during a science activity. Consider how the child will obtain materials, use those materials, and participate in any cleanup. Remember, a partner should only be proposed if the child is unable to work effectively because of hand coordination or spasticity problems.

Learning Activity 9–5

Adapting Science Content to the Intellectually Handicapped Child

Describe how you would develop any two of the following concepts in the fourth grade classroom with an intellectually handicapped child who is reading on a first grade level:

1. The sun gives us heat.
2. A prediction tells what we think will happen in the future.
3. An animal needs food, water, and air in order to survive.
4. A machine makes work easier.
5. Electricity can make a light bulb light.
6. Matter takes up space and has weight.
7. Ice will melt when it is heated.
8. We grow and change.
9. A plant has roots, stems, and leaves.
10. Water, milk, and orange juice are all liquids.

Science and the Culturally Different Child

The Role of Science in the Education of the Culturally Different Child

The culturally different child is any child who comes to the classroom from a home environment distinctly different from the mainstream of society. The difference may be one of race, economic level, ethnic background, religious persuasion, or language. We tend to think of the black child from a poverty-level home as the typical culturally different child. In reality, the child from Appalachia, the bayous of Louisiana, the French-speaking community of northern Maine, or from an Hispanic, Italian, or German background may be as culturally different from the mainstream as the newly arrived Asian immigrant. The culturally different child by definition has an experiential and linguistic background different from the typical child in the classroom.

Using science in the elementary grades, the teacher can help the child from a distinctly different background develop an experiential base similar to that of other children in the classroom without coming into conflict with the traditional mores of the culture.

In addition, the science program can help the culturally different child develop a vocabulary that is appropriate to the mainstream of society. Children coming from poverty-level environments often acquire a vocabulary, particularly for parts and functions of the human body, that is inappropriate for the mainstream of society, although such talk is perfectly appropriate in the child's cultural setting. Through the science program the child can be introduced to terminology appropriate for use in mainstream cultural settings.

Third, the culturally different child, particularly those from a poverty-level Hispanic or black background, tends to have little sense of causal relations and of control over events. The child tends to see himself as a pawn with little control over his or her own destiny. Mary Budd Rowe (1973) has shown that an activity-oriented program in science where the child is able to see and assess his or her effect on a system can help that child to develop a sense of control that will carry over into other spheres of life.

Learning the processes and the problem solving strategies of the elementary science program can also help the culturally different child to learn strategies that will enable him or her to sort out many extraneous sounds and experiences and to focus on the important aspects of a situation. Problem solving skills can also help the child to cope more effectively with the environment outside of the child's specific culture.

Last, the inclusion of science in the program for the culturally different child provides an additional career choice for the culturally different child. Children from diverse backgrounds who show an aptitude for and an interest in science should be encouraged to pursue such a career. This encouragement can come both from the teacher and from guest speakers who are scientists and have the various cultural backgrounds represented in the classroom.

Teaching Science to the Culturally Different Child

Adapting Teaching Methods. The ordinary demonstration, guided discovery, and open inquiry techniques are all appropriate to the culturally different child. Each of these techniques provides a concrete basis from which the teacher can develop the content of the science program. When using expository teaching and exposition with interaction, the teacher should be certain to provide advance organizers and to base the content of the expository teaching on the experiential background of the students. If there are children in the classroom who have little foundation in English, be certain to illustrate the exposition with pictures and drawings to help the child understand the content. During a discussion, the teacher should not constantly correct the child's incorrect grammar. Such continual corrections will quickly make the child stop participating and will carry the additional connotation that the child's language is somehow "bad" and should not be used. The discovery demonstration should be presented after the children have developed an ability to use the processes of science and have engaged in the problem solving of a more structured guided discovery lesson.

Adapting Activities. The activities of the elementary science program should be appropriate for the culturally different child. If the materials are totally unfamiliar to the child, the teacher should provide time for the child to investigate the materials in an unstructured setting. The teacher should also allow time on field trips for the culturally different child to investigate and familiarize himself with a new environment prior to the structured learning activity. If the child does not first become familiar with materials, the novelty of the materials may interfere with the child's ability to carry out the planned experience. If English is a child's second language and if the child does not easily use it, the teacher should consider having the instructions for an activity written in both English and the child's primary language. A high school language teacher or other individual who is fluent in the child's primary language may be called on to help with the translation.

Adapting Content. The content of the science program may need to be adapted for the culturally different child if the experiential background of the child is significantly different from that of the dominant culture. In general, this will mean moving from material appropriate to the child's background and understanding to more technical material. A pretest or a discussion will help the teacher to determine the child's understanding about a particular topic and the child's misconceptions, so that the teacher may make plans suitable to the child. If the cultural difference is based in the child's religious persuasion, the teacher should be careful to respect the child's beliefs and to refrain from attempting to challenge those beliefs. However, the teacher should never sacrifice scientific integrity and accuracy to avoid topics like evolution, the human body, or Earth history.

Adapting Verbal Material. Verbal material will need to be adapted if the child's reading level is substantially different from that of the average child or if the child cannot function well in English. In the former case, the teacher can provide materials written on an appropriate grade level by using additional grade levels of the textbook series or by using tradebooks. In the latter case, the teacher should consider providing materials written in the child's primary language as well as in English. A child should not fail to learn science because he or she is unable to read English. In working with the vocabulary of science, the teacher should be prepared to work from the child's culturally defined vocabulary to the standard vocabulary of science. Any vocabulary development for the culturally different child should move, when possible, from a basis in concrete experience to the use of the standard scientific term.

Learning Activity 9–6

The Culturally Different Child in the Classroom

Interview a teacher or other individual who works consistently with culturally different children.

Ask how the school program has been adapted to accommodate the children, how cultural traits of the various groups are integrated into the school programs, what problems the teacher has encountered, and which teaching techniques have been found to be most effective with the culturally different child.

Science and the Gifted Child

Role of Science in the Education of the Gifted

The gifted child tends to be characterized by certain traits that set him or her apart from the average child. The gifted child tends to have many broad interests, to have an insatiable desire to learn, to be able to do several things at once, to have a wide vocabulary and great verbal fluency, to be able to reason abstractly, and to be persistent in pursuing a task. In addition, the gifted child tends to be able to draw generalizations and to see interrelationships among diverse ideas. Although gifted persons should be distributed throughout the population, children from high socioeconomic levels tend to be identified as gifted more frequently than do children of low socioeconomic groups. A problem in the identification of gifted children from lower socioeconomic groups and from minorities may lie in the cultural biases of the tests commonly used. For the most part children who are identified as academically gifted tend to perform at a high level in the classroom. There are, however, some who do not appear to reach their potentials. This may be due to the social environment — high achievement may not be socially acceptable — or to a lack of stimulation from the school program.

Academically gifted children can benefit from an elementary school science program geared to their level of achievement. In particular, the science program can promote development in four areas.

First, the elementary science program can contribute to the development of abstract reasoning ability. The experimental processes, in particular, are geared to the use of abstract reasoning. The gifted child can be encouraged not only to carry out experiments but also to attempt to develop a causal theory consistent with the results of those experiments. Abstract reasoning includes the ability to hypothesize, to reason from a premise, to make multiple inferences, and to test those inferences. All of these abilities are a part of the process nature of the science program.

Second, the elementary science program can help the gifted child to develop problem solving skills and an objective viewpoint. Of particular importance to the gifted child is acquisition of the ability to use the problem solving skills gained in the classroom in real-life situations. A science program based on information that is practical as well as basic to scientific understanding can aid in this area.

Third, the science program can develop research skills in the gifted child that will permit that child not only to pursue topics of interest but also to create an individualized program commensurate with his or her needs.

And last, for the child who is particularly gifted in science, the elementary science program should permit the gifted child to develop interests leading to a career in the sciences. To think that all gifted children will automatically be interested in science, however, is incorrect. The child whose abilities lie in language may be encouraged to apply this linguistic skill to the science curriculum but should not be forced into science simply because he or she is a gifted child.

Teaching Science to the Gifted Child

Adapting Teaching Methods. The gifted child may be the most likely to understand and recall information given during expository teaching, but these methods are not the most appropriate to the gifted child. Rather, guided discovery, open inquiry, and discovery demonstrations are the most appropriate. Guided discovery and open inquiry allow the gifted child to investigate the phenomena of the elementary science program at an appropriate level without being concerned about being ahead of everyone else. In the discovery demonstration, the gifted child's ability to reason abstractly and to draw generalizations make him or her a likely candidate to present a solution to the problem. In the Socratic method and the discussion, care should be taken that the gifted child, if he or she has facile verbal ability, does not dominate the lesson. The gifted child may be chosen to lead a particular discussion or to work in the debate format. Two methods that we have not previously mentioned in this chapter are also highly appropriate for the gifted child: simulation games and computer programs and programming.

Adapting Activities. The teacher need not adapt the activities presented in the science program for use with the gifted child in the classroom. The child should, however, be given ample opportunity to adapt those activities himself or herself by pursuing more sophisticated experiments or more in-depth activities. Open-ended activities will allow the gifted child to pursue interests within the regular program.

Adapting Content. We tend, when working with the gifted child, to assume that the child has already acquired general background knowledge and that the child is always ready to go further than the content of the textbook or program. This assumption is not always correct. The gifted child may have glossed over background knowledge he or she will need in order to understand more advanced content. Gifted children should be pretested prior to a unit of work in science just like the rest of the class. In this way the teacher can find and remedy deficiencies. Once the basics have been developed one of two approaches can be taken with the gifted child: enrichment or acceleration.

Enrichment. Enrichment means that the gifted child will work with the same content as the other children in the class but will be able to pursue that content to a greater depth. Depth may include both an extended knowledge of the regular classroom content and an opportunity to pursue interesting side issues. An enrichment program can be highly individualized with the child working on planned reports on a contract basis or with a teacher-sequenced series of individualized activities.

Acceleration. Acceleration allows the child to move through the planned curriculum for a particular grade level and on into the curriculum for the next grade level. In this way the fourth grade child may be working on a sixth grade level in science and may even join the sixth grade during science class. An additional way to provide acceleration for the gifted child in science is to use a mentor: a high school student, another teacher, a high school teacher, or even a university professor who is willing to work with the gifted child on an individual basis. The mentor may change with the subject matter in which the child is working.

Adapting Verbal Material. The gifted child tends to have a large vocabulary and to be facile in the use of that vocabulary. This may be misleading in some cases, because the child may have the words but have little basis in experience. The gifted child should work in a concrete mode when vocabulary is developed, in order to assure that his or her verbosity has understanding behind it. In written reports, the gifted child should have a great deal of leeway for creativity, speculation, hypothesizing, and development of argument. Rather than presentation of strictly factual material, the gifted child should demonstrate the application of that material as well as the relationships between the material of the report and other areas of learning. A wide variety of books, magazines, and newspapers should be available to the child. The school library should be available to the child on an as-needed basis rather than at a strictly scheduled time period. Finally, reports of the experiments conducted by the gifted child should show a greater use of mathematics than is found in the average child's reports.

For the gifted child who is conducting independent research in a particular area, the teacher should encourage the child to present the results of that research to the rest of the class; the child, thus, gains in ability to speak before a group, and the rest of the class gains the benefit of the research.

Before you read the next section, take a sheet of paper and draw a picture of a scientist doing whatever it is that a scientist does. Not until you have finished your drawing should you go on.

Science and Girls

The Image of the Scientist

Look at your drawing of a scientist (see page 287). How many of the following characteristics have you included?

1. holding a test tube or other container,
2. in a laboratory,
3. wearing a lab (white) coat,
4. pencils and pens in the coat pocket,
5. wearing glasses,
6. fly-away hair or bald,
7. large head,
8. male.

Probably the most outstanding characteristic of impromptu drawings of scientists is that they are usually males. Few individuals draw a picture of a female scientist and if they do the females drawn tend to be homely with their hair up in "buns."

Women and science do not seem to be connected in most people's minds. In fact, recently a girl of nine told me that science was her favorite subject in school but that she knew she could never be a scientist because scientists are all boys.

Stereotypes in Science

Although the stereotypic notion that some subjects are for boys and some for girls is gradually disappearing, the feeling persists that science, like math, is a male subject. This viewpoint is apparent in the comment of a physics professor who told the only female in his class that "women should not be in the sciences," or the action of the paleontology professor who tried to convince the two female members of his class that they could not go on a weekend field trip, or the elementary classroom teacher who commented: "I don't worry when the girls don't do well on a science quiz. Girls don't need to learn science the way boys do." Films and filmstrips show a high frequency of males in science careers, and the only female scientist many people can name is Marie Curie.

If our society fosters through words, actions, or pictures the idea that science is a male subject, girls will be cut off from highly paid careers in science and industry. Recent research has shown that by the age of nine girls had consistently fewer science experiences than boys, even though they had similar or greater desires to participate in science activities. In addition, girl's responses to questions dealing with science indicated narrow perceptions of what science was and of the usefulness of science research. By the age of thirteen girls were found to have a generally negative attitude toward science and science careers (Kahle and Lakes, 1983).

As a consequence, in 1980 only 11 percent of the undergraduate students in engineering were female, only 26 percent of those in physical science were female, and in biological science 46 percent were female. This latter figure seems quite high until one realizes that nursing, a traditionally female profession, is included in the figure. In graduate schools the percentages drop drastically with only 7 percent in engineering, 18 percent in physical science, and 35 percent in biological science. By comparison, 52.9 percent of the students in fine and applied arts are women, 64.5 percent in foreign language, and 54.8 percent in English, as well as 79.9 percent in library science. These areas have long been considered appropriate for women. By high school only 1 percent of senior women indicate any interest in physical science and only 3.6 percent indicate any interest in biological science as a field for college (Directorate, 1980).

Clearly we should treat the female in the science class as a kind of special student. If the girl in the elementary classroom is not shown that science is an interesting and appropriate subject matter for girls as well as boys, that girl will be excluded from a large part of the curricula of the college or university.

Working with Girls in Science

The science curriculum needs no adaptation to meet the needs of girls in science. Rather, the teacher needs to show that the subject matter of science is as appropriate for girls as it is for boys.

Because teachers in the elementary grades are predominantly female (94 percent in grades kindergarten through three, and 76 percent in grades four through six) the teacher can have a definite impact on the attitudes of girls toward science. The teacher serving as a model is of great importance. The girl who sees that her teacher is interested and knowledgeable in science, and is as well a female, may develop the attitude that science is "OK" for girls.

Other ways of enhancing the attitudes of girls toward science include:

1. maintaining the same expectations in science for girls as for boys;
2. including the study of female as well as male scientists as a part of the curriculum;
3. encouraging girls who show special aptitude toward science by using independent work and presentations to the class;
4. suggesting careers in which science plays an important part: nurse, doctor, engineer, chemist, biologist, physicist, dietician, astronomer, veterinarian, meteorologist, pharmacist, radiologist, lab assistant, medical technician, therapist, x-ray technician, lens grinder, surveyor, geologist, paleontologist, and many more; and when considering the various occupations, having female as well as male practitioners come to talk to the class;
5. giving equal treatment to both boys and girls in terms of time, questions asked, and rewards given for science;
6. acting as a model of science behaviors and attitudes (especially if female);

7. being careful of the kinds of comments made about science, especially those that indicate that men are scientists and women are not;
8. inviting female scientists to come as guest speakers to discuss their work as well as to provide content material;
9. screening teaching materials including textbooks, tradebooks, films, and filmstrips for stereotypes showing males as scientists but not females.

With the scientific attitudes of open-mindedness and objectivity as a part of the curriculum, it is difficult to present a science program for the elementary grades that includes these attitudes yet continues to convey the notion that women are not scientists. In the coming society in which today's children will be adults, the role of science will be great. Even if a child is not destined for a career in science, the program of the elementary school should include all children in an appropriate science program.

Summary

Although science has frequently been excluded from the education of handicapped children, the latest trend is not only to include science in the curriculum but also to encourage those children with interest and ability to pursue careers in science. To allow the handicapped child to develop science skills and concepts, the most appropriate teaching means appears to be hands-on activities presented with the teaching methods of open inquiry or guided discovery.

The culturally different child as well as the gifted child has the right to a science program suited to his or her needs. In both of these cases the program should meet the needs of the child. For the culturally different child this may mean beginning with the child's experiential background and vocabulary and developing the program in science from there. For the gifted child, adaptations may mean provision for the child to work more quickly than the average child or for the child to work in more depth than the average child.

Lastly, to break down the stereotype of the male scientist we must give the girls in the elementary classroom special consideration when it comes to science. Girls should grow to perceive science as an area that is as appropriate for their study as it is for boys. To foster this attitude, the female teacher can do a great deal by acting as a model of scientific competence.

Selected References

Banks, J. A. *Multiethnic Education.* Boston: Allyn and Bacon, 1981.

Bennett, L. M. Science and special students. *Science and Children, 15,* 4, 1978.

Bennett, L. M. and K. Downing. Science education for the mentally retarded. *Science Education, 55,* 1978.

Billings, G. W., E. Cupone, and L. Norber. Lighting up science for the visually impaired. *Science Teacher, 47,* 1980.

Brophy, J. Successful teaching strategies for the inner city child. *Kappan, 63*, 4, 1982.

Bybee, R. W. Helping the special student fit in. *Science Teacher, 7*, 1979.

Campbell, R. L. Intellectual development, achievement, and self-concept of elementary minority school children. *School Science and Mathematics, 81*, 1981.

Directorate for Science Education. *Science Education Databook*. Washington, D.C.: National Science Foundation, 1980.

Eichenberger, R. Special students: Teaching science to the blind student. *Science Teacher, 41*, 1974.

ERIC/SMEAC. What research says: Females and mathematics. *School Science and Mathematics, 82*, 6, 1982.

Firth, G. H., and J. W. Mitchell. Value of science education for the mentally retarded: Empirical data for backing. *Science Education, 64*, 1980.

Fraser, B. J. Enquiry skill proficiency and socioeconomic status. *School Science and Mathematics, 81*, 1981.

Glass, R. M., J. Christiansen, and J. L. Christiansen. *Teaching Exceptional Children in the Regular Classroom*. Boston: Little, Brown, 1982.

Heimberger, M. J. *Teaching the Gifted and Talented in the Elementary Classroom*. Washington, D.C.: National Education Association, 1980.

Hensen, F. O. *Mainstreaming the Gifted*. Austin, Texas: Learning Concepts, 1976.

Hoffman, H. H., and K. S. Ricker. *Science Education and the Physically Handicapped*. Washington, D. C.: National Science Teachers Association, 1979.

Kahle, J. B., and M. K. Lakes. The myth of equality in science classrooms. *Journal of Research in Science Teaching, 20*, 2, 1983.

Levine, D. U. Successful approaches for improving academic achievement in inner city elementary schools. *Kappan, 63*, 8, 1982.

Lincoln. E. A. Tools for teaching math and science students in the inner city. *School Science and Mathematics, 30*, 1980.

Linn, M. C. Science education for the deaf: A comparison of ideal resource and mainstream settings. *Journal of Research in Science Teaching, 16*, 3, 1979.

Lombardi, T. P., and P. E. Balch. Science experiences and the mentally retarded. *Science and Children, 13*, 6, 1976.

Marsh, G. E., B. Price, and T. Smith. *Teaching Mildly Handicapped Children: Methods and Materials*. St. Louis: Mosby, 1982.

McIntyre, M. Science is for all children. *Science and Children, 13*, 6, 1976.

Menhusen, B. B., and R. O. Gromme. Science for the handicapped children — why? *Science and Children, 13*, 6, 1976.

Miller, T. L., and E. E. Davis. *The Mildly Handicapped Student*. New York: Greene and Stratton, 1982.

Nash, R. W., C. Borman, and S. Colson. Career education for gifted and talented students. *Exceptional Children, 46*, 5, 1970.

Rowe, M. B. *Teaching Science as Continuous Inquiry*. New York: McGraw-Hill, 1973.

Stephens, T., A. E. Blackhurst, and L. Magliocco. *Teaching Mainstreamed Students.* New York: Wiley, 1982.

Tuttle, F. B., and L. Becker. *Characteristics and Identification of Gifted and Talented Students.* Washington, D.C.: National Education Association, 1980.

Van Osdol, W. R., and D. G. Shane. *An Introduction to Exceptional Children.* Dubuque, Iowa: Brown, 1982.

Walsh, E. Laboratory classroom: Breaking the communication barrier. *Science, 196,* 1977.

Whitmore, J. R. *Giftedness, Conflict, and Underachievement.* Boston: Allyn and Bacon, 1980.

Wilson, J. T., and J. Karan. Science curriculum materials for special students. *Educating and Training of the Mentally Retarded, 8,* 1973.

Too much reading is a handicap mainly to people who have the wrong attitude of mind. Freshness of outlook and originality need not suffer greatly if reading is used as a stimulus to thinking and if the scientist is at the same time engaged in active research.

— Beveridge, 1950

10 Textbooks and Programs for Elementary Science

Chapter Objectives:

Upon completion of this chapter you should be able to

1. trace the development of science education in the United States from the colonial period to the present;
2. compare and contrast the major curriculum projects of the 1960s;
3. discuss the characteristics of the three major curriculum projects on the basis of program development, psychological basis, content orientation, locus of control, evaluation techniques, and current status of the program;
4. discuss the general characteristics of a textbook as they are found in the teacher's edition;
5. describe how a textbook is appropriately used in the teaching of elementary school science;
6. describe the use of microcomputers in the science classroom;
7. describe how to evaluate microcomputer software for classroom use.

Although teachers must make a tremendous number of decisions about how appropriately to present science lessons, two decisions that most teachers do not have to make are what to teach and what sequence to use with the prescribed topics in science for their grade level. These two decisions are made for the teacher by the writers of the school's curriculum, by the authors of the textbook, or by the developers of the science program. The curriculum or the textbook or program prescribes in detail both the scope and the sequence of science content for each grade level in the elementary school.

But why certain material is included at the fourth grade level rather than at the sixth grade level, why plants and animals are so frequently encountered, why experimentation is left to the intermediate grades, and why some topics are not included at all in the science program, all these decisions are not left to the whim of the authors. Rather, the current science curriculum has developed over a period of years during which it has expanded, changed, been modified, and sometimes even returned to the original. Decisions on what to include in the elementary science curriculum are based on psychology and science as well as on tradition.

Because so many decisions have already been made about the science curriculum, many teachers feel that they cannot adapt this science material to the needs of a particular class. Such adaptations can and should be made so that the science program is appropriate for the children in the class.

To help teachers make appropriate decisions about how to teach and adapt the prepared curriculum of their school, this chapter will present information on how the current science curriculum developed, will discuss some of the programs that contributed to changes in the traditional elementary science textbook, will demonstrate how a textbook should be used, and will introduce the use of the microcomputer in science teaching.

A Brief History of Science Education

The Colonial Period Through 1850

As the United States was emerging from colonial status and growing into a nation, science was also emerging from its reliance on the philosophers of the past and growing into a dependence upon the experimenters of the present. Galileo Galilei (1564–1642) had looked through his telescope at the craters of the moon and had seen four of the moons of Jupiter. Christian Huygens (1629–1695) had suggested that clouds covered the surface of Venus, had elucidated the nature of the rings of Saturn, and had expounded the wave nature of light. Carl von Linne (1707–1778) had outlined a system for biological classification. Isaac Newton (1647–1721), in isolation to escape the plague, had discovered the wave nature of light, had invented differential and integral calculus, and had developed the universal law of gravitation. In the field of chemistry, Joseph Priestly (1733–1804) had shown the necessity for accurate measurements in chemistry and had developed the theory of combustion. Anton van Leeuwenhoek (1632–1723) had seen protozoa in a drop of water and Robert Hooke (1635–1723) had seen cells in a piece of cork. Gregor Mendel (1822–1884) had demonstrated the laws of genetics with garden peas. And from 1831 to 1836, aboard the H.M.S. *Beagle*, Charles Darwin (1809–1882) was gathering the data that would revolutionize man's thinking about life on the Earth.

The early history of the United States coincided with a time when science was developing with a rapidity never before seen. This excitement, however, did not penetrate to the schools of Colonial America. Until about 1880, science was not considered a necessary part of the school program. Reading, writing, spelling, arithmetic, and perhaps geography were the fare of the schools. Science was the domain of the wealthy until the end of the nineteenth century.

Although inclusion of science was suggested for the school curriculum beginning in 1830, and suggestions were made for courses in physiology, botany, mineralogy, and geology, little was actually done to implement the suggestions. When science was taught, it was for reasons that had little to do with the true nature of science. First, science was taught in order to deepen the child's understanding of God and of the Bible. Second, science was taught to strengthen the mind. The concept of the brain as a muscle was strong during the early years of the United States. Educators thought that the study of difficult subjects, like science and mathematics, would cause the brain to increase in strength and power. Finally, science was taught to show its practical applications: applications to farming and industry. The theoretical and the searching nature of science was totally omitted.

The Period from 1850 Through 1890

The second period in the history of science education in the United States saw two developments that strongly influenced science education: object lessons and Nature Study.

As we have seen, proponents of the Nature Study movement saw the predominant content of science as biological. But Nature Study also contained the beginnings of a thrust toward the use of real objects and materials in the study of science.

This same emphasis on first-hand experience with real objects was found in the object lessons of Johan Pestalozzi (1746–1827) and the stress on observation and experimentation advocated by Wilbur Jackman.

Object Lessons. Object teaching or object lessons were based on the use of observation, analysis, and generalization. Following this method, the child was given an object like a chunk of sandstone and asked to observe its color, texture, hardness, grain, and shape. Following this observation, the child would observe, say, granite and analyze the differences between sandstone and granite. Finally, the child would make generalizations from the observations and analysis about the possible origin of the piece of sandstone. The object lesson, as originally advocated by Pestalozzi, emphasized the activity of the child's mind during the learning process. According to this viewpoint, the child was thought to learn by doing rather than by listening.

Wilbur Jackman. Wilbur Jackman (1855–1907) was strongly influenced in his approach to the teaching of elementary science by the American philosopher John Dewey. Like Dewey, Jackman saw the child as an active participant in the learning process through contact with real materials in real situations. Also like Dewey, Jackman emphasized the role of practicality in the solution of problems applicable to the science curriculum. We see these influences in Jackman's emphasis on the use of scientific generalizations as an organizational framework for the science curriculum; these generalizations were to enable the child to see interrelationships within science content and to allow the child to use the content of science in problem solving. In addition, Jackman suggested that these scientific generalizations be developed through the use of first-hand observation and experimentation.

As the first period of science education was characterized by a lack of science teaching in the elementary schools, the second period, 1850–1890, was characterized by the introduction of science and a call for first-hand experiences for children as a way of learning.

The Period from 1890 Through 1957

The period from 1890 through 1957 was influenced strongly by two men and catalyzed by one event. Henry Armstrong, Gerald S. Craig, and the launch of Sputnik all combined to make this period a pivotal one in the history of elementary science education.

Henry Armstrong. In 1910, Henry Armstrong took one step further along the path advocated by Dewey, Pestalozzi, and Jackman. Armstrong proposed the heuristic method of science teaching. According to this method, children acted in the role of discoverer: planning their own methods for attacking a problem whose solution was unknown. Today, Armstrong's heuristic method is known as discovery teaching. But, although Armstrong advocated discovery teaching, he also realized that children could not be expected to discover all of scientific knowledge and so considered discussion and lecture necessary parts of the science program. Armstrong's approach to the teaching of science was highly realistic.

Gerald S. Craig. The second individual who affected science education greatly during the 1890 to 1957 period was Gerald S. Craig. We have already considered his cognitive approach to science content, but he also advocated the inclusion of attitudes and processes in science.

Although Craig argued for the inclusion of more than content and the use of more than reading in the science program, the textbooks of the period did not reflect the desires of science educators. The 1950 edition of *Going Forward with Science* by Craig himself and June E. Lewis is typical the textbooks of this period: based on reading, storybook in format, and without the discovery and first-hand activity suggested by science educators.

The Launch of Sputnik. The launch of Sputnik in 1957 by the Soviet Union provided a catalyst for change in the nature of science education for the elementary school. The immediate reaction to this blow to American national pride was a period of verbalization and memorization in science teaching that effectively concealed the innovations of Pestalozzi, Jackman, Armstrong, and Craig. The resulting emphasis on the physical sciences dealt a blow to Nature Study, which caused its proponents to re-evaluate their goals and resurface in a new form in later years.

Although the immediate reaction to the perceived lack of excellence in science was emphasis on memorization, the more prudent reaction appeared only three years later when the National Society for the Study of Education published its fifty-ninth yearbook. This yearbook reflected the thinking of the psychologists, scientists, and educators of the late fifties who met in a conference at Woods Hole. The content emphasis of the late fifties, according to the yearbook, should be replaced by an approach to science that considered the structure of the discipline. Once again, the child was to be viewed as a discoverer and given the opportunity to explore the environment using a variety of materials.

Those who argued for the structure of the discipline approach and for the role of discovery first turned their attention to the secondary school science programs. The Biological Sciences Study Committee, the Physical Sciences Study Committee, and Harvard Project Physics brought about changes in the high school curriculum to make it more closely illustrate the nature of science. As a result of these secondary school science projects and others, the elementary school science curriculum also saw great changes.

A variety of projects for the teaching of elementary school science appeared during the 1960s both in the United States and in Great Britain. These elementary school science projects were distinguished from the textbooks of the previous decade by being child-oriented, activity-oriented, and process-oriented. Textbooks were out; kits and projects were in.

Of the projects developed during the 1960s, three are considered prime examples of the thinking and of the teaching methods advocated: *Science — A Process Approach, The Science Curriculum Improvement Study,* and *Elementary Science Study*. Although not extensively used in classrooms, these three programs were, along with many others of the period, highly influential in changing the nature of textbooks and in changing the nature of science teaching in the elementary school.

The National Curriculum Projects

Commonalities Among the Three Projects

Although differences do exist among *Science — A Process Approach, The Science Curriculum Improvement Study,* and *Elementary Science Study,* as representative programs of the sixties, many common features appear in their programs and in their development.

1. *All three programs were experimental in nature.* They were developed over a period of several years during which all program materials were tested with children, refined, and retested prior to marketing for national use.
2. *All three programs were initiated by teams of scientists, psychologists, and science educators.* The final programs represented the most advanced thinking in the area.
3. *All three programs rejected the traditional textbook.* Rather than placing a textbook in the hands of each child, the projects developed written materials for the teacher and laboratory workbooks for the students. Other projects placed no written materials at all in the hands of students, relying instead on concrete materials and class discussions to develop the concepts of the program.
4. *All projects were committed to individual and/or small-group direct experience with materials.* The role of the teacher was no longer to direct and instruct a large group of children but rather to provide for experiences that children could use to identify the concepts to be learned for themselves.
5. *All three programs were based on learning theory.* Rather than basing the science program on what had traditionally been taught, or on what an authority in science education claimed was appropriate, developers based their programs on the theories of Gagne, Piaget, and Bruner. From these learning theories, both the content of a program and the sequence of that content were derived.
6. *Fewer content areas were included than the many content areas found in the traditional textbook.* Emphasis was placed on thoroughness of coverage rather than on comprehensiveness of coverage.
7. *Mathematics was integrated into the program wherever appropriate.* The integration of mathematics into the program made the elementary science program better reflect the nature of science. The program became quantitative rather than qualitative.
8. *Technology was reduced and theory was emphasized.* Rather than considering the practical and technological aspects of science, such as its use in health care and maintenance, classes considered the theories, laws, principles, and processes of science.
9. *Activities were made more open ended.* Rather than asking students to look for a single correct answer or a single correct procedure, the projects al-

lowed students to pursue a variety of approaches to the solution of a problem. This approach resulted in an emphasis on problem solving skills.

10. *Rather than being commercially funded by publishers the projects received federal funding from the National Science Foundation.*
11. In commercial form the projects included:
    a. a basic program manual giving the program philosophy, background, and overview;
    b. a series of instructional guides for helping teachers guide students through their science learning experiences;
    c. equipment kits to assure sufficient quantities of the appropriate materials for children to use in hands-on learning experiences.

The projects of the 1960s were a reaction on the part of scientists to the simple memorization being used as a means for teaching science in the elementary school. This was not the true nature of science, according to the scientist, and it did not permit children to develop the understanding they needed to achieve scientific literacy.

Although the three representative projects were all designed to demonstrate the true nature of science as a pursuit of knowledge through the use of processes, the designers of each chose to approach this nature in a different manner.

Science: A Process Approach

Program Development. In 1962, the Commission on Science Education appointed by the American Association for the Advancement of Science with funds from the National Science Foundation, began work on *Science — A Process Approach* (SAPA).

During the spring and summer of 1962, two eight-day conferences were held during which scientists, teachers, and school administrators reviewed the available research on science education and made a decision to recommend the development of science materials beginning at the kindergarten level that would emphasize the processes of science rather than the content.

By the 1963–1964 school year, Parts One through Five of SAPA had been prepared. These materials were tested by 106 teachers and 3,000 children. The results of this testing were taken into account in 1964 for revisions, development of additional materials, and the development of competency measures.

During 1964–1965, Parts One through Six of SAPA were tested by teachers, kindergarten through grade five, and 7,000 children. Some of these children were in the first year of the program, while others were in their second year.

By 1967, a third experimental edition had been produced and tested. At this point, Xerox Corporation was selected to further develop the materials. It was, however, not until 1969 that the final materials of the SAPA program were submitted to Xerox for production.

Psychological Basis of the Program. SAPA was based on the behavioristic approach to learning developed by Robert Gagne. Following this approach, designers broke the material to be accomplished into the smallest possible units. These units were then arranged into a hierarchical pattern so that the learner accomplished the simplest steps, built upon this, and finally accomplished the most complex tasks. This hierarchical approach, in which learning is sequenced from simple to complex in a step-by-step pattern, is the basis of the entire SAPA program. Each of the processes taught in SAPA was developed throughout the program by means of sequential lessons. In addition, the use of behavioral objectives, in the form of competency measures, reflects the behavioristic psychology of SAPA.

Content Orientation of the Program. The approach to content taken by the SAPA program was a radical departure from that of the traditional science program for the elementary school. Rather than follow the traditional science concepts contained in the average textbook, SAPA's designers chose to organize the program around the processes of science, choosing the content only to illustrate and to allow use of the processes. Consequently, the focus of the program became process rather than content.

In the primary grades, children using SAPA were to engage in the processes of observing, using numbers, predicting, inferring, classifying, communicating, using space/time relationships, and measuring. The primary lessons were arranged in a hierarchy so that children attained a certain level of ability with each of the processes before moving on to the next lesson dealing with that process.

In the intermediate grades, the hierarchically arranged lessons were designed to teach the processes of formulating hypotheses, interpreting data, controlling variables, experimenting, and defining operationally. Each of these intermediate grade processes built upon the primary grade processes and allowed the child more fully to experience the nature of science.

The emphasis on process in the SAPA program, however, meant a corresponding de-emphasis of content. Students were not asked to learn and remember particular facts or principles. Rather, children were taught the skills used by a research scientist in the laboratory.

The SAPA program was based on the proposition that an understanding of the nature of science and of science itself depended on being able to look at the world in the same way that a scientist looked at the world. The processes were, therefore, considered to be intellectual skills. General intellectual development, was, in turn, expected to result from the cumulative effect of an orderly progression of learning activities.

The orderly progression of activities was assured by the hierarchy. This hierarchy was a unique aspect of the SAPA program and it was used as the rationale for selecting and ordering activities. The hierarchy used by SAPA showed the interrelationships between an activity and those which preceded or those which followed. SAPA's hierarchy diagrams showed the prerequisites for the current lesson, showed what the child was to learn in the current lesson, and showed what the current lesson prepared the child to undertake in later lessons.

Upon completion of the SAPA program, children were expected to show certain characteristics. The child would be able to apply the scientific method of thought to a wide range of problems including social problems, be able to distinguish facts from inferences, and be able to identify the procedures required to obtain verification of hypotheses and problem solutions. Given a printed account of an experiment, SAPA students were to be able to identify the question being investigated; the variables being manipulated, controlled, and measured; the hypothesis being tested; how such a test related to the results being obtained; and the conclusion which could be legitimately drawn from the data. The SAPA student was also expected to develop the ability to design and carry out an experiment which would test a hypothesis relevant to a particular problem. Finally, the SAPA student was expected to show an appreciation of and an interest in scientific activities by choosing such science topics for reading, entertainment, and other kinds of leisure-time pursuits.

Locus of Control. The SAPA program placed control firmly in the hands of the program and of the teacher. The program controlled events of the classroom through the hierarchy of the lessons. The program also controlled the teacher through explicit instructions as to what he or she was to say and do. The teacher in turn controlled what the students could or could not do with the materials. The SAPA program was so firmly in control of what occurred in the classroom that the student had little to say about what would be learned or how it would be learned.

Evaluation Techniques. Each SAPA lesson was evaluated with competency measures in which each child was given particular tasks to complete and which the teacher would evaluate according to the criteria listed by the program. The use of competency measures was entirely consistent with the behavioristic approach of the program. The competency measures determined whether a child had attained a particular process skill and whether the child and the class were ready to move on to the next lesson.

Current Status of the Program. Currently, SAPA is used in approximately two percent of the kindergarten through grade three classrooms in the United States. It is used in approximately three percent of the fourth through sixth grade classrooms (Directorate, 1980).

Since its inception, SAPA has been changed extensively. It is now correctly termed SAPA-II. SAPA-II consists of 105 modules that can be arranged in a variety of ways rather than in the simple hierarchical structure of the original program. This attempt to reduce the rigidity of the original program offers a choice among several different modules dealing with the same topic and among alternative activities within each of the modules.

More individualization of activities is evident in SAPA-II, including individualized activities with self-checking work sheets. This individualization has made the original, highly structured program more child centered and humanistic. Science is presented as a tool for learning and as a way to satisfy curiosity rather than simply as a series of lessons. Along with this change toward the humanistic has come the inclusion of values in the program.

The subordination of content to process found in the original SAPA program has been modified in SAPA-II so that the processes of some of the modules are used to teach content. Extensive material on the environment is now included in the program so that the processes of science can be applied to environmental issues.

The structure of SAPA-II has been modified so that the program can be used in three different ways. Modules can be used in graded sets of sequences of fifteen modules designed to teach a particular process skill. Or, the various modules can be combined so that a particular area of content is addressed by the modules and the activities of the modules. Finally, SAPA-II can be used as individual modules for enrichment exercises or as a part of a school-developed program in science education.

Learning Activity 10–1

Investigating Science: A Process Approach

Review the materials for either SAPA or SAPA-II. Follow one of the processes of the program throughout the entire program to determine how it is handled from one lesson to another. Also consider the content being addressed as a vehicle for the learning of a process.

Choose one of the lessons for the process that you have selected and prepare to teach the lesson to a group of your peers or to a group of children.

After teaching the lesson evaluate it. How successful was the lesson? What could you do to make the lesson more exciting? What suggestions could you make for adapting this lesson to the various categories of mainstreamed children?

The Science Curriculum Improvement Study

Program Development. The original program for the Science Curriculum Improvement Study (SCIS) was initiated in 1959 by Richard Karplus. By the initiation date, Karplus had spent three years with the Elementary School

Science Project at the University of California and was already attuned to the problems of elementary school science education. In 1962, the National Science Foundation initiated support for the project.

In general, eight steps were used in the development of a SCIS unit. First, a draft version of the unit was prepared that included lesson materials, a teaching plan, and a list of suggested materials. This draft unit then went to schools for teaching in a laboratory setting. The draft version, on the basis of the feedback from the schools, was revised in step three into a complete unit which included a teacher's guide, student manuals, teaching materials, and a list of equipment. The revised unit then underwent testing for one to two years by SCIS staff members and regular elementary school teachers. In the fifth step, the unit as a whole was reconsidered on the basis of feedback from both the first and second trials. The content and methods of the unit were again revised. In the last three steps, field testing, revisions, and another field testing took place. Only after four field tests in elementary schools were the SCIS materials considered ready for use: a total of four to seven years of testing.

Psychological Basis of the Program. The Science Curriculum Improvement Study made a conscious attempt to base its program on the work of Jean Piaget. The four stages of development identified by Piaget were translated by the SCIS developers into three levels of conceptual development.

The first level in conceptual development of the SCIS program consisted of concepts of matter, living things, variation, conservation of matter, all of which are directly observable and concrete. This concrete level led into a more abstract second level of conceptual development that included concepts of interaction and causality along with relativity and geometrical relations. The third and final level contained abstractions which were based upon the more concrete understandings of the first two levels. In level three, concepts of energy, equilibrium, and steady state as well as the behavior, reproduction, and speciation of living things were considered.

Also on a Piagetian basis, the instructional sequence used by the SCIS program provided children with first-hand experience in a laboratory setting. Instead of leaving pupils to learn concepts through abstractions they had read or heard, the SCIS program developed concepts through experiences with concrete materials.

Content Orientation of the Program. The primary emphasis of the SCIS program was on the development of concepts, but attention was also given to the development of attitudes, abilities, and skills such as making observations, methods for recording observations and experiences, discrimination of differences, and recognition of similarities along with the ability to obtain quantitative data and to use appropriate vocabulary. The SCIS program presented a balance among the three aspects of science education designed to produce a scientifically literate individual.

The SCIS program also presented a balance among the biological and physical sciences. Two units of work were developed for each grade level from first through sixth grade with one unit emphasizing the biological sciences and the second unit emphasizing the physical sciences.

Each of the units was designed to provide a foundation for the unit that would be taught in the following grade. In other words, the SCIS program was developmental in nature. The SCIS units at each grade level developed more depth and used more abstract concepts than those of the previous level, so that the program moved from the simple to the complex and from the concrete to the abstract. Table 10–1 shows the units developed by the SCIS program for use in grades one through six.

But, the content orientation and the teaching methods of the SCIS program were not designed to teach only content. Rather, the SCIS program was designed to promote scientifically literate individuals. Scientific literacy was considered to be a blend of knowledge, skills, and attitudes that would be evident in three major ways.

1. The scientifically literate individual would have an understanding of scientific concepts that would allow him or her to develop plausible theories about the interactions occurring in the environment.
2. The scientifically literate person would have enough familiarity with the processes of science to be able to develop a means for testing his or her theories.
3. The scientifically literate person would be one who is curious about the environment and who possesses an attitude that convinces him or her that scientific investigations are personally meaningful.

These characteristics of the scientifically literate person were to be developed through the teaching methods of the program as well as through the content of the program.

Table 10–1 Content of the SCIS program

GRADE LEVEL	BIOLOGICAL SCIENCE	PHYSICAL SCIENCE
First Grade	Organisms	Material objects
Second Grade	Life cycles	Interaction and systems
Third Grade	Population	Subsystems and variables
Fourth Grade	Environments	Relative position and motion
Fifth Grade	Communities	Energy sources
Sixth Grade	Ecosystems	Models of electric and magnetic induction

Locus of Control. In the SCIS program the student was a more active participant and the teacher was a more passive participant. In contrast to the traditional role of the teacher as a purveyor of information, the SCIS teacher was seen as having three roles.

In her or his first role, the SCIS teacher was to act as a guide for the children. The teacher was to help the children to organize their experiences into concepts, which would be useful in further study.

In her or his second role, the SCIS teacher was to listen to the children in order to determine what they were learning so that further experiences could be provided for the children. Rather than listening for the purpose of determining whether a child had attained or not attained a particular concept, the teacher listened to determine where the child and the class as a whole stood in the development of a concept.

Finally, the role of the SCIS teacher was to enhance the openness of the situation rather than to provide closure for the lesson. In this case, the teacher did not need to feel that all loose ends had to be tied together. Rather the teacher was to show that questions could be left without answers, that everything in science did not have a final, identifiable conclusion.

In conducting the activities of a SCIS unit, the teacher led the students through three phases: exploration, invention, and discovery.

Exploration. Practicing exploration, the children were free to explore the materials without the constraint of learning some particular concept. Rather, the children had the opportunity to familiarize themselves with unfamiliar materials and to identify problems that could be investigated in later lessons.

Invention. At the invention stage, the children were introduced to new concepts. The teacher provided experiences through which the children would be able to develop an understanding of a concept. They developed a concrete definition of the concept with the aid of concrete materials, demonstrations, textual materials, and audiovisual materials. Also during the invention stage, the children had the opportunity to review and to discuss the validity of the applications of the concept being developed. At this stage, the concept was given a verbal label in order to help with communication and to insure stability for the concept.

Discovery. In the discovery stage, the children tested the concept they had learned during the invention stage through experimentation and explanation. The purpose of the experimentation was to test the consequences of the concept in a variety of situations. During this stage, the child had to keep the concept clearly in mind, so that he or she could apply it to many situations rather than to any one example. The bulk of any SCIS unit was to be spent in the discovery phase.

In general, the child controls the SCIS unit, because he or she is never told what to learn. Rather, the child analyzed his or her own information and interprets his or her own data. In this way the child was to approach a desired scientific literacy.

Current Status of the Program. SCIS is now SCIIS or SCIS Two. Since its inception, SCIS has changed in a number of ways. Earth Science has been added to the units so that each of the major sequences of units is currently called Physical/Earth Science and Life/Earth Science.

At level five, the Physical/Earth Science unit has been modified to include information dealing with solar energy, while the Life/Earth Science unit for the same level now includes the concepts of the pyramid of numbers and of competition.

At level six, the Physical/Earth Science unit has undergone a major modification changing from Electric and Magnetic Induction to Scientific Theories. This unit now includes electricity, magnetic fields, and light rays as a part of the content.

The new material of the units emphasizes the student's physical relationship to the Earth as well as the ecological nature of this relationship. In addition, more individualization is possible through "Extending Your Experience" cards designed for use as enrichment activities.

The SCIIS program has also been extended downward so that a unit is now included for the kindergarten level. Beginnings, the kindergarten unit, includes material from both the physical and the biological sciences and serves as a basis for the development of process skills.

Another addition to the SCIIS program is the inclusion of evaluation procedures. These procedures are included in the appendix of each teacher's guide and serve as a basis for the evaluation of both content and process. In addition, the student record books and the observations made by the teacher as students are engaged in activities provide a means for student evaluation.

At the current time, the Life/Earth Science units are being used in about four percent of the kindergarten through third grade classrooms and the Physical/Earth Science units in about two percent of classrooms at those grade levels. In the fourth through sixth grades, the Life/Earth Science units are used in about three percent of classrooms and the Physical/Earth Science units in about two percent of the classrooms (Directorate, 1980.)

Learning Activity 10–2 Investigating the Science Curriculum Improvement Study

Review the materials for one grade level of the SCIS or SCIIS program. Then, review a textbook for the same grade level.

1. What similarities in content do you find between the two sets of materials?

2. What similarities in teaching techniques do you find between the two sets of materials?
3. The SCIS program tends to be highly successful in developing both the content and the processes of science. What suggestions might you make to the author(s) of the textbook which would allow the textbook to develop both of these areas more successfully?
4. Look at the activities of the textbook then choose one. How might you adapt this activity to reflect the exploration, discovery, and invention stages of learning advocated by the SCIS program?

The Elementary Science Study

Program Development. The Elementary Science Study (ESS) began in 1960 as an extension of the secondary science program development of the Physical Science Study Committee. With the aid of Educational Services and support from the National Science Foundation, the ESS materials were generated during summer conferences, developed in classroom exploration to see how children responded to a variety of experiences, and finally placed in trial editions of each of the teaching units.

In 1965, field testing was done with revised materials, revisions were made on the basis of the tests, and the ESS materials were commercially published in 1966. The criteria for each of the units developed included scientific accuracy, understandability by both teachers and children, and the addition of a significant dimension to the child's science experiences.

Psychological Basis for the Program. Although the materials were not developed on the basis of any particular psychological outlook, the ESS program is representative of both the Piagetian point of view and that of Jerome Bruner. The use of concrete materials within all of the units, the wide variety and range of material found within each unit, and the child-centered approach to learning all point to a developmental basis.

Concrete Materials. According to the developmental perspective, children in the elementary grades learn most effectively when they can do so through the use of concrete materials. Each of the ESS units, which come in kit form, are based on materials that permit the child to investigate the phenomena of the unit on a first-hand basis, whether it is creating musical instruments, investigating the life cycle of mosquitoes, or putting together the skeleton of a cat.

Variety of Ranges. ESS units are nonsequential and are designed to be used by a wide variety of grade levels. For example, the Musical Instrument Recipe Book contains activities appropriate for children from grades kindergarten through nine. This wide variety assures that children, who develop cognitively at differing rates, will be able to work with concepts that are appropriate to their current cognitive abilities.

Child-Centered Approach. The ESS program allows students the freedom to explore the materials found in the units in a variety of ways. Although some of the units are meant to be teacher directed, others permit the child to work independently and so assure that the child is cognitively ready for the material presented.

Content Orientation of the Program. The ESS program blends content, process, and attitudes into a well-rounded program in science. This three-area orientation is evident in the five program goals of the ESS program:

1. *Rational thinking processes will be developed by the students.* This includes skills in observation, classification, measurement, data collection and organization, inference and prediction, variable identification and control, making and testing hypotheses, and process synthesis leading to the ability to carry out a scientific investigation and report on its results.
2. *Manipulation skills will be developed.* This involves the ability to assemble and use appropriate types of equipment when investigating a scientific problem.
3. *Communication skills will be developed.* Students will develop both the ability to use written and oral communication skills and also the ability to present data with graphic and mathematical symbols.
4. *Conceptual knowledge will be developed.* An understanding of the facts, laws, principles, and theories of science will be developed.
5. *Scientific attitudes will be developed.* The attitudes of curiosity, persistence, willingness to participate, accept evidence, and value critical thinking; and the development of self-confidence are stressed.

Scope and sequence, factors of great importance to the other science projects as well as to textbooks, are not important to ESS. The developers believed that there was no way to know what content would be of importance in the future, and they did not attempt to predict this by establishing a sequence for particular content to be learned by everyone. Also, the developers considered it the prerogative and the responsibility of the school system to develop its own program in science.

ESS has more than fifty units prepared for grades kindergarten through nine. The majority of the units are concentrated in grades four, five, and six although at least sixteen of the units are suitable for kindergarten through third grade and twelve of the units are suitable for grades seven through nine. Some of these units are process oriented, some are content oriented, and some are oriented toward the development of certain thinking skills. Some of the units are designed for use by the entire class at the same time. These units frequently consist of student work sheets and films as well as teacher's guides and pupil materials kits. The units that fall into this category are listed in Table 10–2.

Other units are less definitive and may include only a teacher's guide, which suggests activities, and simple materials, which are obtainable locally or from equipment supply houses. Units of this type may involve the entire class or a part of the class. They may or may not be taught as a series of connected lessons. The units in this category are found in Table 10–3.

The final category of ESS units is designed for individual or small-group work. These units lend themselves well to meeting the individual needs and interests of different children. The design of these units requires an informal and flexible classroom organization where individuals or groups of students can work at different units at the same time. The units in this category are found in Table 10–4.

Locus of Control. The classroom using ESS is not one in which the teacher is an authority figure purveying information to the children. Rather, the ESS teacher is a consultant, guide, and catalyst. The teacher advises, listens, diagnoses, and gives aid when the child is unable to do something alone. In order to use the ESS program effectively, the teacher must turn control of learning

Table 10–2 ESS units designed for full class use

Gases and airs	Balloons
Batteries and bulbs	Kitchen physics
Microgardening	Colored solutions
Balancing	Optics
Growing seeds	Slips and slides
Heating and cooling	Sink or float
Ice cubes	Rocks and charts
Pendulums	Small things

Table 10–3 ESS units designed for total class or small-group use

Bones	Mapping
Mealworms	Match and measure
Mystery powder	Musical instrument recipe book
Eggs and tadpoles	Clay boats
Pond water	Starting from seeds
Mosquitoes	Life of beans and peas
Brine shrimp	Butterflies
Structures	Daytime astronomy
Where is the moon?	Tracks
Animal book	Peas and particles
Light and shadows	Mobiles
Changes	

Table 10–4 ESS units designed for small-group or individual use

Attribute games and problems	Spinning tables
Geo blocks	Mirror cards
Pattern blocks	Balance book
Tangrams	Mobiles
Sand	Printing press
Animal activity book	Drops, streams, and containers
Batteries and bulbs II	

over to the children. The ESS program is firmly in the hands of the learner rather than in the hands of the teacher.

Evaluation Techniques. Evaluation under the ESS program is not viewed in the traditional manner. The developers felt that the materials were thoroughly tested and that they did fulfill the goals of the program. Because ESS was not traditional in its approach to the teaching-learning situation, it could not be evaluated using the usual pencil-and-paper evaluation. Instead, it was suggested that the teacher use either a subjective approach to evaluation in which the teacher considered the child's efforts, contributions, and performance then made judgments on the basis of those considerations. This approach was termed the "honest appraisal approach" by the ESS program.

Recognizing that most schools have to give some formal evaluation in science as in other subjects, however, the ESS program developers also suggested that behavioral objectives could be used for evaluation. In this case, the teacher would develop specific objectives and evaluate according to a checklist developed for the specific class.

Current Status of the Program. The ESS program has now stabilized at fifty-six units and is commercially available. The kindergarten through third grade units are used in less than two percent of the classrooms across the United States. The fourth through sixth grade units have the same rate of use.

Learning Activity 10–3

Investigating the Elementary Science Study

The ESS program can be used by a school district or by an individual school to develop an individual science curriculum.

Using the ESS materials and the constraint that you may choose only ten units, develop a program that you feel would be appropriate for either the kindergarten through third grade or the fourth through sixth grade level. Be prepared to defend your choice of materials for your science curriculum.

The Textbook in Science Teaching

The Abused Textbook

The projects previously discussed in this chapter developed as a reaction to the typical science program being taught in the elementary schools across the United States. With some exceptions, teachers were using textbooks in the only way that most knew how to use textbooks—as an additional reading book. Pre-1960s textbooks lent themselves to a reading approach, because they were written as readers with a few activities scattered throughout the pages. These activities were fully discussed in the textual material; they could be, and usually were, omitted.

The use of the science textbook as a reading book has continued in many classrooms, particularly when materials are lacking and money is simply not available for science equipment. The back-to-basics movement with its emphasis on reading and mathematics has also eroded the activity-oriented science program. And once again science is becoming another reading lesson.

Many teachers say that they have a textbook and must teach what is in the textbook. Many claim that they do not have time for activities because they have to get through the textbook by the end of the year. These cries and claims indicate that the teacher has not really learned to use a textbook or activities effectively in the classroom. The teacher who excludes activity because the text content must be covered is abusing the textbook and the science program.

Not only is the reading approach an abuse of the modern, process-oriented textbook, but it is also an abuse of the nature of science. But to use nothing but activities is to deny the necessity of reading to the development of the scientist. It would be impossible for the mature scientist to maintain his or her knowledge of a particular scientific field without reading journals in that field. Journal articles are constantly reporting new discoveries and new theories, which may relate to the scientist's current research project.

But it is also an abuse of the nature of science and of the intent of the textbook author and publisher to consider science only as reading, only as an additional means to improve reading skills. This omits the process nature, the experimental nature of science. Consequently, both the reading only and the activity only approaches to science distort the science program of the elementary school.

Textbook reading and concrete activity should complement one another, so it is important that the teacher know how to use a textbook effectively in the classroom. The purpose of this section of this text is to illustrate the most appropriate use of the elementary science textbook. This use involves consideration of the teacher's edition as an overview of the total program and of the teacher's edition as a guide for teaching.

The Content and Organization of the Teacher's Edition

The purpose of the teacher's edition is to direct the teacher in how the textbook can be used, the outcomes that will result if the textbook is used correctly, the types of evaluation that are appropriate, and any additional teaching aids that may, or may not, be used. Each of these aids to the teacher is found grouped with the others in a separate section of the teacher's edition, usually bound in the front of the book and frequently printed on a different colored paper. The information in the teacher's edition is generally divided into:

1. the program overview or rationale,
2. the program objectives,
3. the textbook organization,
4. the role of the teacher,
5. suggestions for teaching,
6. instructional materials and background information,
7. evaluation techniques.

Each of these sections contains specific information that will help the teacher who is about to use the textbook for the first time. Each of these sections will be discussed on the following pages, in order to alert you to what can be found within the introductory material of the textbook.

The Program Overview or Rationale. Each textbook will describe for the teacher the rationale of the program, that is, it will detail the way in which the program is organized, comment on the balance of the content, and remark on the most recommended teaching method.

> Gateways to Science is a balanced science program that enables students to study a broad range of topics in the three major divisions of science — the biological sciences, the physical sciences, and the Earth-Space Sciences. (Holmes, et al., 1979)

> The Laidlaw Exploring Science Program has been designed and developed to provide pupils with relevant, effective learning experiences in both the knowledge and processes of science. (Blecha, et al., 1979)

> The study of science should call for children to master and employ certain scientific processes. (Brewer, et al., 1974)

These examples indicate the kind of information you will find within the overview or rationale of the textbook. This section gives the essential beliefs of the authors about science teaching and how the teacher can best put those beliefs into practice.

The Program Objectives. The introductory material found in the teacher's edition will also include the objectives for the textbook's program in science. These objectives, not usually presented in behavioral or performance terms, indicate what is to be accomplished by the program. In some cases, these objectives are written as a part of other materials. For example, the program objectives may be listed as the processes and conceptual schemes that will be learned as a result of the program. In other cases, they are listed under the heading of objectives:

> to provide an exciting study of science by appealing to pupil interest and curiosity. (Blecha, et al., 1979)
>
> to provide a basis for the development of positive values and attitudes toward science in people's everyday lives. (Blecha, et al., 1979)
>
> understand the diverse interrelationships among living and nonliving things in the environment. (Holmes, et al., 1979)

The teacher should be thoroughly familiar with the program objectives in order to know what direction his or her teaching should take. These program objectives will help the teacher to determine what is important in the program and thus he or she should emphasize, as well as what the teacher can briefly consider or omit if time is at a premium. Omissions should, however, be undertaken only with extreme caution.

Textbook Organization. In this section of the teacher's edition the way in which the authors have chosen to organize the textual materials will be discussed. This section should indicate whether a unit approach or a chapter approach has been taken. In addition, this section should indicate whether the chapters can stand alone or whether a spiral approach to content development has been taken. Once again, as with the objectives, the organization of the textbook can give the teacher an indication of what should be taught in depth and what can be treated more lightly.

The Role of the Teacher. This section of the teacher's edition attempts to show the most effective teaching methods for accomplishing the objectives of the program.

The section dealing with the teacher's role will probably indicate that inquiry or discovery is the major teaching method of the textbook. At this point, the teacher's edition may also indicate possible room arrangements, grouping practices for effective teaching, questioning strategies for use in inquiry situations, and patterns of learning among children. This section of the teacher's edition should be studied thoroughly, so that the teacher can present the textbook in its intended manner.

Suggestions for Teaching. Sometimes called teaching helps, this information is generally found within the teacher's edition located on pages corresponding to those found in the student's textbook. The most common form is to reproduce a page of the student text and in the margins of the page to show how that particular page is to be taught. These suggestions will usually include:

1. the main concepts of the chapter,
2. sample answers to questions asked in the text,
3. sample answers for questions that call for thought on the part of the students,
4. teaching helps for the activities of the chapter which include the processes being used, sample findings for the activity, and the generalization that may be inferred as a result of the activity,
5. new vocabulary words,
6. suggestions for discussions,
7. objectives for the chapter or section.

Instructional Materials and Background Information. The teacher's edition should also include a section in which the teacher is given a list of reference materials for her or his use, a list of materials for the use of the children, a list of films or recorded materials that could be obtained, and an overview of the unit so that the teacher has some background information on the topic. There should also be a list of the concrete materials the teacher will have to obtain if the children are to do the activities contained in the unit.

This section of the teacher's edition will provide the teacher who is uncertain of his or her background in a particular content area with the resources with which he or she can develop the necessary background. The teacher interested in using audiovisual materials to enhance learning is given suggestions for materials that will most effectively match the areas covered in the textbook. The teacher preparing to work with a unit for the first time is given a listing of the materials he or she must acquire.

Evaluation Techniques. Finally, the teacher's edition of the textbook will include suggested evaluation techniques. Usually, these are in the form of chapter or unit tests, which the teacher may duplicate and use with the class. The tests generally reflect the content the authors consider of the greatest importance. Some texts include a checklist of objectives rather than written tests. These objectives are often more process oriented than are the written tests of other texts.

The introductory material in the teacher's edition of a textbook gives the teacher valuable information as to how the textbook is to be used, the outcomes expected, and the content considered. A thorough review of this material is vital before the teacher actually begins to prepare the first unit of material for presentation to the class.

Using a Textbook Appropriately

Once the teacher has reviewed the introductory material of the teacher's edition and determined the approach preferred by the textbook, the next step is to determine how most effectively to use that textbook in the classroom. Textbooks are written for the mass market — for the average school and the average child. As a teacher you will need to determine what adaptations you have to make to fit this average textbook to your unique situation.

First Steps in Textbook Use. The first steps you take in using a textbook in the science class are the same as those you would take for any textbook in any subject area:

1. *Read the textbook.* Only by reading through the entire textbook can you know where you are going and what points are necessary for an understanding of the material covered from one chapter or unit to the next. Reading the textbook from cover to cover will also help you determine where you will need to do some additional reading in order to feel more confident in your teaching.

2. *Review the activities.* Good science activities should teach, not simply review, what is contained in the textual material. Try to think of ways to make the "cookbook" activities you find more discovery oriented and more open ended. Try to add additional activities that will effectively teach the content to be covered. Read to determine where the activity can be most effectively incorporated into the textual material.

3. *Review the evaluation materials.* Determine the kinds of procedures the textbook suggests and when those evaluation procedures are used.

4. *Determine the prerequisite knowledge children are expected to have.* Textbooks assume that students have mastered certain understandings and concepts prior to beginning each chapter. These are generally assumed to have been developed at previous grade levels or in previous units of the textbook. The only way to be certain that children do have this prerequisite knowledge is to pretest. Review as needed so that you are not handicapping children because they have not studied or have forgotten the prerequisite material.

5. *Compare the textbook to the curriculum guide.* This comparison will tell you what to emphasize at a particular grade level and what can be treated lightly.

Figure 10–1 Using a textbook—magnets

WHAT ARE MAGNETS MADE OF?

Science Background

There are many kinds of magnets. The first magnetic material discovered was lodestone, which is a naturally magnetic iron ore. It is not known when the magnetic property of lodestone was first discovered. Ancient Greeks knew that lodestone attracted other pieces of lodestone and iron. They knew that lodestone did not attract bronze, silver, gold, or copper. The Greeks also knew that a piece of lodestone when suspended at its center by a piece of string would swing around so that one end always pointed in the same direction. For this reason people began to use lodestone to guide ships at sea.

The permanent magnets that are most familiar are made of steel. More-powerful magnets may be made of alnico—a mixture of iron, aluminum, nickel, and cobalt. Pure nickel is magnetic. Cobalt is only weakly magnetic in its natural state. Aluminum is not magnetic at all; it was selected for use because of its lightness.

Main Concepts (pages 72–73)

Some magnets are made of iron or steel.

Natural magnets are made of a material called lodestone, which is found in the ground.

Performance Objectives

After studying the information provided in this lesson, the pupils should be able to

—identify magnets made by people;
—identify a magnet found in the ground;
—pick out magnets made by people and magnets that are natural.

Important Words

magnet iron steel

Teaching Helps for the Pictures

When your pupils looks at the pictures on this page, you may want to ask them what the magnets in the pictures are made of. They may say that the magnets are made of iron. Tell them many magnets are also made of steel. (Steel is iron that has been refined. In making steel some carbon is added to iron to form an alloy to improve its performance. Steel is very hard but malleable under suitable conditions.)

If there is an opportunity for your pupils to handle natural magnets from lodestone, this will provide an excellent learning opportunity. You may wish to have your pupils suspend a piece of lodestone by a thin string and notice its property of pointing in a certain direction.

SOURCE: Blecha, M. K., Gega, P. C., and Green, M. *Laidlaw Exploring Science Program, Brown Book Teacher's Edition.* Laidlaw, 1982, pp. 72–73. Reprinted by permission of Laidlaw Brothers, A Division of Doubleday and Company, Inc.

Once he or she has taken the first steps, the teacher should begin to prepare for more specific teaching, considering four areas: objectives, activities, content, and evaluation.

Objectives. Once you have read and reviewed the entire textbook, develop your objectives for the first unit or chapter of material. Consider the objectives of each chapter outlined in the teacher's edition. These will probably be general in nature. It will be up to you to adapt the objectives to the class by making them more specific and by determining the level which children should reach.

Also, as you write objectives for a particular unit, try to work with a variety of levels from Bloom's taxonomy. It is important for children to acquire certain facts, but it is also important for children to be able to apply those facts in various situations, and for children to be able to evaluate the appropriateness and accuracy of their experiments and activities. Also, since much of what is learned in science is applicable to daily life, children should be able to apply knowledge to real situations and to evaluate the consequences of actions that stem from scientific understandings.

It may be important to know the operation of an electric power plant. It is also important to be able to evaluate the ramifications of steadily increasing power use. Students should be aware of the various vitamins and minerals needed for human nutrition, but they should also be able to apply that information to their own diets.

Only the teacher can determine the appropriate objectives for a particular class of children. This determination of objectives should be based on the rationale of the textbook, but should not depend entirely on a textbook written for general use rather than for your specific situation.

Activities. Activities in textbooks can generally be divided into two classes: verbal activities and concrete activities. Verbal activities can, in turn, be divided into those requiring discussion and those requiring reading.

Verbal Activities. Children frequently have difficulties in science because they are unable to read the textbook. This problem arises for two reasons. First, children may find reading difficult and may be unable to read material on the grade level at which they have been placed. The fifth grade science textbook will, of course, be too difficult for the child who is in fifth grade but reading on the second grade level. Second, science textbooks introduce a great deal of vocabulary that is not introduced in the basal reading program.

Reading Levels. Although textbook authors and publishers do carefully monitor the vocabulary of the textbooks and do write at a level appropriate to a particular grade level, every child will not necessarily be able to read the text.

Figure 10–2 Using a textbook—plants

PLANTS MAKE FOOD

Science Background

Plants are called producers because they are able to produce their own food inside their leaves by a process called photosynthesis. Plants contain a green substance called chlorophyll that helps them make sugars and starches, using water and minerals from the soil and carbon dioxide from the air. The energy that plants need to make their food comes from the sun. Some of the energy that plants get from the sun is stored in the food the plants make. The sun is the source of all the energy used by plants and animals.

Main Concept (pages 164–165)

Plants are producers.

Performance Objectives

After studying the information provided in this lesson, the pupils should be able to

—state that plants do not have to get food;
—explain that plants make food;
—identify the things that plants need to make their own food.

Important Words

plants	leaves	gas
sunlight	water	air

Teaching Helps for the Pictures

After the pupils have looked at the pictures on these pages, ask them where the plants in these pictures are growing. Then ask them where they have seen plants growing. They may say plants grow in their yard, in their house, or in a flower shop.

Suggested Discussion

After discussing "Plants Make Food," you may wish to ask your pupils these questions: "Where would you keep a plant in your house?" "What would happen to the plant if it did not get water?" (Sample answers: I would keep a plant near a window or where it would get light. The plant would dry up and die.) These questions may help to bring out that even though plants do not have to get food, they need light and water to help them make their food.

Additional Information

Fungi such as molds and mushrooms, which were once classified as plants, are no longer classified as plants by many biologists. Fungi do not contain chlorophyll and cannot make their own food. Only green plants are classified in the plant kingdom.

SOURCE: Blecha, M. K., Gega, P. C., and Green, M. *Laidlaw Exploring Science Program, Gold Book Teacher's Edition*. Laidlaw, 1982, pp. 164–165. Reprinted by permission of Laidlaw Brothers, A Division of Doubleday and Company, Inc.

As children with reading difficulties progress through the grade levels, their reading skills become even more problematic. In the first grade, children tend to have little difficulty with the textbook. Most of the material is presented in pictorial form and actual reading is minimum. Children in the first grade can succeed in the textbook based program. By the fifth grade, some children may still be reading at the first grade level, although some could be reading at the high school level. For the majority of the children in the class the reading level of the textbook will be appropriate. However, for the poorer readers in the class, the teacher should consider:

1. rewriting portions of the textbook that are necessary for the child's success, putting the material into words and sentences the child will be able to read and understand;
2. using a variety of textbooks and tradebooks in the classroom so that the student can select readable materials; picture books, textbooks from lower grades, and teacher written materials can all be included;
3. tape recording the material so that the child can listen to the material rather than being frustrated by reading.

On the other end of the scale, children who read well can be challenged with material written for a more complex level or with more detail. Again, the use of a variety of levels of materials rather than a single textbook can be beneficial to the advanced student.

Vocabulary. The vocabulary of science is important because it permits discussion of concepts unique to science. The correct vocabulary should be used, but use should be based on understanding. The child who uses science terms without understanding has not really learned; he or she is only able to return material much like a parrot that has been taught to speak. But the individual who has not learned the proper vocabulary is at a disadvantage when a concept is discussed and he or she does not know the term.

It may be easier for children to talk about the "little pieces that make up heavy things," but they will not understand the same concept when it is presented as "atoms and molecules are the building blocks of matter."

In the development of ordinary, daily-use vocabulary, a dictionary definition may be all the child needs to understand the meaning of a word and to use that word appropriately in conversation. It may be enough to define a pediatrician as a "doctor who treats children." Such a definition will permit the correct use of the term. It is not enough to define inertia as "the tendency of an object in motion to remain in motion and the tendency of an object at rest to remain at rest unless acted upon by an outside force." This definition really does not develop the concept of inertia.

How then is scientific vocabulary developed? Most scientific terms are operational. That is, the term was developed to describe or to designate a particular observable or inferrable phenomenon. In developing scientific vocabulary, the teacher should return to the phenomenon being named, work concretely with that phenomenon, and after the concept has been developed give the concept or phenomenon its correct name. This technique — working with the concept concretely and then adding the correct term — is more effective than looking for a dictionary definition, memorizing it, then reading about the concept.

When new vocabulary is introduced in the textbook, look for ways to use an activity to develop the term, then use the textbook material to refine and clarify the definition.

Concrete Activities. This second category of activities includes those in which the child is actively involved in the use of materials. These activities should predominate in the elementary school science program. Unfortunately, the usual textbook does not offer a lot of activities except in the primary grades, particularly first and second grade. The teacher's role is to supplement the text with activities that will help to elucidate the reading material presented.

In addition, the teacher should be reconsidering those activities presented in the textbook, so that they can be made more open ended and more likely to teach than to simply review the material presented in written form. A general suggestion is to do the activities, omitting written explanations of what will happen, then go to the written material in order to review and consolidate what was learned through the activity. This procedure will both reinforce the child's learning and aid in retention.

Process and Content in Activities. Although the activities of most textbooks are designed to elucidate the content of the textbook, it is well to remember that the activities of textbooks deal with the processes of science. The teacher preparing to use a textbook should also study the activities of a textbook in order to determine the processes used. This will allow the teacher to add additional process-oriented activities as they are needed in order to develop a total science program.

It is important for the teacher to recall that answers for activities that are based on evidence collected by the students must be considered correct. According to the process orientation, the student should be able to succeed even if the final answer does not reflect scientific thought. Such unusual answers can be checked against the textbook, and a discussion can arise as to why the concrete evidence could differ from the written presentation of the material.

Content. When determining the relationship between the curriculum guide and the textbook, we gave some consideration to content. The purpose of this comparison was to determine the relative importance of material and to determine from that the amount of time we should be devoting to each topic. Content, however, should also be considered in other ways.

Content Accuracy. Most of the content included in the elementary science textbook is unlikely to change in the next few years. It is unlikely that the basic understanding of the difference between a mammal and a fish will change. It is unlikely that the molecular theory will be replaced or that the concept of gravity will be eliminated. However, in other areas understanding is advancing at such a pace that it is impossible to keep up in the textbook.

Astronomy is advancing at a phenomenal pace as space probes and advances in the development of telescopes bring in new information on a daily basis. No longer is Saturn the only planet with rings. No longer is Pluto an unknown body without a moon. The Earth is no longer the only part of the solar system with which man has had direct contact. It is up to the teacher to keep pace with some of the newest advances in science and maintain content accuracy.

The teacher can monitor changes in scientific knowledge through newspapers and popular science magazines written for the layman. These changes also support the concept that science is far from being a finished enterprise. Even a recent copyright date cannot assure that the material in the textbook is accurate. Information may have changed yesterday or even this morning.

Supplementing Content. The textbook can only include a certain amount of information. The curriculum guide for the school or the interests of the students may indicate that more depth is needed in a particular area. At this point, the teacher needs to supplement the content. Try to maintain a list of additional tradebooks, films, resource persons, and newspaper or magazine articles that can be included in the program to appropriately increase content depth.

Controversial Content. The content of science programs is constantly challenged by various parent and community groups. Material dealing with evolution, with the age of the Earth, with the human body, and with alcohol and drugs is currently considered the most objectionable. If such material is a part of the textbook and the curriculum guide, it cannot, and should not, be omitted just to avoid controversy.

Science has always been controversial, from the sun-centered concept of the solar system which Galileo was forced to recant, to the evolutionary theory of Darwin, to the use of nuclear energy for the generation of electrical energy. It is the nature of science to consider all aspects of the physical world. It is the nature of science to incite controversy.

Pseudoscientific areas such as astrology, UFO's, and "monsters" can be considered with the view of showing how science operates to support a particular theory of a phenomenon. Where science overlaps with religious beliefs, the teacher needs to accept the fact of such beliefs and to show the way in which science may differ and the evidence on which the scientific point of view is based, but in no way should the teacher ridicule religious beliefs at the expense of the child or enhance those beliefs at the expense of scientific accuracy.

Evaluation. Textbook evaluations tend to be rather limited in scope. The pencil-and-paper test is the most frequently used means of evaluation, whether it is called unit test, chapter check, or "testing what you know." Looking carefully at these evaluations reveals that they tend to include the content of the program at the expense of the process and attitudinal aspects of the program. Textbook evaluations also tend to include only the knowledge and comprehension levels of Bloom's taxonomy with occasional forays into the application level. Multiple choice questions or questions with single-word or short-phrase answers predominate; these also tend to be found word-for-word in the text making it easy for students to locate answers by looking for key words.

Content Evaluation. Probably the easiest way to evaluate content is to give a test or quiz. Using the textbook suggested evaluation as a basis, the teacher should determine the levels of the questions asked. If the majority of the questions fall into the knowledge and comprehension levels, the teacher will need to supplement with questions from the application, analysis, synthesis, and evaluation levels. If the teacher has included more information than is in the text, due to the emphasis of the curriculum guide or the interests of the children, he or she will have to devise additional questions in the content evaluation.

A variety of types from multiple-choice, to true-false, to matching, ordering, short-answer, and essay questions should be included, and the type of question should be appropriate both to the taxonomic level of the question and to the children. First and second graders do not write essays; fifth and sixth graders have difficulty writing more than a few sentences.

Process Evaluation. Other than requesting the definition of a process or selection of processes out of a description of an activity, pencil-and-paper tests are not good ways to evaluate processes. In order to determine whether or not a child is able to use a particular process, the teacher should see the child using the process. To evaluate whether or not a child can experiment, have the child conduct an experiment and report, orally or in writing, on the procedures and the results. Use of a checklist is also an effective way to evaluate a child's ability to use the processes of science. The checklist is especially effective when coupled with the child's written or oral activity report.

A written report may tell whether the child has used a particular process at the direction of the teacher. An observation of the child at work, guided by a checklist indicating the points to be observed, can help the teacher to determine whether the child is able to select the appropriate process for a given situation and then follow through on the use of the process.

Attitude Evaluation. The most difficult area to evaluate is that of attitudes. Frequently, the means for evaluating attitudes is indirect and involves the use of anecdotal records rather than direct measures. Curiosity may be inferred if the child takes books on a particular subject out of the library, asks questions, or brings in a newspaper article dealing with the topic under study. Open-mindedness can be inferred if the child listens to a different point of view without interrupting or contradicting. Skepticism may be inferred if the child questions what is in the textbook on the basis of evidence. The teacher should keep anecdotal records that provide him or her with evidence of a child's attainment or progress in the various scientific attitudes.

Total evaluation in the science program should include all three areas of science. The textbook can be used as a starting point for evaluation, but the teacher needs to evaluate the suggested evaluation procedures themselves to determine whether they are appropriate for the class and the total program.

The Role of the Textbook in the Total Program for Science

Most elementary teachers will be provided with a textbook for teaching science. A good textbook is detailed enough that the beginning teacher will have little difficulty in beginning to work in science. The suggestions of this chapter should provide additional aid for the beginning teacher.

The textbook should serve as an organizing tool for the total science program. It provides the teacher with a basis for decision making and for conceptual development. In addition to these two functions the textbook can be uniquely used in a number of ways:

1. The textbook can provide background information that will permit the students in the class to design their own experiments and activities.
2. The textbook can be a source of information when determining which of two or more activities or experiments demonstrate the more scientifically correct results.
3. The textbook can serve as a springboard for discussion.
4. The textbook can provide suggestions for research topics for children to pursue.
5. The textbook can provide a basis for consideration of how the content of science has changed over time.
6. The textbook can provide reinforcement of content information learned during activities and can provide definitions of vocabulary terms against which operational definitions can be compared.

Many teachers say that it is easy to teach science: "I just follow the book." But rather than blindly following the textbook, the skillful teacher should fit the textbook into the pattern most appropriate for his or her class. Adherence to the textbook without consideration of other materials and ideas is easy, but it is an abuse of the textbook, an abuse of the nature of science as inquiry, and an abuse of the child, who is being bypassed because he or she cannot read the textbook or because he or she has read the reports of the Saturn fly-by and knows that the textbook is not correct. Rather than follow the textbook blindly, the conscientious teacher should adapt the textbook to his or her classroom situation.

Learning Activity 10–4 Investigating Science Textbooks

Obtain a copy of the textbook series currently used in your state or local school district.

Choose one of the grade levels of that textbook series and review the teacher's edition of the textbook. Consider each of the points indicated in this chapter as found in the teacher's edition. Write a summary of the major points found in the teacher's edition.

Learning Activity 10–5 Investigating a Science Course of Study

Obtain the textbook series currently being used for science in your state or local school district. Also obtain a copy of the course of study or curriculum guide that is in use in the schools.

Considering one primary grade and one intermediate grade, compare the textbook series to the course of study or curriculum guide. What similarities and differences do you find between the two?

Learning Activity 10–6 Preparing for Textbook Use

Select a textbook for any grade level from first through sixth. Pretend that the textbook which you have chosen is the one that you will be using as a first-year teacher. Following the guidelines in this chapter, prepare to teach one of the units in the textbook.

1. Compare the textbook to the state or local course of study or curriculum guide.

2. Evaluate the content.
3. Assume that you have at least two nonreaders and one gifted child in the classroom. How will you adapt the textbook to these children so that they can achieve a high level of success?
4. Review the activities. What additional activities could you include to make the unit more process oriented? What processes are already included in the chapter?
5. Make a listing of additional trade books, films, filmstrips, resource persons, and other sources that could be used to enhance the unit.
6. Consider the scientific attitudes. What attitudes are being developed as a result of the unit? How could you be certain that these attitudes are being enhanced?
7. How would you evaluate the unit? Present examples of the evaluations which you would use in order to determine achievement in process, content, and attitude.
8. What adaptations might be needed for mainstreamed children using this textbook: mentally retarded, visually handicapped, hearing handicapped?
9. Do you see any evidences of sex bias in the text? If so, what?

The Microcomputer in Science Teaching

Microcomputers and Computer Literacy

The Microcomputer. During the 1960s computers first came into education with the beginnings of programmed instruction and with the use of computers for administrative and managerial functions. These early uses in education were generally confined to linear or branching programs in which the student read a small piece of information, answered a question, then continued on to the next question. Errors were handled by having the student either review previous frames of information or by having the student move into a branch of the program which would reteach the material. The early use of programmed instruction via computers was hindered by several factors: expense, the need for time sharing, the size of the computer which frequently required special housing, and the frequent preemption of the computer for managerial use (ASCD, 1983).

The first appearance of microcomputers for home use in 1977 brought about an upsurge in the use of computers in education. These microcomputers were small enough to be brought into any classroom, inexpensive enough to be affordable by school districts, and easy enough to use that both children and their teachers could learn to use preprogrammed software and to program the machines themselves.

This explosion of the use of microcomputers in education, at home, and in the workplace requires that children become literate in the use of computers.

Computer Literacy and Computing Literacy. Computer literacy is generally defined as the ability to express an idea in such a way that a computer can carry out a particular set of instructions. L. The (1982) took the concept of computer literacy one step further by proposing the concept of computing literacy. According to The, computer literacy is too limited because the computer becomes an end to itself. Computing literacy, on the other hand, requires that the individual have the knowledge and ability to use larger computering systems as tools for the enrichment of personal and professional life.

Computing literacy is a combination of skills for software use and develops in three stages:

1. using them (computers) as machines, as a clerk doing data entry does;
2. using them as tools, as a manager doing financial analysis does;
3. using them as creative instruments, as a writer or programmer does. (The, 1982, p. 60)

The science curriculum provides many opportunities for the development of computer literacy and computing literacy in children. The use of computer software in a variety of situations within the science classroom is one step on the road to the development of literacy.

The Uses of Microcomputers in the Classroom

The uses of microcomputers in the classroom can be divided into three categories: computer assisted instruction, computer managed instruction, and programming or problem solving. The two areas of most interest to the teaching of science are those of computer assisted instruction and programming or problem solving.

Computer Assisted Instruction. Computer assisted instruction in science deals with the use of a microcomputer for teaching and learning, frequently as a substitute for the teacher or the textbook. The student involved in computer assisted instruction engages in interaction with a computer program in order to reach some particular skill or understanding. This type of instruction can be divided into six different areas.

Drill and Practice. This type of program, which assumes previous knowledge of the subject on the part of the user, presents information in a repetitive manner that tests periodically for retention of the material. An example of this type of program would be one designed to reinforce the names of the parts of the digestive system. The *URSA* program for grades five through twelve, which drills on constellation names, is an example of this type of program. *URSA* is available through Minnesota Educational Computing Consortium (MECC).

Tutorial. The tutorial program presents information in small segments to a user who is assumed to have no knowledge in that particular area. This type of program requires active participation on the part of the user and is frequently structured in a question and answer format. Tutorial can be used for diagnosis, remediation, enrichment, or acceleration. An example of this type of program is one in which the student is introduced to the skill of graphing and is actually taught to develop a bar graph. *Our Bodies,* for the second grade level from Right On Programs, is an example of the tutorial program.

Simulations. Simulations are programs in which a model of a real system or situation is presented and the user is placed in the situation. The user then controls the outcomes of the situation through answers to questions. The program responds to the user by presenting the ramifications of each decision. An example of this type of program would be one in which the student is placed in a particular environment, perhaps as an animal common to that environment, and attempts to survive. The *Odell Lake Program* for grades five through twelve, available from Apple, is an example of this type of program.

Instructional Games. These programs include some kind of a scoring system in which competition with other students or one's own performance is used. These programs tend to motivate students and to cause great interest. An example is a program in which students compete with each other to answer the greatest number of questions about sound. The *Sharing Science Program* for grades two through six from MECC includes instructional games.

Informational. Informational programs provide background information on a topic and allow children to develop questions leading to further research. An example might be a program where a student reads about stars and planets and develops a question which he or she will research. An example of this type of program is *Active Reading: World of Nature* for grades two through five from Micro Media.

Demonstration. These programs use the graphic and simulation capabilities of the microcomputer to make a visual learning aid. In this case, students might learn about the process by which blood circulates through the heart. An example is *Basic Electricity* for grades two through eight from Micro Media.

Programming and Problem Solving. These uses allow for more student-oriented and creative uses of the microcomputer than does computer assisted instruction. Programming provides the opportunity for students to learn to program the computer, to convert their ideas into programs. Problem solving permits the use of programs to solve problems and to study the methods of problem solving.

A wide variety of materials are available to help both adults and children learn to use the various computer languages. The most commonly used language for children is BASIC, which is used on all the available classroom microcomputers. In addition, LOGO, which was developed for use in problem solving, is an easy language for children to learn and use.

Programming and problem solving uses not only lead the child to computing literacy but also permit a child to work in a particular cognitive style, which the teacher could identify and use to develop child-appropriate learning materials (Pappert, 1979).

The Benefits of Microcomputer Use

Whether used for computer assisted instruction or for programming and problem solving, the microcomputer in the science classroom has been found to increase enthusiasm, offer more lively and interesting applications of problems, enhance student feelings of freedom, and enhance feelings of control among students (Scherer, 1979; Inman, 1979; and Bell, 1979). In particular, these benefits accrue when students work in groups of two or three.

Such groups are, of course, a necessity when there is a limited number of microcomputers available, but are most successful when students are fairly well matched in learning ability. When too great a discrepancy in ability is evident the less able student tends to be left out (Cox and Berger, 1981).

This is not, however, to say that only the gifted student should have access to the microcomputer. Slower students using microcomputers in the science class showed gains in motivation, persistence, and self-confidence as well as in subject matter (Cox and Berger, 1981).

Another benefit of the use of microcomputers is the development of problem solving skills. Students can use the microcomputer to find solutions to problems more difficult than those of the usual drill and practice found in the textbook. Low and high achievers both benefit from this approach to problem solving: skill and confidence in approaching real-life situations develop.

Last, the teacher benefits by being able to use the microcomputer to develop a more individualized science program. The right choice of software for the microcomputer can permit the development of a remedial drill and practice or tutorial program for slower students or a simulation, problem solving, and programming approach for the more able. The major problem is the selection of computer software adequate for educational use.

Evaluating Computer Software for Science Teaching

The evaluation of computer software is probably the most difficult task that the science teacher will face in using the computer in the classroom. Because of the relative newness of computer use for the classroom, there tends to be a good deal of material that was developed by computer experts rather than educators. Consequently, much of this material is not oriented to the realities of running a classroom (ASCD, 1983).

In addition, the majority of the available computer software is aimed toward the junior and senior high school levels rather than toward the elementary school. Those which have been produced for the elementary school science program tend to be produced by Right On Programs and as of this writing cost from $13 for a cassette version to $15 for a diskette version. Programs for elementary science use are also available from Micromedia, Apple, MECC, and Radio Shack.

The teacher's evaluation of computer software should include three major areas in addition to basic program information: system requirements, program uses, and program evaluation. When determining whether to purchase a particular piece of software for the classroom, the teacher would be wise to view the entire program rather than a demonstration diskette. Only by seeing the entire program can the teacher evaluate the total program, rather than a selection of bits and pieces showing the outstanding parts and omitting the less appropriate.

Program Information. An evaluation of computer software for the science class should begin with the basic information, apart from content: the title, the edition or volume number, the cost, the average running time for the program, the distributor, whether or not a purchase warranty is included, and where a review or recommendation may be found.

Some sources for reviews and recommendation about computer software are:

1. Courseware Report Card
   150 W. Carob Street
   Compton, CA 90220
   This is published five times a year and includes an edition which is primarily for kindergarten through sixth grade. Each issue contains twenty to twenty-five reviews including a description of the product, a grading of the program for ease of use, error handling, appropriateness, and overall educational value.
2. EPIE Institute
   P.O. Box 620
   Stoney Brook, NY 11790
   The reviews are called PRO/FILES and the subscriber receives about sixty software and ten hardware PRO/FILES each year as well as *Computing Teacher Magazine*.
3. Microsift
   300 S.W. 6th Ave.
   Portland, OR 97204
   A part of the Northwest Regional Education Laboratory that publishes software evaluations. About eighty-five evaluations have been published

with about twenty-five new evaluations each year. These are commonly available through state departments of education.

4. School Microware Reviews
   P.O. Box 246
   Dresden, ME 04342
   Published about three times a year with in-depth reviews by teachers along with manufacturer comments. Also available is the School Microware Directory listing 2,000 software packages for all subject areas and grade levels.

System Requirements. System requirements include those factors which describe what hardware is needed if the program is to be used. The user should first consider the memory capacity of the microcomputer on which the program is to be run. Also, the number of disk drives required as well as whether the program is available on cassette, if the hardware handles only cassettes should be considered. Last, the user should determine whether a printer is required or desirable. Also, the teacher should determine whether the program is compatible with the particular type of microcomputer available. A school should investigate the software available for a particular brand of microcomputer prior to the purchase of that microcomputer.

Program Uses. To evaluate this area, a simple checklist is all that is necessary. The various uses of programs in teaching science have already been considered. The teacher evaluating a piece of software for use in the science classroom should work through the program to determine into which category the program falls: drill or practice, tutorial, simulation, instructional gaming, problem solving, informational, demonstration.

Program Evaluation. As the teacher works through the program, he or she should consider and evaluate certain characteristics.

Written Instructions. The instructions for the program should be included in the program and should be easily available to the user.

User Friendly. The program should be such that it gives praise for a correct response, using the individual's name if possible, and gives a simple "incorrect" if the response is not correct. A user-friendly program says "Good work, Jimmy," whereas a user-nonfriendly program says "Boo, you made a mistake, Eric."

Quality of Directions. The written instructions for use of the program and for the participation of the user should be in clear, easy-to-read, logical steps allowing the user to follow the program with a minimum of assistance from the teacher.

Instructional Content. The content should be appropriate to the grade level and to the subject matter. This should be carefully considered for those programs said to be appropriate for a wide variety of grade levels.

Degree of User Control. The user should be able to control the speed at which the program operates. The user should also be able to interact fully with the program rather than being a minimal participant.

Simplicity of User Input. The program should be easy for the user to work with. The user would not need a great deal of knowledge of computer language to operate and succeed in using the program.

User Modifiable. Some provision should be made for the teacher to modify the program to make it appropriate for the particular classroom.

Reading Level Appropriate. The level of vocabulary and the general reading level should be appropriate to the grade level. Be certain that children with reading difficulties will be able to use the program easily.

Graphics Appropriate and Direct. Graphics should be clearly and concisely related to the subject matter. Graphics should be employed to indicate correct answers only, rather than for both correct and incorrect answers.

Menu Complete. A menu is a listing of a program's or lesson's parts. Programs should begin with a master menu that allows users to select the desired parts. The program should also contain submenus throughout that allow users to return to the master menu at any point.

Content Accurate and Well Designed. Programs should be free of content errors and misspellings. Lessons should be interesting to use and contain activities appropriate to the age range of the users.

Complete Learning Package. A good educational software package should use most of the computer's capabilities in order to present children with a well-balanced learning experience. All materials necessary for use of the program should be included in the package.

Other Factors. Other factors which should be considered in evaluating the program but which are self-explanatory are:

1. ease of error handling,
2. ease of bringing the program on line,
3. operating speed,
4. program works as planned,
5. effectiveness of the program in teaching the material, as compared to other methods.

A form for the evaluation of programs is included in Table 10–5 as a guide for the teacher.

Available Software for Teaching Elementary Science

Most of the available software for the teaching of science is geared to the junior and senior high school level. In the latest Apple II/III catalogue, ninety-five programs were listed for science, but only ten of these were appropriate for the

Table 10–5 Software evaluation form

I. *Program Information*

Title:________________________________

Edition or volume:________________ Cost:________________

Average running time:________________

Distributor:________________________________

Purchase warranty:________________________________

Review or recommendation:________________________________

____

____

II. *System Requirements*

Memory required:________________

Disk drives required:________________ Cassette available:________________

Printer required:________________ Desirable:________________

Other requirements:________________________________

III. *Program Uses*

Drill and practice________

Tutorial________

Simulation________

Instructional game________

Informational________

Demonstration________

IV. *Program Evaluation*

	POOR				SUPERIOR
Written Instructions	1	2	3	4	5
User Friendly	1	2	3	4	5
Quality of Directions	1	2	3	4	5
Instructional Content	1	2	3	4	5
Degree of User Control	1	2	3	4	5

Table 10–5 continued

	POOR				SUPERIOR
Simplicity of User Input	1	2	3	4	5
User Modifiable	1	2	3	4	5
Reading Level Appropriate	1	2	3	4	5
Graphics Appropriate and Direct	1	2	3	4	5
Menu Complete	1	2	3	4	5
Content Accurate and Well Designed	1	2	3	4	5
Complete Learning Package	1	2	3	4	5
Ease of Error Handling	1	2	3	4	5
Ease of Bringing Program on Line	1	2	3	4	5
Operating Speed	1	2	3	4	5
Program Works as Planned	1	2	3	4	5
Program Effectiveness as Compared to Other Methods	1	2	3	4	5

elementary grades. The latest catalogue for the Radio Shack TRS-80 list seventy-three entries under science, with only one for grades four through six. Other catalogues listing programs for science teaching show a similar lack of programs appropriate for the elementary school science program.

A recent directory of textbooks for elementary science did not list any software especially produced for any textbook series. As of 1983, teachers of elementary science have to select from available software that which will complement the textbook or program in use. When such software is selected, the particular program should be carefully evaluated for compatibility with the textbook, so that the student is not merely rereading what is included in the text but is being introduced to more in-depth concepts or, even better, to applications of science concepts through the use of simulations and gaming as well as problem solving. In addition, the teacher should consider learning to do more than just operate a software package; he or she should become as proficient as possible in one of the computer languages so as to be able to develop his or her own class-appropriate teaching materials.

Summary

The modern elementary school science curriculum has developed over a long period and has frequently reflected current thinking about children, learning, and science. The earliest science programs considered science as a difficult subject that would improve the learner's mind, much as exercise improves the tone of a muscle. Activities were advocated, and gradually the science program for the elementary school came to acknowledge the need of children for hands-on experiences. The Nature Study movement advocated biological science as the appropriate content of an elementary school program, whereas the work of Gerald S. Craig indicated the need for a more balanced program in science. The programs of the 1960s caused the greater inclusion of process and attitudes to go along with the content of the traditional textbook, called attention to the need for a psychological basis for science teaching, and demonstrated the need for hands-on experiences if children were to learn science effectively. Although SAPA, SCIS, and ESS were not adopted as extensively as their devleopers had hoped, they did serve to change the face of science education.

The programs of the sixties caused changes in the traditional textbook for elementary school science, so that emphasis on content decreased and emphasis on process increased. Even though the modern textbook in elementary science does include the needed aspects of science, the teacher needs to carefully consider the textbook chosen for the school, determine where there may be deficiencies, adapt the textbook to the class being taught, and decide on the best method for teaching rather than blindly follow the textbook.

Finally, the textbook is no longer the only means for presenting the content of science to children. The newest tool available to the science teacher is the microcomputer with programs that allow for tutorials, simulations, remediation, and gaming. This tool has great potential for use in science teaching, but, at this time, the teacher needs carefully to evaluate any software and determine whether a given computer program meets the criteria established for a sound educational program.

Selected References

Apple II/III Software Directory, vol. 2. Overland Park, Kansas: Advanced Software Technology, 1983.

Association for Supervision and Curriculum Development. Educators finding software a hard choice. *ASCD Update*, *25*, 2, 1983.

Bell, F. H. Classroom computers: Beyond the three r's. *Creative Computing*, *5*, 1979.

Blecha, M. K., P. C. Gega, and M. Green. *Exploring Science Series*. River Forest, Illinois: Laidlaw, 1976.

Blecha, M. K., P. C. Gega, and M. Green. *Laidlaw Exploring Science Program, Brown Book Teacher's Edition*. River Forest, Illinois: Laidlaw, 1982.

———. *Laidlaw Exploring Science Program, Gold Book, Teacher's Edition*. River Forest, Illinois: Laidlaw, 1982.

Bork, A. *Science and Engineering Policies in the United States*. Irvine, California: Educational Technology Center, April 3, 1980.

———. *Compendium of Bad but Common Practices in Computer Based Learning*. Irvine, California: Educational Technology Center, November 1, 1982.

Brewer, A. C., N. Garland, T. F. Edwards, A. Marshall, and J. J. Notkin. *Elementary School Science Learning by Investigating*. Chicago: Rand McNally, 1974.

Cox, D., and C. F. Berger. Microcomputers are motivating. *Science and Children, 19*, 1, 1981.

Directorate for Science Education. *Science Education Databook*. Washington, D.C.: National Science Foundation, 1980.

Educational Software Directory. Manchaca, Texas: Swift, 1983.

Educational Software Sourcebook. Radio Shack, 1983.

Elementary Science Study Materials. New York: McGraw-Hill, 1978.

ERIC-SMEAC. Science Education Fact Sheet No. 3. Microcomputers and science teaching. Columbus, Ohio: Clearinghouse for Science, Math, and Environmental Education, 1982.

Garner, D. Educational microcomputer software: Nine questions to ask. *Science and Children, 19*, 6, 1982.

Gring, S. R. Introducing computer literacy. *Educational Leadership, 40*, 1, 1982.

Hakansson, J. How to evaluate educational courseware. *Journal of Courseware Review, 1*, 1, 1981.

Hill, S. A. The microcomputer in the instructional program. *Arithmetic Teacher, 3*, 6, 1982.

Holmes, N. J., J. B. Leake, and M. W. Shaw. *Gateways to Science Series*. New York: McGraw-Hill, 1979.

Martin, K. The learning machines. *Arithmetic Teacher, 29*, 3, 1981.

Noonan, L. Computer simulations in the classroom. *Creative Computing*, 7, 10, 1981.

Paldy, L. G. *SCIS II Sampler Guide*. Boston: American Science and Engineering, 1978.

Pappert, S., D. Watt., A. di Sessa, and S. Weir. *Final Report of the Brookline LOGO Project*. Cambridge: Artificial Intelligence Lab, MIT, 1979.

Rogers, R. E., and A. M. Voelker. Programs for improving elementary science instruction in the elementary school: Elementary science study. *Science and Children, 8*, 1, 1970.

Romney, E. *A Working Guide to the Elementary Science Study*. Newton, Mass.: Educational Development Center, 1971.

Rowbotham, N. Using a microcomputer in science teaching. *School Science Review, 63*, 222, 1981.

Scherer, D. R. The microcomputer in a small school and at the university. *Interface Age, 4*, 1979.

Science — A Process Approach Materials. Lexington, Mass.: Ginn, 1979.

SCIIS Materials. Chicago: Rand-McNally, 1980.

SCIS Sampler Guide. Chicago: Rand-McNally, 1970.

The, L. Squaring off over computer literacy. *Personal Computing*, 6, 9, 1982.

Winkle, L. W., and W. M. Matthews. Computer equity comes of age. *Kappan, 63*, 5, 1982.

Part IV

Activities for Teaching Science

11 Activities for the Basic Processes of Science

The activities in this chapter are designed to develop children's abilities to use the basic processes of science. These activities are, therefore, supplementary to Chapter 3.

The activities emphasize those processes most appropriate for the preschool, kindergarten, or primary grade child. However, because so many intermediate grade children are unable to use the processes effectively, activities are included that will allow these children to develop the basic process skills they may lack.

All of the activities of this chapter should be followed by a discussion of the major processes covered by the lesson. Both convergent and divergent questions should be posed in the discussion, so that children can be helped not only to identify the process but also to understand the use of the process in other situations.

Each of the activities for the basic processes, except for the process of operational questions, includes the activity instructions, the content area most closely related, adaptations for mainstreamed children, and suggestions for correlation with other subject areas.

In this chapter are activities dealing with observation, classification, communication, number relations, space relations, and operational questions.

Activity 11–1: Adopt a Tree

(Appropriate for all grade levels)

Purpose: The purpose of this activity is to isolate the process of observation. In addition, the processes of communication and space relations are used.

Materials: A small outdoor tree or shrub that changes with the seasons, camera and slide film, white drawing paper and crayons, powdered borax and cornmeal if flowers are present or will develop during the course of the year.

Procedure:

1. During the first week of school, choose a small tree or large shrub to "adopt."
2. Observe the tree or shrub as carefully as possible using as many of the senses as are appropriate.
   a. A fruit tree or sassafras tree can allow the sense of taste to be included in the observations.
   b. Make any possible measurements, such as height and diameter of the trunk or low branches.
   c. Make bark rubbings using the paper and crayons.
   d. If flowers are present, dry them by covering with a mixture of one part Borax and three parts cornmeal. After four days, check the flowers. If they are still moist, leave them in the mixture and check again in a few days.
   d. Take one or more slides of the tree or shrub.
   e. Have the class write a story about the tree, write a poem, or draw a picture of the tree or shrub.
3. Each month, on approximately the same date as the original observations, repeat the observations including one or more new slides.
   a. If changes occur more quickly, the observations should be repeated more frequently than once a month.

Adaptations: No adaptations for mainstreamed children should be necessary because all senses are used for observations. If the class should contain an orthopedically handicapped child, choose a tree or shrub which is easily accessible.

Related Content: This activity is closely related to the study of plants, the four seasons, or the concept of change.

Suggestions:

1. A display including pressed leaves, dried flowers, pictures, and written materials can be useful in keeping observations in mind and current.

2. Correlate with social studies by looking into the various uses of trees and plants.
3. The process of prediction could also be included by having the students try to predict what changes will occur before their next actual observation.

Activity 11–2: Color Match

(Preschool and primary grades)

Purpose: The purpose of this activity is to isolate and emphasize the process of observation. Classification is also used in the activity.

Materials: This activity is designed for use with a group of ten to fifteen children. Needed are circles of construction paper about nine inches in diameter and in the following colors: red, orange, yellow, green, blue, violet, white, black. Only one circle of each color is needed.

Procedure:

1. Hold up each circle of color individually, having the children name the various colors.
2. Choose one child to stand and have a second match the color the child is wearing to one of the circles.
   a. Repeat until all children have had a chance to stand and to match colors.
3. Lay the circles out on a table or on the floor.
   a. Have the children gather objects from around the classroom that belong with each colored circle.

Adaptations:

1. The blind child will not be able to participate; however, the partially sighted child should be strongly encouraged to work with colors.
2. Fewer colors may be necessary for mildly or moderately retarded children.
3. Children who speak a second language should be encouraged to share the color names with the class.

Related Content: This activity can be related to the five senses or to material dealing with vision during a study of the human body.

Suggestions:

1. Preschool and kindergarten children enjoy simply naming and identifying colors. Older children could be involved in graphing:
   a. the number of objects of each color found in the classroom,
   b. colors that are found in clothing,
   c. favorite colors.

2. This can be correlated with an art activity or with writing poetry which deals with the colors.

Activity 11–3: Investigating a Watermelon

(Appropriate for all grade levels)

Purpose: The purpose of this activity is to isolate and emphasize the process of observation. In addition, the processes of communication and number relations are used.

Materials: One watermelon, one sharp knife, paper towels, newspaper

Procedure:

1. Place the newspapers on the floor so that a large space is covered. Place the whole watermelon on the papers in full view of the children. Make any observations of the melon that are possible using the senses of hearing, touch, smell, and sight.
   a. Record the observations on tape or in writing.
2. Cut the watermelon in half and observe as the cutting is done.
   a. Record all observations made.
3. Give each child a slice of the watermelon to eat.
   a. Continue to record the observations.
   b. Save the seeds to be counted later as a part of the observations.

Adaptations: No adaptations should be necessary for this activity.

Related Content: This activity is related to the study of plants, particularly to the idea that the fruit is a container for seeds, or to a unit on nutrition.

Suggestions:

1. If at all possible, do this outside on the playground.
2. Try some of the following extension ideas:
   a. Plant some of the seeds and make predictions of how many seeds will grow as well as observations of the growth of seedlings.
   b. Weigh the whole melon, then weigh what is left after eating to find out how much of a watermelon can be used for food.
   c. Write an operational definition of either the word fruit or the word watermelon.
   d. Try doing the same activity using a dill pickle for each student.

Activity 11–4: Listen, Listen, Listen

(Primary grades)

Purpose: The purpose of this activity is to isolate and emphasize the process of observation. In addition, the process of communication is used.

Materials: For each group of three or four children supply: an apple, orange, or pear; paper or tape recorder for recording observations; a sharp knife (teacher use only).

Procedure:

1. Review the process of observation through the use of sight, touch, taste, and smell by having the children observe the piece of fruit both whole and in pieces they can taste.
2. After the observations have been made, ask what sense was not used in observing the fruit.
   a. Have the children describe the sounds they heard as they ate their piece of fruit.
   b. Have the children try to describe the sounds rather than naming them.
3. Listen quietly to the sounds in the room; describe them rather than naming the object making the sound.
   a. As a class, gather a list of all of the sounds that were heard by each of the small groups.
4. Repeat the sound observations outdoors and in at least one other location in the building.
   a. Make a class list of the descriptions of the sounds heard. Again, try not to name the object that made the sound but to describe the noise.

Adaptations: Auditorily handicapped children with residual hearing should be encouraged to participate as fully as possible. Deaf children could use other senses or could make drawings of the various locations to illustrate places where the sounds were heard or objects which made the sounds.

Related Content: This activity could be related to the study of sound as well as to material on the five senses, the human body or the environment.

Suggestions:

1. Working with small groups will make the movement from location to location easier to accomplish.
2. Correlate this activity with music by listening to and describing the sounds of various instruments.

Activity 11–5: Rough or Smooth?

(Kindergarten and primary grades)

Purpose: The purpose of this activity is to isolate and emphasize the process of observation. In addition, the processes of communication and classification are included.

Materials: For each child: Six to ten sheets of paper cut into rectangles about 4.5 x 6 inches (the exact size is not important, but the pieces should be small enough to handle easily.); crayons; two objects — one rough and one smooth.

Procedure:

1. Before presenting the activity to the children make two crayon rubbings by placing a piece of paper over an object and rubbing the flat side of a crayon over the paper. Use one very smooth object and one rough object. Have the objects used available but hidden or unidentified.
2. Display the rubbings for the children and have the children try to guess what objects were used to make the textured patterns.
3. Demonstrate how to make rubbings and show in particular that the wax crayon needs to be rather thickly applied in order to capture the texture.
   a. Have the children choose any objects they wish and make rubbings.
   b. If possible, objects both indoors and outdoors can be included.
4. After the rubbings are finished, have the children classify their rubbings as smooth or rough.
   a. The two original rubbings can be used for comparison or to develop an operational definition of smooth and rough with the children.

Adaptations:

1. Visually handicapped children should be able to feel textural differences in the rubbings if the crayon is applied heavily enough.
2. Children with weak or spastic hands may be assigned a partner who can make the rubbing of the object chosen by the handicapped child. The object and the rubbing could both be brought to the child to be touched and classified.

Related Content: This activity can be related to the study of the human body and nervous system or to the study of the five senses.

Suggestions:

1. Classification of the rubbings should not be stressed in this activity; however, the children can be encouraged to find other ways than

just smooth and rough to use for classifications. Some possibilities include: color, straight lines or curved lines, lines or dots, types of object from which the rubbing was made, location of the object, etc.

2. This can be correlated with art by turning the rubbings into pictures or by using the rubbings in a collage.

Activity 11–6: What Does an Animal Do All Day?

(Intermediate grades)

Purpose: The purpose of this activity is to isolate and emphasize the process of observation. In addition, the processes of communication and number relations are used.

Materials: Any small animal or animals that can be kept in the classroom for a period of time: fish, gerbil, hamster, mouse, bird, turtle, snake, chameleon. Any one, or a number, of these could be considered.

Procedure:

1. Set up an area where children can go singly and observe the animal for a ten- to fifteen-minute period daily for a period of one week.
2. Provide a list of simple questions to guide the observations:
    a. What do you see the animal doing
    b. What does the animal look like?
    c. What do you hear?
    d. What do you smell?
3. Encourage the children to be as specific as possible, timing or counting activity repetitions as necessary and appropriate.
4. If more than one type of animal is available, have the children observe the different types.

Adaptations:

1. Visually handicapped children can work with a partner who can interpret sounds heard. The visually handicapped child might also be given special permission to handle the animal briefly.
2. Cages or aquaria should be in locations that are easily accessible to orthopedically handicapped children.

Related Content: This activity is closely related to the study of animals and their needs.

Suggestions:

1. Keep small animals caged rather than allowing children to handle them freely. This will not only prevent scratches and bites as well as the accidental spread of disease, but will also prevent the animals from being "loved to death."

2. This can be related to language arts by having the children write factual reports about animal habits or imaginative stories about what it is like to be one of the animals observed. Reading can be encouraged of tradebooks about the various types of animals.

Activity 11–7: Color Fast, Color Slow

(Intermediate grades)

Purpose: The purpose of this activity is to isolate and emphasize the process of observation. In addition, the process of communication is used.

Materials: For each child or pair of children supply: two baby food jars or clear plastic cups, ice water, warm water, container of food coloring — either a dropper bottle or a container and a medicine dropper—ruler, felt-tip marker or rubber band, paper towels.

Procedure: The following directions can be given to the children either orally or in written form.

1. Obtain a set of materials.
2. Using the ruler, measure up 4cm or 1½in from the table and mark this height on the jar using the magic marker or rubber band.
3. Pour ice water into one of the jars until it reaches the marked height.
4. Carefully put two or three drops of food coloring into the ice water. Do not stir or shake.
   a. Observe the food coloring in the water for five minutes. Write down any observation that you can make or draw pictures of what you see.
5. Into the second container, pour warm water to the marked level.
6. Carefully put two or three drops of food coloring into the warm water. Do not stir or shake.
   a. Observe the food coloring in the water for five minutes. Write down your observations. Make drawings of what you see.
7. Compare the observations of the warm and the cold water.

Adaptations: If partially sighted children are present, try this activity using a clear glass cake pan placed on an overhead projector. The water is placed in the pan and dark food coloring added. The pattern will be projected onto the screen, allowing some partially sighted children to see it.

Related Content: This activity can be related to the study of heat energy or to the study of color.

Suggestions:

1. Use the top section of a styrofoam egg carton as a tray for the materials and set everything out ready for use. The carton will also catch any minor spills.
2. Gallon plastic milk jugs make easy-to-use containers for bringing water into a classroom that lacks running water.
3. This can be related to art by mixing various colors of food coloring in the containers and observing the resulting colors.
4. To be certain it is the motions of the molecules of water causing the spreading of the food coloring, have the children wait until the water is still in the containers before adding the coloring.

Activity 11–8: An Environment in a String

(Intermediate grades)

Purpose: The purpose of this activity is to isolate and emphasize the process of observation. In addition, the process of classification is used.

Materials: For each group of three or four children supply: four meters of string tied into a loop, magnifier, spoon or trowel, jars or plastic bags, thermometer (optional), paper for collecting data, an outdoor area — a meadow or woodland.

Procedure:

1. Review with the class the meaning of the term environment.
   a. Have the children name some things that are a part of the classroom environment.
2. Prior to going to a previously chosen outdoor area, give the students the following directions in both written and oral form:
   a. With your partners, find an area where you can spread out your string into a circle.
   b. The area you have chosen is your environment. Try to observe it, and the area directly above the circle of string, as carefully as you possibly can. Include observations of different types of plants, any animals, the soil, rocks, and the atmosphere.
      (1) Use the thermometer to take the air and soil temperatures.
      (2) Use the magnifiers to make any observations of small insects or seeds.
      (3) Use the jars or bags to collect any interesting objects to share with the class.
3. At the end of the activity have the groups share their most interesting observations of the objects they collected.

Adaptations: Be certain the outdoor area is accessible to the orthopedically handicapped child. If the area is not accessible to a wheelchair or to canes, a wagon can be helpful.

Related Content: This activity can be related to the area of ecology and can be used to develop the concept of an environment.

Suggestions:

1. The purpose of this activity is to observe. No attention need be given to naming and identifying plants, animals, or rocks. However, curious children may want to use identification books, so have them available.
2. Discuss ground rules for behavior before getting to the site, then review those rules once there. Children who know what is expected of them are less likely to misbehave.
3. Magnifiers and thermometers are not required. The observations can be done just as successfully without them.
4. *Cautions:*
   a. In measuring soil temperature, have children dig a small hole, place the thermometer, then gently cover the thermometer bulb with soil. *Do not* let them attempt to force the thermometer into hard soil; it will shatter and puncture cuts will be likely.
   b. Use only *alcohol* thermometers (the red kind); mercury is poisonous. There is always the possibility of a broken thermometer.
   c. When outdoors, keep the children within an easily observed area. Children should not have the opportunity to stray.
   d. Prior to going out to the site, visit the area to be certain there are no poisonous plants and that the area is free from broken glass, etc.

Activity 11–9: Button, Button

(Primary grades)

Purpose: The purpose of this activity is to isolate and emphasize the process of classification. In addition, the processes of communication and observation are used.

Materials: A box of buttons that differ in size, shape, color, number of holes, and material; a small pie plate or top from a styrofoam egg carton for each child; one-quarter cup measuring cup; aluminum or other type of tray.

Procedure:

1. Shake the closed box of buttons and have the children try to guess what is inside it.
   a. Have the children make observations describing what they hear.
2. If no one guesses the contents of the box, have one or two children close their eyes and reach into the box to feel what is inside.
   a. Have those children make observations of what they feel.
3. Finally, pour the buttons onto the tray.
4. Give the children time to look at and to handle the buttons.
   a. Have each child pick two buttons from the tray that he or she particularly likes.
   b. Have the children describe how their buttons are alike or different.
5. After the children have mentioned as many similarities and differences as they can, give each child a pie plate and about one-fourth cup of buttons.
   a. Have the children find a way of putting their buttons into two piles that are the same in some way.
6. After the children have classified their buttons, have the group come together so that the children can share their classification methods.

Adaptations:

1. If the buttons are sufficiently different in size, texture, or material, the visually handicapped child should have no difficulty in participating in this activity.
2. Although the hearing handicapped child may not be able to tell how his or her groups were made, he or she could show the groups and have others guess the characteristics which were used.
3. Hearing handicapped children who cannot hear the sounds made by the moving box could be among those who reach inside to feel the buttons.
4. Intellectually handicapped children may need assistance in determining groups. If possible, the buttons given to these children should evidence striking characteristics.

Related Content: This activity can be related to the concept that matter has certain properties.

Suggestions: If buttons are not available, a mixture of dried peas and beans works well: lentils, navy beans, pinto beans, blackeyed peas, yellow peas, lima beans, and kidney beans.

Activity 11–10: A Tasting Party

(Appropriate for all grade levels)

Purpose: The purpose of this activity is to isolate and emphasize the process of classification. In addition, the process of communication is used.

Materials: Five to ten foods: About half of the samples should be salty and about half should be sweet. A small piece should be available for each child as well as a few extra pieces.

Procedure:

1. Before showing the children the food that they will be tasting, have them think about their favorite foods.
   a. Discuss with the children what it is that they like about their favorites.
2. Introduce the idea that some of the foods that were mentioned were salty and some were sweet.
3. Bring out the food samples and determine with the class that it is necessary to taste the foods present to decide which are salty and which are sweet.
   a. Have the children taste one food at a time and make a decision as to whether it is salty or sweet.
   b. As a class group, classify the foods using one of the extra pieces to put in the group as the foods are classified.
4. After the foods have been classified, have the students contribute the names of other foods which could go into the salty or sweet groups.

Adaptations: None should be needed for this activity.

Related Content: This activity could be related to the study of the five senses and to the study of nutrition.

Suggestions:

1. For intermediate grades, extend the activity to more groupings and have students determine their own classification systems.
2. If possible, children should suggest foods that they particularly enjoy so that the teacher can obtain samples of those foods. This is also a good way for the culturally different child to share their culture's foods with the rest of the class.
3. Before doing this activity, check with parents to be certain that there are no food allergies.

Activity 11–11: Where Do You Fit?

(Intermediate grades)

Purpose: The purpose of this activity is to isolate and emphasize the process of classification. In addition, the process of communication is used.

Materials: Children in the class and a large diagram of the hierarchical classification system shown below

Procedure:

1. Discuss with the class some of the characteristics that make them similar to and different from their classmates.
2. Using the diagram of a hierarchical classification system and adapting it as necessary, have the class work as a group to find a way to classify everyone in the room.

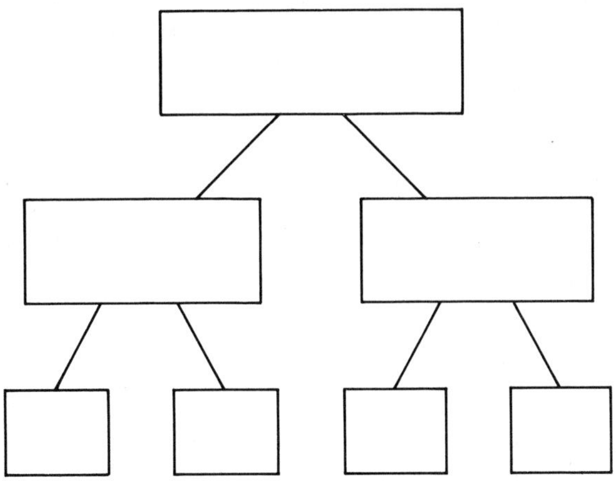

3. After placing everyone in the classification system, have the class break into small groups and have each group develop a second system of their own to classify everyone in the group. Have the groups share their systems.

Adaptations: None should be needed for this activity.

Related Content: This activity can be related to the study of the human body.

Suggestions:

1. This activity could be done outside on the playground where the classification chart could be drawn in chalk, and the children could actually place themselves in the appropriate categories as they are classified.

2. An instant camera could be used to take photographs of each child. These photographs could then be placed into the hierarchy and the entire system displayed.
3. Hierarchical classification is not easy for children. Be prepared to offer a great deal of help and to show through examples where problems are occurring.

Activity 11–12: Classifying Junk

(Intermediate grades)

Purpose: The purpose of this activity is to isolate and emphasize the process of classification. In addition, the process of communication is used.

Materials: Five shoe boxes containing a variety of objects. There should be at least twenty-five objects to a box and the boxes need not contain the same materials. Drawing paper for each group.

Procedure:

1. Review with the class the development of a hierarchical classification system.
2. Divide the class into groups giving one of the shoe boxes of materials to each of the groups.
3. Have each group classify the materials in the boxes drawing a diagram of their classification systems and listing the objects in the final categories.
4. Each group should then present its system to the rest of the class for critiquing.

Adaptations: For the intellectually handicapped child, the categories for the system could be given and the child asked to determine which objects would fit into each of the given categories.

Related Content: This activity could be related to the study of the properties of matter.

Suggestions: Materials that could be included in the boxes include plastic tableware, string, yarn, various types of paper, bottle caps, jar lids, erasers, pencils, pens, blocks, wrapped candy, corks, paper clips, stones, small toys, plastic bottles, old keys, crayons, chalk, etc.

Activity 11–13: Classifying Nonsense Words

(Intermediate grades)

Purpose: The purpose of this activity is to isolate and emphasize the process of classification. In addition the process of communication is used.

Materials: Sets of index cards holding one each of the following nonsense words. (Supply one set of cards for each pair of students.)

Int	Lep	Mimsey
Ablaf	Freep	Krum
Crepf	Mome	Blaaf
Drap	Sych	Kartoof
Hrap	Brillig	Arl
Gimble	Bret	Ernal
Beemish	Tof	Chickenitza
Xedni	Vorpal	Outgrabe
Eot	Qubl	Slithey
Orf	Trimble	Dribbleblitzen
Ritl	Skrooch	Teoteewhoican

Procedure:

1. Review with the class the idea of a hierarchical classification system.
2. Divide the children into groups of two giving each group a pack of cards.
   a. Have the children look through the packs of cards trying to decide on some of the ways in which they could be classified.
   b. Make a list of some of the possible ways of classifying the words.
3. Have each of the groups develop a hierarchical classification system for their words.

Adaptations: For the visually handicapped child, have the words taped including their spelling, written in Braille if the child is a Braille reader, or assign the child a partner who will read the word and the spelling to the child.

Related Content: Rather than being closely related to scientific content, this activity is closely related to the language arts.

Suggestions:

1. The most common ways of classifying these words are by beginning letters, ending letters, number of letters, number of vowels, number of consonants, and number of syllables.
2. If permitted to work creatively, children can also develop their classifications around parts of speech (they develop their own sentences to show use) or will develop a purely imaginary system in which the words are names for cars, foods, animals, flowers, colors, etc.

Activity 11–14: Classifying Living Things

(Intermediate grades)

Purpose: The purpose of this activity is to isolate and emphasize the process of classification. In addition, the process of communication is used.

Materials: A large selection of pictures of plants and animals mounted and ready for children to handle, some should be familiar and others unfamiliar.

Procedure:

1. Review with the class the development of a hierarchical classification system.
2. Display ten of the pictures from the collection including some plants and some animals.
   a. As a class develop a classification system for the pictures displayed.
   b. Discuss the other possible ways for classifying the displayed pictures.
3. Divide the class into groups of four and provide each group with a pile of pictures to classify.
   a. After the classification system is developed, have the children share their classifications.

Adaptations: The visually handicapped child will need to work with a group that will describe the pictures fully

Related Content: This activity is directly related to the study of biological science and to the biological classification system.

Suggestions:

1. Research skills developed in the language arts can be used in looking for information about the unfamiliar plants and animals.
2. This activity could be separated into two activities, one dealing only with plants and one dealing only with animals.
3. More advanced classes, or gifted children, could be encouraged to compare their classifications with the actual classification system used in biology.

Activity 11–15: Pinwheels

(Primary grades)

Purpose: The purpose of this activity is to isolate and emphasize the process of communication. In addition, the process of observation is used.

Materials: Pinwheel pattern (see page 355), pencils with erasers, stapler, straight pins, crayons

Procedure:

1. Have each of the children make a pinwheel following the pattern and your directions.

Pinwheel pattern

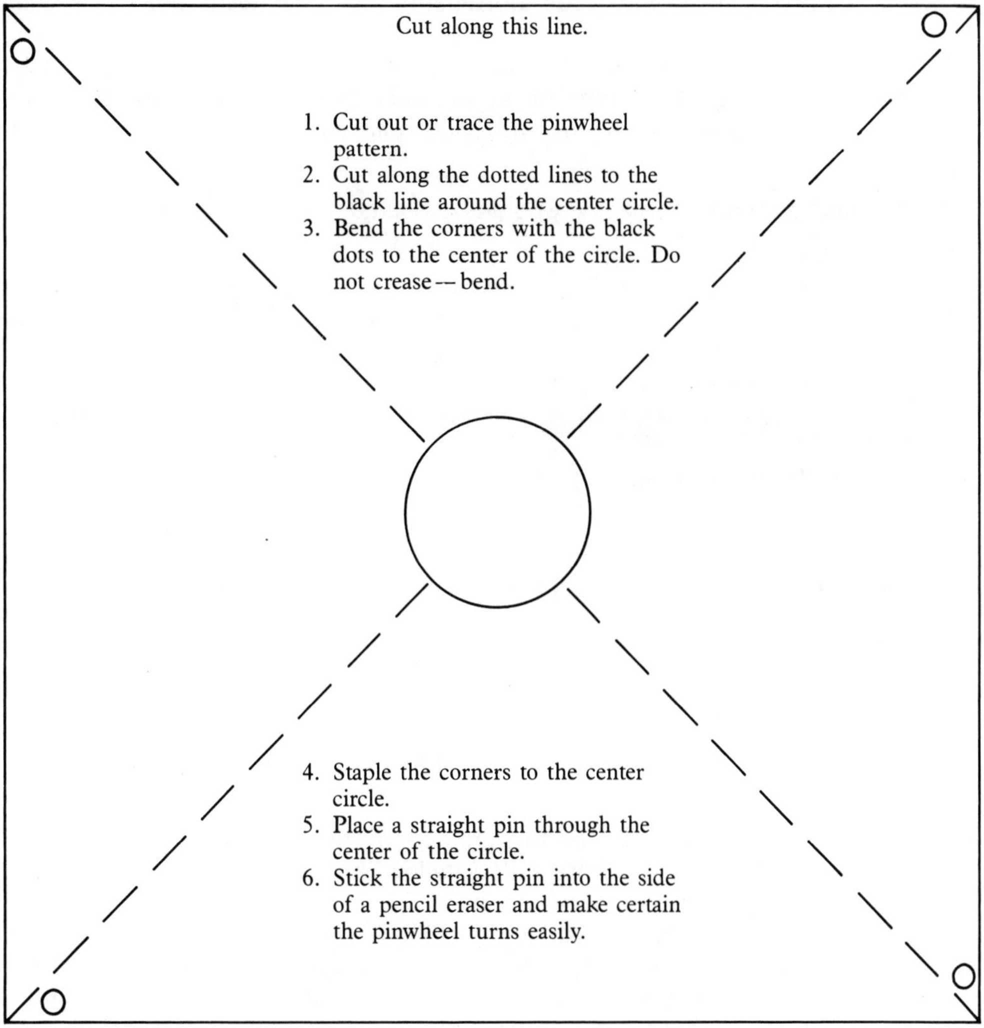

Cut along this line.
1. Cut out or trace the pinwheel pattern.
2. Cut along the dotted lines to the black line around the center circle.
3. Bend the corners with the black dots to the center of the circle. Do not crease — bend.
4. Staple the corners to the center circle.
5. Place a straight pin through the center of the circle.
6. Stick the straight pin into the side of a pencil eraser and make certain the pinwheel turns easily.

2. After the children have made the pinwheels:
   a. Ask: How many ways do you think you can find to make a pinwheel turn? How could you get it to turn very fast? How could you get it to turn slowly?
   b. Give the children a chance to work with the pinwheels trying to find as many ways as possible to get them to turn.
   c. After about fifteen minutes, bring the children back together to discuss and demonstrate the various methods they discovered.

Adaptations:

1. For children with poor coordination, the pinwheels could be already made and ready to use.
2. Orthopedically handicapped children could be assigned a partner who would try some of the possibilities that the child might be unable to do. Visually handicapped children might also be given a partner.

Related Content: This activity could be related to the study of energy.

Suggestions:

1. For reading and language arts, children could dictate a story about pinwheels to the teacher or into a tape recorder for later transcription.
2. For young children, the pinwheels could already be made so that time is not used in construction which could be better used in activity.
3. Try this outdoors if possible.

Activity 11–16: An Ice Cube Race

(All grade levels)

Purpose: The purpose of this activity is to isolate and emphasize the process of communication. In addition, the process of observation is used.

Materials: An ice cube for each child, newspaper, paper towels

Procedure:

1. Place one ice cube on the table before the children.
   a. Ask: What will happen if I allow this ice cube to sit on the table until the end of the day?
   b. Discuss the ideas that the children have.
   c. Watch the ice cube for about a minute, and collect on the chalkboard or on an experience chart any of the observations that the children make.
2. Say: This does not seem to be melting very fast. What do you think we could do to get it to melt faster?
   a. Again discuss the possibilities recording ideas on the chalkboard or experience chart.
3. Give each child an ice cube. Challenge the children to find ways to make the ice cubes melt as fast as possible.
   a. Use the newspaper to protect desk or floor areas.
4. Have the children describe their methods for the class.

Adaptations: All children should be able to participate fully in this activity.

Related Content: This activity could be related to the study of the states of matter or to the study of energy.

Suggestions:

1. Do this activity outdoors if possible.
2. Children could be encouraged to write about their method or to write creatively about what it is like to be a melting ice cube.

Activity 11–17: A Crystal Garden

(All grade levels)

Purpose: The purpose of this activity is to isolate and emphasize the process of communication.

Materials: One shallow, open glass dish; coal, coke, or charcoal to cover the bottom of the dish; water, laundry bluing, ammonia, salt, food coloring

Procedure:

1. Show the children the materials. Have them describe the materials. *Do not permit them to smell the ammonia.*
2. As the children watch, follow the directions given in Step 3.
   a. Periodically stop and have the children describe what has been done.
   b. When all the materials have been mixed, place the container in a location where it will not be disturbed but will be easily seen.
   c. Have the children discuss the changes they see from day to day as the crystals grow. Older children should keep a written or pictorial record.
3. Make a crystal garden:
   a. Place the coal, coke, or charcoal in the dish.
   b. Pour two tablespoons each of water, laundry bluing, and salt over the coals. Add each of these ingredients separately. Dot the coals with drops of food coloring.
   c. Let stand for twenty-four hours.
   d. After twenty-four hours, add two more tablespoons of salt.
   e. On the third day, add two tablespoons of ammonia.
4. After about five days of observation, discuss with the children what they have seen happen.

Adaptations: Because this is based strictly on vision and the resulting crystals are too fragile to touch, the visually handicapped child will not be able to participate.

Related Content:

1. This activity may be related to a study of chemical changes.
2. The activity may also be related to the growth of crystals.

Suggestions: The ammonia will give the crystals a fluffy appearance. The chemical reaction that occurs will form coral-like crystals that will be colored by the food coloring. These crystals will continue to grow until all of the liquid has been used. They are very fragile and need to be located where strong breezes will not destroy them.

Activity 11–18: Animal Tracks

(All grade levels)

Purpose: The purpose of this activity is to isolate and emphasize the process of communication. In addition the processes of observations and inference are used.

Materials: Animal track patterns cut from differing colors of paper (the number depending on the track pattern made)

Procedure:

1. Make animal tracks from the patterns on pages 360–363. On the classroom, hallway, or gym floor, or on the outdoor play area, form paths as shown in the diagram on page 359.
   a. If the play area is used, colored chalk could be used to form the tracks rather than the construction paper patterns.
2. Have the children make observations of the track patterns.
   a. Divide the class into groups of four.
   b. Give time for each of the groups to make up a story that will fit the pattern made by the tracks.
   c. Have each group act out their story for the other groups emphasizing the sequential nature that the story should have.

Adaptations: Visually handicapped children could be given a partner who will walk him or her through the track pattern. In addition, extra tracks should be available for the visually handicapped child to touch while walking the path.

Related Content: This activity could be related to the study of animal habits.

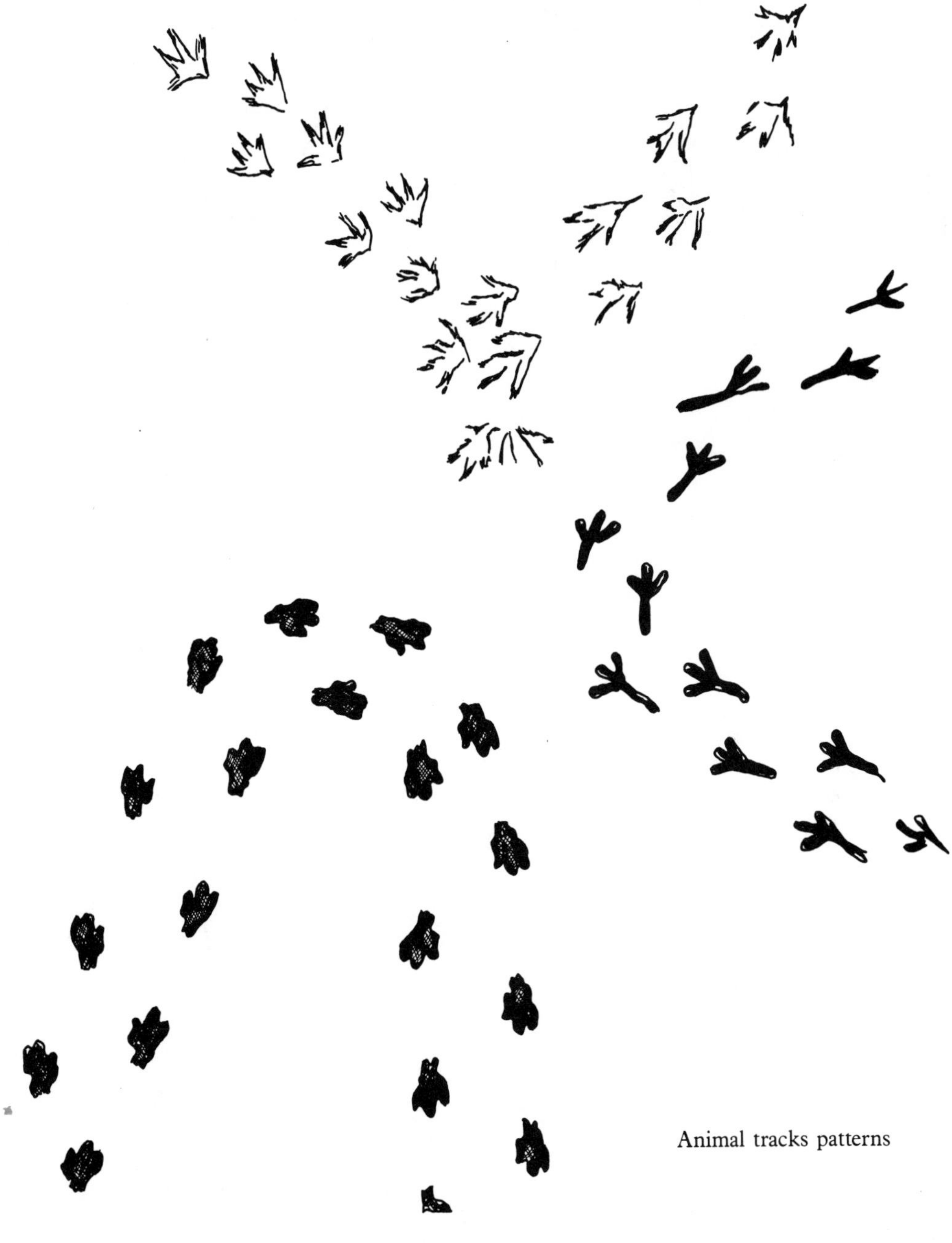

Animal tracks patterns

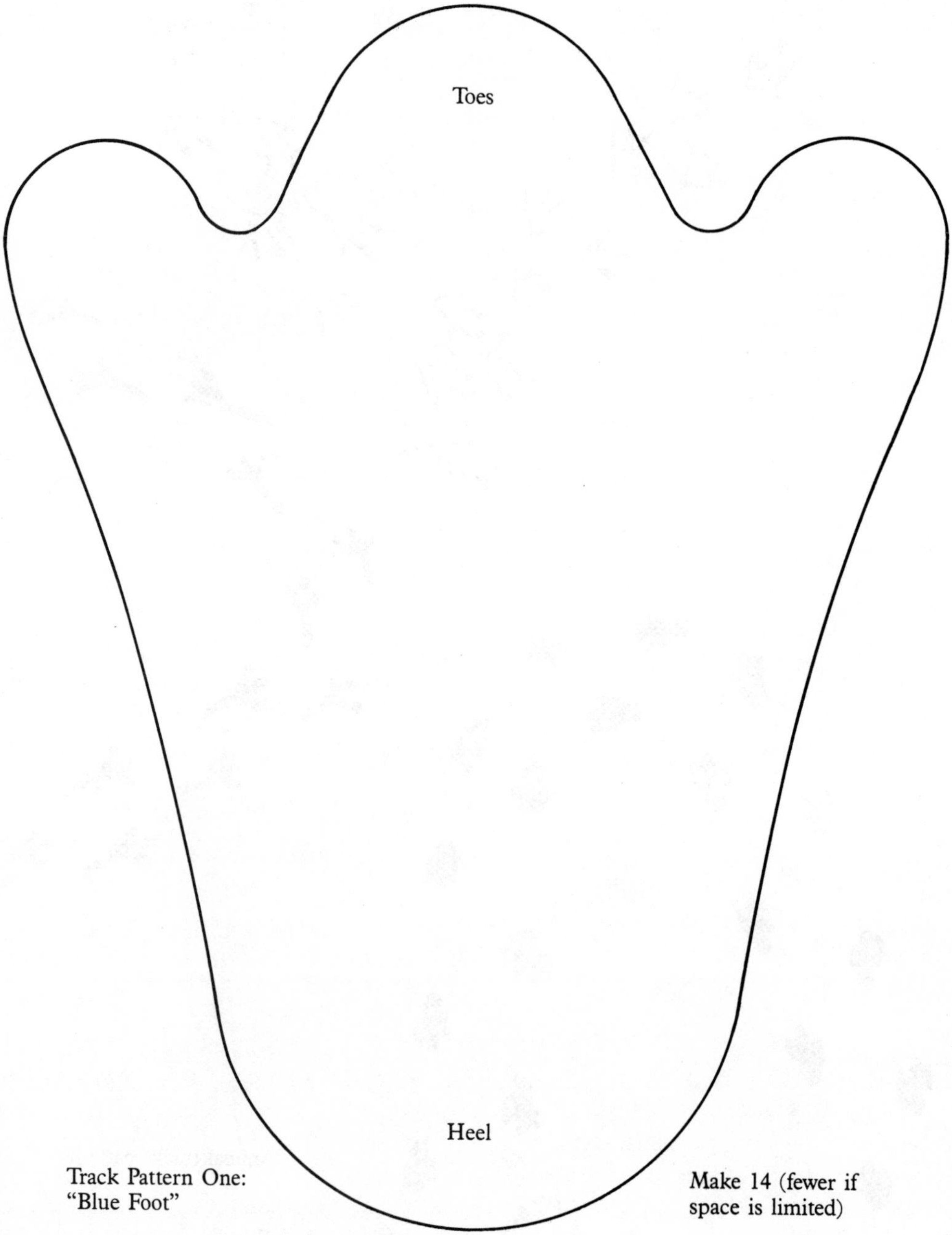

Track Pattern One:
"Blue Foot"

Make 14 (fewer if space is limited)

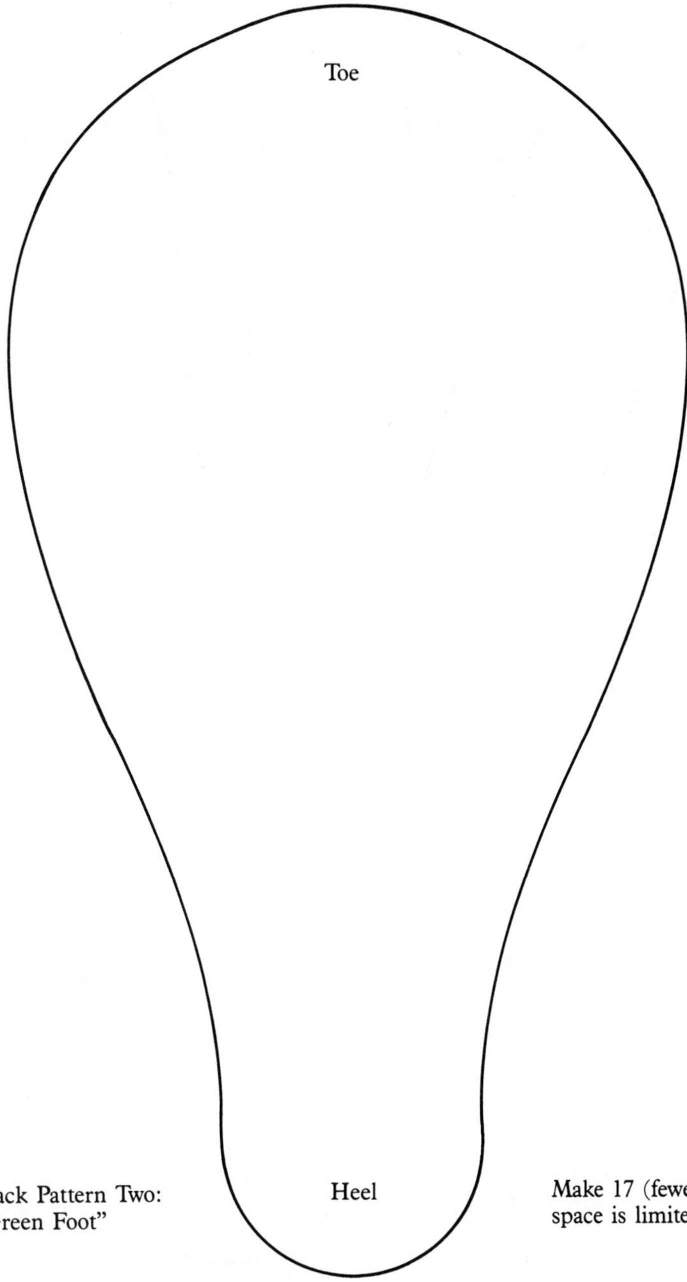

Track Pattern Two:
"Green Foot"

Make 17 (fewer if space is limited)

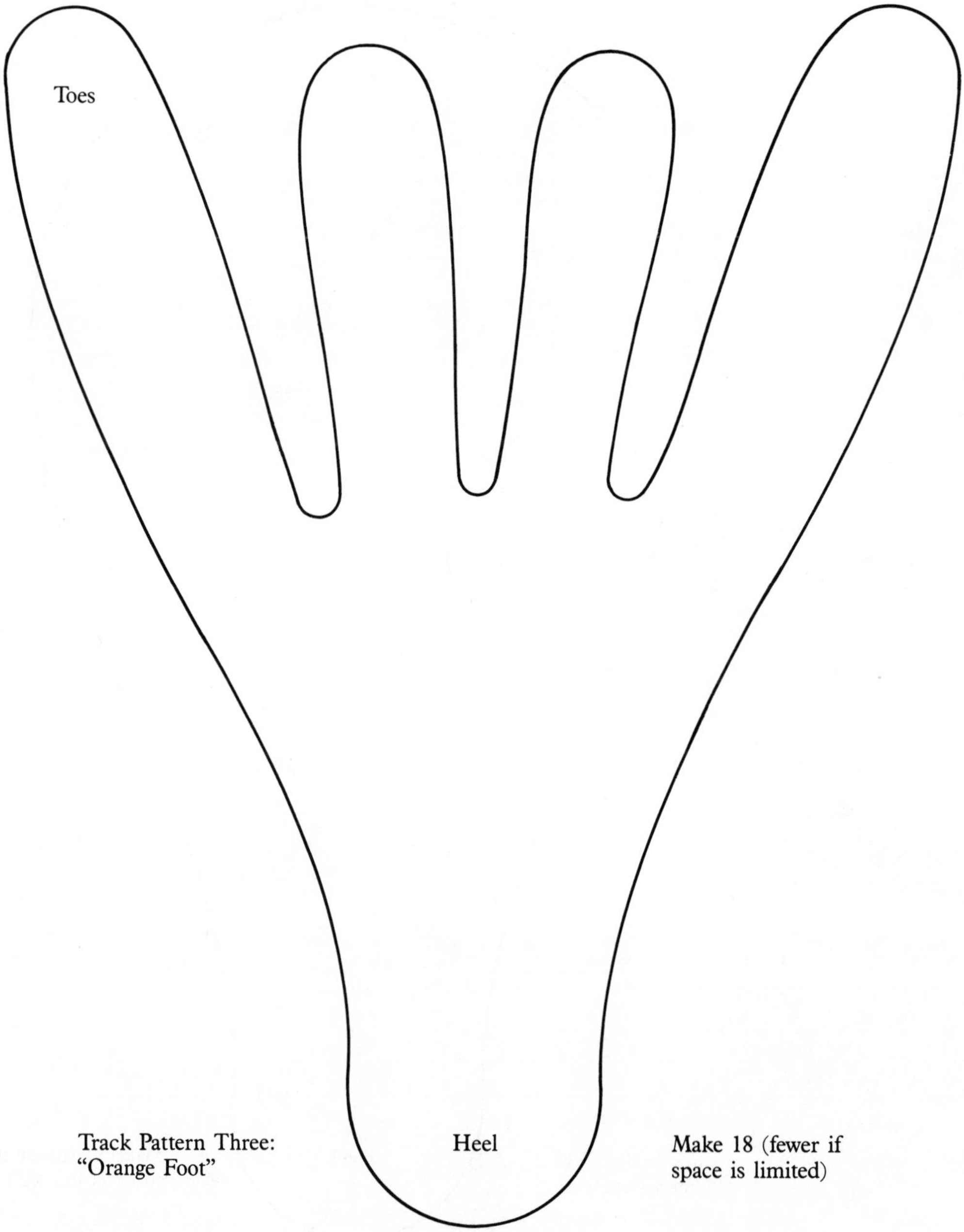

Track Pattern Three: "Orange Foot"

Make 18 (fewer if space is limited)

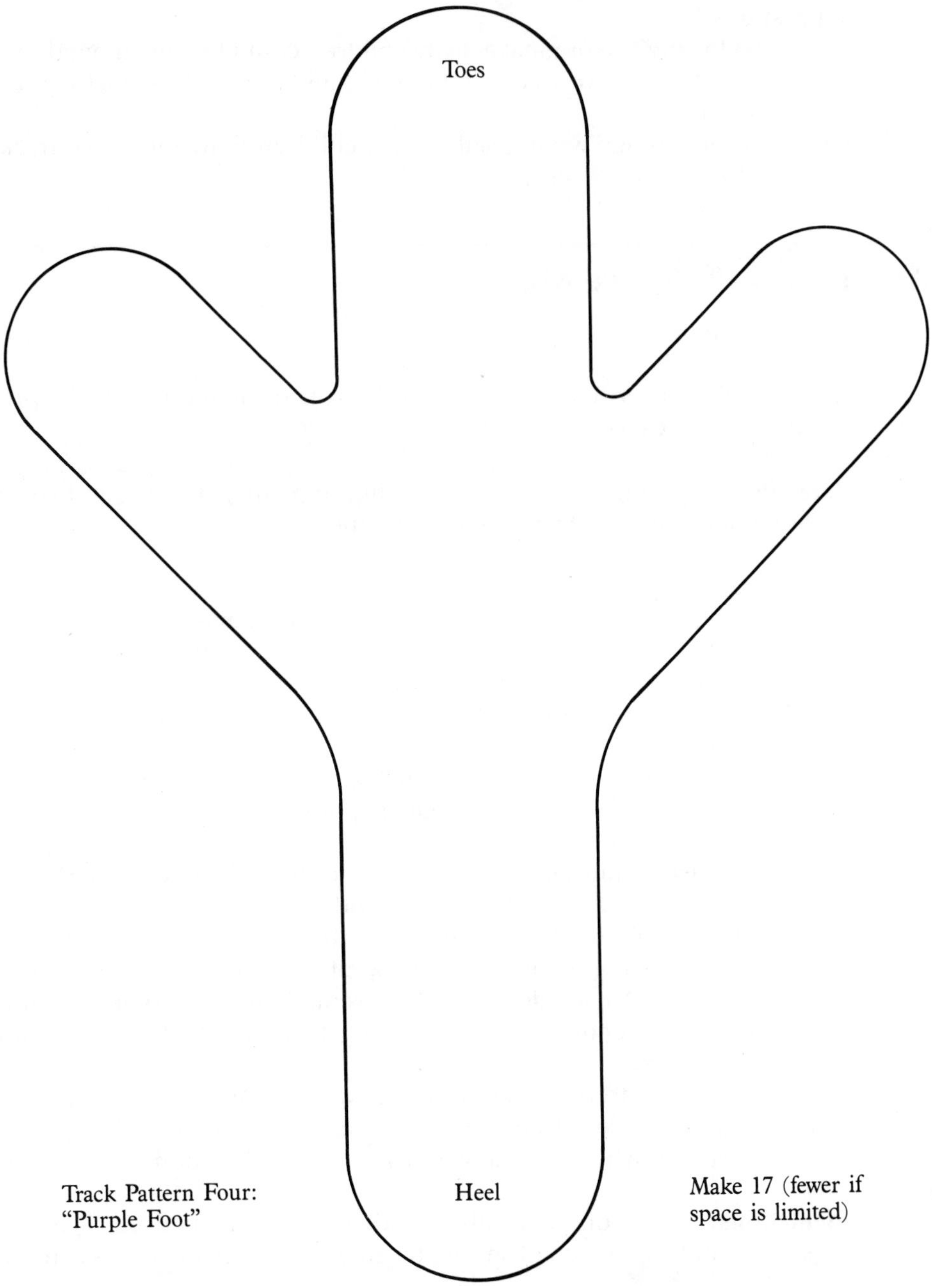

Track Pattern Four:
"Purple Foot"

Make 17 (fewer if space is limited)

Suggestions:

1. Following the original activity children could be encouraged to make up different stories using the tracks and to place the tracks according to the story.
2. To encourage writing skills, have children draw their own track pictures and write stories about them.

Activity 11–19: Space Man

(All grade levels)

Purpose: The purpose of this activity is to isolate and emphasize the process of communication.

Materials: Modeling clay or papier-mâché, or paints, crayons, and construction paper, or a combination of all of them

Procedure:

1. Using the story in Step 2, have the children make an extraterrestrial.
   a. Have the children then write a story about the creature and its adventures on its home planet.
   b. Have the stories and the creatures displayed for others to see and read.
   c. Younger children could dictate the tale to the teacher or into a tape recorder for later transcription.
2. Story:
   Four astronauts take off from Earth for the planet Antares. When they land there, they immediately send home word that the planet is rather small, but that there is air to breathe and water to drink. Even more amazing is the fact that the planet Antares has "people." The people of Antares look very different from the people of Earth, but they are friendly and one is going to return to the Earth with the astronauts.

   It is up to you to try to decide what an Antarean would look like. Make a model of an Antarean. Then, write a story about what the Antarean, who is very adventurous, does while home on Antares.

Adaptations: If clay or some other modeling material is used, even the visually handicapped child should be able to participate in this activity.

Related Content: This activity could be related to the study of other planets in the solar system, by making the creature the inhabitant of one of the actual planets and having the children use their knowledge about the planet in creating their creatures.

Suggestions: This activity is closely related to both art and to creative writing. Children should be given as much freedom as possible to exercise their creativity.

Activity 11–20: Swingers

(Primary grades)

Purpose: The purpose of this activity is to isolate and emphasize the process of number relations.

Materials: String, keys, washers, or paper clips; clock with a sweep second hand; paper for recording data

Procedure:

1. Make pendula from the string and paper clips, keys, or washers for each pair of children in the class.
2. Show how a pendulum swings back and forth with a regular motion by using one of the pendula and having the children watch.
   a. Decide as a group how to count the number of swings of the pendulum.
   b. Time for one minute and count the number of swings together as a class.
3. Give each of the groups a pendulum to use.
   a. Have the children decide on the length that they will use.
      (1) Groups should be encouraged to have different lengths.
   b. Have the children count the number of swings of the pendulum for one minute.
4. Make a record of the activity by gluing or taping the pendula to a large sheet of paper and writing beneath each the number of swings.
   a. Try to place the pendula in order from the longest to the shortest.
   b. Discuss with the class any trends in the data that they see.

Adaptations:

1. The visually handicapped child might be the one in the pair to hold the string while the pendulum swings. The motion of the pendulum can be felt in this way.
2. Mentally handicapped children may need help in counting. Assign a partner who can count accurately and help the child to count the number of swings.

Related Content: This activity is related to the study of motion and energy.

Suggestions:

1. If possible, have one pendulum that is attached to the ceiling and reaches to the floor to compare with the smaller pendula used by the children.

2. The results can be made into a bulletin board display dealing with the activity.

Activity 11–21: A Throw of the Dice

(Intermediate grades)

Purpose: The purpose of this activity is to isolate and emphasize the process of number relations. In addition the process of communication is used.

Materials: One die for each trio of children, paper for recording data, clock with a second hand

Procedure:

1. Begin by asking the children how many of them have played a game like Monopoly where you throw a die or pair of dice to determine how far to move in the game.
   a. Discuss whether they can tell which number is going to turn up next.
2. Give the following directions:
   a. Choose two partners.
   b. Choose one person to time, one to record, and one to throw the die.
   c. As the timer times for one minute, the thrower should quickly throw the die, call out the number on the upper side, then throw the die again. This should continue for one minute. The recorder should write down the number of times the thrower calls out each of the numbers from one to six.
      (1) The recording is easy to do if the recorder has a sheet of paper numbered from one to six. All that is needed, then, is to place a tally mark next to the number.
   d. After one minute switch jobs. The switch should be repeated twice so that each person has the opportunity to time, to throw, and to record.
3. At the end, tally up the number of times each number was seen on the top of the die.
   a. Each group should then find the total number of times a number was seen and then find the average number of times each number appeared.
4. As a class, find the average number of times that each of the numbers was seen on the die.
   a. The results should come close to being the same for each of the numbers since there is an equal probability for each of them.

b. Discuss with the class why they think the numbers for the averages were so similar or why they were so different when they should be the same.

Adaptations:

1. Visually handicapped children can participate by having one of the other members of the group call out the number which appears on the die.
2. Children with orthopedic handicaps affecting the use of the hands can have a partner throw the die while the handicapped child calls out the number.

Related Content: This activity can be related to probability and to the relationship of probability to genetics.

Suggestions:

1. This activity is closely related to the mathematical concepts of mean and of probability and can be used to reinforce those ideas.
2. Flipping two coins at one time and recording the results as two-heads, two-tails, or one-head, one-tail, and then tallying those combinations can also show the concepts of probability.

Activity 11–22: Taking a Survey

(Intermediate grades)

Purpose: The purpose of this activity is to isolate and emphasize the process of number relations. Concluding is also used.

Materials: Graph paper, crayons or markers

Procedure:

1. Take a survey of the class or of a number of classes within the school tallying the number of children who fall into each of the following groups:
   a. brown hair, blond hair, red hair;
   b. brown eyes, green eyes, blue eyes, hazel eyes;
   c. month of birthday;
   d. number of brothers or sisters;
   e. favorite color;
   f. favorite television show;
   g. favorite motion picture.
2. Divide the class into groups so that each group has two sets of data to work with.
   a. Have each group graph their data.
   b. Have each group show its graph to the rest of the class.

3. As a class, discuss the graphs and write a profile of the class or of those in the group that participated in the survey.

Adaptations: All children should be able to participate in this activity.

Related Content: This activity can be related to the study of the human body.

Suggestions:

1. The larger the population which can be surveyed, the better this activity is. Try to arrange with other teachers at the same grade level to allow the children to survey their classes.
2. The drawing of conclusions about a large number of children can be used as a language arts experience by having the children write an "official report" about their class or grade level.

Activity 11–23: How Fast Does It Sink?

(Primary grades)

Purpose: The purpose of this activity is to isolate and emphasize the process of number relations. In addition, the process of communication is used.

Materials: Clear plastic basins or aquaria filled with water, five or more jar lids of varying sizes, white paper 12 × 18 inches, felt-tipped markers

Procedure:

1. Place one of the aquaria or basins with water in front of the children.
   a. Show one of the jar lids. Ask what might happen if the lid was placed into the water.
   b. Show that the lid will float if placed gently on the water and sink if placed just below the surface.
   c. Demonstrate how to record how long it takes for the lid to sink when gently placed in the water by having one of the children draw a line slowly along a piece of white paper starting when the lid is placed in the water and ending when the lid reaches the bottom of the container.
2. Divide the children into pairs to make their line drawings of how long it takes each of the lids to sink. Each child should have the opportunity to place the lids in the water as well as to draw.
   a. Have the children label each of the lines by numbering the lids or naming the type of lid.
3. The children have now produced a graph that shows the length of time needed for each of the lids to sink in the water.
   a. Discuss the graphs made using questions to elicit the kinds of information that can be obtained from a graph.

Adaptations: The visually handicapped child should be able to participate in this activity if assigned a partner who will clearly tell when to start and stop the line. Placing the paper between two meter sticks can help the child to maintain a straight line. When the visually handicapped child places the lids in the water, he or she can place one hand on the bottom of the container and call for a halt to the drawing when the lid touches the underwater hand.

Related Content: This is directly related to text chapters dealing with sinking and floating.

Suggestions:

1. The deeper the containers, the better this will work.
2. If children can also graph small objects falling through other media such as liquid detergents, shampoo, oil, and glycerine many other comparisons can be made.
3. Be certain to caution the children to always draw at about the same rate.

Activity 11–24: How Big Is It?

(Primary grades)

Purpose: The purpose of this activity is to isolate and emphasize the process of space relations.

Materials: Paper for recording data collected

Procedure:

1. Seat the children in a line that parallels the longest dimension of the room beginning at one wall and extending as far as possible to the opposite wall.
   a. Ask the children how they could determine how long their room is.
   b. Collect as many ideas as possible writing them on the chalkboard or on chart paper.
   c. Begin the measuring of the room by finishing the distance to the wall and counting the number of seated children needed to measure that distance.
2. Divide the children into groups of three or four.
   a. Have each of the groups decide on three ways they could use, from the list made or other ways, to measure the length of the room.
   b. Have the children measure the room and record their measurements.

3. Discuss the different measurements obtained for the same room focusing on why they are different.
4. Have the children try to think of a method that they could use to measure their own heights.
   a. Discuss and list the ideas, then use some of them to measure the children.

Adaptations: All children should be able to participate fully in this activity.

Related Content: This activity is related to the study of measurement.

Suggestions:

1. For young children, this lesson can be used to reinforce counting skills by having one child measure and the others count.
2. The results of this activity could be graphed using simple bar graphs in which one block of a piece of graph paper is colored for each step, hop, jump, etc., taken in measurement.
3. Children might also draw a plan of the classroom and measure off the various room measurements and desk placements by using whatever measurements they wish.

Activity 11–25: Giving Directions

(Preschool and kindergarten)

Purpose: The purpose of this activity is to isolate and emphasize the process of space relations.

Materials: Objects in the classroom

Procedure:

1. Review to be certain that all children understand the terms: in front of, behind, left, right, forward, backward, beside, and under.
   a. A game such as Simon Says can be effective for such a review.
2. Pick up one object in the room and choose one child.
   a. Say: I want ________ to be able to come and get this ________. But, he (she) cannot do it unless the rest of us give him (her) some directions.
   b. Have the children give the chosen child directions, one step at a time until the child reaches the object.
      (1) Be certain to emphasize the various directional words listed in the review step.
3. Repeat with various objects and children.

Adaptations:

1. Be certain that the area is not too cluttered if a visually handicapped child is to participate.

2. Hearing handicapped children may be given signs or signals as well as the oral directions.
3. Bilingual children might be encouraged to share their second language words with the other children and those words incorporated into the directions.

Related Content: Can be related to directionality using compass directions.

Suggestions: Even with preschool and kindergarten children, the directional words used in this activity could be printed on cards. This is not to teach reading, but to develop the concept that written and spoken words do have a connection.

Activity 11–26: Measuring

(Primary to intermediate grades)

Purpose: The purpose of this activity is to isolate and emphasize the process of space relations.

Materials: Pencils, chalk, soft drink cans, paper clips, coat hangers, and straws

Procedure:

1. Present the class with a situation in which all of the rulers in the entire world have been lost and no more are available.
   a. Ask the children what they might use to determine how big their room is without a ruler.
   b. Try out some of the ideas listing the various measurements on the chalkboard.
2. Display the items listed in the materials section.
   a. Present the idea that, since these items are very common all over the world, they are going to be used instead of rulers.
   a. Develop a list of items that could be appropriately measured with each of the items.
   b. Have the children work in pairs to measure ten of the items found in the total list.
3. After the measurements are made, discuss with the class why, even though the same objects were used, there are still differences in the measurements.

Adaptations: All children should be able to participate in this activity.

Related Content: This activity can be used to develop a concept of measurement for later use in developing metric measurement.

Suggestions: Almost any object can be used as a nonstandard form of measuring device. Children, particularly young children, especially like measuring with parts of their bodies.

Activity 11–27: Making Shapes

(Intermediate grades)

Purpose: The purpose of this activity is to isolate and emphasize the process of space relations.

Materials: Straws, clay, pins

Procedure:

1. Without giving precise instructions as to how to construct each of the figures, challenge the children to use the straws to construct each of the following shapes:
   a. a shape with three sides the same length,
   b. a shape with three sides but one side longer than the other two,
   c. a shape with four sides the same length,
   d. a shape with four sides but with two of the opposite sides longer than the other two,
   e. a shape with five equal sides, eight equal sides, and twelve equal sides.
2. Discuss the characteristics of each of the shapes that were constructed including the names of the shapes.
3. Again without giving precise instructions, challenge the children to use clay to construct each of the following shapes:
   a. a shape that has six squares for its sides,
   b. a shape that has two squares and two rectancles for its sides,
   c. a shape that has one square and three triangles for its sides,
   d. a shape that has five pentagons for its sides,
   e. a shape that uses any of the shapes made in step one.
4. Discuss the characteristics of the various shapes naming any which can be easily named.

Adaptations: All children should be able to participate in this activity.

Related Content: This can be related to the concept of properties in the study of matter.

Suggestions:

1. Children should be given as little guidance as possible in the construction of the shapes. Allow them to discover their own methods.
2. Relate this to the study of geometry in mathematics.

Activity 11–28: Looking for Shapes

(Primary grades)

Purpose: The purpose of this activity is to isolate and emphasize the process of space relations. In addition the processes of observation and communication are used.

Materials: Any outdoor area

Procedure:

1. Review with the children the names of the basic plane and solid shapes: circle, square, triangle, rectangle, oval, cube, pyramid, ovoid (egg), and rectangular solid (box).
2. Take the children on a "shape walk" to look for examples of the various shapes found in nature.
   a. Whenever possible, collect a sample of the shape to bring back to the classroom.
   b. Keep a list of the objects and the shapes seen.
3. After the walk, discuss the various objects found and their shapes.
   a. Draw pictures of the objects for display and name the shapes.

Adaptations:

1. For the visually handicapped child, allow the child to touch objects when appropriate so that the shape can be felt.
2. Be certain that the area chosen for the walk will be accessible to the orthopedically handicapped child. Use a wagon for transportation if necessary.

Related Content: This activity can be directly related to the study of the characteristics of plants and animals.

Suggestions:

1. Although a wooded area is particularly nice for this activity, it is usually easier to find the various shapes in an urban setting. Either situation can be used effectively.
2. Relate this to the study of geometry in mathematics.

Activities 11–29 through 11–37

The activities that follow are suitable for all grade levels; they provide a starting point for children to develop the ability to use operational questions in science. All of the basic processes of science will be used so that these activities also provide a means for consolidating the child's ability to use the primary processes.

Each of the activities is presented in the form of a starting question and a list of materials that would be needed for each child or pair of children in order to investigate the original question. Other materials that could be required by the children as they write and investigate their operational questions are also included.

In general, the procedure should be to present the children with the starting question, have them solve the problem posed by the question, write any additional questions that they would like to investigate, then allow the children to investigate the questions they write.

Activity 11–29: Investigating Bubbles

Question: What is a bubble?

Materials: Liquid detergent, straws, bubble blowing pipes or hoops, paper towels, paper cups

Additional Materials: Light-weight cardboard, aluminum foil, empty jars, food coloring, water, bubble liquid, salt

Activity 11–30: Investigating Splashes

Question: How far does water splash?

Materials: Plastic containers, marbles, water, newspaper, meter sticks

Additional Materials: Various sized objects, salt, other liquids, various sized plastic containers

Activity 11–31: Investigating Salt

Question: How much salt will dissolve in water?

Materials: Clear glass or plastic containers, water, measuring cups or graduated cylinders, salt, balances, stirring rods or spoons

Additional Materials: Warm water, ice water, sugar, epsom salts; other solids like sugar, corn starch, baking soda; other liquids such as oil, vinegar, soft drinks, various sized containers

Activity 11–32: Investigating Seeds

Question: How does a seed grow?

Materials: Radish seeds, sponges, paper towels, plastic bags, water

Additional Materials: Various types of seeds, various types of containers, soil, meter sticks or rulers

---

Activity 11–33: Investigating String

Question: How strong is a piece of string?

Materials: Thin string (crochet cotton works well), books, balance

Additional Materials: Thread, twine, cord, yarns of various types, rope, water, spring scales, pound or kilogram masses

---

Activity 11–34: Investigating Soil

Question: How much water does soil hold?

Materials: Garden soil, paper cups, measuring cups or graduated cylinders, water

Additional Materials: Sand, humus, potting soil, vermiculite, clay soil, gravel

---

Activity 11–35: Investigating Mice

Question: How smart is a mouse?

Materials: Mice, cardboard for mazes, masking tape, carrots, clock

Additional Materials: Other small animals and additional cardboard

---

Activity 11–36: Investigating Sound

Question: How can the pitch of a sound be changed?

Materials: Rubber bands, small boxes

Additional Materials: Various sized rubber bands, various sized boxes, old guitar or violin strings, wire, oatmeal boxes, balloons, string, scissors, tape or glue, musical instruments

---

Activity 11–37: Investigating Leaves

Question: What is a leaf?

Materials: Any outdoor area with lots of plants

Additional materials: Meter sticks, thermometers, balances, collecting jars

Selected References

Brock, J. A. M., D. W. Paulsen, and F. T. Weisbruch. *Patterns and Processes of Science, Laboratory Text One.* Lexington, Mass.: Heath, 1969.

———. *Patterns and Processes of Science, Laboratory Text Two.* Lexington, Mass.: Heath, 1969.

Butts, D. P. *Teaching Science in the Elementary School.* New York: Macmillan, 1973.

Divito, A., and G. H. Krockover. *Creative Sciencing: Ideas and Activities for Teachers and Children,* 2nd ed. Boston: Little, Brown. 1980.

Feifer, N. *Adventures in Chemistry.* New York: Sentinal, 1959.

Hone, E. B., J. Alexander, E. Victor, and P. Brandwein. *A Sourcebook for Elementary Science.* New York: Harcourt, 1962.

Sund, R. B., B. W. Tillery, and L. W. Trowbridge. *Elementary Science Lessons: The Biological Sciences.* Boston: Allyn and Bacon, 1970.

———. *Elementary Science Lessons: The Earth Sciences.* Boston: Allyn and Bacon, 1970.

———. *Elementary Science Lessons: The Physical Sciences.* Boston: Allyn and Bacon, 1970.

12 Activities for the Causal Processes of Science

The activities of this chapter are designed to enable children to develop their abilities in the use of the cause-and-effect processes. These activities emphasize those processes that are best addressed after the child has become skilled in the use of the basic processes. The child must be able to observe, use number relations, and communicate, as well as use the other basic processes, before he or she can easily draw conclusions or identify cause-and-effect relationships.

All of the activities of this section should be followed by a discussion of the major processes of the activity, in order to develop the child's ability to use the process effectively. In addition, the teacher should emphasize other areas where the process is used, so that the child develops the ability to transfer knowledge into other subject areas.

Each of the activities for the cause-and-effect processes includes the activity instructions, the content area most closely related, adaptations for mainstreamed children, and suggestions for working with correlated subject areas.

In this chapter are activities dealing with inference, conclusion, prediction, cause and effect, and interaction and systems. The processes of cause and effect and interactions and systems are closely related and are combined in the activities.

Activity 12–1: What Do Commercials Really Say?

(Intermediate grades)

Purpose: The purpose of this activity is to isolate and emphasize the process of inferring.

Materials: Advertisements cut from magazines, newspapers, and product brochures; tape recordings of television and radio commercials

Procedure:

1. Ask the children what commercials they recall from listening to the radio or watching television.
   a. Discuss what these commercials are asking the buyer to infer about the product being sold.
2. Listen to tape recordings of some of the commercials from radio and television.
   a. Again make inferences about what the buyer is supposed to believe about the product as a result of the commercial.
   b. Pick out the observations that buyers would make that cause these inferences to be made.
3. Give each student one or two of the advertisements taken from magazines, newspapers, or product brochures.
   a. Have each student make inferences about the product.
4. Discuss why advertisers might use the kind of advertisements that allow listeners to make such inferences.

Adaptations:

1. Intellectually handicapped children may have difficulty making inferences from the advertisements. They could be given the easiest of the advertisements and some aid in picking out the inferences.
2. Visually handicapped children will be able to participate in this activity provided that there are some taped examples.

Related Content: The discussion should revolve around the difference between observations and inferences as they apply to experiments in science.

Suggestions:

1. Toothpaste, deodorant, and mouthwash commercials are particularly good for this activity.
2. This can be related to social studies and the way in which material can be slanted to show a particular point of view.

Activity 12–2: Circuit Boxes

(Intermediate grades)

Purpose: The purpose of this activity is to isolate and emphasize the process of inferring.

Materials: Shoe boxes, wire, "D" batteries, paper brads, bulbs and sockets

Procedure:

1. Prepare the inferences boxes before the lesson (see diagram below).
   a. Punch two rows of equally spaced holes in the lid of the shoe box. Each row should have five or six holes, and the rows should be parallel.

Diagram of a Circuit Box

Inside

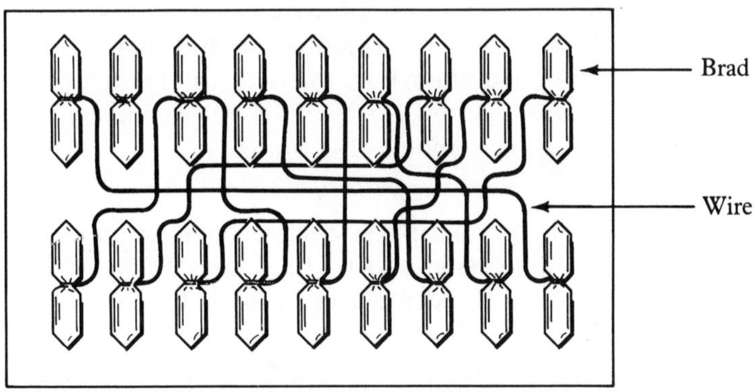

Outside

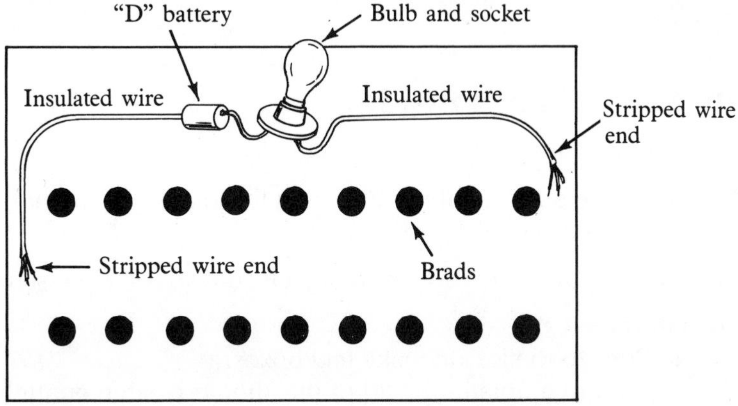

b. Push a paper brad through each hole and open the prongs of the brad so that it will not fall out.
c. On the inside of the lid, wire the brads together in pairs using a separate piece of wire for each of the pairs.
(1) Vary the pattern in each of the boxes.
(2) Do not consistently wire the brads across from one another.
d. Place the lid on the box and seal the box so that it cannot be opened.
e. Tape the battery to the top of the box so that the terminals at each end are easily accessible.
f. Place the bulb in the socket and attach a wire to each of the screws. Attach one wire to a battery terminal.
g. Attach an additional piece of wire to the other terminal of the battery.
(1) There should be two ends of wires unattached.
h. If the box is correctly made, touching the loose ends of the wires to brads which are connected should cause the bulb to light.

2. Give a box to each group of two or three children.
a. Explain that the brads are wired and that if two wired brads are touched with the wires, the bulb will light.
b. Have the children work with the boxes to try to find the pattern of wires that connects the brads.

Adaptations:

1. Intellectually handicapped children and visually handicapped children should be assigned a partner.
2. Also, a buzzer could replace the bulb for the visually handicapped child.

Related Content: This activity is directly related to the study of circuits.

Suggestions: Children should also be given the materials and asked to develop their own inference boxes for others to try to solve.

Activity 12–3: What's Inside?

(Intermediate grades)

Purpose: The purpose of this activity is to isolate and emphasize the process of inferring.

Materials: Shoe boxes, common objects, old socks, tape, scissors

Procedure:

1. Prior to the lesson make feel boxes.
a. Cut a hole in the lid of the shoe box large enough to accommodate a child's hand.

   b. Cut the top off a sock and attach it to the hole so that the hand passes through the sock to get inside the box.
      (1) The sock helps to eliminate peeking.
   c. Place one or more common objects in the box and seal the box.
2. Provide one box for each group of two or three children.
   a. Have each member of the group place a hand into the box and feel the object or objects.
   b. Each member of the group should then write three observations of the object and make three inferences based on the observations as to what could be in the box.
   c. Trade boxes among groups and repeat with as many boxes as time permits.
3. Discuss the inferences made including the idea that many inferences can be made from the same observations.

Adaptations: Provided that some easy-to-recognize objects are included for the intellectually handicapped child, all children should be able to participate in this activity.

Related Content: This activity could be related to the properties of matter as well as to the concept of a theory versus a fact.

Suggestions:
1. Be careful that the objects do not have any sharp, rough, or splintered edges that could cause cuts or scratches.
2. Some suggested objects: toothbrush, pine cone, eraser, plastic bag of salt or sugar, various shapes of blocks, unsharpened pencils, tape rolls or dispensers, plastic bottles, yarn or string balls, foil balls, stones, feathers, various types of cloth, small toys

---

Activity 12–4: Why Does It Live There?

(Intermediate grades)

Purpose: The purpose of this activity is to isolate and emphasize the process of inferring.

Materials: Pictures of a wide variety of plants and animals from various habitats from desert to ocean

Procedure:
1. Review with the children the various types of habitats with which they are familiar: desert, woodland, stream, ocean, forest, pond, mountain.
2. Provide each group of four or five children with a pile of pictures.
   a. Have the children try to place the animals and plants into the various habitats.

b. After each of the pictures is placed, have each group describe the inferences that they made as they placed the animals.
   (1) These inferences should be based on the characteristics of the animals the children observe. For example: The frogs are brown and green so that they can hide easily on the leaves and dirt on the forest floor.

Adaptations: Because the activity is done in groups, all children should be able to participate in the activity.

Related Content: This activity is directly related to the study of habitats and of adaptations of plants and animals.

Suggestions:

1. The wider the variety of pictures, including many unfamiliar plants and animals, the better this activity will be.
2. This could be related to social studies by including a study of where each of the habitats could be found on the Earth or in the country.
3. Research skills from language arts could be included by having students look for information on unfamiliar animals and plants or for information on misplaced animals and plants.

Activity 12–5: What Lives on Jupiter?

(Intermediate grades)

Purpose: The purpose of this activity is to isolate and emphasize the process of inferring.

Materials: Reference books dealing with the planets, drawing paper

Procedure:

1. Have each group of four or five children choose a planet to research.
2. Discuss with each group the characteristics of each of the planets that they found through their reading.
3. Challenge each of the groups to design three animals and two plants that could live on the planet they researched.
   a. Have the children draw their plants and animals.
   b. Have each group describe for the rest of the class the plants and animals that they designed for the planet.
      (1) Each group should bring out the characteristics of the planet used as the basis for each of the characteristics developed for the creatures.

Adaptations: Rather than drawing their animals, visually handicapped children could be encouraged to model them from clay.

Related Content: This activity is closely related to both the study of the planets and to the study of biology.

Suggestions:

1. If possible, modeling materials should be made available so that three-dimensional models could be constructed by all children.
2. This activity could be continued in art by having children develop dioramas for their models.

Activity 12–6: Fading Colors

(Intermediate grades)

Purpose: The purpose of this activity is to isolate and emphasize the process of concluding.

Materials: Various colors of construction paper cut into squares about ten centimeters to a side, piece of partly faded paper

Procedure:

1. Display the partly faded paper for the students and make inferences as to what could have caused the partial color change evident in the paper.
2. Display the various colors of paper and ask the students whether they think all of the colors will fade in the same way as the sample.
   a. As a class devise a method that could be used to determine whether each of the colors will fade equally.
3. Divide the class into groups of three or four.
   a. Have each group carry out the activity designed by the class.
4. When the activity is over, collect the data from each of the groups into a common data pool on the board.
   a. Discuss the data and draw a conclusion as to the way in which various colors of construction paper will fade.
      (1) Be certain to retain an example of the original paper for comparison if necessary.

Adaptations: Visually handicapped children will have difficulty participating in this activity. Even a partner will not be too helpful. Try to find an alternative for the visually handicapped child.

Related Content: This activity is closely related to a study of light and to a study of energy in general.

Activity 12–7: Growing Mold

(Intermediate grades)

Purpose: The purpose of this activity is to isolate and emphasize the process of concluding.

Materials: Moldy loaf of bread, nonmoldy slices of bread, water, plastic wrap, aluminum foil, jars or plastic containers with lids

Procedure:

1. Display the moldy loaf of bread for the children and allow time for observations.
2. Ask the students to infer where the bread might have been kept that it got so moldy.
   a. Divide the class into groups of three or four children.
   b. Have each group develop a method which could be used to find out where bread is likely to develop mold.
      (1) Have each group carry out the activity.
3. Once the various activities have been completed, collect the data from each of the groups into a class collection of data.
   a. From the information collected, draw a conclusion as to where mold is most likely to develop on bread.

Adaptations: All children should be able to participate in this activity.

Related Content: This activity is directly related to the study of molds.

Suggestions:

1. This activity can be extended by providing a variety of kinds of foods for children to work with and to develop a conclusion as to the kinds of food that will develop molds.
2. In language arts, children could be encouraged to write stories dealing with what it would be like to live in a world where the only kinds of plants were molds.

Activity 12–8: Picking Up the Pieces

(Intermediate grades)

Purpose: The purpose of this activity is to isolate and emphasize the process of concluding.

Materials: Plastic and metal spoons, nylon combs, cotton, wool, and fur scraps, confetti-sized bits of paper, styrofoam pieces, iron filings, balloons

Procedure:

1. Begin by asking how many in the class had ever touched a doorknob and received a shock.
   a. Have students describe their experiences, especially what they did just before the "shock."
   b. Rub a balloon against a wool sweater or against your hair and place it against the wall; the balloon will stick to the wall.
      (1) Have the students describe what you did to get the balloon to stick. Use the term *static electricity* if the children do not.
2. Present the following two questions to the children:
   a. What objects will develop a static charge?
   b. How strong is static electricity?
3. Have the children work in pairs or in groups of three or four to find answers to the questions using the provided materials.
4. After the activity, collect all of the data and draw two conclusions: one to answer each question.

Adaptations: All children should be able to participate in this activity.

Related Content: This activity is directly related to the study of static electricity.

Suggestions:

1. Provide a variety of materials so that each child can work with materials rather than having to wait for someone to finish.
2. Although children rarely have problems in finding a way of measuring the strength of a static charge, some possibilities are: How large a piece of styrofoam can be picked up? How many pieces of confetti are picked up? What amount of iron filings are picked up? How long will a balloon stick to the wall?

Activity 12–9: How Far Can You Jump?

(Intermediate grades)

Purpose: The purpose of this activity is to isolate and emphasize the process of concluding.

Materials: Large, open space like a hallway or playground; a meter stick; calculators

Procedure:

1. Ask: How far do you think someone your age can jump?
   a. What are some things which could affect how far a person can jump?

b. What information would we need to collect in order to answer the question about how far a person can jump?

2. Set up an activity in which each child makes five different kinds of jumps: on one foot; on both feet with arms across the chest; on both feet with arms swinging; hop-skip-and-jump; and from a running start.
   a. Measure each child's jumps.
   b. Collect all of the data.
   c. Divide the class into five groups giving each group a calculator and one set of data.
      (1) Have each of the groups find the average distance jumped for each of the type of jumps.
   d. Collect the resulting averages.
   e. Draw a conclusion that reflects the data collected.

Adaptations:

1. Visually handicapped children should be permitted to participate as fully as possible in the activity. A partner may be needed for those jumps which require a moving start.
2. Orthopedically handicapped children will not be able to participate if wheelchair bound. These children can be made the official recorders or measurers.

Related Content: This activity can be related to the study of the human body.

Suggestions:

1. Divide the class into groups of four or five for quicker handling of the measurements.
2. Relate this activity to mathematics by reviewing the use of an average and the means of calculating averages.
3. Extend the activity by asking students if there is any other information they could obtain from the data collected.
4. Graph the data for easier consideration of the information.

Activity 12–10: Fingerprints

(Intermediate grades)

Purpose: The purpose of this activity is to isolate and emphasize the process of concluding.

Materials: Clear tape, pencils, fine sandpaper, feathers, magnifiers, index cards

Procedure:

1. Begin by asking if any of the children have ever watched a detective program on television or have read a detective story.
   a. Discuss some of the things a detective does in order to solve the crime.
   b. Be certain to bring out that detectives usually look for fingerprints.
2. Give the following directions for taking fingerprints:
   a. Cut five pieces of tape about four centimeters long.
   b. Rub the pencil point across the sandpaper until there is a pile of black pencil lead.
   c. Obtain a feather and an index card.
   d. Roll the fingerprint side of your little finger over the sticky side of the first piece of tape.
   e. Remove your finger and very gently sprinkle some of the pencil dust on the tape.
   f. Gently dust the fingerprint with the feather to remove any extra dust.
   g. Tape the print onto the card. Label it with the correct name.
   h. Repeat with each of the fingers.
3. Using the magnifier, examine your fingerprints and those of at least four other classmates:
   a. What observations can you make?
   b. What conclusion can you draw about fingerprints?
4. Discuss with the class the results of the activity and draw a conclusion about fingerprints.

Adaptations: The visually handicapped child will not be able to participate in this activity.

Related Content: This activity is directly related to the study of the human body.

Suggestions: This would be a good activity to follow up with a visit from a police officer who could show how fingerprints are taken by the police and discuss the use of fingerprints in police work.

Activity 12–11: How Fast Will They Grow?

(Intermediate grades)

Purpose: The purpose of this activity is to isolate and emphasize the process of prediction.

Materials: Various types of seeds, paper towels, plastic wrap, water, paper cups

Procedure:

1. Place the various types of seeds into paper cups so that each of the students receives at least three or four of each seed type.
2. Ask the students to examine the seeds, making any observations they can.
   a. Have some of the students orally present their observations to the class.
   b. Have the students make predictions on the basis of the observations as to the order in which the seeds will sprout.
      (1) Be certain that the predictions are backed up by any observations the students made.
3. Divide the class into groups of three or four.
   a. Have each group decide on a method that they could use to test their predictions.
   b. Have the students carry out their method.
4. After the seeds have sprouted have the students compare the actual occurrences to their predictions.
   a. Have the students make inferences as to why they may have predicted incorrectly in some cases.

Adaptations: All children should be able to participate in this lesson.

Related Content: This activity is closely related to the study of plants and plant growth.

Suggestions:

1. Seeds that are easy to work with and easy to obtain include dried lima beans, popping corn, radish seeds, grass seed, birdseed, and dried peas.
2. Students should be encouraged to find a variety of methods to test their predictions.

Activity 12–12: The Final Temperature

(Intermediate grades)

Purpose: The purpose of this activity is to isolate and emphasize the process of prediction.

Materials: Styrofoam cups, thermometers, water, ice cubes, heat source, measuring cups or graduated cylinders.

Procedure:

1. Prior to the activity, heat one cup or 250 ml of water to boiling. Also have ready ice water and a thermometer.
   a. While the class watches, take the temperature of the boiling

water and record the temperature on the chalkboard. Then take the temperature of the ice water and record it on the chalkboard.

b. Tell the class that you are going to mix one-half cup of the ice water with the cup of boiling water.
   (1) Have the students make predictions as to what the temperature of the two will be when they are mixed.
   (2) Once the predictions have been made, quickly pour the cold water into the boiling water, remove from the heat, and find the temperature. Check the actual temperature against the prediction.

2. Have the students work with varying amounts of warm and cold water, recording starting amounts and temperatures, predicting the final temperature, and then finding the final temperature.
3. Discuss why predictions may not have been found to be correct.

Adaptations: Provided that the visually handicapped child is assigned to a partner who will read the various temperatures, all children should be able to participate in this activity.

Related Content: This activity can be related to the study of matter and energy.

Suggestions:

1. Under no circumstances should children be permitted to use boiling water.
2. Using two styrofoam cups, one within the other and a plastic lid with a hole for the thermometer will retain the heat longer than an open cup. A thermos bottle is even better.
3. This could be related to math by having children find the actual relationship between the resulting temperature, the original temperatures, and the quantities of water.

Activity 12–13: Heads or Tails

(Intermediate grades)

Purpose: The purpose of this activity is to isolate and emphasize the process of prediction.

Materials: Pennies

Procedure:

1. Flip a coin. Have the children predict whether it will be heads or tails.
   a. Repeat a number of times keeping a record of how many times heads is tossed and how many times tails is tossed. Also keep a record as to how often the students have been correct in their predictions.

2. Have the students predict how many times two heads will show when two coins are flipped together. Repeat the predictions for two tails and for one head and one tail.
   a. Have the students each flip their coins twenty-five times, keeping a record of the result of each toss.
   b. Collect the results from all students on the chalkboard.
   c. Have the students determine the relationship in the data and check it against the prediction.

Adaptations: All children should be able to participate in this activity provided the visually handicapped child has a partner who will tell the child which combination has appeared.

Related Content: This activity can be related to the study of genetics.

Suggestions:

1. This activity should be related to the study of probability in mathematics.
2. Other materials which could be used to extend the activity include dice, playing cards, various colored marbles to be picked out of a bag, and pieces of paper of various colors.

Activity 12–14: Spinning Colors

(Intermediate grades)

Purpose: The purpose of this activity is to isolate and emphasize the process of prediction.

Materials: Cardboard circles about five centimeters in diameter with a large, blunt-ended yarn needle through the center forming a top; five centimeter circles of white paper; plastic pen tops; crayons or poster paints; nine clear plastic glasses or nine babyfood jars; water; red, blue, and yellow food coloring. See diagram, page 391, for spinner construction.

Procedure:

1. Begin the activity with a demonstration of what happens when the three primary colors are mixed in pairs.
   a. Collect the observations that red + yellow = orange, blue + yellow = green, and red + blue = violet.
   b. Ask the class what they think will happen if other colors are mixed.
2. Show how to spin the cardboard top by holding the needle by the eye and pushing the edge of the disk. The disk and pen top should rotate freely on the blunt point of the needle.

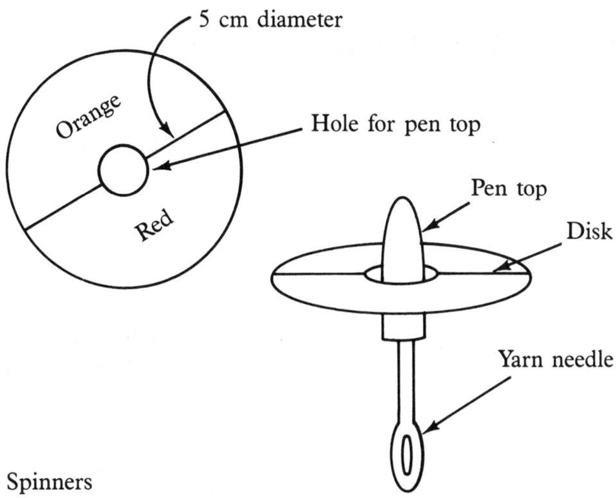

Spinners

a. Each of the white circles can be colored with two or more different colors. When the colored paper is placed over the needle eye and on the cardboard, spinning the top will blend the colors so that the result can be seen.
b. Divide the class into groups of two or three to try various combinations of colors.
   (1) Each group should list the color combination being tested followed by the predicted color during the spinning.
c. Discuss the results.

Adaptations:
1. Visually handicapped children will not be able to participate in this activity.
2. If an orthopedically handicapped child has difficulty using the hands, assign a partner to spin the object and to color at the child's direction.

Related Content: This activity is directly related to the study of light. It may also be used in considering sight during a unit on the human body.

Suggestions:
1. Prior to the activity, children should discuss and come to a conclusion as to the kind of data that should be collected.
2. Mathematics could be correlated with this activity by having students measure certain segments of the circle to be colored using a protractor.

Activity 12–15: Make It Sink

(Intermediate grades)

Purpose: The purpose of this activity is to isolate and emphasize the process of prediction.

Materials: Aluminum foil, basins, water, clay, balance

Procedure:

1. Divide the class into groups of two or three. Provide each group with a basin, a piece of aluminum foil about 10cm square, water, and clay.
   a. Have each group make a foil boat that will float on the water in the basin.
   b. Once the boats have been made, have each group use the clay to find out how much weight the boat will hold before it sinks.
      (1) The balance can be used to find the exact weight.
2. As a class, make a list of some of the factors that could affect how much an aluminum boat will hold before it sinks.
   a. Have each group test these factors, or some of the factors, first predicting whether the new boat will hold more or less than the original, then testing each prediction.

Adaptations: All children should be able to participate in this activity.

Related Content: This activity is directly related to concepts of buoyancy and density.

Suggestions:

1. This activity could lead to research in the area of social studies dealing with shipping.
2. Integrate mathematics into the lesson by finding the average amount the original boat would hold using the data collected by the entire class.
3. If children appear to be using very small amounts of clay in testing for the amount a boat will hold before sinking, suggest that they start with a piece of clay the size of a pea or more.
4. This activity could be extended by using other materials for construction of the boat and testing the relative carrying capacities of various materials.

Activity 12–16: Conductors and Nonconductors

(Intermediate grades)

Purpose: The purpose of this activity is to isolate and emphasize the process of prediction.

Diagram of Circuit for Testing Conductors and Nonconductors

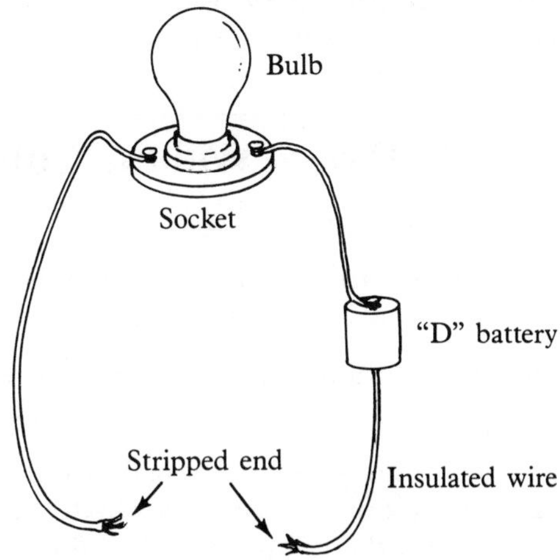

The object to be tested is placed in the gap between the ends of the wire, one wire touching each side of the object.

Materials: Wire, socket, bulb, battery, assorted objects both metal and nonmetal

Procedure:

1. Divide the class into groups of two or three and have each group set up a circuit of a bulb and socket, battery, and two wires between which other objects can be placed to determine whether they are conductors or not (see diagram above).
2. Have one member of each group touch the ends of the two wires together to see if the bulb lights.
   a. Discuss why the bulb lights when the wires are touched.
   b. Separate the wires and touch one wire to each end of a pencil.
      (1) Discuss why the bulb will not light in this case.
3. Have each group collect ten small objects from around the room to test in their circuits.
   a. Each group should write the name of the objects and then make a prediction as to whether the bulb will light. Each prediction should then be tested.

Adaptations: Some orthopedically handicapped children and some intellectually handicapped children may need help in constructing the circuit. Either construct one or assign the orthopedically handicapped child to a group where he or she can give the directions to others.

Related Content: This is directly related to the study of conductors and nonconductors of electricity.

Suggestions: Although children should have the opportunity to decide on the objects that they wish to test, a prearranged collection of objects could be assigned to each group.

Activity 12–17: Where Will the Color Go?

(Intermediate grades)

Purpose: The purpose of this activity is to isolate and emphasize the processes of cause and effect and interaction and systems.

Materials: Two identical bottles, index card, food coloring, water

Procedure:

1. This is done as a demonstration.
2. Fill each of the bottles to the top with water.
3. Add food coloring to one of the bottles.
4. Place the index card over the mouth of the clear bottle and carefully invert it over the bottle of colored water. The rims of the bottles should match, but *do not remove the card.*
5. Ask the class what they think will happen when the card is removed.
   a. Collect all answers making a listing on the chalkboard.
6. Carefully remove the card. Even though the coloring is in the bottom bottle and both are full, the top bottle will become colored as well.
7. Discuss what has occurred, focusing on the parts of the system and the interactions that have occurred among the parts.
   a. It is not necessary to explain the cause.

Adaptations: Provided that the teacher describes the materials and the outcome for any visually handicapped children, all children should be able to participate in this lesson.

Related Content: This activity can be related to the study of matter and molecular activity.

Suggestions:

1. Practice removing the card a few times before doing this in front of a class. Even then, do it over a container to catch spills.
2. The triangular shaped mouthwash bottles work well for this demonstration.

Activity 12–18: How Does It Work?

(Intermediate grades)

Purpose: The purpose of this activity is to isolate and emphasize the process of cause and effect and the process of interaction and systems.

Funnel and jar diagrams

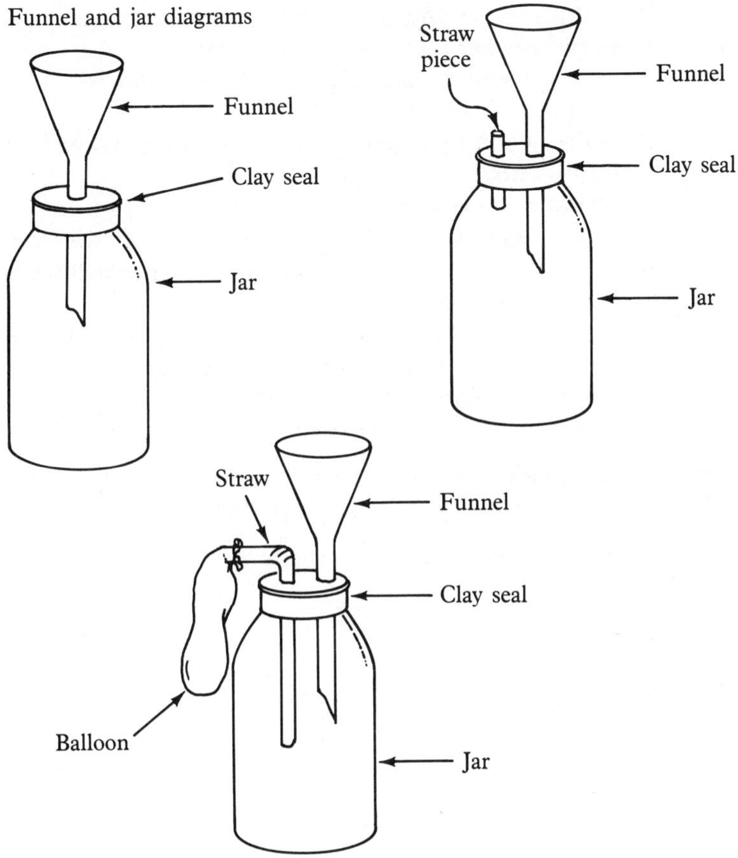

Materials: Three narrow-mouthed jars, funnel, plastic straws that will bend, water, food coloring, clay, balloon, tape

Procedure:

1. This is done as a demonstration (see above for diagram).
2. Prior to the demonstration prepare three bottles:
   a. In the first bottle place the funnel and seal the space between the funnel and the bottle neck securely with clay.
   b. In the second bottle place a funnel and a small piece of straw in the mouth of the bottle and seal securely with clay.
      (1) The straw should be concealed by the clay but open at both ends.
   c. In the third bottle place a funnel and a full length straw in the mouth of the bottle and seal securely with clay.
      (1) Bend the straw and attach a balloon to the end.
   d. Color the water with food coloring so it can be seen.

3. Place the first jar and funnel before the class. Ask what will happen if you pour water into the funnel. Do it.
   a. If the bottle is securely sealed the water will not flow into the bottle.
4. Place the second jar before the class. Ask what will happen if water is poured into the funnel. Do it.
   a. Water will pour in unless you place a finger over the concealed straw. Do this a few times to stop and start the flow of water.
5. Place the third jar before the class. Ask what will happen if water is poured into the funnel. Do it.
   a. The water will go into the jar and the balloon will expand.
6. Discuss what the class has seen in terms of the systems demonstrated and the interactions that occurred.
   a. It is not necessary to explain what has happened.

Adaptations: Provided that the teacher describes each bottle and what occurs, all children should be able to participate in this activity.

Related Content: This activity is directly related to the concept that air is matter.

Suggestions:
1. Be certain that the seals are airtight. If they are not, the demonstration will not work properly.
2. Mouthwash bottles with wide openings work very well for this demonstration.
3. If the bore of the funnel is large, some air will escape and some water will pour into the jar. This is an interesting effect and only adds to the demonstration.

Activity 12–19: How Far Does It Move?

(Intermediate grades)

Purpose: The purpose of this activity is to isolate and emphasize the processes of cause and effect and interaction and systems.

Materials: Rulers, aluminum foil, meter sticks, paper for recording data, small blocks or rubber erasers

Procedure:
1. Prior to starting the activity, hold a ruler at the edge of a desk so that the ruler hangs over by about ten centimeters. Roll a piece of foil, about ten centimeters square, into a ball (see diagram, page 397).

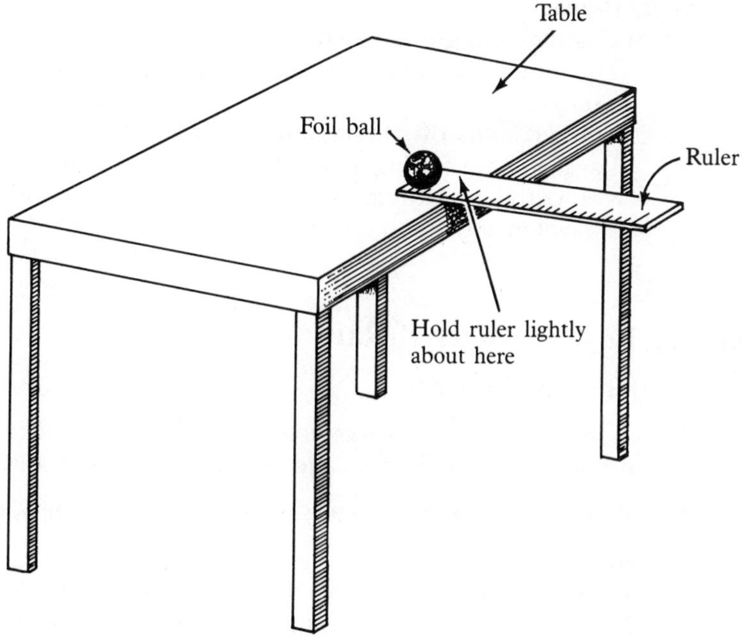

a. Have the children predict what will happen if the ball of foil is placed on one end of the ruler and the other end of the ruler is tapped.
   (1) A finger placed over the ruler will prevent it from flying along with the ball of foil.
   (2) Try it a few times and measure the distance the ball travels. Find the average.

2. Ask the students what might cause a difference in the distance the ball will move. Collect these ideas on the chalkboard.
3. Divide the class into groups of three or four.
   a. Using the eraser or block as the fulcrum of the ruler, have the students find the average distance their ball of foil will move.
      (1) Be certain a finger is placed over the fulcrum to keep the rulers from flying along with the foil.
   b. Have the students test one or more of the factors to see their effect on the distance moved.
4. Discuss the activity in terms of the system used and the interactions that occurred.

Adaptations: Since this activity is done in groups, all children should be able to participate.

Related Content: This activity is directly related to the study of levers as well as to the study of energy.

Suggestions:

1. Assign each group to a different area of the room so that the foil balls do not fly toward anyone, and be certain that the rulers are held securely.
2. Other kinds of papers and soft, small objects could also be made available for testing and comparison to the foil.
3. To correlate with mathematics, have students find average distances traveled and graph the results.

Activity 12–20: Make It Rain

(Intermediate grades)

Purpose: The purpose of this activity is to isolate and emphasize the processes of cause and effect and interaction and systems.

Materials: Hot plate, pan, water, cookie sheet, ice cubes, thermometers

Procedure:

1. This should be done as a demonstration (see diagram below).
2. Fill the pan about halfway with water. Take the starting temperature of the water and the starting temperature of the ice.

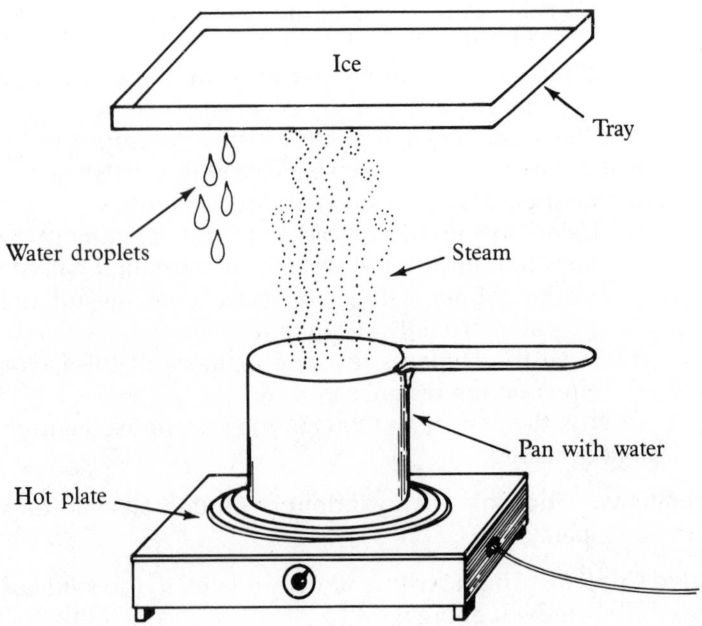

3. Heat the water to boiling, taking the temperature when it begins to boil.
4. Place the ice on the cookie sheet and hold it about 60cm above the boiling water so that the steam hits the underside of the sheet.
   a. Allow the water to condense and fall back.
   b. A few drops might be allowed to drip onto the hot plate and sizzle.
5. Have the students describe what they saw.
   a. Discuss the demonstrations in terms of the systems involved and the interactions that occurred.

Adaptations: Provided the teacher describes what is being done and what happens for a visually handicapped child, all children should be able to participate in this activity.

Related Content: This activity is a demonstration of the water cycle and can be related to that content.

Suggestions:

1. Do not allow children to work with boiling water. This should be a demonstration only.
2. If no visually handicapped children are present in the classroom, this demonstration can be done as a discovery demonstration.

Activity 12–21: Observing an Aquarium

(Intermediate grades)

Purpose: The purpose of this activity is to isolate and emphasize the processes of cause and effect and interaction and systems.

Materials: An established aquarium including fish, plants, gravel, snails, water pump and filter, light, etc.

Procedure:

1. Have students observe the aquarium as a small environment that is easily observed and maintained.
   a. As students observe, have them record any interactions between the living parts of the aquarium as well as between the living and nonliving parts of the aquarium.
   b. From the observations of interactions, have the students infer the various systems in the aquarium.

Adaptations: Visually handicapped students should be assigned a partner for this activity.

Related Content: This activity is directly related to the study of the environment.

Suggestions:

1. This activity might also be done in an outdoor setting using a lake, stream, pond, or other body of water.
2. Children might use their writing skills to write a log of their observations and inferences over a period of time.

Selected References

Brock, J. A. M., D. W. Paulsen, and F. T. Weisbruch. *Patterns and Processes of Science, Laboratory Text One*. Lexington, Mass.: Heath, 1969.

———. *Patterns and Processes of Science, Laboratory Text Two*. Lexington, Mass.: Heath, 1969.

Butts, D. P. *Teaching Science in the Elementary School*. New York: Macmillan, 1973.

Divito, A., and G. H. Krockover. *Creative Sciencing: Ideas and Activities for Teachers and Children*, 2nd ed. Boston: Little, Brown, 1980.

Feifer, N. *Adventures in Chemistry*. New York: Sentinal, 1959.

Hone, E. B., J. Alexander, E. Victor, and P. Brandwein. *A Sourcebook for Elementary Science*. New York: Harcourt, 1962.

Sund, R. B., B. W. Tillery, and L. W. Trowbridge. *Elementary Science Lessons: The Biological Sciences*. Boston: Allyn and Bacon, 1970.

———. *Elementary Science Lessons: The Earth Sciences*. Boston: Allyn and Bacon, 1970.

———. *Elementary Science Lessons: The Physical Sciences*. Boston: Allyn and Bacon, 1970.

13 Activities for the Experimental Processes of Science

The activities of this chapter are designed to help children develop their abilities to use the experimental processes. These activities emphasize those processes best taught and used in the fifth and sixth grades.

Each of the activities of this chapter should be considered as a starting point from which the children can develop their own experiments. If children are not familiar with the experimental processes, the class as a whole, under teacher direction, should develop the experiment. Gradually, as children become better able to use the experimental processes, they should be given more freedom to develop their own experiments, either for one person or for a small group to conduct.

Rather than separate the processes, these activities are designed to permit the child to incorporate all of the experimental processes into a single experimental design. The intention is to leave the activities open ended enough that children will be able to develop their own hypotheses, decide which variables to manipulate, and draw any warranted conclusions.

In each experiment developed by the children as a result of these activities, the child should use all of the experimental processes.

Activity 13–1: Paper Airplanes

(Upper intermediate grades)

Purpose: The purpose of this activity is to provide a starting point for the use of the experimental processes.

Materials: Variety of types of paper, meter sticks, paper for collecting data, scissors, tape, paper clips

Procedure:

1. Have one student demonstrate how to fold a standard paper airplane.
   a. Working in groups of two or three, have each group make an airplane, fly it five times, and find the average distance the plane flies.
      (1) An operational definition of "distance a plane flies" could be developed to be certain all groups were measuring the same thing.
   b. Using the averages, find the class average for the distance a standard airplane flies.
2. Discuss with the class, and make a list of, the factors that could affect the distance a paper airplane will fly.
3. Have each group choose one of the factors and develop an experiment to test the effect of that factor on the distance a paper airplane will fly.
   a. Be certain that each experiment contains all of the parts and includes an identification of the variables and constants.

Adaptations: Intellectually handicapped children may not have reached the stage in development where experimentation is possible. The option to return to an activity that does not emphasize control of variables should be available to these children.

Related Content: This activity is closely related to the study of flight.

Suggestions:

1. Suggested papers include: old ditto sheets, faded construction paper, pages from old telephone books, old newspapers, pages from old magazines, waxed paper and aluminum foil.
2. Review each of the groups' experimental procedure before they begin. Be certain that they are controlling all variables and that they are changing only one variable at a time.
3. The process of operational definitions may not be needed. Also, the need for operational definitions may not be seen until after the experiment is started.

Activity 13–2: Investigating Evaporation

(Upper intermediate grades)

Purpose: The purpose of this activity is to provide a starting point for the use of the experimental processes.

Materials: Assorted containers; water and assorted other liquids; masking tape; plastic wrap

Procedure:

1. Divide the class into groups of four or five and provide each group with the same type of container, water, and a piece of masking tape, metric rulers
   a. Pour enough water into the container so that the level of the water is at least five centimeters above the bottom of the container or the container is at least half full.
   b. Use the tape to mark the original level of the water.
   c. Place the containers in the same location.
      (1) For the next three days, keep a record of the water level by measuring up from the bottom of the container.
      (2) At the start of the fourth day, find the average rate of evaporation per day (or hour) for the water.
2. Discuss with the children some of the factors that could affect the rate of evaporation of water, listing these on the board.
3. Have each group choose one of the factors and develop an experiment to test the effect of that factor on the evaporation of water.
   a. Each experiment should contain an hypothesis, an identification of the dependent, independent, and constant variables, a means for collecting data, a conclusion, and any operational definitions needed.

Adaptations: Intellectually handicapped children may not have reached the stage in development where experimentation is possible. The option to return to an activity that does not emphasize control of variables should be available to these children.

Related Content: This activity is closely related to the study of matter.

Suggestions:

1. Containers can include paper cups, styrofoam cups, glasses, jars, basins, buckets — anything that will hold water.
2. Other liquids which could be tried include: vinegar, oil, soft drinks, juices, paints, and various colors of water using food coloring.

Activity 13–3: Affecting Plant Growth

(Upper intermediate grades)

Purpose: The purpose of this activity is to provide a starting point for the use of the experimental processes.

Materials: Various types of seeds; potting soil, paper cups or flower pots, water, fertilizers, other types of soils, household chemicals, graph paper, rulers

Procedure:

1. Divide the class into groups of four or five.
   a. Have each of the groups plant three or four of the same types of seeds in precisely the same manner.
   b. During the next week (longer if the seeds do not sprout) keep a daily record of the height of each of the seedlings by graphing the data.
   c. At the end of the week, find the average rate of growth for the particular type of plant.
2. Discuss with the class the factors that might affect the rate at which a plant grows. List these on the chalkboard.
3. Have each group choose one of the factors and develop an experiment to test the effect of that factor on the rate at which a plant grows.
   a. The experiment should contain an hypothesis, an identification of the constants and variables, a means for collecting data, a conclusion, and any necessary operational definitions.

Adaptations: Intellectually handicapped children may not have reached the stage in development where experimentation is possible. The option to return to an activity that does not emphasize control of variables should be available to these children.

Related Content: This activity is directly related to the study of plants and plant growth.

Suggestions:

1. Good seeds with which to start are radish seeds that will sprout very quickly. Other seeds might include lima beans, popping corn, lettuce, grass seeds, and marigold seeds.
2. Household chemicals include: vinegar, baking soda, oil, milk, juices, various spices, literally anything found in the ordinary kitchen.
3. Plant growth is an area where control of variables is very difficult.

Students should also discuss factors they could not control in their experiments no matter how carefully the experiment was planned.

Activity 13–4: Bouncing Balls

(Upper intermediate grades)

Purpose: The purpose of this activity is to provide a starting point for the use of the experimental processes.

Materials: Assorted balls, adding machine tape, meter sticks, paper, colored pencils, masking tape

Procedure:

1. Divide the class into groups of three and provide each group with the same type of ball, two meters of adding machine tape, colored pencils, masking tape, and a meter stick.
   a. Have each group tape the adding machine paper to a wall vertically.
   b. Using at least five trials, have each group find the average height to which a ball will bounce by bouncing the ball, marking the height on the paper, then measuring the height.
   c. Collect the averages from each of the groups and find a total average height to which a ball of that type will bounce.
2. Discuss with the class, and make a list of, the factors that could affect the height to which a ball will bounce.
3. Have each group choose one of the factors and develop an experiment to test the effect of that factor on the height to which a ball will bounce.
   a. Each experiment should contain an hypothesis, an identification of the dependent, independent, and constant variables, a means for collecting data, a conclusion, and any operational definitions needed.

Adaptations: Intellectually handicapped children may not have reached the stage in development where experimentation is possible. The option to return to an activity that does not require control of variables should be available to these children.

Related Content: This activity could be related to a study of the properties of matter.

Suggestions: The selection of balls might include tennis balls, golf balls, ping-pong balls, "super" balls, baseballs, soccer balls, basketballs, foam balls, whiffle balls, and playground balls.

Activity 13–5: Candles and Jars

(Upper intermediate grades)

Purpose: The purpose of this activity is to provide a starting point for the use of the experimental processes.

Materials: Glass jars, plasticine, candles, matches, metal containers, clock with sweep second hand

Procedure:

1. As a demonstration, place a candle in plasticine and stick it firmly to a nonflammable tabletop.
   a. Show the class the largest jar available. Have them predict how long it will take for the candle to go out in the jar.
   b. Cover the candle with the inverted jar. Try this a few times finding the average amount of time needed for the candle to go out.
2. Discuss with the class the factors which could affect how long it takes for a candle to go out.
   a. Divide the class into pairs. Have each of the pairs plan an experiment to test one of the factors.
3. After the experiments have been planned, have one member of the group tell you what to do. Carry out the experiment as a demonstration.
   a. Have the entire class contribute to collecting the data and drawing the conclusions.
   b. Try as many of the experiments as time permits.

Adaptations: All children should be able to participate in this activity.

Related Content: This activity is directly related to the study of combustion.

Suggestions:

1. Although most schools do not permit children to work with open flames as is required in this activity, if children are able to carry out their experiments themselves do the following:
   a. Show children how to correctly strike a match by moving it away from their bodies.
   b. Use metal containers for the used matches.
   c. Use rubber bands to hold back long hair.
   d. Caution children not to light the candle until necessary.
   e. Although breakage of the jars is unlikely, have children wear safety goggles.
   f. Have a blanket and a fire extinguisher in case of accidents.
   g. Remove all flammable materials from the area of the experiment.
   h. Tolerate no clowning around when flames are being used.

Activity 13–6: A Swing and a Hit

(Upper intermediate grades)

Purpose: The purpose of this activity is to provide a starting point for the use of the experimental processes.

Materials: String, balls of plasticine about 2.5cm in diameter, one-inch wooden blocks, white paper, meter sticks

Procedure:

1. Make the pendula for this about two days ahead of time by rolling the ball of plasticine clay around the end of about two meters of string.
   a. Allowing these to sit in the open for a day or two causes the clay to become hard. It will, however, soften again with the heat of hands.
2. Divide the class into groups of three or four and provide each of the groups with a pendulum, block, meter stick and paper (see diagram).
   a. Tape the paper to the floor and place the block at one edge. Draw around the block and find the center point.
   b. Measure the pendulum so that the entire length is about fifty centimeters. Pull back about fifteen centimeters from the edge of the paper and practice hitting the block with the pendulum bob.
      (1) Once the group has become proficient with hitting the block measure the distance the block travels five times and find the average.

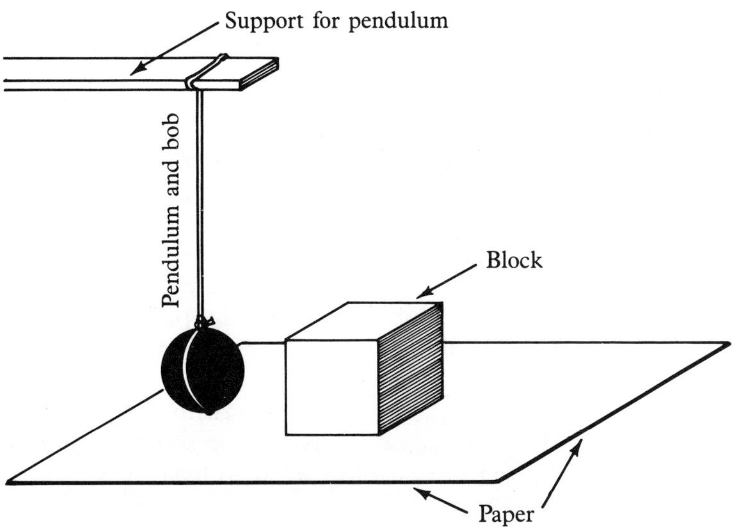

c. Have each group identify five factors which could affect how far the block will move when hit by the pendulum.
d. After the factors have been identified, have each group design an experiment to test one of their factors.
   (1) Each experiment should contain an hypothesis, an identification of the dependent, independent and constant variables, a means for collecting data, a conclusion, and any operational definitions needed.

Adaptations: Intellectually handicapped children may not have reached the stage in development where experimentation is possible. The option to return to an activity that does not require control of variables should be available to these children.

Related Content: This activity is directly related to the study of energy.

Suggestions:
1. If possible, stands should be used for the pendula.
2. This activity might be better divided into two days of classes so that children can design their experiments and collect their materials prior to use.

Activity 13–7: Investigating Magnetic Strength

(Upper intermediate grades)

Purpose: The purpose of this activity is to provide a starting point for the use of the experimental processes.

Materials: Magnets, cardboard, plastic sheets, aluminum foil, cloth, iron or steel pie tin or cookie sheet, paper clips, thread, books or other support for one magnet

Procedure:
1. Tie one end of the thread to a paper clip and place the other end under the books. Using the magnet, suspend the paper clip in the air, having at least one inch between the paperclip and the magnet (see diagram on page 409).
   a. Ask the class to predict what will happen if a sheet of paper, a piece of cardboard, a sheet of plastic, the cookie sheet, and the aluminum foil are placed between the magnet and the clip.
   b. Try each object.
   c. Tell the students that each of the objects, as well as the cookie sheet will cause the paper clip to fall if something is done.
   d. As a group develop an hypothesis as to what would need to be done.

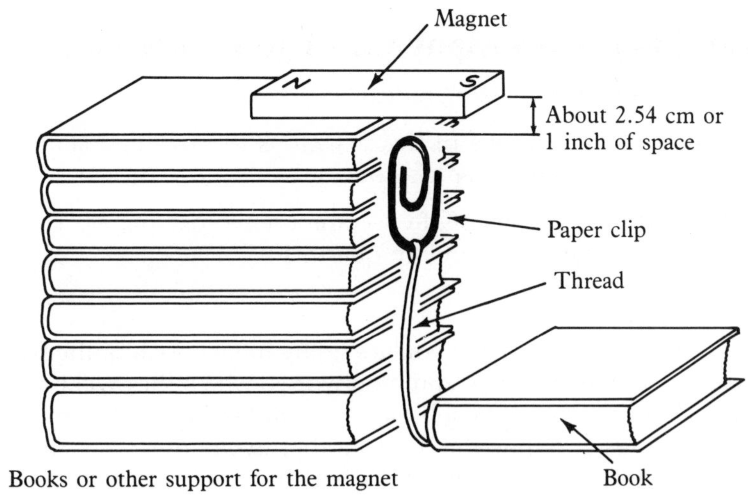

2. Divide the class into groups of three or four to design an experiment that will test the hypothesis developed by the class.
   a. The children should show the variables controlled, the means for collecting the data, a conclusion, and any necessary operational definitions.
   b. Once the experiment has been developed, each group should collect the materials and carry out the experiment.

Adaptations: Intellectually handicapped children may not have reached the stage in development where experimentation is possible. The option to return to an activity that explores magnets and what they will attract should be available to these children.

Related Content: This activity is related to the study of magnetism.

Suggestions:

1. Probably the easiest hypothesis to test in this activity is: If the thickness of the material is increased, then the paper clip will fall. However, other hypotheses developed by the children should also be tested.
2. For the suspended paper clip to work, the magnet needs to be very strong. Also, the length of the thread should be kept under thirty centimeters unless the magnet is exceptionally strong.

Activity 13–8: How Many Can You Remember?

(Upper intermediate grades)

Purpose: The purpose of this activity is to provide a starting point for the use of the experimental processes.

Materials: List of twenty-five common words, paper, clock with second hand, index cards cut into quarters

Procedure:

1. Tell the class that you are going to give each of them a sheet of paper with twenty-five common words, which they will be able to study for two minutes. When the two minutes are up, they must turn the paper over and they will have another two minutes to write all of the words that they remember. When the second two minutes are up, they should compare their own lists to the original list. On the small card, they should then write how many words were recalled and give it to the teacher. Spelling will not count.
   a. The teacher should tally the number of words remembered and find the class average.
2. Once the average has been found, discuss with the class, and list on the board, the factors that could affect the average number of words recalled.
3. Divide the class into four groups, each one with a different factor.
   a. Each group should develop an experiment to try with the class which contains an hypothesis, and identification of the dependent, independent, and constant variables, a means for collecting data, a conclusion, and any operational definitions needed.
4. Have each of the groups try their experiments with the class, collect their data, and draw their conclusions.
   a. The conclusions should then be shared with the entire class.

Adaptations: For the visually handicapped child, the words could be taped for the child to listen to with earphones. The child could then dictate the words recalled into the tape recorder or to the teacher. This procedure could also be used with intellectually handicapped children with poor reading and writing skills.

Related Content: This activity is directly related to the study of the human body.

Suggestions:

1. Data in the form of the number of words recalled should be anonymously submitted to the teacher who will then give it to the various

groups for interpretation. There should be no opportunity for children to be ridiculed because they could recall only a few words.

Activity 13–9: Remembering Pictures

(Upper intermediate grades)

Purpose: The purpose of this activity is to provide a starting point for the use of the experimental processes.

Materials: Index cards showing about twenty various geometric shapes and simple patterns (enough decks for one half of the class); drawing paper, clock with a second hand

Procedure:

1. Divide the class into pairs.
2. Tell the class that one of the two children in the pair will show the cards to the other during a three-minute period. After the three minutes is up, the child who watched the cards should draw each of the shapes recalled. The shapes drawn should be checked against the cards and the number drawn correctly indicated on the paper and given to the teacher.
   a. The second member of the group should then be shown the cards and the procedure repeated.
   b. The first child to show the cards should not look at the cards or at his or her partner's drawings.
   c. Find the average number of shapes recalled.
3. Discuss with the class, and list on the board, the factors that could affect the average number of drawings recalled.
4. Divide the class into four groups to develop an experiment around one of the factors chosen. Each group should choose a different factor.
5. Have each of the groups try their experiments with the class, collect their data, and draw their conclusions.
   a. The conclusions should then be shared with the entire class.

Adaptations: If a visually handicapped child is present, the set of cards for this child could be made with string glued over the patterns. The child could then be given a second pile of cards that includes some shapes or patterns not previously given and asked to identify as many as possible that were in the original group.

Related Content: This activity is directly related to the study of the human body.

Suggestions:

1. If Learning Activity 13–8 has been done, students could compare the data from the two activities and draw conclusions about differences in recall of words versus recall of pictures.
2. The number of pictures recalled should be tallied by the teacher to prevent any discomfort on the part of children.

Activity 13–10: Changing Your Pulse Rate

(Upper intermediate grades)

Purpose: The purpose of this activity is to provide a starting point for the use of the experimental processes.

Materials: Watch or clock with second hand, calculator

Procedure:

1. Have the class sit quietly for a few minutes while you demonstrate how to take pulse rate. Have each student find the pulse at either wrist, throat, or temple.
   a. Once each child has found the pulse, tell them to count the number of beats from the time you say go to the time you say stop.
   b. Time for six seconds. Have children multiply the number of beats counted by ten in order to find the pulse rate per minute.
   c. Collect the pulse rates for each child and use the calculator to find the average pulse rate.
2. Discuss with the class some of the factors which could affect average pulse rate.
   a. As a class, design an experiment to test the factor including an hypothesis, control of variables, and means for collecting data.
   b. Carry out the experiment, collecting all of the data.
   c. As a class, draw a conclusion from the data.

Adaptations: If the factor tested is the effect of exercise, have the orthopedically handicapped child participate in whatever manner possible. The participation is more important than doing the exact form of exercise.

Related Content: This activity is directly related to the study of the human body.

Suggestions: If exercise is chosen as the independent variable, move the class to the gym or playground where there is plenty of room.

Activity 13–11: Investigating the Growth of Algae

(Upper intermediate grades)

Purpose: The purpose of this activity is to provide a starting point for the use of the experimental processes.

Materials: Various containers including some glass jars, one container of water with an overgrowth of algae, household chemicals, algae

Procedure:

1. Divide the class into groups of three or four providing each of the groups with a jar of algae-filled water.
   a. Tell the children that they have five minutes to think of any questions they would like to ask about the algae in the jars.
   b. After the five minutes is up, answer any of the questions which the children developed.
2. Tell the class that it is up to them to find a method to keep the water in a second container as clear as possible of algae. Their original materials will include a container of water, an eyedropper into which they will draw about two centimeters of algae water to place into the clear container, and their own ideas.
3. Have each of the groups develop an experimental procedure with which they could try to prevent the growth of algae.
   a. In addition to the standard parts of an experiment, each of the procedures should include a control group.
   b. Have each group carry out the experiment and present the results to the class at the end of the experiment.

Adaptations: Intellectually handicapped children may not have reached the stage in development where experimentation is possible. These children might be encouraged to observe the algae carefully using magnifiers and report their findings to the class.

Related Content: This activity is directly related to the study of simple green plants.

Suggestions:

1. Prior to developing the experiments review the concept of a control group with the class.
2. Students may also need to do additional research into the conditions under which algae grows prior to developing the activity.

Activity 13–12: What Do You Feed a Mouse?

(Intermediate grades)

Purpose: The purpose of this activity is to provide a starting point for the use of the experimental processes.

Materials: Four pairs of mice, cages, food, balance, graph paper, reference materials

Procedure:

1. Review with the class the basic food needs of human beings and why foods from a variety of sources are necessary for health.
2. Show the children the four cages of mice and ask them what they think would be the *best possible diet* for a mouse.
   a. Discuss how it would be possible to tell whether a particular diet was best. Write the ideas on the chalkboard.
3. Divide the class into three groups providing each group with a pair of mice. For the next three days have the students maintain the original diet of the mice while they apply each of the criteria listed on the board.
4. While the mice are being observed, have the students research the food requirements of mice and write an experimental procedure to try to determine whether a particular diet they develop as a result of the research is better than the current diet.
5. Have each group carry out the experiment and report the results to the class.

Adaptations: All children should be able to participate fully in this activity.

Related Content: This activity is related to the study of nutrition and to the study of mammals.

Suggestions:

1. Be certain that the diets developed by the children are based on research and contain nothing that could be harmful to the animals.
2. Review all experimental procedures to be certain that the experiments could cause no harm to the animals.
3. If the animals seem to be suffering under the diet or the experimental procedure, the experiment should be terminated and that result used in drawing the conclusions.
4. If the children handle the mice, be certain that they handle them carefully and that they wash their hands afterwards.

Activity 13–13: The Life of a Mealworm

(Upper intermediate grades)

Purpose: The purpose of this activity is to provide a starting point for the use of the experimental processes.

Materials: Mealworms, glass containers, colored construction paper, graph paper, tweezers, trays, ice

Procedure:

1. Divide the class into groups of four and give each group a tray with four or five mealworms.
    a. Have the students observe the behavior of the mealworms for a few minutes, then write down their observations.
    b. Have the students present their observations to the rest of the class until a composite picture of the behavior of mealworms is developed.
2. Present the class with the following two operational questions and have each of the groups develop two experiments, one for each of the questions.
    a. Each experiment should contain an hypothesis, an identification of the dependent, independent, and constant variables, a means for collecting data, a conclusion, and any operational definitions needed.
3. Once the experiments have been completed the results should be added to the composite picture of a mealworm.
4. Questions:
    a. How does heat affect the behavior of a mealworm?
    b. How does color affect the behavior of a mealworm?

Adaptations: Be certain that one member of the group describes the behavior of the mealworms to any visually handicapped children.

Related Content: This activity is directly related to the study of insects and their behavior.

Suggestions:

1. Some children do not care to handle mealworms. The tweezers should be provided as an alternative. Children should not be forced into handling the mealworms if they do not care to do so.
2. Once the profile of a mealworm is completed, the students should be encouraged to research the mealworm and to compare their findings to the research materials.

Activity 13–14: Dry, Dryer, Driest

(Upper intermediate grades)

Purpose: The purpose of this activity is to provide a starting point for the use of the experimental processes.

Materials: Various types of cloth cut into squares about 10cm on a side, various kinds of liquids, blow dryer, clock

Procedure:

1. Dampen one of the pieces of cloth and display it before the class. Ask the class what could affect how long it would take for the cloth to dry.
   a. Develop an operational definition of "dry."
   b. Collect the various ideas on the chalkboard.
   c. Choose one of the ideas to try. Develop a procedure that would be used by everyone.
2. Divide the class into groups of four and give each group a square of the same type of cloth, water, and the instructions.
   a. Have each group carry out the experiment.
   b. When everyone has finished, collect the group data and draw a class conclusion.
3. Keeping the same groups, have each of the groups choose a second factor to test.
   a. Each of the groups should design an experiment with an hypothesis, procedure, means for data collection, and a conclusion.
   b. Have each group report its findings to the rest of the class.

Adaptations: All children should be able to fully participate in this activity.

Related Content: This activity is related to the study of matter and of change of state.

Suggestions:

1. Any type of cloth can be used. This is a good time to tear up old sheets or to find someone who sews and has a box of scrap material.
2. Any type of non-poisonous household liquids should be used.
3. The hairdryer should be used by students only with teacher supervision.

Activity 13–15: Making Work Easier: The Pulley

(Upper intermediate grades)

Purpose: The purpose of this activity is to provide a starting point for the use of the experimental processes.

Materials: Various sized pulleys, both single and double; string, spring scales, books or other heavy objects

Procedure:

1. Tie two books together with string then lift them straight off the table using the spring scale (see diagram below).
   a. Record the mass of the books.
   b. Set up a single, fixed pulley and again lift the books from the table (see diagram).
      (1) Record the amount of force needed to lift the books from the table as indicated on the scale.

Procedure: Step 1

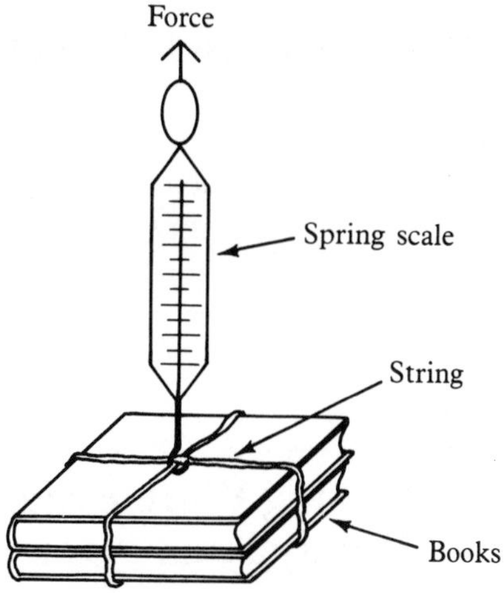

Procedure: Step 1b

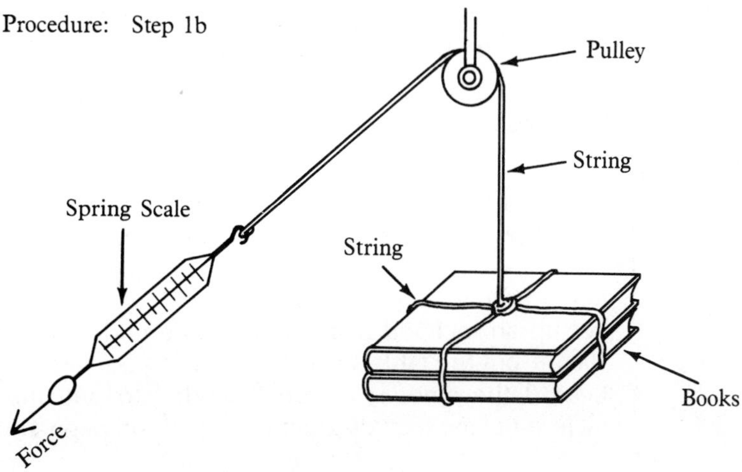

2. Discuss what happens to the amount of force needed to lift an object when a pulley is used.
   a. Make a listing of some possible changes that could be made in the pulley system to affect the force needed to lift an object.
3. Divide the class into groups of three or four.
   a. Have each of the groups choose one of the ideas discussed and plan an experimental procedure which they will use to test the factor.
   b. Each experimental procedure will include the hypothesis being tested, the procedure, a means for collecting the data, and a conclusion as well as any operational definitions needed.
4. Discuss the results presented by each of the groups as a class.

Adaptations: All children should be able to participate in this activity.

Related Content: This activity is directly related to the study of simple machines.

Suggestions:

1. Prior to the activity, be certain to check the mass of the books using the spring scales to be certain that they are not too heavy for the scales.
2. Reference books dealing with pulleys should be made available so that students can research the use of pulleys as they design their experiments.

Activity 13–16: Making Work Easier: The Inclined Plane

(Upper intermediate grades)

Purpose: The purpose of this activity is to provide a starting point for the use of the experimental processes.

Materials: Books, boards or other flat surfaces that can be made into inclines, spring balances, string

Procedure:

1. Tie two books together with a piece of string then lift them straight off the table using the spring scale (see diagram of Step 1 on page 419).
   a. Record the mass of the books.
   b. Set up an inclined plane so that one end of the plane is about 10cm from the table surface.
   c. Record the amount of force needed to pull the book up the inclined plane (see diagram of Step 1b on page 419).

Procedure: Step 1

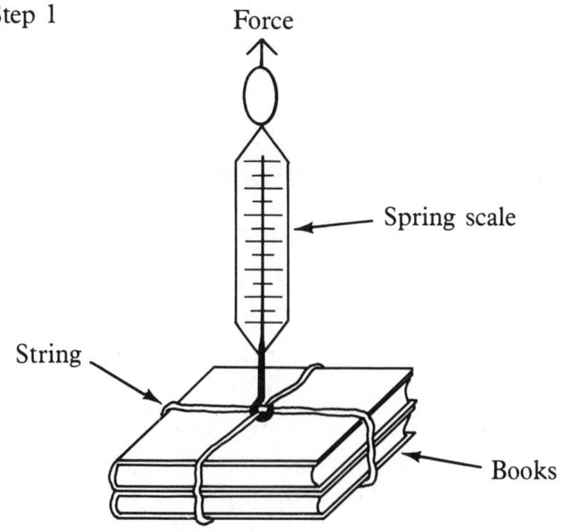

Procedure: Step 1b

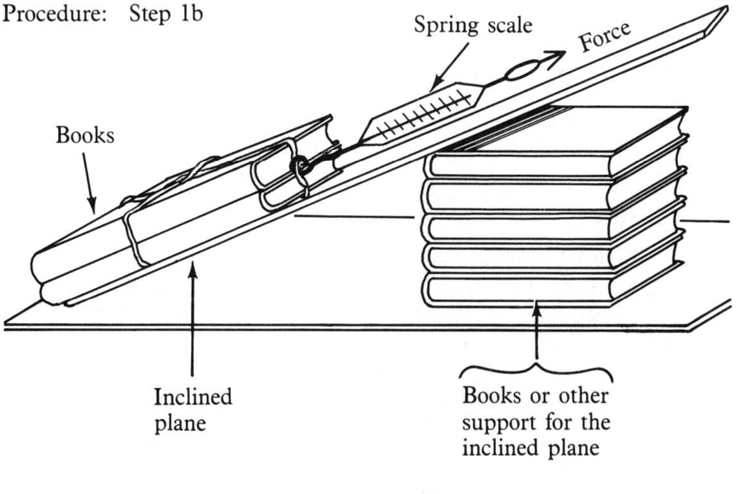

2. Discuss what happens to the amount of force needed to lift an object when an inclined plane is used.
   a. Make a listing of some possible changes which could be made in the inclined plane system that could affect the force needed to lift an object.
3. Divide the class into groups of three or four.
   a. Have each of the groups design an experimental procedure that they will use to test one of the factors discussed.
   b. Each experimental procedure should include the hypothesis

being tested, the procedure, a means for collecting the data, and a conclusion as well as any operational definitions needed.
4. Each of the groups should then present its findings to the class as a whole.

Adaptations: All children should be able to participate in this activity.

Related Content: This activity is directly related to the study of simple machines.

Suggestions:
1. Boards make good inclined planes. If they are too rough they can be covered tightly with plastic wrap or aluminum foil.
2. Toy trucks can also be used instead of books. These could provide a means for getting variable weights without changing other factors.
3. Various materials could also be provided for changing the surface of the inclined plane: different types of papers, sand, salt, wax, or oil.

Selected References

Brock, J. A. M., D. W. Paulsen, and F. T. Weisbruch. *Patterns and Processes of Science, Laboratory Text One*. Lexington, Mass.: Heath, 1969.

———. *Patterns and Processes of Science, Laboratory Text Two*. Lexington, Mass.: Heath, 1969.

Butts, D. P. *Teaching Science in the Elementary School*. New York: Macmillan, 1973.

Divito, A., and G. H. Krockover. *Creative Sciencing: Ideas and Activities for Teachers and Children*, 2nd ed. Boston: Little, Brown. 1980.

Feifer, N. *Adventures in Chemistry*. New York: Sentinal, 1959.

Hone, E. B., J. Alexander, E. Victor, and P. Brandwein. *A Sourcebook for Elementary Science*. New York: Harcourt, 1962.

Sund, R. B., B. W. Tillery, and L. W. Trowbridge. *Elementary Science Lessons: The Biological Sciences*. Boston: Allyn and Bacon, 1970.

———. *Elementary Science Lessons: The Earth Sciences*. Boston: Allyn and Bacon, 1970.

———. *Elementary Science Lessons: The Physical Sciences*. Boston: Allyn and Bacon, 1970.

Bibliography

Allen, T. E. A study of two groups of descriptive children when taught with contrasting strategies: Directive vs. nondirective teaching. Doctoral Dissertation, Florida State University, 1976.

American Association for the Advancement of Science. *Science — A Process Approach.* Lexington, Mass.: Ginn, 1975.

American Association for the Advancement of Science, Committee on Opportunities in Science. *Science Education for Handicapped Youth: A Background Paper for Meeting of the Office of Opportunities in Science.* Washington, D.C., 1978.

Amidon, E., and N. A. Flanders. The effects of direct and indirect teacher influence on dependent-prone students learning geometry. In *Interaction Analysis: Theory, Research, and Application.* Eds. E. Amidon and J. B. Hough. Reading, Mass.: Addison-Wesley, 1967.

Anderson, C., and D. Butts. A comparison of individualized and group instruction in a sixth-grade electricity unit. *Journal of Research in Science Teaching, 17,* 2, 1980.

Anderson, J. R. *Language, Memory, and Thought.* Hillsdale, New Jersey: Erlbaum, 1976.

Apple II/III Software Directory, vol. 2. Overland Park, Kansas: Advanced Software Technology, 1983.

Association for Supervision and Curriculum Development. Educators finding software a hard choice. *ASCD Update, 25,* 2, 1983.

Asimov, I. *Asimov's Guide to Science.* New York: Basic Books, 1980.

Aspy, D. N., and F. N. Roebuck. Affective education: Sound investment. *Educational Leadership, 39,* 7, 1982.

Ausubel, D. P. *Psychology of Meaningful Verbal Learning.* New York: Greene and Stratton, 1963.

———, and F. G. Robinson. *School Learning: An Introduction to Educational Psychology.* New York: Holt, Rinehart, and Winston, 1969.

Ayers, J. B., and C. Price. Children's attitudes toward science. *School Science and Mathematics, 75,* 4, 1975.

Banks, J. A. *Multiethnic Education.* Boston: Allyn and Bacon, 1981.

Barron, R. Modifying science instruction to meet the needs of the hearing impaired. *Journal of Research in Science Teaching, 15,* 2, 1978.

Barrow, L. H. The basics — communicating, thinking, and valuing. *School Science and Mathematics, 79,* 8, 1979.

Bath, J. B. The reception of elementary students to inquiry science. Paper presented at National Association for Research in Science Teaching, March, 1975.

Baust, J. A. Spatial relationships and young children. *Arithmetic Teacher, 26,* 1, 1981.

———. Teaching spatial relationships using language arts and physical education. *School Science and Mathematics, 82,* 7, 1982.

Beane, J. A. Self-concept and self-esteem as curriculum issues. *Educational Leadership, 39,* 7, 1982.

Bell, F. H. Classroom computers: Beyond the three r's. *Creative Computing, 5,* 1979.

Bellamy, M. L. What is your theory? *Science Teacher, 50,* 2, 1983.

Bem, D. J. *Beliefs, Attitudes, and Human Affairs.* Belmont, California: Brookes-Cole, 1970.

Bennett, L. M. Science and special students. *Science and Children, 15,* 4, 1978.

———, and K. Downing. Science education for the mentally retarded. *Science Education, 55,* 1978.

Billings, G. W., E. Cupone, and L. Norber. Lighting up science for the visually impaired. *Science Teacher, 47,* 1980.

Blankenship, T. Is anyone listening? *Science Teacher, 49,* 9, 1982.

Blecha, M. K., P. C. Gega, and M. Green. *Exploring Science Series.* River Forest, Illinois: Laidlaw, 1976.

Bloom, B. S., ed. *Taxonomy of Educational Objectives. The Classification of Educational Goals. Handbook I: The Cognitive Domain.* New York: David McKay, 1956.

———, ed. *Taxonomy of Educational Objectives. The Classification of Educational Goals. Handbook II: Affective Domain.* New York: David McKay, 1964.

Blosser, P. E. *How to Ask the Right Questions.* Washington, D.C.: National Science Teachers Association, 1975.

Bork, A. *Science and Engineering Policies in the United States.* Irvine, California: Educational Technology Center, April 3, 1980.

———. *Compendium of Bad but Common Practices in Computer Based Learning.* Irvine, California: Educational Technology Center, November 1, 1982.

Bornstein, M. H., and W. Kessen, eds. *Psychological Development from Infancy.* Hillsdale, New Jersey: Erlbaum, 1979.

Boulanger, F. D. Instruction and science learning: A quantitative synthesis. *Journal of Research in Science Teaching, 18,* 4, 1980.

Boyd, E., and K. D. George. The effect of science inquiry on the abstract categorization behavior of deaf children. *Journal of Research in Science Teaching, 10,* 5, 1973.

Brath, H. M. An investigation of two methods of science instruction and teacher attitudes toward science. *Journal of Research in Science Teaching, 14,* 6, 1977.

Breen, M. J. Teacher interest and student attitude toward four areas of the elementary school curriculum. *Education, 100,* 1, 1979.

Brewer, A. C., N. Garland, T. F. Edwards, A. Marshall, and J. J. Notkin. *Elementary Science: Learning by Investigating*. Chicago: Rand McNally, 1974.

Brock, J. A. M., D. W. Paulsen, and F. T. Weisbruch. *Patterns and Processes of Science, Laboratory Text One*. Lexington, Mass.: Heath, 1969.

———. *Patterns and Processes of Science, Laboratory Text Two*. Lexington, Mass.: Heath, 1969.

Brophy, J. Successful teaching strategies for the inner city child. *Kappan, 63*, 4, 1982.

Bruner, J. *The Process of Education*. New York: Vintage, 1963.

Bruni, J. V. Problem solving for the primary grades. *Arithmetic Teacher, 29*, 6, 1982.

Buggey, L. J. A study of the relationship of classroom questions and social studies achievement in second grade students. Unpublished Doctoral Dissertation, University of Washington, 1971.

Burns, M. How to teach problem solving. *Arithmetic Teacher, 29*, 6, 1982.

Bussis, A. M. Burn it at the casket: Research, reading instruction, and children's learning. *Kappan, 64*, 4, 1982.

Butts, D. P. *Teaching Science in the Elementary School*. New York: Macmillan, 1973.

Bybee, R. W. The ideal elementary science teacher: Perceptions of children, pre-service, and in-service elementary science teachers. *School Science and Mathematics, 75*, 3, 1975.

———. Helping the special student fit in. *Science Teacher, 7*, 1979.

———, and P. A. Hendricks. Teaching science concepts to preschool deaf children to aid language development. *Science Education, 56*, 1979.

Campbell, R. L. Intellectual development, achievement, and self-concept of elementary minority school children, *School Science and Mathematics, 81*, 1981.

Carin, A. A., and R. B. Sund. *Teaching Modern Science*. Columbus, Ohio: Merrill, 1980.

Chiapetta, E. L. A review of Piagetian studies relevant to science instruction at the secondary and college levels. *Science Education, 60*, 1976.

Chinn, P. C., C. J. Drew, and D. R. Logan. *Mental Retardation — A Life Cycle Approach*. St. Louis: Mosby, 1975.

Clarke, S. A., and J. Koch. *Children: Development through Adolescence*. New York: Wiley, 1983.

Coble, C. R., and D. R. Rice. Rekindling scientific curiosity. *Science Teacher, 50*, 2, 1983.

Comstock, A. B. *Handbook of Nature Study*. Ithaca, New York, 1911.

Cooke, L. L. Science for the disadvantaged student — Problems and opportunities. *Science Teacher, 42*, 1975.

Coulter, D. J. New paradigms for understanding the properties and functions of the brain: Implications for education. A Research Project. Greeley, Colorado: University of Northern Colorado, 1981.

Cox, D., and C. F. Berger. Microcomputers are motivating. *Science and Children, 19*, 1, 1981.

Craig, G. S. *Certain Techniques Used in Developing a Course of Study in Science for the Horace Mann Elementary School.* Bureau of Publication, Teachers College, Columbia University, Contributions to Education, No. 276. New York, 1927.

———, and J. E. Lewis. *Going Forward with Science.* Boston: Ginn, 1950.

Craig, R. P. The child's construction of space and time. *Science and Children, 19,* 3, 1981.

Crisci, P. E. The role of teachers and administrators in providing for positive mental health. *The Journal of School Health, 8,* 9, 1978.

Damarin, S. K. What makes a triangle. *Arithmetic Teacher, 29,* 1, 1981.

Davis, J. D., ed. *Our Forgotten Children: Hard of Hearing Pupils in the Schools.* Minneapolis: Audio Visual Library Services, 1977.

Davis, J. M., and D. W. Ball. Utilization of the elementary science study with educable mentally retarded students. *Journal of Research in Science Teaching, 15,* 1978.

Directorate for Science Education. *Science Education Databook.* Washington, D.C.: National Science Foundation, 1980.

Divito, A., and G. H. Krockover. *Creative Sciencing: Ideas and Activities for Teachers and Children,* 2nd ed. Boston: Little, Brown, 1980.

Dunfee, J. Investigating children's science learning. *The Education Digest, 36,* 5, 1971.

Educational Software Directory. Manchaca, Texas: Swift Publishing, 1983.

Educational Software Sourcebook. Radio Shack, 1983.

Egleston, J. C., and D. Mercaldo. Science education for the handicapped: Implementation for the hearing impaired. *Science Education, 59,* 1975.

Eichenberger, R. Special students: Teaching science to the blind student. *Science Teacher, 41,* 1974.

Elementary Science Study Materials. New York: McGraw-Hill, 1978.

Epstein, H. T. Growth spurts during brain development: Implications for educational policy and practices. In *Education and the Brain.* Chicago: University of Chicago Press, 1979.

ERIC/SMEAC. Science Education Fact Sheet No. 3. *Microcomputers and science teaching.* Columbus, Ohio: Clearinghouse for Science, Math, and Environmental Education, 1982.

———. What research says: Females and mathematics. *School Science and Mathematics, 82,* 6, 1982.

Ericsson, K. A., W. G. Chase, and S. Faloon. Acquisition of memory skill. *Science, 208,* June, 1980.

Erikson, E. H. *Childhood and Society.* New York: Norton, 1950.

Falmagne, R. J., ed. *Reasoning: Representation and Process.* Hillsdale, New Jersey: Erlbaum, 1975.

Farley, J. R. Raising student achievement through the affective domain. *Educational Leadership, 39,* 7, 1982.

Feifer, N. *Adventures in Chemistry.* New York: Sentinal, 1959.

Finley, F. N. Science processes. *Journal of Research in Science Teaching, 20,* 1, 1983.

Firth, G. H., and J. W. Mitchell. Value of science education for the mildly retarded: Empirical data for backing. *Science Education, 64,* 1980.

Flavell, J. H. *The Developmental Psychology of Jean Piaget.* New York: Van Nostrand, 1973.

Floriani, B. P., and J. C. Cairns. Assessing combining forms in science. *Science and Children, 19,* 4, 1982.

Follis, H. D. and G. H. Krockover. Selecting activities in science and mathematics for gifted young children. *School Science and Mathematics,* Jan. 1982.

Fowler, T. W. An investigation of the teacher behavior of wait-time during an inquiry science lesson. Paper presented to National Association for Research in Science Teaching, Los Angeles, 1975.

Fraser, B. J. Enquiry skill proficiency and socioeconomic status. *School Science and Mathematics, 81,* 1981.

Fried, N. S., and K. J. Holyoak. *Induction of Category Distributions: A Framework for Classification Learning.* Chicago/Michigan Cognitive Science Technological Report, 1981.

Gail, M. D., B. Dunning, and R. Weathersby. *Higher Cognitive Questioning: Minicourse 9. Teacher's Handbook.* Beverly Hills: Macmillan Educational Services, 1971.

Gallagher, J. J. Basic skills common to science and mathematics. *School Science and Mathematics, 79,* 8, 1979.

Garigliano, L. J. The relation of wait-time to student behaviors in the science curriculum improvement study lessons. Doctoral Dissertation, Columbia University, 1972.

Gaskel, J. Discrimination against the handicapped. In *Science Technology and the Handicapped.* American Association for the Advancement of Science report number 76-R-11. Washington, D.C.: American Association for the Advancement of Science, 1976.

Garner, D. Educational microcomputer software: Nine questions to ask. *Science and Children, 19,* 6, 1982.

Gaudry, E., and C. D. Spielberger. *Anxiety and Educational Achievement.* New York: Wiley and Sons Australasia, 1971.

Gauld, G. The scientific attitude and science education: A critical reappraisal. *Science Education, 66,* 1, 1982.

Gerlich, J. A., G. Downs, and G. Mangrane. How essential is science at the elementary level. *Science and Children, 19,* 3, 1981.

Ginsberg, H., and S. Opper. *Piaget's Theory of Intellectual Development: An Introduction.* Englewood Cliffs, New Jersey: Prentice-Hall, 1979.

Glass, R. M., J. Christiansen, and J. L. Christiansen. *Teaching Exceptional Children in the Regular Classroom.* Boston: Little, Brown, 1982.

Goldberg, L. Elementary school science: Learning how to learn. *Science and Children, 9,* 7, 1982.

Good, R. G. *How Children Learn Science: Conceptual Development and Implications for Teaching.* New York: Macmillan, 1977.

Greeno, J. G. Trends in the theory of knowledge for problem solving. In D. T. Tuma and F. Reif, eds. *Problem Solving and Education: Issues in Teaching and Research.* Hillsdale, New Jersey: Erlbaum, 1980.

Gring, S. R. Introducing computer literacy. *Educational Leadership, 40,* 1, 1982.

Geschwind, N. Specialization of the human brain. *Scientific American,* September, 1979.

Gusert, P. The coercive use of affective objectives. *Science Education, 61,* 2, 1978.

Hakansson, J. How to evaluate educational courseware. *Journal of Courseware Review, 1,* 1, 1981.

Hammil, D. D., and N. R. Bartel. *Teaching Children with Learning and Behavior Problems.* Boston: Allyn and Bacon, 1975.

Hardman, M. L., M. W. Egan, and E. D. Landau. *What Will We Do in the Morning? The Exceptional Student in the Regular Classroom.* Dubuque, Iowa: Brown, 1981.

Hasan, O. E. An investigation into factors affecting science interest in secondary school students. *Journal of Research in Science Teaching, 12,* 9, 1975.

Heimberger, M. J. *Teaching the Gifted and Talented in the Elementary Classroom.* Washington, D.C.: National Education Association, 1980.

Hensen, F. O. *Mainstreaming the Gifted.* Austin, Texas: Learning Concepts, 1976.

Hilgard, E. R., and G. H. Bower. *Theories of Learning.* Englewood Cliffs, New Jersey: Prentice-Hall, 1975.

Hill, S. A. The microcomputer in the instructional program. *Arithmetic Teacher, 3,* 6, 1982.

Hoffman, H. H. An assessment of eight-year-old children's attitudes toward science. *School Science and Mathematics, 77,* 8, 1977.

Hofman, H., ed. A working conference on science education for handicapped students. Proceedings. Washington, D.C., April, 1978.

Holmes, N. J., Leake, J. B., and Shaw, M. W. *Gateways to Science Series.* New York: McGraw-Hill, 1979.

Hone, E. B., J. Alexander, E. Victor, and P. Brandwein. *A Sourcebook for Elementary Science.* New York: Harcourt, 1962.

Hunt, M. *The Universe Within.* New York: Simon and Schuster, 1982.

Hymes, J. L. *Teaching the Child Under Six.* Columbus, Ohio: Merrill, 1981.

Inhelder, B., and J. Piaget. *The Growth of Logical Thinking from Childhood to Adolescence.* New York: Basic Books, 1964.

———. *The Early Growth of Logic in the Child.* New York: Harper and Row, 1964.

Inman, D. Apples, computers, and teachers. *Interface Age, 4,* 1979.

Jaus, H. H. The effects of activity oriented science instruction on children's attitudes toward science and school. Paper presented at National Association for Research in Science Teaching, March, 1975.

Johnson, R. T., F. L. Ryan, and H. Schroeder. Inquiry and the development of positive attitudes. *Science Education, 58,* 1974.

Johnson, V. R. Myelin and maturation: A fresh look at Piaget. *Science Teacher, 49,* 3, 1982.

Johnson-Laird, P. N. Mental models in cognitive science. Paper presented at La Jolla Conference in Cognitive Science. University of California at San Diego, 1979.

Kagan, J. Do infants think? *Scientific American,* March, 1972.

———. Structure and process in the human infant: the ontogeny of mental representation. In Bornstein and Kessen, 1979.

———. Jean Piaget's contributions to education. *Kappan, 62,* 4, 1980.

Kahle, J. B., and M. K. Lakes. The myth of equality in science classrooms. *Journal of Research in Science Teaching, 20,* 2, 1983.

Kendig, F. A conversation with Isaac Asimov. *Psychology Today, 17,* 1, 1983.

Kennedy, K. A. The effectiveness of comparative advance organizer in the learning and retention of metric system concepts. Paper presented at National Association for Research in Science Teaching, March, 1975.

Klausmeir, H. J., and R. E. Ripple. *Learning and Human Abilities.* New York: Harper and Row, 1971.

Kohlberg, L. Development of moral character and moral ideology. In L. Hoffman and M. Hoffman, eds. *Review of Child Development Research.* New York: Russell Sage Foundation, 1964.

Konya, B. A. The effects of higher and lower order questions on the frequency and type of student verbalization. Unpublished Doctoral Dissertation, University of Tennessee, 1972.

Krulik, S., and J. Rudnik, eds. *Problem Solving: A Handbook for Teachers.* Boston: Allyn and Bacon, 1980.

Kuhn, D. J. A study of varying modes of topical presentation in elementary college biology to determine the effect of advance organizers on knowledge. Unpublished Doctoral Thesis. Purdue University, 1967.

Kurzwell, Z. E. *Anxiety and Education.* New York: Thomas Yorseloff, 1968.

Lake, J. H. The effects of higher and lower order questions on the frequency and type of student verbalizations. Unpublished Doctoral Dissertation, University of Tennessee, 1972.

Lawson, A. E. The development and validation of a classroom test of formal reasoning. *Journal of Research in Science Teaching, 15,* 1, 1978.

———. Formal reasoning, achievement, and intelligence: An issue of importance. *Science Education, 66,* 1, 1982.

Lawrenz, F. The relationship between science teacher characteristics and student achievement and attitude. *Journal of Research in Science Teaching, 12,* 10, 1975.

Lee, K. S. Guiding young children in successful problem solving. *Arithmetic Teacher, 29,* 5, 1982.

Levin, T., and R. Long. *Effective Instruction.* Alexandria, Virginia: Association for Supervision and Curriculum Development, 1981.

Levine, D. U. Successful approaches for improving academic achievement in inner city elementary schools. *Kappan, 63,* 8, 1982.

Levy, J. Research synthesis on right and left hemispheres: We think with both sides of the brain. *Educational Leadership, 39,* 1, 1983.

Lincoln, E. A. Tools for teaching math and science students in the inner city. *School Science and Mathematics, 30,* 1980.

Linn, M. C. Science education for the deaf: A comparison of ideal resource and mainstream settings. *Journal of Research in Science Teaching, 16,* 3, 1979.

———, and R. W. Peterson. The effect of direct experiences with objects on middle class, culturally diverse, and visually impaired young children. *Journal of Research in Science Teaching, 20,* 2, 1973.

Lloyd, S. E., and I. D. Brown. Investigation of children's attitudes toward science fostered by a field-based science methods course. *Science Education, 63,* 5, 1979.

Lombardi, T. P., and P. E. Balch. Science experiences and the mentally retarded. *Science and Children, 13,* 6, 1976.

Lowrey, L. F. An experimental investigation into the attitudes of fifth grade students toward science. *School Science and Mathematics, 67,* 1967.

Lunzer, E. A. Problems of formal reasoning in test situations. In *Cognitive Development in Children.* Five monographs of the Society for Research in Child Development. Chicago: University of Chicago Press, 1970.

Markle, G. Generating good vibrations for science. *Science and Children, 49,* 4, 1982.

Marsh, G. E., B. Price, and T. Smith. *Teaching Mildly Handicapped Children: Methods and Materials.* St. Louis: Mosby, 1982.

Martin, K. The learning machines. *Arithmetic Teacher, 29,* 3, 1981.

Mayor, J. R., and A. H. Livermore. A process approach to elementary school science. *School Science and Mathematics, 69,* 5, 1969.

McAnarney, H. How much space does an object take up? *Science and Children, 19,* 4, 1982.

McIntyre, M. Science is for all children. *Science and Children, 13,* 6, 1976.

McMillian, J. H., and M. J. May. A study of factors influencing attitudes of fifth grade students toward science. *School Science and Mathematics, 67,* 1967.

Menhusen, B. B., and R. O. Gromme. Science for the handicapped children — Why? *Science and Children, 13,* 6, 1976.

Miller, T. L., and E. E. Davis, eds. *The Mildly Handicapped Student.* New York: Greene and Stratton, 1982.

Minstrell, J. Getting the facts straight. *Science Teacher, 50,* 1, 1983.

———. Conceptual development research in the natural setting of the classroom. In *Education in the 80's: Science.* Ed. Mary Budd Rowe. Washington, D.C.: National Education Association, 1982.

Moore, R. W. Open-mindedness and proof. *School Science and Mathematics, 82*, 6, 1982.

Nash, R. W., C. Borman, and S. Colson. Career education for gifted and talented students. *Exceptional Children, 46*, 5, 1970.

National Science Teachers Association Curriculum Committee. *Theory into Action in Science Curriculum Development*. Washington, D.C.: National Science Teachers Association, 1964.

Newell, A., and H. A. Simon. *Human Problem Solving*. Englewood Cliffs, New Jersey: Prentice-Hall, 1972.

Neuman, D. B. Promoting reading readiness through science. *Science and Children, 19*, 1, 1981.

Nicodemis, R. B. *An Evaluation of Elementary Science Study and Science: A Process Approach*. Washington, D.C.: Department of Health, Education and Welfare, 1968.

Noonan, L. Computer simulations in the classroom. *Creative Computing, 7*, 10, 1981.

Olsen, R. C. A comparative study of the effect of behavioral objectives on class performance and retention in physical science. *Dissertation Abstracts*, 33, 1: 224A, 1972.

Owsley, P. J. Teaching science to deaf children. *American Annals of the Deaf, 107*, 1962.

———. Development of the cognitive abilities and language of deaf children through science. Curriculum: Cognition and content. *Volta Review*. Washington, D.C.: Bell Association, 1968.

Padilla, M. J., J. R. Okey, and F. G. Dellashaw. The relationship between science process skills and formal thinking abilities. *Journal of Research in Science Teaching, 20*, 3, 1983.

Paldy, L. G. *SCIS II Sampler Guide*. Boston: American Science and Engineering, 1978.

Pallrand, G. J. The transition to formal thought. *Journal of Research in Science Teaching, 16*, 5, 1979.

Palmer, G. A. Teaching the nature of scientific enterprise. *School Science and Mathematics, 79*, 1, 1979.

Pappert, S., D. Watt, A. di Sessa, and S. Weir. *Final Report of the Brookline LOGO Project*. Cambridge: Artificial Intelligence Lab, MIT, 1979.

Partington, J. R. *A Short History of Chemistry*. New York: Harper, 1960.

Pepir, M. K. A science activity teaching plan. *School Science and Mathematics, 80*, 5, 1980.

Perlmutter, M. What is memory the aging of? *Developmental Psychology, 14*, 1978.

Piaget, J. *The Psychology of Intelligence*. Totowa, New Jersey: Littlefield, 1963.

———. *The Child's Conception of Physical Causality*. Totowa, New Jersey: Littlefield, 1972.

———. *Judgment and Reasoning in the Child*. Totowa, New Jersey: Littlefield, 1972.

———. *The Origins of Intelligence in Children.* New York: New York University Press, 1974.

———. *The Child's Conception of the World.* Totowa, New Jersey: Littlefield, 1975.

———, and B. Inhelder. *The Child's Conception of Space.* London: Routledge and Kegan Paul, 1956.

———, and B. Inhelder. *The Growth of Logical Thinking from Childhood to Adolescence.* New York: Basic Books, 1958.

Renner, J. W., M. P. Abraham, and D. G. Stafford. Evaluation in science education: Affective studies. *A Summary of Research in Science Education.* New York: Wiley, 1976.

Rice, D. R., and W. P. Dunlap. Introducing the ways and means of scientific inquiry. *Science Teacher, 59,* 3, 1982.

Riley, J. P. The effects of preservice teacher's cognitive questioning level and redirecting on student science achievement. *Journal of Research in Science Teaching, 18,* 4, 1979.

Ringness, T. A. *The Affective Domain in Education,* Boston: Little, Brown, 1975.

Robinson, M. L. Attitudes and achievement: A complex relationship. March, 1975, ERIC Document 111 678.

Rogers, R. E. and A. M. Voelker. Programs for improving elementary science instruction in the elementary school: Elementary science study. *Science and Children, 8,* 1, 1970.

Romney, E. *A Working Guide to the Elementary Science Study.* Newton, Mass.: Education Development Center, 1971.

Rosch, E., and B. B. Lloyd. *Cognition and Categorization.* Hillsdale, New Jersey: Erlbaum, 1978.

Rowbotham, N. Using a microcomputer in science teaching. *School Science Review, 63,* 222, 1981.

Rowe, M. B. *Teaching Science as Continuous Inquiry.* New York: McGraw-Hill, 1973.

Rowe, M. B. Wait-time and rewards as instructional variables, their influence on language, logic, and fate control: Part one, wait-time. *Journal of Research in Science Teaching, 11,* 2, 1974.

———. Relationship of wait-time and rewards to the development of language, logic, and fate control: Part two, rewards. *Journal of Research in Science Teaching, 11,* 4, 1974.

———. Pausing phenomena: Influence on the quality of instruction. *Journal of Psycholinguistic Research, 3,* 3, 1974.

———. *What Research Says to the Science Teacher, Volume I.* Washington, D.C.: National Science Teachers Association, 1978.

———. *What Research Says to the Science Teacher, Volume II.* Washington, D.C.: National Science Teachers Association, 1979.

Russel, T. L. Analyzing arguments in science classroom discourse: Can teacher's questions distort scientific authority? *Journal of Research in Science Teaching, 20,* 1, 1983.

Sadker, M., and J. Cooper. Increasing student higher order questions. *Elementary English, 51*, 4, 1974.

Safford, P. L. *Teaching Young Children with Special Needs*. St. Louis: Mosby, 1978.

Sagan, C. *Broca's Brain*. New York: Random House, 1974.

———. *Cosmos*. New York: Random House, 1980.

Sanders, N. M. *Classroom Questions: What Kinds?* New York: Harper, 1966.

Savage, T. V. A study of the relationship of classroom questions and social studies achievement of fifth grade children. Unpublished Doctoral Dissertation, University of Washington, 1972.

Saxon, D. S. Liberal education in a technological age. *Science, 218*, 4575, 1982.

Schlenker, R. G. The effects of an inquiry development program on elementary school children's learnings. Doctoral Dissertation, New York University, 1970.

Schlichter, C. L. The answer is in the question. *Science and Children, 20*, 5, 1983.

Schneider, L., and J. W. Renner. Concrete and formal teaching. *Journal of Research in Science Teaching, 17*, 6, 1980.

Scherer, D. R. The microcomputer in a small school and at the university. *Interface Age, 4*, 1979.

Schultz, J. E. *Mathematics for Elementary School Teachers*. Columbus, Ohio: Merrill, 1982.

Science — A Process Approach, Materials. Lexington, Mass.: Ginn, 1979.

SCIIS Materials. Chicago: Rand-McNally, 1980.

SCIS Sampler Guide. Chicago: Rand-McNally, 1970.

Shaw, J. M., and M. Cliatt. Searching and researching. *Science and Children, 19*, 3, 1981.

Shayer, M., and P. Adey. *Towards a Science of Science Teaching*. Exeter, New Hampshire: Heineman, 1981.

Shepard, S. *The Disadvantaged Child*. New York: Praeger, 1968.

Smart, M., and R. C. Smart. *Preschool Children: Development and Relationships*, 3rd ed. New York: Macmillan, 1982.

Smith, W. S. Engineering a classroom discussion. *Science and Children, 20*, 5, 1983.

Soar, R., and R. Soari. Emotional climate and teacher management: A paradigm and some results. In *Conceptions of Teaching*. Eds. H. Walbert and P. Peterson. Berkeley, California: McCutchan, nd.

Stephens, T., A. E. Blackhurst, and L. Magliocco. *Teaching Mainstreamed Students*. New York: Wiley, 1982.

Suchman, J. R. *The Elementary School Training Program in Scientific Inquiry*. Champaign/Urbana: University of Illinois Press, 1962.

Sullivan, R. Student interest in specific science topics. *Science Education, 63*, 5, 1979.

Sund, R. B., B. W. Tillery, and L. W. Trowbridge. *Elementary Science Lessons: The Biological Sciences*. Boston: Allyn and Bacon, 1970.

———. *Elementary Science Lessons: The Earth Sciences*. Boston: Allyn and Bacon, 1970.

———. *Elementary Science Lessons: The Physical Sciences.* Boston: Allyn and Bacon, 1970.

Sund, R. B. and A. J. Picard. *Behavioral Objectives and Educational Measures: Science and Mathematics.* Columbus, Ohio: Merrill, 1972.

Suydam, M. Update on research on problem solving: Implications for classroom teaching. *Arithmetic Teacher, 29,* 6, 1982.

The, L. Squaring off over computer literacy. *Personal Computing, 6,* 9, 1982.

Tisher, R. R. Verbal interaction in science classes. *Journal of Research in Science Teaching, 8,* 1, 1977.

Tobin, K. G. The effect of extended wait-time on concept formation and problem solving in science for children in senior primary grades. Unpublished Doctoral Dissertation, Florida State, 1977.

———, and W. Capie. Lessons with an emphasis on process skills. *Science and Children, 19,* 6, 1982.

Tuttle, F. B. and L. Becker. *Characteristics and Identification of Gifted and Talented Students.* Washington, D.C.: National Education Association, 1980.

Van Osdol, W. R. and D. G. Shane. *An Introduction to Exceptional Children.* Dubuque, Iowa: Brown, 1982.

Victor, E. The inquiry approach to teaching and learning: A primer for the teacher. *Science and Children, 12,* 2, 1974.

Wager, W. Instructional design and attitude learning. *Educational Technology, 19,* 2, 1979.

Walsh, E. Laboratory classroom: Breaking the communication barrier. *Science, 196,* 1425, 1977.

Wason, P. C., and P. N. Johnson-Laird. *Psychology of Reasoning: Structure and Content.* Cambridge, Mass.: Harvard University Press, 1972.

Webb, R. A. Concrete and formal operations in very bright six to eleven year olds. *Human Development, 17,* 1974.

Welch, W. W. Inquiry in school science. In *What Research Says to the Science Teacher, Volume III.* Washington, D.C.: National Science Teachers Association, 1981.

Weishan, M. W., and B. R. Gearheart. *The Handicapped Child in the Regular Classroom.* St. Louis: Mosby, 1976.

White, E. P. Why self-directed learning? *Science and Children, 19,* 5, 1982.

Whitmore, J. R. *Giftedness, Conflict, and Underachievement.* Boston: Allyn and Bacon, 1980.

Wilson, J. T., and J. Karan. Science curriculum materials for special students. *Educating and Training of the Mentally Retarded, 8,* 1973.

Winkle, L. W., and W. M. Matthews. Computer equity comes of age. *Kappan, 63,* 5, 1982.

Wittrock, M. C. *The Brain and Psychology*. New York: Academic, 1980.

Wolfinger, D. M. *Interaction of Young Children with Science Materials in a Free Setting*. Unpublished manuscript, 1982.

———. The effect of science teaching on the young child's concept of Piagetian physical causality: Animism and dynamism. *Journal of Research in Science Teaching, 19*, 7, 1982.

Wollman, W., B. Eylon, and A. E. Lawson. An analysis of premature closure in science and developmental stage. *Journal of Research in Science Teaching, 17*, 2, 1980.

Worth, J. Problem solving in the intermediate grades: Helping your students solve problems. *Arithmetic Teacher, 29*, 6, 1982.

Zweng, M., T. Turner, and J. Geraghty. *Children's strategies of solving verbal problems*. Final report, NIE Grant No. G-78-0094. August, 1979 (ERIC document number ED 178 359).

Index